Visualising far-right environments

Manchester University Press

Global Studies of the Far Right

Series editors:
Dr Eviane Leidig, Dr William Allchorn, Dr Ariel Alejandro Goldstein

We are living in an unprecedented moment of uncertainty and chaos. The edifice of the old liberal order is starting to crack and a new, illiberal order is appearing on the horizon. The complexity and seriousness of these changes is such that now more than ever scholars are needed to weigh in on – and make sense of – these 'shifting sands'.

This series showcases innovative research from established and early career scholars working on the far right, providing fresh insights on emerging trends and themes within this field of study. It features high-quality single-authored books and edited volumes.

The series is multi-disciplinary, taking in the fields of political science, cultural studies, communication studies, sociology and international relations. More importantly, it aims to be broad in geographical scope, looking at both the Global North and the Global South, as we see new illiberal and authoritarian populist actors increasingly across the globe.

Forthcoming titles:
Irma Kinga Allen, Kristoffer Ekberg, Ståle Holgersen and Andreas Malm (eds)
Political ecologies of the far right: Fanning the flames

Visualising far-right environments

Communication and the politics of nature

Edited by Bernhard Forchtner

MANCHESTER UNIVERSITY PRESS

Published by Manchester University Press
Oxford Road, Manchester M13 9PL

www.manchesteruniversitypress.co.uk

British Library Cataloguing-in-Publication Data
A catalogue record for this book is available from the
British Library

ISBN   978 1 5261 6538 1   hardback
ISBN   978 1 5261 9131 1   paperback

First published 2023
Paperback published 2025

EU authorised representative for GPSR:
Easy Access System Europe – Mustamäe tee 50,
10621 Tallinn, Estonia
gpsr.requests@easproject.com

Typeset
by New Best-set Typesetters Ltd

Contents

List of figures   vii
List of tables   x
List of contributors   xi
Acknowledgements   xv

Studying the far right's natural environments: towards a visual
turn – Bernhard Forchtner   1

1 Right as rain: affective publics and the changing visual
   rhetoric of the far right in South Africa – Scott Burnett   24

2 The exclusivist claims of Pacific ecofascists: visual
   environmental communication by far-right groups in
   Australia and New Zealand – Kristy Campion and
   Justin Phillips   43

3 The National Socialist Movement of the United States and
   the turn to environmentalism: greenfingers or brownshirts?
   – Daniel Jones   63

4 The environmental semiotics of Spanish far-right
   populism: Vox's visual rhetoric strategies online
   – Carmen Aguilera-Carnerero   83

5 Purity and control: gender and visual environmental
   communication by the extreme right in Cyprus
   – Miranda Christou   104

6 The new Russian civilisation: Arctic fossil fuels, white
   masculinity and the neo-fascist visual politics of the
   Izborskii Club – Sonja Pietiläinen   125

7 Not so green after all: visual representation of green issues
   by the far-right Kotlebovci – People's Party Our Slovakia
   – Radka Vicenová, Veronika Oravcová and Matúš Mišík   146

  8 From metapolitics to electoral communication: visualising
     'nature' in the French far right – Zoé Carle   166
  9 The murky world of ideologies: the (un)troubling overlaps
     in visual communication between Hungarian greens and
     far-right ecologists – Balša Lubarda   186
 10 Homeland, cows and climate change: the visualisation of
     environmental issues by the far right in India – Mukul Sharma   206
 11 Double vision: local environment and global climate change
     through the German far-right lens – Bernhard Forchtner and
     Jonathan Olsen   229
 12 Talking heads and contrarian graphs: televising the Swedish
     far right's climate denialism – Kjell Vowles   253
 13 The (paranoid) style of American climate politics: a
     comparative visual rhetoric analysis of web design by
     far-right and left conspiracists in the United States
     – Lauren Cagle   274
Looking back, looking forward: some preliminary conclusions
on the far right's visualisation of its natural environments
– Bernhard Forchtner   294

Index   302

Figures

0.1 On the left, video by Spanish Vox (www.youtube.com/
watch?v=RaSIX4-RPAI&t=0s, accessed 8 February 2022).
On the right, a poster for a German neo-Nazi party (www.
materialvertrieb.de/produkt/umweltschutz-ist-heimatschutz-
a3/, accessed 25 April 2021) 2
1.1 Twitter banner of Suidlanders (https://twitter.com/
suidlanders, accessed 30 November 2021) 25
1.2 'Die Land', father and son share an affectionate moment as
they tend cattle (www.youtube.com/watch?v=Kf_BIm2SndE,
accessed 30 November 2021) 34
1.3 'Die Land', kissing in the rain (www.youtube.com/
watch?v=Kf_BIm2SndE, accessed 30 November 2021) 36
2.1 Screenshot of the NSN webpage, 'Australia for the white
man' (NSN, 2021a) 49
2.2 Screenshot from Telegram, 'Planting the Flag on the Hill'
(NSN, 2021b) 51
2.3 Screenshot of part of the home page of Action Zealandia
website (AZ, 2021a) 55
2.4 Screenshot from Telegram, AZ members exploring
Maukatere (AZ, 2021b) 57
3.1 Neo-Nazis picking litter; image from 'NSN Missouri Active
on the Streets', Stormtrooper #32 (2009: 7); copyright:
National Socialist Movement 68
3.2 NSM photo of the Sonoran Desert; image from 'National
Socialist Movement Border Operations: January Through
May 2012', NSM Magazine Summer/Fall (2012: 5);
copyright: National Socialist Movement 71
3.3 Neo-Nazis with their flags and dogs; image from 'NSM
Sept. 10th, 2016' NSM Grassroots Action Gallery on the

NSM Website (https://web.archive.org/
web/20180812060801/http:/gallery.nsm88.org/
displayimage.php?album=71&pos=1, accessed 29
September 2021); copyright: unknown   75

4.1 'Perhaps now Spaniards realise we can live without
puppeteers but not without farmers and cattle breeders',
tweet published on 20 March 2020 by @vox_es   93

4.2 Shot from the promotional video for the 2018 Andalusian
elections 'Andalucía por España' (Andalusia for Spain),
posted on Twitter on 12 November 2018 by @vox_es   95

4.3 Shot taken from Vox's video with the caption reading
'[thanks to the presence of Vox in the Parliament], the
totalitarian left and separatism do not advance more',
posted on Instagram on 29 February 2020.   98

5.1 Ammochostos, the 'ghost city,' buried in the sand (ELAM,
2020a)   115

5.2 Cyprus with the thirteen blocks of Exclusive Economic
Zone, surrounded by Turkish ships (©Pantelis Valtadoros,
Reproduced with permission)   116

5.3 ELAM volunteer putting out a fire (ELAM, 2020b)   118

6.1 'People of the polar dream' (Prokhanov, 2016a: 2)   134

6.2 '50 years of victory' (Prokhanov, 2016b: 17)   136

6.3 'Arctic as scientific laboratory' (Peterman, 2016: 62) 138

7.1 Distribution of issues, articles (left axis), sentences and
images (right axis) by year; no newspapers were published
in 2015   152

7.2 Number of sentences on green issues in ĽSNS newspaper   154

7.3 Emotional versus rational charges   156

7.4 Visual highlighting of the text (green issues: left axis,
non-green: right axis)   157

8.1 'Nature as our bedrock', promotional video by *Institut
Iliade*, posted on 12 April 2020 (www.youtube.com/
watch?v=WNTcJeYoIFs, accessed 23 May 2021)   174

8.2 'Duty'. Instagram @Academia Christiana, posted on 4
December 2019 (www.instagram.com/p/B5qb5mUK2Ps/,
accessed 17 September 2021)   178

8.3 'Back from RN [*Rassemblement National*] Congress: We
are forced to notice the massive presence of wind-turbines
in our beautiful Mediterranean landscapes', tweeted on
4 July 2021 (https://twitter.com/HerveJuvin/status/
1411769027534356483, accessed 30 October 2021)   181

9.1 Overview of Themes/Images: Our Homeland   192

9.2 Our Homeland Facebook page: 'People may live on
    different levels, but will drown in trash equally' (GH)   195
9.3 Overview of Themes/Images: LMP   197
9.4 LMP Facebook page: 'One Nation Trianon'   198
10.1 RSS's chief with top functionaries (*Organiser*, 22 June
    2014: 44)   210
10.2 Mother Ganga descending from the heavens (*Organiser*, 24
    February 2019: 43)   215
10.3 'PM Modi taking holy dip' (*Organiser*, 7 April 2019: 21)   223
11.1 Hell on Earth (Beleites, 2020: 11)   240
11.2 '»Against the selling out of the homeland« – bioregional
    identity contra the disappearance of place' (Eichberger,
    2020: 14)   246
12.1 The top pane shows the graph used in SwebbTV taken
    from the book *Falskt alarm*; the graph is based on a figure
    in the first IPCC report 1990 (middle pane) which is a
    reconstruction of Central England temperatures; in the
    SwebbTV-version, the *x*-axis has been compressed, making
    the medieval warm period look warmer; this is a case of
    cherry-picking an obsolete graph, showing temperature at
    one specific location, rather than using global temperature
    reconstructions available in later IPCC reports (bottom
    pane); credits: top pane: Pettersson (2020); middle pane:
    IPCC (1990); bottom pane: Masson-Delmotte et al. (2013)   263
12.2 Annual mean sea level as measured by tide gauge at the
    Battery, New York; credit: Permanent Service for Mean Sea
    Level and National Oceanic and Atmospheric
    Administration   264
12.3 Graph claiming to show temperature changes over
    millennia; credit: Randy Mann and Cliff Harris   266
13.1 Page one of the six-page ICLEI conspiracy theory flyer
    found in Lexington, KY   275
13.2 Side-by-side comparison of MH Corporate WordPress
    template (left) and freedomadvocates.org (right), which is
    based on that template   285
13.3 Side-by-side comparison of Weebly Light theme (left) and
    democratsagainstunagenda21.com (right), which is based
    on that template   286

Tables

5.1 Three themes in ELAM's visual communication of the environment   114

11.1 Topics present in the visual climate change communication of the German far right   237

11.2 Frames conveyed via the visual climate change communication of the German far right   238

11.3 Topics present in the visual communication of nature of the German far right   242

11.4 Frames conveyed in the visual communication of nature of the German far right   243

Contributors

Carmen Aguilera-Carnerero received her PhD at the Department of English and German Philology at the University of Granada (Spain) where she currently teaches. Her postdoctoral research has focused on the study of the extremist speech online, especially on CyberIslamophobia, the online discourse of the post-war ethnic conflict in Sri Lanka, the online rhetoric of the far-right, the semiotics of terrorism and the communicative force of graffiti.

Scott Burnett is an assistant professor of African Studies and Women's, Gender, and Sexuality Studies at the Pennsylvania State University. His research takes an intersectional approach to race, gender and discourses of the land in traditional and social media texts. He is the author of *White Belongings: Race, Property and Land in Post-Apartheid South Africa* (Lexington Books, 2022) and has published in a number of leading journals, including *Men and Masculinities*; *Sexualities*; *Discourse, Context & Media*; and *Environment and Planning E: Nature and Space*.

Lauren Cagle is an associate professor of writing, rhetoric, and digital studies and associate faculty in Environmental and Sustainability Studies at the University of Kentucky. Her research focuses on overlaps among digital rhetorics and scientific and technical communication. Cagle frequently works with local and regional environmental and technical practitioners, including the Kentucky Division for Air Quality, the Kentucky Geological Survey, the University of Kentucky Recycling Program and the Arboretum, State Botanical Garden of Kentucky. Cagle's work has appeared in *Technical Communication Quarterly*, the *Journal of Technical Writing and Communication*, *Rhetoric Review* and *Computers & Composition*.

Kristy Campion is a senior lecturer and discipline lead of terrorism studies at the Australian Graduate School of Policing and Security, Charles Sturt University (Australia). She researches terrorism and extremism in Western democratic contexts, with a focus on transhistorical and transnational threat natures, ideological systems underpinning political violence, right- and left-wing threats, and strategic evolution. Her research has been published in leading journals such as *Perspectives on Terrorism, Terrorism and Political Violence* and *Critical Studies on Terrorism*. She recently authored the first comprehensive history of terrorism in Australia, titled *Chasing Shadows: The Untold and Deadly Story of Terrorism in Australia*.

Zoé Carle is an associate professor in semiotics and discourse analysis at the University of Paris 8 – Vincennes Saint Denis. After working on revolutionary slogans and graffitis in contemporary Egypt, she is now working on the metapolitics of the far right in France, with a special focus on environmental issues. Publications includes *Poétique du slogan révolutionnaire* (Presses de la Sorbonne Nouvelle, 2019).

Miranda Christou is an associate professor of sociology of education at the University of Cyprus. Her research interests focus on questions of nationalism, globalisation and the expansion of radical-right youth movements. She has worked on European projects such as: 'INCLUD-ed: Strategies for Inclusion and Social Cohesion in Europe from Education' (FP6, 2006–2011) and 'SOLIDUS: Solidarity in European Societies: Empowerment, Social Justice and Citizenship' (Horizon2020–2015–2018). She has published in various journals, including *Current Sociology, Qualitative Inquiry* and *British Journal of Sociology of Education*, and has co-edited (with Spyros Spyrou) the book *Children and Borders* (Palgrave Macmillan, 2014).

Bernhard Forchtner is an associate professor at the School of Media, Communication and Sociology, University of Leicester (United Kingdom), and has previously worked as a Marie Curie Fellow at the Institute of Social Sciences at the Humboldt University in Berlin (Germany), where he conducted a project on far-right discourses on the environment (project number 327595). Publications include 'Climate change and the far right' (*WIREs Climate Change*, 2019), 'Nation, nature, purity: Extreme-right biodiversity in Germany' (*Patterns of Prejudice*, 2019) and the edited volume *The Far Right and the Environment* (Routledge, 2019).

Daniel Jones is Researcher in Far Right Studies Post 1945, an associate lecturer in history and the Searchlight Collections Officer in the Department of Culture, University of Northampton (United Kingdom), and an associate fellow of the Royal Historical Society. Previous publications include 'The National Socialist Group: A case study in the groupuscular right', co-authored with Paul Jackson within the edited volume *Tomorrow Belongs to Us: The British Far Right since 1967* (Routledge, 2018).

Balša Lubarda is a visiting fellow at the Center for Right-Wing Studies, UC Berkeley, and the founder and former head of the Ideology Research Unit at the Centre for Analysis of the Radical Right. He completed his PhD at Central European University (Austria) where he examined the links between the far right and the environment. He is the author of a book based on his doctoral research, *Far-Right Ecologism: Environmental Politics and the Far Right in Hungary and Poland* (Routledge, 2023).

Matúš Mišík is an associate professor at the Department of Political Science at Comenius University in Bratislava. His main research interests include energy security and decarbonisation in the European Union. He is the author of *External Energy Security in the European Union* (Routledge, 2019) and co-editor of *From Economic to Energy Transition: Three Decades of Transitions in Central and Eastern Europe* (Palgrave, 2021) and *Energy Humanities: Current State and Future Directions* (Springer, 2021). He has published articles in peer-reviewed journals including *Nature Energy*, *Energy* and *Energy Policy*.

Jonathan Olsen is professor and chair of the Department of Social Sciences and Historical Studies at Texas Woman's University. He has held previous appointments at the European University Viadrinna (Frankfurt-Oder), the University of Potsdam and the University of Muenster. Publications include *Nature and Nationalism: Right-Wing Ecology and the Politics of Identity in Contemporary Germany* (St. Martin's Press/Palgrave, 1999), *The Left Party in Contemporary German Politics* (with Dan Hough and Michael Koss, Palgrave, 2007) and *Left Parties in National Governments* (Palgrave, 2010).

Veronika Oravcová is a research assistant at the Department of Political Science at Comenius University in Bratislava and a research fellow at the Slovak Foreign Policy Association. Her research interests are centred on energy transition and energy security in Central and Eastern Europe, and she is a co-editor of *From Economic to Energy Transition: Three Decades of Transitions in Central and Eastern Europe* (Palgrave, 2021), several chapters on energy transition and several papers on energy policy in Visegrad countries.

Justin Phillips is a political scientist and senior lecturer in the School of Social Sciences at the University of Waikato, New Zealand. He specialises in political communication research, particularly on social media utilising big datasets. His recent articles on traditional and social media have been published in *Mass Communication and Society*, *Politics & Gender*, the *Australian Journal of Political Science* and the *Journal of Language and Politics*. Justin's ongoing collaborative and individual research has been funded by Facebook, the Royal Society Te Apārangi and the Ministry of Business, Innovation and Employment.

Sonja Pietiläinen is a doctoral researcher at the Geography Research Unit, University of Oulu, Finland. Her doctoral research investigates the political geographies of the far right, focusing on the relationships between space, power and nature in far-right movements' mobilisation in Finland and Russia.

Mukul Sharma is a professor of environmental studies at Ashoka University (India). He was a professor of development communication at the Indian Institute of Mass Communication. He has published several books in English and Hindi, the latest being, *Caste and Nature: Dalits and Indian Environmental Politics* (2017) and *Green and Saffron: Hindu Nationalism and Indian Environmental Politics* (2012). His research interests lie in examining the relations between nature, culture, politics, policy and power. His forthcoming book is *Dalit Ecologies: Caste and Environment Justice* (Cambridge University Press).

Radka Vicenová is a postdoctoral fellow at the Department of Political Science at the Comenius University in Bratislava as well as a Research Fellow at the Slovak National Centre for Human Rights. Her research interests focus on the contemporary far right, particularly in the central and eastern European region. Her latest publication activity has been related mostly to the issue of far-right paramilitarism and vigilantism. She has also participated in a research project focused on how the topics of environmentalism and ecologism are (mis)used in the narratives of the far-right political actors.

Kjell Vowles is a PhD candidate at the division of Science, Technology and Society and the Department of Technology, Management and Economics, Chalmers University of Technology (Sweden). He is conducting his research within the Centre for Climate Change Denialism. Before enrolling in the PhD programme, he was a journalist writing extensively about climate change for Swedish magazines and newspapers. Publications include 'Scare-quoting climate: The rapid rise of climate denial in the Swedish far-right media ecosystem' (with Martin Hultman, *Nordic Journal of Media Studies*, 2021).

Acknowledgements

Scrolling through my mailbox, I am reminded that the idea behind *Visualising Far-Right Environments: Communication and the Politics of Nature* emerged in March 2020, around the time the World Health Organization declared COVID-19 to be a global pandemic. What started in uncertain times became a project defined by the virus – with the manuscript submitted to Manchester University Press a little under two years later and with many contributors still being affected by the pandemic. During this time, Manchester University Press, and especially Robert Byron, have been very supportive: thank you. Furthermore, I would like to express my gratitude to the editors of the Global Studies Far Right series – Eviane Leidig, William Allchorn and Ariel Alejandro Goldstein – for their support and giving me this valued opportunity to publish this volume. I also wish to thank everyone at the Käte Hamburger Kolleg/Centre for Global Cooperation Research (Duisburg, Germany) for an inspiring, indeed fantastic, time as a Senior Fellow in 2023, when this volume was finalised. In particular, I wish to thank Research Group Leaders Katja Freistein and Christine Unrau, as well as Chair of the Managing Board, Sigrid Quack, to whom I am truly indebted. Yet I am even more grateful to all the authors who submitted chapters in exceptional circumstances while caring for friends and families, and I wish all of them the best as we now (hopefully) exit the pandemic.

Studying the far right's natural environments: towards a visual turn

Bernhard Forchtner

Introduction

A middle-aged, bearded man roams the countryside, picking his way through a lush forest before reaching a majestic mountaintop. A hand protectively holds an oak sapling. While such images (Figure 0.1) may seem to be mundane visualisations of the natural environment, both in fact depict far-right political projects. In the case of the former, the leader of the Spanish far-right party Vox, Santiago Abascal, enjoys the beauty of the nation's countryside as a voice-over narrates the party's vision to 'make Spain great again' in a short video, while the latter depiction is part of a poster for a German neo-Nazi party, accompanied by a call to 'Protect the environment & the homeland! An intact nature is the foundation of our people! Take part!'[1] Indeed, ideas and assumptions concerning the relationship between 'the land' and 'the people' have long informed far-right imaginaries, signifying how 'ideal' far-right subjectivities, both communal and personal, should live their lives (Kølvraa and Forchtner, 2019). And it is in this context that the two aforementioned depictions, as well as images of, for example, 'native' non-human animals threatened by 'invasive' ones, landscapes overshadowed by wind turbines and the denigrating of climate activists, can play a powerful role. Thus, to understand and address far-right environmental communication and its potential impacts, there is a need to approach the visual not simply as something 'extra' or 'illustrative'. Rather, it is a key means in positioning *us* and *them*, in (re)producing (emotional) bonds comprising, for example, love for the homeland, fear of its despoliation and disgust for cosmopolitan hysterics who endanger it. Against this background, *Visualising Far-Right Environments: Communication and the Politics of Nature* offers original and systematic analyses of the real-world centrality of images and their interplay with other modes, first and foremost the written one, that

0.1 On the left, video by Spanish Vox. On the right, a poster for a German
neo-Nazi party.

is, of multimodal constructions of contemporary far-right environmental
politics.

The intersection of worsening environmental crises and rising far-right
politics has led to a number of publications addressing how the contemporary
far right – a multifaceted continuum spanning anti-liberal-democratic,
radical-right actors to anti-democratic, extreme-right ones (see Mudde, 2019)
– engages with the natural environment (for recent, book-length contributions,
see Forchtner, 2019a; Malm and The Zetkin Collective, 2021; Moore and
Roberts, 2022; for earlier accounts, see Olsen, 1999; Biehl and Staudenmaier,
2011 [1995]; Sharma, 2012; Voss, 2014). Studies charting this terrain have
deepened our understanding of the ways in which far-right ideas and interests
interact in relation to environmental issues, from denial and belittling to
apparently sincere claims to protect the natural environment. Yet the role
of images and other visual aspects, such as text formatting, has hardly been
touched upon. Indeed, even though ongoing cultural and technological
changes keep increasing the significance of 'the visual', systematic engagement
with images (from photographs to scientific figures, cartoons, infographics
and artistic representations) in these articulations has been largely missing.
This is surprising because, first, the persuasiveness of images has long been
noted (more later); and, second, there have long been developments towards
the visual mode becoming more central in societies across the world and
even of shifts towards what has been aptly termed 'image-centricity' (Stöckl
et al., 2021). This rise can be understood in terms of, for example, living
within a society of the spectacle in which images mediate the social relationships of otherwise impoverished, fragmented lives of isolated individuals in
capitalist societies (Debord, 1994), and in terms of the post-modern as a

visual culture (Mirzoeff, 1998: 4; see also Evans and Hall, 1999 and Heywood and Sandywell, 2012 on collections dealing with visual culture). However, while theorising visuality today is beyond the remit of this volume and while the 'balance of power' between word and image remains an empirical question – with Bateman (2014: 11) rightly stating that the written word is still with us – the significance of diverse multimodal practices makes it vital to approach the contemporary far right as producers and products of images. This includes its visual representations of the natural environment, the subject of this volume. In other words, at a time when our planet is literally burning, there is a need for a concerted effort towards implementing a systematic 'visual turn' in the study of contemporary far-right communication about the environment in order to understand the ways in which this political force constructs its politics of nature visually.

Thus, this volume considers, for example, strategic mobilisations of the natural environment, the polysemic nature of images and articulations of 'ideal' subjectivities. More generally, this volume asks such questions as: What themes characterise far-right visual environmental communication? How do historically and culturally resonant ideas of nature, for example Romantic, *völkisch* or overtly fascist ones, feature in such imagery? How do far-right actors depict local/regional/national sites vis-à-vis global ones, such as landscapes and climate change? What emotions are at play? And might we even identify overlaps between far-right and centrist/left-wing visual communication?

In response to these timely questions, this volume offers analyses of images (and, at times, other visual aspects) and contributes to our knowledge about the intersection of the environment and the far right more broadly. Yet it also adds to our more general understanding of the roles played by images employed by the far right and showcases a wide variety of methodological approaches to analysing them. Importantly, this volume goes beyond a myopic focus on (western) European cases. Although there are good reasons to consider the latter, the far right has long been a global phenomenon. In consequence, insights from around the world are urgently needed as categories and hypotheses employed in existing studies cannot be assumed to be of similar relevance in other contexts.

Setting the scene for this endeavour, this introduction brings together scholarship bearing upon the aforementioned questions, starting with a brief recap of the link between the far right and the natural environment, before connecting this to aesthetic concerns more broadly. This is followed by considering the significance of imagery, especially in terms of its emotiveness, and a review of studies on visual communication to support stronger foci on visuals in the analysis of far-right politics of nature. I close with an outline of subsequent chapters.

Eco-communion and the aesthetic

As mentioned earlier, the far right spans a continuum from anti-liberal-democratic, radical-right actors to anti-democratic, extreme-right ones. While the conceptual distinction between these two poles remains useful, the increasing complexity of far-right politics suggests the adoption of far right as an umbrella term (Pirro, 2022), especially when working empirically. Definitions of this continuum have been notoriously varied; for the purpose of this introduction, and building on Mudde (2019), I approach the far right as ethnonationalist and authoritarian.[2] The latter goes beyond forms of government, but denotes the view that authority is to be respected and that infringements of authority are to be punished severely (think of law-and-order policies). Ethnonationalism (instead of speaking, like Mudde, of nativism), in turn, points to a range of exclusionary elements to be mobilised and a rich literature on the 'organic' relationship between people and land. Of course, elements such as anti-Americanism and anti-Semitism, ethnopluralism, revisionism and Islamophobia might be present too – though they are not necessary.

While not all far-right actors have shown an interest in environmental protection, there is an ideologically driven inclination towards a particular type of environmental concern (for a review, see Forchtner, 2019a). Its history has been eloquently told, albeit still focused on Germany and, to a lesser extent, on other Western countries. Thus, I limit the following to a brief overview of key aspects.[3] These aspects include Romantic views which integrally connect ethnic communities and 'their' nature (homeland), as well as colonial ideas of pristine lands (such as in the United States) and ideas justifying the reshaping of 'Annexed Eastern Areas' by Nazi Germany. It includes Social Darwinist and eugenic views related to 'racial deterioration' in proximity to concerns over nature by the likes of the German Ernst Haeckel and the American Madison Grant, respectively. In fact, the latter not only talked about ethnic replacement but also about races and their alleged adjustment to specific environmental conditions in *The Passing of the Great Race* (first published in 1916) – a book Hitler called his bible. Indeed, the Third Reich is arguably the single most extensively discussed case of the nexus of the far right and the natural environment. Linking race and conservation, it drew on and added to especially Romantic views and the *Heimatschutz* (homeland protection) movement (the latter – ultimately institutionalised as the Association for Homeland Protection in 1904 – appears to have, though not exclusively, been significant for the reproduction of *völkisch* ideas). Although its ideological affinity towards the protection of nature (to protect the *Volk*) featured environment-friendly elements, National Socialism largely subordinated these to productivist/war efforts. Extensive environmental management in support of political aims and claims to regenerate 'the people' were also visible in southern European fascisms, while fascist forces in the United Kingdom proposed environmental ideas around healthy environments and farming which, ultimately, found their way into the post-war environmental movement.

During the second half of the twentieth century, the far right–environment intersection often revolved around, for example, neo-Malthusian ideas of 'overpopulation' and anti-immigration environmentalism (in the United States associated with the likes of John Tranton), as well as the ideas of the New Right (initially in France before influencing a significant German contingent and beyond). During the early twenty-first century, far-right environmental concerns resurfaced, for example in France and Germany as well as Hungary and Poland, but also among prominent thinkers of the 'alt right' in the United States, such as Richard Spencer and Greg Johnson. The far-right desire for purity appears to be, furthermore, present beyond 'the West', for example in India. Yet, it was through outright violent terrorism, most prominently in the case of Christchurch (New Zealand) in 2019, that 'ecofascist' concerns for the natural environment received widespread public attention. Having said that, a fixation on this label and the most extreme version of the nation–nature nexus prevents a substantive understanding of the complexities of far-right politics of nature, a politics which not only has a multifaceted history but, today, has the potential to become particularly consequential through visualisation.

This politics is best understood as particularistic; that is, committed to a specific, bounded piece of land. Accordingly, it is different from the universalist and global outlook of most contemporary environmentalism. This should come as no surprise, given the ethnonationalist and authoritarian core of the far right, which strongly emphasises the role of territory. This is an ideological background against which eco-naturalism (nature as a blueprint for the social order, providing laws not subject to the zeitgeist) and eco-organicism (nature and society viewed in organicist terms, as interdependent and consisting of parts which develop and decay) have been identified as principal components (Olsen, 1999; Lubarda, 2020a). While, once again, environmental protection has often been ignored or even sabotaged by far-right actors, there exists an affinity with the natural environment in far-right thought which resides in a sense of ethno-communal rootedness.

This perceived relationship between the nation and its homeland in far-right environmentalism spans a 'cultural' relationship to one imagined as 'biological' (the infamous *Blut und Boden*, Blood and Soil). In both cases, this ethnicised relationship between people and land turns natural space into sacred territory; an 'ancestral homeland' and 'ethnoscape' (Smith, 1999). As such, the idea – and *feeling* – of the rootedness of a particular community in 'its' land is central. It is this exclusionary, particularistic relationship I propose to understand in terms of *eco-communion*. Drawing upon Anderson's (1983: 6) characterisation of the nation as an 'imagined community' whose members do not know each other directly – 'yet in the minds of each lives the image of their communion' – this notion directs our attention to a motivating source of environmental concern.[4] While Anderson points to the (emotional) bond connecting 'the people', those taking the relationship between nation and homeland seriously view this bond as not only binding the nation as people, but, to varying extents, extend the communion between human animals to non-human animals and beyond, to potentially all actants that are part of this ecosystem. It is this awareness and the feeling of being part of such a system which can motivate concern for the natural environment. This might include a preference for environmentally friendly farming (Lubarda, 2020b) as well as calls to prevent the loss of actants and to avoid the (too radical) addition of actants, whether human immigrants or non-human 'invasive species' (Hultgren, 2015; Forchtner, 2019b; Turner and Bailey, 2021). That is, it simultaneously serves as a boundary mechanism. Indeed, eco-communion is central to the far right's environmental/ecological imaginary (see Kølvraa, 2019 and Forchtner, 2019b, respectively), motivating its exclusionary concerns over and the embeddedness of 'the people' in 'their homeland'.[5] Such a bounded eco-communion asserts a desire for purity, order and (relative) stability, something visible in the 2017 assertion by the leader of the French party National Rally (the erstwhile Front National), Marine Le Pen: 'France is a living reality of men and women, lands and seas, trees and birds, rivers and forests, flavours and words (quoted in Boukala and Tountasaki, 2019: 79) and that '[t]he fight for [a] French identity is a fight to keep our gardens, mountains, companions, flowers, birds, butterflies' (quoted in Boukala and Tountasaki, 2019: 82). Such imaginaries, with their varying degrees of anthropocentrism, are reproduced through written and spoken words, as well as, among others, images. Consequently, they are, in manifold ways, implicated in strategic environmental communication and the articulation of 'ideal' far-right subjectivities. Indeed, all this, including Le Pen's claim above, points to aesthetic concerns (Forchtner and Kølvraa, 2015) and, thus, returns us to this volume's very agenda: Visual environmental communication by the far right and its ability to transform far-right ideas on the environment into affective, emotive and 'easily digested' images.

How can such eco-communion be squared with the widely noticed (though not uniformly present) scepticism on the far right towards (anthropogenic) climate change, related scientific knowledge creation/decision-making processes and policy responses connected to this phenomenon (for a recent article on climate change acceptance and obstruction, see Forchtner and Lubarda, 2022; for book-length discussions, see Malm and The Zetkin Collective, 2021; Moore and Roberts, 2022)? Why is it that an actor with an ideological affinity with the natural environment is not at the forefront of tackling what is likely to have severe effects on the 'national ecosystem'? These effects are increasingly visible, from changing tree populations and razed forests to changing rain seasons and mountains without glaciers. The reasons for evading these truths are many, from strategic calculations related to the political field and, for example, the alleged economic interests of those working in the fossil fuel industry to perceptions of climate policies as threats to 'petro-masculinity' (Daggett, 2018) and 'industrial/breadwinner masculinities' (Hultman et al., 2019) and a set of ideological factors concerned with the global (Forchtner and Kølvraa, 2015; Lockwood, 2018). The latter feeds into well-known far-right opposition to 'globalism', be it envisaged in the actions of a 'liberal-left cosmopolitan elite', attacks on national sovereignty or 'internationalist' values associated with the global nature of climate change. After all, the climate crisis has humanity as its referent and calls for global solidarity; it is thus manifestly different from an exclusivist type of solidarity marking far-right eco-communion. Finally, the far right is unlikely to feel much affinity with images of 'banal globalism' (Szerszynski et al., 2000: 110), for example depictions of the Antarctic ice shelf, instead favouring more local, contextualised depictions of the community's ecosystem that highlight the symbolic significance and beauty of 'the people's' piece of land.

Taking a step further, we might consider both the beautiful, which facilitates a restful and contemplative mind, for example an edelweiss in the Austrian Alps or the quiet scenery of a beach in Denmark, and the sublime, that is, the vast and magnificent capable of moving the mind, such as a massif or a tempestuous sea (see Kant, 1797 [1764]). Indeed, the sublime might be equally (or even more) powerful in evoking 'our' nature, and supporting the articulation of an 'ideal' subjectivity. The commitment to an exclusionary, particularistic, ethno-communal ecosystem is connected to a special type of (initially Romantic) appreciation of, even sensibility towards, the environment (Hinchman and Hinchman, 2007). Such a commitment also finds its expression in the natural environment as a site of 'banal nationalism' (Billig, 1995) or 'everyday nationalism' (Fox and Miller-Idriss, 2008). This may range from an edelweiss on a coin to the ordinary social practices of people through which community is actively performed. Attempts to keep 'the land' beautiful through 'eco-actions', such as clean-ups, are thus not unheard of on the far right (for example, Tarant, 2019), and find a historical predecessor in, for example, early twentieth-century German *Heimatschutz's* (homeland protection's) aesthetic concerns (Rollins, 1997). This affection contrasts sharply with global depictions of the climate, which is commonly visualised via, for example, scientific graphs, global elite-driven processes and iconic representations revolving around 'no man's land', such as Antarctica, and distant animals, such as polar bears. This context makes it arguably more difficult to visualise the climate as being part of 'us' – but is there more to say about the diverse ways in which the far right has made aesthetic sense of environmental issues?

Here, it is worth taking a step back and connecting far-right subjectivity and imagery to the extreme end of the far-right spectrum, to fascism, which Paxton (2004: 9) described as the 'most self-consciously visual political formation', and more specifically to fascist aesthetics. Walter Benjamin's (1996) concern over the 'aestheticisation of politics' in 'The Work of Art in the Age of Mechanical Reproduction', originally published in 1935, can serve as an entry point to consider presentation and perception in far-right politics. According to Benjamin, fascist aestheticisation diverts people's attention away from how society is materially organised and towards perception, which results in enjoyment and inspiration. Perhaps most famously, he referred to Marinetti's celebration of war being beautiful, though his wider point is that such aestheticisation aims for stability against a background of modernity's liquifying tendencies. Such spectacle aims for closure in a world in flux and, thus, allegedly contrasts with open genre that are fragmentary and dynamic. However, more recent scholarship has pointed out that Italian Futurists' montages had already objected to harmony and reconciliation, as well as to closure (Affron and Antliff, 1997). Rather, they wished to reinvigorate society, to imagine an alternative time and to mould new, genuinely fascist subjectivities, rituals and symbols.

Fascism's aesthetic politics was thus both semiotically significant and overpowering. Yet this should not imply the existence of a shared repertoire, nor even a shared aesthetic strategy. As Thomas (2020: 9) has recently argued, fascism's 'visual tactics were effective because they were diverse, opportunistic, and incoherent'. Similarly, Eley (2020: 287) notes that the visualisations provided by fascism concerned not only the 'large-scale public machinery of spectacles' but also 'small-scale sentimentality too'. This is where these considerations connect to celebrations of both beauty and the sublime by the far right today. While only some of the cases discussed in this volume are properly described as fascist, *Visualising Far-Right Environments* highlights that contemporary far-right imagery of nature too does not eschew a single style or set of aesthetic strategies. Accordingly, contributions to this volume illustrate both commonalities and differences between far-right actors' visualisations of the natural environment today and ways in which these attempt to be transformative.

The real-world significance of images

It is here that we need to return to images that may facilitate such a trans-formation – both in terms of effectively communicating political agendas and imagining alternative, 'ideal' subjectivities. As suggested earlier, not only have images become ever more prevalent – a development now driven especially by the ease with which they can be produced, consumed and circulated – but their impact is well documented too. As Harper (2002: 13) argues, 'images evoke deeper elements of human consciousness than do words; exchanges based on words alone utilise less of the brain's capacity than do exchanges in which the brain is processing images as well as words'. O'Neill (2013: 10) thus views images as particularly persuasive, especially in terms of their ability 'to draw in audiences through vivid and emotive portrayals [...] they can portray highly ideological messages, and act as normative statements portraying a particular way of viewing the world'. Likewise, Blair (2004: 59) highlights the immediacy, verisimilitude and concreteness of visuals, while Joffe (2008: 217) speaks of their emotive, vivid and memorable character which 'proves' the authenticity of the depicted and, thus, their potential power to create, alter or reinforce actions and beliefs. Undoubtedly, the emotiveness of images can result in both the simplification of complex arguments and the amplification of the force of a text's claim. As I mentioned at the beginning of this introduction, images might evoke love for the homeland, fear of its despoliation and disgust for those (cosmopolitan hysterics) who endanger it. In so doing, they not only represent but act as devices that tie together networks of associations and affects (Carah, 2014: 138). They thus act as powerful loci in boundary-making. All this is connected to Berger's (1972) contention that 'seeing comes before words'. Yet Berger also reminds us that the effect an image might have does not simply reside in what is seen, but is invariably affected by the viewing subject. Indeed, instead of solely considering the image itself, the 'act of seeing' too is sociocultural, constituted through histories of knowledge, power and domination.

The persuasiveness of images is connected to their particularly polysemic nature. The latter can be strategically mobilised in coded semiosis, for example in what Wodak (2013) has referred to as calculated ambivalence. Due to their polysemy, the meaning of images is regularly 'anchored' to the written mode. However, images might alternatively have an equal status, as in Barthes' (1977: 38–41) original proposal on text–image relations; or, indeed, the written text might be subordinated as in Stöckl et al.'s (2021) aforementioned discussion of image-centricity. Furthermore, the persuasiveness of images derives from their ability to position via the creation of imaginary social relations between the viewer and the subject represented (Kress and van Leeuwen, 2006). For example, images may raise a 'demand' through direct eye contact between the subject represented and the viewer. Alternatively, images may 'offer' – by positioning the viewer as an 'invisible onlooker' – turning the depicted into an object of one's gaze. Similarly, viewers can also be positioned through frame size, from being close enough to touch to close enough to interact with; or being further away. Furthermore, an image angle can convey hierarchy, from a low angle indicating the superiority of the subject represented to a high angle doing the opposite, from a frontal angle which invites full involvement to a more sideways angle (or even shots from behind). Besides and beyond the aspects already mentioned, there is a semiotic richness to moving images, as illustrated recently by van Leeuwen (2021). The latter takes as its subject news read by a Dutch national broadcaster, in which corona viruses floated over a blue space, 'seemingly weightless and slowly moving, mostly towards the right and slightly upwards'. In this representation, direction signifies the viruses' threatening progress. In short, there is ample indication of the significance of images in positioning viewers and this no doubt also applies to visualisations of the natural environment by the far right. Hence, the visual mode can play a primary role in normalising far-right views and thus has to play a central role in analyses of such politics of the natural environment.

Resources for a 'visual turn'

Against this background, scholarship on the particularities of visual environmental communication by the far right is urgently required – that is, scholarship on far-right communication which fosters eco-communion and obstructs environmental protection. True, there has been research on the historical far right and imagery (recent work includes O'Shaughnessy, 2017; Thomas and Eley, 2020), but research relating to the contemporary far right and the natural environment has seldom explored the role of visuals in detail. That said, there have been important exceptions, including Turner-Graham (2012), who describes (but does not feature) local images of the landscape in her discussion of the youth wing of the Freedom Party of Austria's online presence. Similarly, Pettersson et al. (2022) describe and analyse humour and irony in a misogynist, climate change-related campaign video by the Finns Party, while Malm and The Zetkin Collective (2021) open *White Skin, Black Fuel* with a description of a climate-related cartoon by what was back then the True Finns party. With complementary arguments derived from analyses of the written mode, Bogerts and Fietz (2019) include an image as they mention nature and family in their analysis of memes of the German far right, while Awad et al. (2022) include an example of landscape in their analysis of boundary construction by the Danish People's Party and Turner and Bailey (2021) present two images which portray immigration as a threat to the natural environment in their conceptualisation of 'ecobordering'. Forchtner et al. (2018) feature the cover pages of German far-right magazines concerned with climate change, while Hurd and Werther (2016) comment on a series of images in their study on German neo-Nazi environmentalism and Hughes et al. (2022) present a range of images to illustrate ideological themes by ecofascist circles on Twitter and Telegram. More detailed analysis is found in Westberg and Årman's (2019) work on aesthetics in Swedish neo-Nazism and Forchtner and Kølvraa's (2017) examination of the construction of authority and intimacy through visuals about, for example, nature.

As such, visual analysis of far-right natural environments has only just begun. No doubt, emerging work will especially benefit from two extant bodies of literature. On the one hand, this concerns the field of visual environmental communication. On the other hand, research on images in far-right communication offers valuable resources.

Analysing visuals has become an increasingly buoyant area of research in environmental communication (for reviews, see Hansen, 2018; O'Neill and Smith, 2014). Much recent work has dealt with climate change (for a review, see Wang et al., 2018), but crucial work has also been done on visual branding (Porter, 2013; Takach, 2013), offering insights from fields not usually included in the study of the far right. This focus on branding speaks, moreover, to how older imaginaries of the natural environment can affect contemporary visualisation, with both Porter (2013) and Takach (2013) pointing to, for example, the presence of Romantic associations/a Romantic gaze. Another study (Meisner and Takahashi, 2013) offers a content analysis of visualisations of environmental affairs on the covers of *Time* magazine. The authors suggest that the written mode anchors the meaning of visuals. By contrast, DiFrancesco and Young (2011), in their analysis of visual communication in print media coverage of climate change in Canada, observe that meanings conveyed through visuals and written text tend to point in different directions (for similar findings, see O'Neil et al., 2022). Such findings call for similar enquiry regarding the far right and, given the latter's concerns over the 'purity' of the land, may well find inspiration in Peeples' (2013) study of imaging toxins, or Kroma and Flora's (2003) content analysis of pesticide advertising in agricultural magazines.

Turning to resources offered in work on climate change communication, O'Neill (2020) investigates changes in iconic climate imagery between 2001 and 2009 through a content analysis of newspapers in the United States and the United Kingdom, while Born (2019) focuses on the icon of the polar bears in her multimodal critical discourse analysis. The former study also notes that polar bears, smokestacks and wind turbines were increasingly subverted and parodied in right-leaning newspapers (in line with their climate scepticism), findings which could inform comparisons with such visualisations in far-right sources. Indeed, such imagery can be plausibly assumed to act as an emotive basis for far-right polemics. The latter have long been directed towards Al Gore whose film An Inconvenient Truth, or more precisely its trailer, is analysed by Bortoluzzi (2009) in the context of multimodal constructions of emotionally loaded identities.

The reception of images is also a site of relevant research, such as in O'Neill and Nicholson-Cole's (2009) interview- and focus group-based investigation of how fear-inducing imagery can make people recognise the significance of climate change but also disempower them. Chapman et al. (2016) ran structured discussion groups and a survey in the United Kingdom, the United States and Germany in order to see how members of the wider public evaluate climate change imagery. Metag et al. (2016) used Q methodology to argue that perceptions of such imagery are fairly consistent in many parts of 'the West' – an observation which raises the question of whether this is also the case beyond 'the West' and in the far right.

Possibly the richest area of research to be mobilised regards the literature on frame analysis (see Schäfer and O'Neill, 2017 for an overview). For example, Wozniak et al. (2017), based on a combination of semi-structured interviews and content analysis of newspapers, show that the verbal-textual mode in climate change coverage is dominated by traditional authorities, while non-governmental organisations are more successful regarding their visual framing conceptions. Wozniak et al. (2015) propose a multimodal research design for the standardised content analysis of climate change reportage, bringing together framing, narration and visual representation. Rebich-Hespanha et al. (2015) draw upon content and cluster analysis when approaching imagery in news articles in the United States and identify common themes and frames around broad categories of technology and society; nature; and disaster and risk. Arguably, these categories are also relevant to the far right's visual communication. O'Neill (2013) researched images in online articles published by newspapers in the United States, the United Kingdom and Australia by means of content and frame analysis, identifying a contested visual frame as well as a distancing visual frame. In contrast, Hopke and Hestres (2018) offer a quantitative content analysis of visual framing emerging in Twitter debates over the Conference of the Parties meeting in Paris in 2015. A multilevel approach to imagery, also holding promise for the study of far-right visual communication, is offered by Culloty et al. (2019), who propose a four-level analysis of visual climate change analysis: from content to frame, audience and ideological analyses.

Unlike an often quantitative focus of scholarship upon environment communication, studies of visual representations of far-right politics have more typically been qualitatively oriented, and thus offer a different set of insights. For example, Richardson and Colombo (2013) examine the Italian *Lega Nord* (Northern League), particularly the continuities and changes visible in their anti-immigrant posters. Their perspective embraces the discourse-historical approach (DHA) in critical discourse studies and explicitly connects visual and linguistic content. Also drawing upon the DHA, Richardson and Wodak (2009) provide a qualitative analysis of far-right visual communication in Austria and Britain, pointing out implied racist meanings. Similar dynamics are observed by Wodak and Forchtner (2014), who investigate a comic by the Austrian Freedom Party, also within the framework of the DHA. Doerr (2017) conducted a cross-national comparison of anti-immigration cartoon images across Europe, combining multimodal analysis and the DHA, while Doerr (2021) looks at the Alternative for Germany in her multimodal analysis of far-right communication about women's empowerment and LGBT rights. Relatedly, Mehta (2015) also draws on images in her analysis of everyday politics and violence produced by Hindu right-wing women, arguing that these help to negotiate a 'feminine' space within such a political project at large. Focusing on the German far right and fashion, Miller-Idriss (2018) offers analyses of the role played by symbols and images. Turning to online imagery, Hakoköngäs et al. (2020) investigate a corpus of Internet memes circulated by the Finnish far right on Facebook. Following a classification according to the memes' main content, the authors employ multimodal discourse analysis. Another study on the Finnish far right (Hokka and Nelimarkka, 2020) draws upon computational data analysis when investigating the affective economy of such images on Facebook. Turning towards moving images, Ekman (2014) and Peters (2015) analyse YouTube videos by far-right actors in Sweden and Germany, respectively. The former identifies eight thematic categories which are then qualitatively analysed, while Peters focuses qualitatively on a video and a webpage.

While these studies offer vital insights into how to multimodally analyse far-right strategic communication and the interpellation of 'ideal' subjectivities, Bast (2021) adds a quantitative content analysis of (visual) image management on Instagram by leading figures of populist radical-right parties in Europe. The study covered meaning manifest at the surface level plus quasi-manifest content, though not the latent meaning of images. Furthermore, Schmuck and Matthes (2017: 620) conducted a survey-experiment with Austrian citizens to investigate the effect of portrayals of immigrants as economic and symbolic threats, arguing that including 'an attention-grabbing image (...) reinforces the effects of the mere textual appeals on anti-immigrant

attitudes and extends them to a broader population'. This, again, highlights
the need for dedicated scholarly study of *visual* environmental communication
by the far right; and this volume hopes to serve as a springboard for such
an engagement.

Overview of contributions to the volume

In this final section, I introduce the subsequent chapters which present
analyses of a wide range of actors, ranging from radical-right to extreme-right
ones, from metapolitical ones to political parties. These chapters deal with
both new and legacy media and showcase significant methodological variety,
applying both qualitative and quantitative approaches. However, the chapters
are arranged neither according to these categories nor along geographical
lines, for example starting with cases from the Global South before turning
to Europe. Instead, I employ a thematic logic. That is, the chapters move
from a focus on concrete and particular natural environments in which
communities can be rooted (although not the same, this covers local, regional
and/or national place) to the abstract and global issue of climate change.
In so doing, the volume foregrounds the visualisation of far-right engagement
with different types of environmental issues.

The first three chapters concern settler-colonial cases, starting with South
Africa. Here, Scott Burnett introduces a modernised style and vocabulary
when analysing an influential music video which reproduces white masculinity
through depictions of rural life and landscape. In particular, his analysis
stresses the strategic deployment of affect, thus pointing to an important
dimension to consider when analysing such communication. This contribution
is followed by Chapter 2 on visual environmental communication by the
far right in Australia and New Zealand. Drawing on the concept of ecofascism,
Kristy Campion and Justin Phillips reveal how members of the Australian
National Socialist Network and Action Zealandia multimodally express
exclusive entitlement to the land online. In Chapter 3, the first of two
chapters dealing with the United States, Daniel Jones analyses the National
Socialist Movement. He does so by considering the communication of three
campaigns (the adoption of a highway to keep a stretch of roadway clean,
the 'protection' of the Mexican border and the promotion of outdoor activities)
via its website and magazines, and argues that eco-action, custodianship of
'the land' and its border, and outdoorsmanship facilitate the sense of a cultic
milieu.

These chapters are followed by three contributions on similarly 'land-
centred' Eurasian cases. In the first of these chapters, Carmen Aguilera-
Carnerero deals with the Spanish radical-right party Vox. Analysing images
and videos circulated via Twitter and Instagram, she illustrates how the

countryside is multimodally articulated as the backbone of the nation, that is, how it functions as an anchor of Spanish identity, of *us* and *them*. In Chapter 5, Miranda Christou examines images of 'the land' from the website of the extreme-right party National Popular Front in Cyprus. Drawing on ecofeminist theory, she illuminates the party's website communication as presenting the heroic masculinity of a liberator and saviour of a sacred national territory, one which is conceptualised as female, enslaved (by Turks) and endangered (by fires). The last case in this set of contributions is provided by Sonja Pietiläinen, who analyses images concerning the Russian Arctic from the Izborskii Club, an intellectual organisation and one of the most prominent far-right forces in Russia. By investigating the club's magazine, she illustrates how imagery justifies the exploration and exploitation of the region, and reproduces white, masculine notions of national identity.

Chapters 7 to 11 deal, to varying extents, with cases in which the local/regional/national environment and global climate change are addressed. The first of these chapters is authored by Radka Vicenová, Veronika Oravcová and Matúš Mišík and considers the role of nature in the far-right Slovak party Kotlebovci – People's Party Our Slovakia. The authors analyse the party's newspaper as a whole, thus enabling an understanding of the (rather minimal) role the environment plays within the party's wider communication, and point out the symbolic significance of the homeland and the emotional charge/rational argumentation present in this communication. Chapter 8 turns to France as Zoé Carle offers a multimodal analysis of how both far-right metapolitical and party-political actors have put the environment on the agenda. Focusing on webpages and social media platforms, she identifies localism and rootedness as providing common ground for otherwise diverging engagements with the natural environment. In Chapter 9, Balša Lubarda analyses the ideological versatility and semiotic flexibility of visual environmental communication of two Hungarian political parties, the far-right Our Homeland and a left-of-centre green party. Considering relevant Facebook posts, he illuminates overlaps in their environmental communication, ranging from animal welfare to climate change. Moving to India, Mukul Sharma offers insights into far-right Hindu nationalism and how the latter mobilises environmental aspects in Chapter 10. In particular, he focuses on how the magazine of the National Volunteer Organisation multimodally constructs 'self' and 'other' through representation of the Hindu motherland/homeland, the 'sacred' river Ganga and cows, policies related to climate change and renewable energy, and Prime Minister Narendra Modi as an environmental saviour. In the final chapter of this third set of contributions, Bernhard Forchtner and Jonathan Olsen explicitly compare the role of the local/regional/national environment and global climate change by analysing two dedicated subcorpora consisting of articles and related images derived from far-right party and non-party magazines in Germany. While the environment is largely affirmed, they illustrate that climate change and related policies are viewed rather sceptically in the investigated corpus, something they pinpoint as being due to the differently gendered natures of these two domains and a fundamental, ideological aversion towards the global in far-right ideology.

Finally, Chapters 12 and 13 relate to climate change. First, Kjell Vowles offers an analysis of the Swedish YouTube channel SwebbTV. More specifically, he showcases how to analyse the use of graphs; in the case of SwebbTV to convey a contrarian scientific message through showing correct graphs – but claiming that they are false, through misinterpreting correct graphs, through modes of cherry-picking and outright manipulation. In Chapter 13, Lauren Cagle provides a comparative rhetorical analysis of far-right and left-wing climate conspiracists, focusing on the form, not content, of their communication. She introduces the notion of a 'paranoid visual style' and illustrates that conspiracist information by far-right actors might look different from what one might expect.

In a concluding chapter, Bernhard Forchtner considers the findings present across chapters, for example regarding themes characterising far-right visual environmental communication; how historically and culturally resonant ideas of nature, for example Romantic, *völkisch* or overtly fascist ones, feature in such imagery; representations of local/regional/national sites vis-à-vis global ones; the emotions present; and possible overlaps between far-right and centrist/left-wing visual communication, before pointing to a few avenues for future research.

Whether it is politicians posing in the countryside, explicit invocations of the nature–nation nexus or attacks on climate activists and environmental agendas, articulations of the natural environment by the far right are today inconceivable without images. Hence, and given that environmental crises are going to remain key in the public imagination, their persuasive and subjectivity-constituting powers must be taken seriously. *Visualising Far-Right Environments* hopes to respond to this.

Notes

I am grateful to Lise Benoist, Matthew Feldman, Mirjam Gruber, Christoffer Kølvraa, Balša Lubarda, Jonathan Olsen and Julian Matthews for helpful comments on earlier versions of this chapter. All mistakes remain my own.

1 Both for pragmatic reasons and due to public usage, I largely speak of 'environment'/
   'environmental', subsuming other notions such as 'nature' and 'ecology'/'ecological'

under this umbrella (see Radkau, 2014). See Dobson (1999: 235f) for a widely shared differentiation between managerial environmentalism and radical ecologism.

2 As the nation remains the main point of reference for the far right, speaking of ethnonationalism is justified even though exclusionary bonds at other levels ('race'/'civilisation'/region) might be relevant too.

3 This very brief overview draws on, for example, Biehl and Staudenmaier (2011 [1995]), Rollins (1997), Olsen (1999), Brüggemeier et al. (2005), Sharma (2012), Voss (2014), Hultgren (2015), Forchtner (2019a), Jones (2021), Staudenmaier (2021), Moore and Roberts (2022), Armiero *et al.* (2022) and Lubarda (2023). See also subsequent chapters in this volume.

4 Campion (2021: 2) too has drawn upon Anderson's concept of 'imagined community' when defining ecofascism as a 'reactionary and revolutionary ideology that champions the regeneration of an imagined community through a return to a romanticised, ethnopluralist vision of the natural order.' For further, recent thoughts on ecofascism, see, for example, Rueda (2020), Darwish (2021), Szenes (2021), Hughes et al. (2022) and Macklin (2022). See also the aforementioned Moore and Roberts (2022).

5 On the imagination of elements of the Romanian landscape as xenophobic and sentinent, as siding with the nation against 'others', see Cotofana (2022).

References

Affron, M. and Antliff, M. (1997): Art and fascism in France and Italy: An introduction. In: M. Affron and M. Antliff (eds), *Fascist Visions: Art and Ideology in France and Italy*. Princeton: Princeton University Press, 3–24.

Anderson, B. (1983): *Imagined Communities: Reflections on the Origin and Spread of Nationalism*. London: Verso.

Armiero, M., Biasillo, R. and Graf von Hardenberg, W. (2022): *Mussolini's Nature: An Environmental History of Italian Fascism*. Cambridge, MA: MIT Press.

Awad, S., Doerr, N. and Nissen, A. (2022): Far-right boundary construction towards the 'other': Visual communication of Danish People's Party on social media, *The British Journal of Sociology*. https://doi.org/10.1111/1468-4446.12975

Barthes, R. (1977): Rhetoric of the image. In: R. Barthes, *Image, Music, Text*. London: Fontana, 32–51.

Bast, J. (2021): Managing the image: The visual communication strategy of European right-wing populist politicians on Instagram, *Journal of Political Marketing*. https://doi.org/10.1080/15377857.2021.1892901.

Bateman, J. A. (2014): *Text and Image: A Critical Introduction to the Visual/Verbal Divide*. London: Routledge.

Benjamin, W. (1996): Das Kunstwerk im Zeitalter seiner technischen Reproduzierbarkeit. In: M. Opitz (ed.), *Walter Benjamin: Ein Lesebuch*. Frankfurt/Main: Suhrkamp, 313–347.

Berger, J. (1972): *Ways of Seeing*. London: Penguin.

Biehl, J. and Staudenmaier, P. (2011 [1995]): *Ecofascism Revisited*. Porsgrunn: New Compass Press.

Billig, M. (1995): *Banal Nationalism*. London: Sage.

Blair, A. (2004): The rhetoric of visual arguments. In: C. Hill and M. Helmers (eds), *Defining Visual Rhetorics*. Mahwah: Lawrence Erlbaum, 41–61.

Bogerts, L. and Fielitz, M (2019): 'Do you want meme war?': Understanding the visual memes of the German far right. In: M. Fielitz and N. Thurston (eds), *Post-Digital Cultures of the Far Right: Online Actions and Offline Consequences in Europe and the US*. Bielefeld: transcript, 137–153.

Born, D. (2019): Bearing witness? Polar bears as icons for climate change communication, *National Geographic, Environmental Communication*, 13(5): 649–663. https://doi.org/10.1080/17524032.2018.1435557

Bortoluzzi, M. (2009): An Inconvenient Truth: Multimodal emotions in identity construction. In: J. Vincent and L. Fortunati (eds), *Electronic Emotion: The Mediation of Emotion via Information and Communication Technologies*. Bern: Peter Lang, 137–164.

Boukala, S. and Tountasaki, E. (2019): From black to green: Analysing *Le Front National*'s 'patriotic ecology'. In: B. Forchtner (ed.), *The Far Right and the Environment*. London: Routledge, 72–87.

Brüggemeier, F. J., Cioc M. and Zeller, T. (eds) (2005): *How Green Were the Nazis? Nature, Environment, and Nation in the Third Reich*. Athens, OH: Ohio University Press.

Campion, K. (2021): Defining ecofascism: Historical foundations and contemporary interpretations in the extreme right, *Terrorism and Political Violence*. https://doi.org/10.1080/09546553.2021.1987895.

Carah, N. (2014): Curators of databases: Circulating images, managing attention and making value on social media, *Media International Australia*, 150(1): 137–142.

Chapman, D., Corner, A., Webster, R. and Markowitz, E. (2016): Climate visuals: A mixed methods investigation of public perceptions of climate images in three countries, *Global Environmental Change*, 41: 172–182. https://doi.org/10.1016/j.gloenvcha.2016.10.003

Cotofana, A. (2022): *Xenophobic Mountains: Landscape Sentience Reconsidered in the Romanian Carpathians*. Cham: Palgrave.

Culloty, E., Murphy, P., Brereton, P., Suiter, J., Smeaton A. and Zhang, D. (2019): Researching visual representations of climate change, *Environmental Communication*, 13(2): 179–191.

Daggett, C. (2018): Petro-masculinity: Fossil fuels and authoritarian desire, *Millennium*, 47(1): 25–44. https://doi.org/10.1177%2F0305829818775817

Darwish, M. (2021): Nature, masculinities, care and the far-right. In: M. Hultman and P. Pulé (eds), *Men, Masculinities, and Earth Contending with the (m)Anthropocene*. Cham: Palgrave Macmillan, 183–206.

Debord, G. (1994): *The Society of the Spectacle*. London: Rebel Press.

DiFrancesco, D. and Young, N. (2011): Seeing climate change: The visual construction of global warming in Canadian national print media, *Cultural Geographies*, 18(4): 517–536. https://doi.org/10.1177%2F1474474010382072

Dobson, A. (1999): Ecologism. In: R. Eatwell and A. Wright (eds), *Contemporary Political Ideologies*. London: Pinter, 231–254.

Doerr, N. (2017): Bridging language barriers, bonding against immigrants: A visual case study of transnational network publics created by far-right activists in Europe, *Discourse and Society*, 28(1): 3–23. https://doi.org/10.1177%2F0957926516676689

Doerr, N. (2021): The visual politics of the Alternative for Germany (AfD): Anti-Islam, ethno-nationalism, and gendered images, *Social Sciences*, 10(1). https://doi.org/10.3390/socsci10010020

Ekman, M. (2014): The dark side of online activism: Swedish right-wing extremist video activism on YouTube, *MedieKultur*, 56: 79–99. https://doi.org/10.7146/mediekultur.v30i56.8967

Eley, G. (2020): Conclusion. In: J. A. Thomas and G. Eley (eds), *Visualizing Fascism: The Twentieth-Century Rise of the Global Right*. Durham, NC: Duke University Press, 284–292.

Evans, J. and Hall, S. (1999): *Visual Culture: The Reader*. London: Sage.

Forchtner, B. (2019b): Nation, nature, purity: Extreme-right biodiversity in Germany, *Patterns of Prejudice*, 53(3): 285–301. https://doi.org/10.1080/0031322X.2019.1592303

Forchtner, B. (ed.) (2019a): *The Far Right and the Environment*. London: Routledge.

Forchtner, B. and Kølvraa, C. (2015): The nature of nationalism: Populist radical right parties on countryside and climate, *Nature + Culture*, 10(2): 199–224. https://doi.org/10.1080/0031322X.2019.1592303

Forchtner, B. and Kølvraa, C. (2017): Extreme right images of radical authenticity: Multimodal aesthetics of history, nature and gender in social media, *European Journal of Cultural and Political Sociology*, 4(3): 252–281.

Forchtner, B. and Lubarda, B. (2022): Scepticisms and beyond? A comprehensive portrait of climate change communication by the far right in the European Parliament, *Environmental Politics*. https://doi.org/10.1080/09644016.2022.2048556

Forchtner, B., Kroneder, A. and Wetzel, D. (2018): Being skeptical? Exploring far-right climate-change communication in Germany, *Environmental Communication*, 12(5): 589–604. https://doi.org/10.1080/17524032.2018.1470546

Fox, J. and Miller-Idriss, C. (2008): Everyday nationhood, *Ethnicities*, 8(4): 536–576.

Hakoköngäs, E., Halmesvaara, O. and Sakki, I. (2020): Persuasion through bitter humor: Multimodal discourse analysis of rhetoric in Internet memes of two far-right groups in Finland, *Social Media + Society*. https://doi.org/10.1177%2F2056305120921575

Hansen, A. (2018): Using visual images to show environmental problems. In: A. Fill and H. Penz (eds), *The Routledge Handbook of Ecolinguistics*. London: Routledge, 179–195.

Harper, D. (2002): Talking about pictures: A case for photo elicitation, *Visual Studies*, 17(1): 13–26. https://doi.org/10.1080/14725860220137345

Heywood, I. and Sandywell, B. (2012): *The Handbook of Visual Culture*. London: Bloomsbury.

Hinchman, L. and Hinchman, S. (2007): What we owe the Romantics, *Environmental Values*, 16(3): 333–354. http://dx.doi.org/10.3197/096327107X228382

Hokka, J. and Nelimarkka, M. (2020): Affective economy of national-populist images: Investigating national and transnational online networks through visual big data, *New Media & Society*, 22(5): 770–792. https://doi.org/10.1177%2F1461444819868686

Hopke, J. E. and Hestres, L. E. (2018): Visualizing the Paris climate talks on Twitter: Media and climate stakeholder visual social media during COP21, *Social Media + Society*, 4(3): 1–15. https://doi.org/10.1177%2F2056305118782687

Hughes, B., Jones, D. and Amarasingam, A. (2022): Ecofascism: An examination of the far-right/ecology nexus in the online space, *Terrorism and Political Violence*. https//doi.org/10.1080/09546553.2022.2069932.

Hultgren, J. (2015): *Border Walls Gone Green: Nature and Anti-immigrant Politics in America*. Minneapolis: University of Minnesota Press.

Hultman, M., Björk, A. and Viinikka, T. (2019): The far right and climate change denial: Denouncing environmental challenges via anti-establishment rhetoric, marketing of doubts, industrial/breadwinner masculinities enactments and ethnonationalism. In: B. Forchtner (ed.), *The Far Right and the Environment*. London: Routledge, 121–135.

Hurd, M. and Werther, S. (2016): The militant media of neo-Nazi environmentalism. In: H. Graf (ed.), *The Environment in the Age of the Internet: Activists, Communication, and the Digital Landscape*. Cambridge: Open Book Publishers, 137–170.

Joffe, H. (2008): The power of visual material: Persuasion, emotion and identification, *Diogenes*, 217: 84–93.

Jones, R. (2021): *White Borders*. Boston: Beacon Press.

Kant, I. (1797 [1764]): *Beobachtung über das Gefühl des Schönen und Erhabenen*. Graz: Andreas Lenkam.

Kølvraa, C. (2019): Wolves in sheep's clothing? The Danish far right and 'wild nature'. In: B. Forchtner (ed.), *The Far Right and the Environment*. London: Routledge, 107–120.

Kølvraa, C. and Forchtner, B. (2019): Cultural imaginaries of the extreme right: An introduction, *Patterns of Prejudice*, 53(3): 227–235. https://doi.org/10.1080/0031322X.2019.1609275

Kress, G. and van Leeuwen, T. (2006): *Reading Images: The Grammar of Visual Design*. London: Routledge.

Kroma, M. M. and Flora, C. B. (2003): Greening pesticides: A historical analysis of the social construction of farm chemical advertisements, *Agriculture and Human Values*, 20(1): 21–35. https://doi.org/10.1023/A:1022408506244

Lockwood, M. (2018): Right-wing populism and the climate change agenda, *Environmental Politics*, 27(4): 712–732. https://doi.org/10.1080/09644016.2018.1458411

Lubarda, B. (2023): *Far-Right Ecologism: Environmental Politics and the Far Right in Hungary and Poland*. London: Routledge.

Lubarda, B. (2020a): Beyond ecofascism? Far right ecologism (FRE) as a framework for future inquiries, *Environmental Values*, 29(6): 713–732. http://dx.doi.org/10.3197/096327120X15752810323922

Lubarda, B. (2020b): Homeland farming' or 'rural emancipation'? The discursive overlap between populist and green parties in Hungary, *Sociologia Ruralis*, 60(4): 810–832. https://doi.org/10.1111/soru.12289

Macklin, G. (2022): The extreme right, climate change and terrorism, *Terrorism and Political Violence.* https://doi.org/10.1080/09546553.2022.2069928

Malm, A. and The Zetkin Collective (2021): *White Skin, Black Fuel: On the Danger of Fossil Fascism.* London: Verso.

Mehta, A. (2015): The aesthetics of 'everyday' violence: Narratives of violence and Hindu right-wing women, *Critical Studies on Terrorism,* 8(3): 416–438. https://doi.org/10.1080/17539153.2015.1091656

Meisner, M. and Takahashi, B. (2013): The nature of *Time*: How the covers of the world's most widely read weekly news magazine visualize environmental affairs, *Environmental Communication,* 7(2): 255–276. https://doi.org/10.108 0/17524032.2013.772908

Metag, J., Schäfer, M., Füchslin, T., Barsuhn, T. and von Königslöw, K. (2016): Perceptions of climate change imagery: Evoked salience and self-efficacy in Germany, Switzerland, and Austria, *Science Communication,* 38(2): 197–227. http://dx.doi.org/10.1177/1075547016635181

Miller-Idriss, C. (2018): *The Extreme Gone Mainstream: Commercialization and Far-Right Youth Culture in Germany.* Princeton: Princeton University Press.

Mirzoeff, N. (1998): What is visual culture? In: N. Mirzoeff (ed.), *The Visual Culture Reader.* London: Routledge, 3–13.

Moore, S. and Roberts, A. (2022): *The Rise of Ecofascism: Climate Change and the Far Right.* Cambridge: Polity Press.

Mudde, C. (2019): *The Far Right Today.* Cambridge: Polity Press.

O'Neill, S. (2013): Image matters: Climate change imagery in US, UK and Australian newspapers, *Geoforum,* 49: 10–19. https://doi.org/10.1016/j.geoforum.2013.04.030

O'Neill, S. (2020): More than meets the eye: A longitudinal analysis of climate change imagery in the print media, *Climatic Change,* 163: 9–26. https://doi.org/10.1007/s10584–019–02504–8

O'Neill, S. and Nicholson-Cole, S. (2009): 'Fear won't do it': Promoting positive engagement with climate change through visual and iconic representations, *Science Communication,* 30(3): 355–379. https://doi.org/10.1177%2F1075547008329201

O'Neill, S., Hayes, S., Strauß, N., Doutreix, M., Steentjes, K., Ettinger, J., Westood, N. and Painter, J. (2022): Visual portrayals of fun in the sun misrepresent heatwave risks in European newspapers. *The Geographical Journal.* https://doi.org/10.1111/geoj.12487

O'Neil, S. and Smith, N. (2014): Climate change and visual imagery, *WIREs Climate Change,* 5: 73–87. https://doi.org/10.1002/wcc.249

O'Shaughnessy, N. (2017): *Marketing the Third Reich: Persuasion, Packaging and Propaganda.* London: Routledge.

Olsen, J. (1999): *Nature and Nationalism.* New York: St. Martin's Press.

Paxton, R. O. (2004): *The Anatomy of Fascism.* New York: Alfred A. Knopf.

Peeples, J. (2013): Imaging toxins, *Environmental Communication,* 7(2): 191–210. https://doi.org/10.1080/17524032.2013.775172

Peters, R. (2015): Become immortal! Mediatization and mediation processes of extreme right protest, *Conjunctions,* 2(1): 132–152.

Pettersson, K., Martikainen, J., Hakoköngäs, E. and Sakki, I. (2022): Female politicians as climate fools: Intertextual and multimodal constructions of misogyny disguised as humor in political communication, *Political Psychology*. https://doi.org/10.1111/pops.12814

Pirro, A. L. P. (2022): Far right: The significance of an umbrella concept, *Nations and Nationalism*. https://doi.org/10.1111/nana.12860

Porter, N. (2013): 'Single-minded, compelling, and unique': Visual communications, landscape, and the calculated aesthetic of place branding, *Environmental Communication*, 7(2): 231–254. https://doi.org/10.1080/17524032.2013.779291

Radkau, J. (2014): *The Age of Ecology*. Cambridge: Polity Press.

Rebich-Hespanha, S., Rice, R., Montello, D., Retzloff, S., Tien, S. and Hespanha, J. (2015): Image themes and frames in US print news stories about climate change, *Environmental Communication*, 9(4): 491–519. https://doi.org/10.1080/17524032.2014.983534

Richardson, J. E. and Colombo, M. (2013): Continuity and change in anti-immigrant discourse in Italy: An analysis of the visual propaganda of the Lega Nord, *Journal of Language and Politics*, 12(2): 180–202. https://doi.org/10.1075/jlp.12.2.02ric

Richardson, J. E. and Wodak, R. (2009): The impact of visual racism: Visual arguments in political leaflets of Austrian and British far-right parties, *Controversies*, 6: 45–77.

Rollins, W. (1997): *A Greener Vision of Home: Cultural Politics and Environmental Reform in the German Heimatschutz Movement, 1904–1918*. Ann Arbor: University of Michigan Press.

Rueda, D. (2020): Neoecofascism: The example of the United States, *Journal for the Study of Radicalism*, 14(2): 95–126.

Schäfer, M. and O'Neill, S. (2017): Frame analysis in climate change communication. In M. Nisbet, S. Ho, E. Markowitz, S. O'Neill, M. Schäfer and J. Thaker (eds), *Oxford Encyclopedia of Climate Change Communication*. Oxford: Oxford University Press. https://doi.org/10.1093/acrefore/9780190228620.013.487

Schmuck, D. and Matthes, J. (2017): Effects of economic and symbolic threat appeals in right-wing populist advertising on anti-immigrant attitudes: the impact of textual and visual appeals, *Political Communication*, 34(4): 607–626. https://doi.org/10.1080/10584609.2017.1316807

Sharma, M. (2012): *Green and Saffron: Hindu Nationalism and Indian Environmental Politics*. Hyderabad: Orient Blackswan.

Smith, A. D. (1999): *Myths and Memories of the Nation*. Oxford: Oxford University Press.

Staudenmaier, P. (2021): *Ecology Contested*. Porsgrunn: New Compass Press.

Stöckl, H., Caple, H. and Pflaeging, J. (ed.) (2021): *Shifts towards Image-Centricity in Contemporary Multimodal Practices*. London: Routledge.

Szenes, E. (2021): Neo-Nazi environmentalism: The linguistic construction of ecofascism in a Nordic Resistance Movement manifesto, *Journal for Deradicalization*, 27. https://journals.sfu.ca/jd/index.php/jd/article/view/465 (accessed 15 January 2022).

Szerszynski, B., Urry, J. and Myers, G. (2000): Mediating global citizenship. In: J. Smith (ed.), *The Daily Globe: Environmental Change, the Public and the Media*. London: Routledge, 97–114.

Takach, G. (2013): Selling nature in a resource-based economy: Romantic/extractive gazes and Alberta's bituminous sands, *Environmental Communication*, 7(2): 211–230. https://doi.org/10.1080/17524032.2013.778208

Tarant, Z. (2019): Is brown the new green? The environmental discourse of the Czech far right. In: B. Forchtner (ed.), *The Far Right and the Environment*. London: Routledge, 201–215.

Thomas, J. A. (2020): Introduction: A portable concept of fascism. In: J. A. Thomas and G. Eley (eds), *Visualizing Fascism: The Twentieth-Century Rise of the Global Right*. Durham, NC: Duke University Press, 1–20.

Thomas, J. A. and Eley, G. (eds) (2020): *Visualizing Fascism: The Twentieth-Century Rise of the Global Right*. Durham, NC: Duke University Press.

Turner, J. and Bailey, D. (2021): 'Ecobordering': casting immigration control as environmental protection, *Environmental Politics*. https://doi.org/10.1080/09644016.2021.1916197

Turner-Graham, E. (2012): 'An intact environment is our foundation of life': The Junge Nationaldemokraten, the Ring Freiheitlicher Jugend and the cyber-construction of nationalist landscapes. In: A. Mammone, E. Godin and B. Jenkins (eds), *Varieties of Right-Wing Extremism in Europe*. London: Routledge, 233–248.

van Leeuwen, T. (2021): The semiotics of movement and mobility, *Multimodality & Society*, 1(1): 97–118. https://doi.org/10.1177/2634979521992733

Voss, K. (2014): *Nation and Nature in Harmony: The Ecological Component of Far Right Ideology*. Unpublished PhD thesis. Florence: Italy.

Wang, S., Corner, A., Chapman, D. and Markowitz, E. (2018): Public engagement with climate imagery in a changing digital landscape, *WIREs Climate Change*, 9. https://doi.org/10.1002/wcc.509.

Westberg, G. and Årman, H. (2019): Common sense as extremism: The multi-semiotics of contemporary national socialism, *Critical Discourse Studies*, 16(5): 549–568. https://doi.org/10.1080/17405904.2019.1624183

Wodak, R. (2013): Anything goes! The Haiderization of Europe. In: R. Wodak, B. Mral and M. KhosraviNik (eds), *Right-Wing Populism in Europe: Politics and Discourse*. London: Bloomsbury, 1–37.

Wodak, R. and Forchtner, B. (2014): Embattled Vienna 1683/2010: Right-wing populism, collective memory and the fictionalisation of politics, *Visual Communication*, 13(2): 231–255. https://doi.org/10.1177%2F1470357213516720

Wozniak, A., Lück, J. and Wessler, H. (2015): Frames, stories, and images: The advantages of a multimodal approach in comparative media content research on climate change, *Environmental Communication*, 9(4): 469–490. https://doi.org/10.1080/17524032.2014.981559

Wozniak, A., Wessler, H. and Lück, J. (2017): Who prevails in the visual framing contest about the United Nations Climate Change Conferences? *Journalism Studies*, 18(11): 1433–1452. https://doi.org/10.1080/1461670X.2015.1131129

1

Right as rain: affective publics and the changing visual rhetoric of the far right in South Africa

Scott Burnett

Introduction

The far right in South Africa underwent a period of rapid change and adaptation in the first two decades after apartheid. By the time the neo-Nazi *Afrikaner Weerstandsbeweging* (Afrikaner Resistance Movement) leader Eugene Terre'Blanche was murdered in April 2010, the militia he had founded in 1973 was associated with uncoordinated acts of racist brutality and buffoonery. Though the *Afrikaner Weerstandsbeweging* lingers on, still using the infamous three-legged swastika as its insignia,[1] its place as the most threatening paramilitary force on the far right has been eclipsed by a group who call themselves *Suidlanders* (Southlanders). This staunch Christian and mostly Afrikaans-speaking ethnonationalist grouping organises training and logistical support for an imminent 'white genocide' in South Africa, as well as sharing anti-Semitic and anti-vax conspiracy theories on their Twitter account, which is followed by over 12,000 people (Figure 1.1). Founded in 2006, the group has proven media savvy, leaving most of their public utterances to a slick English-speaking spokesperson, and eschewing the overt Nazi references of the *Afrikaner Weerstandsbeweging* in favour of a simple white and blue teardrop emblem.

That the far right in South Africa has coalesced around a droplet of water, a substance which in fascist symbolism tends to be associated with dissolution and femininity (Theweleit, 1987), is a significant change considering the historical centrality of branding and marketing to right-wing organising (see O'Shaughnessy, 2017). Indeed, close attention to an evolving visual rhetoric is crucial for understanding how a new generation of white nationalists is being interpellated through traditional and social media (Forchtner and Kølvraa, 2017; Winter, 2019; Hermansson et al., 2020). The *Suidlanders* droplet appears in different versions that exploit the sign's polysemy. In an animated version of the logo used on a YouTube clip entitled 'United We

1.1 Twitter banner of Suidlanders

Stand', the droplet forms from separate shapes, the walls between which break down, unifying what was previously separate.[2] In the version that appears as a fabricated cut-out on the back wall of their YouTube studio, the sign is etched into the 'a' of *Suidlanders* as a teardrop, signifying (according to its designer) the 'pain and sorrow' of victims of violent crime in South Africa.[3] In the more common form used on Twitter it could signify fresh water, a salient theme given that the pumping of untreated sewage into natural waterways is a major advocacy issue for the group.[4] All three of these meanings are contextually racialised, as it is white unity, white victim-hood and Black pollution that are indexed. The droplet might also signify rain, a powerfully evocative sign in a drought-prone country. But what might the weather have to do with white supremacy?

This chapter contributes to understanding the visual representations of the countryside (whether 'natural' or agricultural) in far-right rhetoric in a context where the visuality of right-wing discourse has received little attention (see Deumert, 2019 for a notable exception). That being said, European taxonomies of social and political movements as populist, far or extreme right have little purchase in South Africa, where virulent white supremacist thinking takes diverse cultural and organisational forms, shapeshifting and attaching to different fractions of the small white minority, who may express ethnonationalist, anti-democratic or separatist ideologies in response to specific developments at specific times, and who account for barely 8 per cent of the population. Identifiably white ethnonationalist discourse will thus be approached not through the political articulations of *Suidlanders* or the *Afrikaner Weerstandsbeweging*, but through a cultural artefact: The music video of the 2019 Afrikaans hit 'Die Land'. Its lead singer, Steve Hofmeyr, is a popular but polarising figure who serves as a key node in expressions of Afrikaner ethnonationalism. He eulogised Terre'Blanche amid waving swastikas at his funeral in 2010, played the central character in a sensationalist film about the murder of white farmers, and regularly retweets *Suidlanders* posts to his nearly 296,000 followers on Twitter. It was Hofmeyr's reputation as a racist that resulted in the 2019 disqualification of 'Die Land' from a high-profile musical award funded by the country's largest entertainment company, MultiChoice, which also refused to broadcast the song. These moves in turn prompted a prominent Afrikaner rights advocacy group (AfriForum, which I introduce later) to declare a 'dispute' with MultiChoice[5] and their allies to organise to distribute the online version of the song as far and wide as they could.[6] Since April 2019 when it was first uploaded, the video has clocked over nine million views on YouTube, an impressive figure considering there are only 2.6 million white Afrikaners. I suggest that this use of a digital medium is key to the formation of an online 'affective public' (Papacharissi, 2015) that has enabled a resurgence in Afrikaner ethnonationalism. It is thus reasonable to read 'Die Land' as a crucial window onto political and semiotic developments in the white right in South Africa.

These developments should be read against a complex history. For this reason, I offer a sketch of the changing nature of the white right in South Africa in the next section, before reviewing scholarship on the links between ethnonationalism and Afrikaner popular culture in the next. After making brief comments on method, I analyse 'Die Land' as a multimodal text. In the conclusion, I discuss the contribution of the analysis to theorising Afrikaner 'enclave nationalism' (van der Westhuizen, 2016) and to global investigation of the visual natures of the far right.

Boer nationalism to the bitter end

After apartheid, the vast majority of whites rejected far-right politicking in favour of centre-right market liberalism (Friedman, 2021). There has thus been limited scholarly interest outside of a spate of op-eds (for example, Bueckert, 2018; van der Westhuizen, 2018; McMichael, 2021) in mapping recent developments or their connection to historical processes. This history goes back at least to Nazi Germany. The entry of white-ruled South Africa into the Second World War as a British ally consolidated the Afrikaner vote in 1948, propelling the National Party into power (Norval, 1996: 47). Prominent National Party politicians had been members of the Nazi-adjacent *Ossewa Brandwag* (Oxwagon Sentinel) which had worked with Germany, spying on and sabotaging the war effort (Kleynhans, 2021). Apartheid South Africa was a safe haven for Nazis on the lam (Lee, 2000: 42) and a source of funding and support for a network of fascists in other countries (Macklin, 2010). Overt references to these ideologies had, however, to be muted as South Africa aligned itself with the liberal West during the Cold War (Hyslop, 2020), arguably sparking the formation of the *Afrikaner Weerstandsbeweging* in 1973, which tapped into global neo-Nazi networks for funding and training (Lee, 2000: 298).

While the democratic transition of the 1990s saw an upsurge in white supremacist acts of terror, parliamentary politics absorbed most of the energies of ethnic nationalisms post-1994. In the twenty-first century, non-violent but also non-parliamentary ethnically demarcated organisations started to rearticulate modernised forms of Afrikaner nationalism. The whites-only Mineworkers Union, historically a cheerleader for apartheid, rebranded as 'Solidarity' in 2001 and developed a stable of new organisations and initiatives, which included from 2006 the increasingly prominent Afrikaner rights advocacy group AfriForum (Boersema, 2012). Instead of positioning themselves as opposed to the multiracial democratic order, these organisations have strategically assumed the role of defenders of the liberal Constitution, in a realm they construct as 'outside' of politics (Holmes, 2019). Historical white supremacy and its crimes tend to be obscured in their discourse, and a bright future for all whites (including English speakers) is articulated, based on an ostensibly anti-communist and shared 'Western', Christian heritage (van Zyl-Hermann, 2018: 2682). More generally, the defeat of an Afrikaans claim to the nation-state as a whole occasioned the rise of geographically distinct, usually private, suburban nodes of Afrikaner consumption, a phenomenon Christi van der Westhuizen (2016) dubs 'enclave nationalism'. The existence of these enclaves as locations of aspirations for self-determination and ethnic self-expression complicates drawing any simple parallels between contemporary Afrikaner and European nationalisms.

Expressions of Afrikaner self-determination have become more strident and less compromising of late in response to proposed Constitutional provisions for the redistributive expropriation of land without compensation (van der Westhuizen, 2018). Organisations aligned with AfriForum furthermore contend with competition from the right, in the form of *Suidlanders*, whose eloquent spokesperson Simon Roche made a highly publicised tour to the United States in 2017, during which he met key far-right figures such as David Duke and Richard Spencer, and participated in the Unite the Right rally (Gedye, 2018). Following hot on his heels, AfriForum CEO Kallie Kriel and his deputy Ernst Roets went to the United States in 2018 on a campaign to highlight 'farm murders' in South Africa (van der Westhuizen, 2018). Roets's interview with Tucker Carlson on *Fox News* made global headlines when Donald Trump tweeted that he would investigate the possibility of humanitarian intervention (de Greef and Karasz, 2018). Attention to the supposed 'extermination' of white farmers by vengeful Blacks in South Africa quickly became a staple of the global conservative and far-right media.

These political developments accompanied important shifts in cultural production. Both AfriForum and *Suidlanders* were launched in 2006, which was also the year that Bok van Blerk's runaway hit song *De la Rey* was released. With its nostalgic retrieval of an injured identity rallying behind the storied Boer general Koos de la Rey, the song purported to be about events in the South African War (Second Anglo-Boer War) which played out between colonial Britain and the fledgling Boer republics, cradles of Afrikanerdom, between 1899 and 1902. The song tapped into a sense of emptiness and crisis in Afrikaner identity since the end of white minority rule (Lambrechts and Visagie, 2009). Singing along to *De la Rey*, young white Afrikaners could once again feel proud of a heritage of resistance to imperial domination that had been 'contaminated by feelings of guilt and shame' (van der Waal and Robins, 2011: 778). The political utility of nostalgia for this sanitised and self-justifying version of the past was grasped by many as an opportunity to reassert a narrow ethnic identity politics (Baines, 2013) and the *De la Rey* phenomenon was associated with a boom in the production of Afrikaner popular music and film. While political hegemony was irrecoverable, white Afrikaans economic power within its enclaves had ensured that the cultural industries remained vibrant and lucrative.

Indeed, white Afrikaans music and film continue to thrive, and play an important political role in shaping identity (Blaser and van der Westhuizen, 2012). As van der Westhuizen (2018) notes, consuming Afrikaans cultural artefacts becomes a way to become an Afrikaner, to enact one's identity, providing a space where people who hold diverse political ideologies can 'meet each other under the sign of the market'. Most Afrikaans film and pop stars – even Bok van Blerk – are, however, not as closely associated with a particular political stance as is Steve Hofmeyr. During his long and successful career, Hofmeyr has repeatedly asserted white blamelessness for apartheid and bemoaned the subsequent victimisation of Afrikaners, especially white farmers. His mere appearance on screen is sufficient to index an injured, racist and defiant white Afrikaans identity (Broodryk, 2016; Marx Knoetze, 2020). This identity does not, however, float free, but is rooted in a particular landscape, an Afrikaner ethnoscape (Smith, 1999) which I situate in the literature on far-right natural imaginaries in the following section.

Nature, farmland, ethnoscape: imagining South Africa as a white man's land

The rhetorical mobilisation of a richly imagined homeland in need of reclamation or protection from external threat or occupation is an important facet of various forms of ethnonationalist politics. A 'key trope' of British post-war fascism, for example, is the 'timelessness of ... "countryside", farmlands and wider rural environment' (Richardson, 2017: 156–157). Contemporary far-right formations across Europe and North America articulate a love for the land that is organised around wilderness and/or agriculture, indigeneity and/or settler incursion, depending on local contingencies (Forchtner, 2019). In South Africa, articulating a white national identity necessitated the 'imaginative appropriation' (Foster, 2008) of the landscape as the rightful home and possession of settlers, and this imaginary came to structure white cultural production. The white literary canon portrayed the land as a patchwork of family farms where the centrality of Black labour was occluded, or as blank, unpeopled and threatening; a landscape of repression (Coetzee, 1988: 5–10). White environmentalists after apartheid mobilised photography of agricultural landscapes to represent the 'pristine' and 'god-given' 'heartland' they seek to protect (Burnett, 2019). Visual evidence of colonial incursion and culture is thus naturalised on the land, producing a white ethnoscape (Burnett, 2022) that asserts settler autochthony and sanctifies landholding patterns.

For Afrikaner identity specifically, the family farm was a key nodal point in the construction of a 'lost' community (Norval, 1996: 16). Though the centrality of the farm faded from the 1960s onwards as Afrikaner identity modernised (van Zyl, 2008), it has enjoyed a twenty-first century resurgence connected to land invasions, the murders of white people in rural areas and threats of expropriation closer to home (Steyn, 2019: 67). In a country plagued by high levels of violent crime, the brunt of which is borne by poor and Black people (Brodie, 2013), the grotesque details of specific murders or assaults of white people is circulated as proof of an ongoing 'white genocide' perpetrated by vengeful Blacks. While Black farm labourers are often also victims, it is bloody and bruised white survivors who make the front page of Afrikaans newspapers (Steyn, 2019: 76–77). The visual representation

of injured white bodies confirms the narrative of victimisation and disad-
vantage since the end of apartheid that Melissa Steyn (2001: 78) dubbed
'This Shouldn't Happen to a White'.

It is in this context that celebrated director Darrell Roodt's film *Treurgrond*
(*Mourning Ground*, 2015) has been critiqued as a thinly veiled marketing
platform for AfriForum, providing 'manipulative' answers to complex social
problem (Weys, 2016). The central role of the white farmer, who is brutally
murdered at the end, is played by Steve Hofmeyr, whose reactionary politics
and cinematic oeuvre of white nostalgia are invoked in his casting (Broodryk,
2016). The film is structured as a morality tale, its central visual device
being to contrast the Edenic paradise of Afrikaner farming life with the
place of terror it becomes as Black violence rains down on it (Steyn, 2019:
58–59). An attack on the farm has thus come to stand for an attack on
Afrikanerdom. The butchered and bloody white bodies pictured in the film
signal 'apocalyptic anticipation' that Titlestad (2016) has argued is in a
dialectic relationship with 'restorative nostalgia'; in this reading, an idealised
Afrikaner agricultural past can only become future again through 'revelatory
violence' (2016: 72) which brings about a new social order. In her analysis
of the 'settler-colonial rhetoric' of *Treurgrond* and other texts, Deumert
(2019) homes in on 'sensational signs': the farm, the cultivator, the graveyard,
the butchered bodies. Sensational signs create sensations that 'stick' differently
to different types of bodies (2019: 476). Building on Sara Ahmed's (2004a;
2004b) theorisation of affective economies, Deumert understands emotions
as actively *doing things* in the world, aligning individuals with communities,
or bodies with social space. The historical circulation of signs has worked
to attach a specific affective value to them, which is traded on in the present,
working to affect bodies through effects of adhesion, which may work to
hold in-groups together (as a cohesive force) but also to form the boundaries/
borders between social groups, where the other becomes the object of fear,
disgust or hatred.

While representations of harm to white bodies may signal the 'invasion
of the body of the [white] nation' (Ahmed, 2004b: 119), they also work
to create group cohesion. The sensational signs of extra-lethal violence on
display in *Treurgrond* have been shown to benefit 'victim' groups (such as
AfriForum) who claim to represent them, attracting funding and swelling
membership through the construction of an 'increased threat environment'
(Holmes, 2020). It is furthermore highly relevant, in tracing how these
affective (and material) economies work, that threat and fear frequently
co-occur with a sense of hope. The murdered farmer's son Lukie is portrayed
as a potential avatar of renewal and rebirth at the end of the film, and
it is telling that AfriForum's Ernst Roets also appears, as himself, in the

film (Steyn, 2019: 78). The strategic deployment of affect allows organised Afrikanerdom to produce itself as the sober voice of common sense, of being the rational solution to a nightmarish problem (Deumert, 2019: 468–469). These institutions are as much a part of the solution as is the suggestion that Lukie will take over the family farm. The sensational signs of *Treurgrond* trace the borders of a 'defensive ethnicity' within a neoliberal logic that must be invested in, and which is in competition with others to expand 'self-contained, ethnically demarcated, comfort zones' (Blaser and van der Westhuizen, 2012: 388). While these Afrikaner enclaves tend to be suburban, or situated in rural towns, it is the consumption of nostalgic myths of rural culture that works on social and traditional media that works to create broader 'affective publics' (Papacharissi, 2015) who become organised across physical distance to attempt to fix a specific Afrikaner identity.

Discourse, rhetoric and multimodality: 'moving' images

In a recent special issue of *Social Semiotics*, Milani and Richardson (2020) argue that much critical discourse analysis has failed to account for the centrality of affect to the (re)production of social categories and relations. They cite Martin's (2014: 120) observation that:

> [E]motions serve to situate subjects in relation to their world, orienting them towards its objects with degrees of proximity and urgency, sympathy and concern, aversion or hostility. These emotional orientations are never fixed or complete but are open to contestation and negotiation, mediated often (though not exclusively) by rhetorical argument.

Exploring rhetoric requires going beyond the propositional content of a discourse to explore other factors that coax affinity from subjects. Though it is possible for visual communication to efficiently encode the logical terms of arguments, images are especially effective at securing their 'ethotic and pathetic' force (Blair, 2012: 274). In my analysis of '*Die Land*' as a multimodal video text below, I use both Ahmed's/Deumert's notion of 'sensational signs' and van Leeuwen's (2008; 2021) work on the visual representation of social actors, and recent taxonomy of the semiosis of movement. Some of the affective dynamics of multimodal representations of movement (for example, on stage, in film, in sculpture) evoke the ambiguities in the verb 'to move'; both a change in the position of some element and a change in emotional state. Thus, I explore how the deployment of raced and gendered social actors, as well as elements of movement such as directedness, expansion and velocity (van Leeuwen, 2021: 110), interact with other visual and multimodal elements to 'sensational' effects on the surfaces of individual bodies and collectivities.

'This land belongs to you'

In this section, I analyse the music video of '*Die Land*' as a multimodal text consisting of moving images, music and the text of the song.[7] The song has a similar structure to many pop anthems in that it starts with two verses (V1 and V2) followed by a chorus (C), which is followed by a third verse (V3) that builds up to the second refrain of the chorus (C-R1), a bridge, and then the final (climactic) refrain of the chorus (C-R2). V1 and V2 consist mostly of a series of rhetorical questions:

> (V1) Where will you play with your friends?
> What path will you take?
> Where will you fall, and stand up and cry and
> Where will you gaze at the sunset that stretches for miles?
> ...
> (V2) What do we leave for our children?
> What will we have left to show one day?
> What is still right or wrong, I want to know.
> What do we do if years of sweat go forgotten?
> ...
> (V3) What happened to the love?
> What happened to the dream?
> Tears of thousands fall on the sand,
> And just let the trees grow stronger in the fields.

While V1 is addressed to a baby or unborn child, it clearly works to evoke a nostalgia for a South African childhood spent outside, exploring and enjoying nature. V2 is directed generally to adults (or fellow parents), bringing into question inheritance and generational achievement. The idea that the fruits of hard toil are threatened by struggle over what 'is still right or wrong' indexes threatened expropriation of white farms without compensation. V3 also evokes a political imaginary: that of the 'love' and 'dream' of a post-apartheid South Africa with hope and possibility for all, now turned into a land of mourning and tears, which paradoxically do not salt the earth but deepen the roots of the trees on an agricultural landscape. This seeming paradox – of great sorrow that fertilises the ground – is echoed in the contrast between the heartbreak and doubt of the verses and the song's uplifting, anthemic chorus:

> (C) I leave to you the sun, and the sea, and the land my child
> Promise you I will be there at the end

My flag will keep waving and I will sow my seeds for you
And keep you safe
I leave to you the sun, and the sea, and the land my child
The Lord hears me, we will make a life
My flag will keep waving and I will sow my seeds for you
I promise you
This land belongs to you

Though I have translated '*land*' as land in English, the Afrikaans word '*land*' maps on to the English 'country'; it is land in the sense of 'homeland' rather than any specific piece of ground. The text thus evokes the narrative of a threat to an expansive inheritance (sun/sea/countryside) successfully resisted through gestures of patriotism (waving a flag) and investments in the future (i.e. the figurative or literal seeds that are sown) that are suffused with religious dedication.

The video consists of interwoven footage from two settings: a theatrical stage with chairs, and scenes of rural life and landscapes. The video starts with a sweeping aerial shot of wide-open plains, where the use of brown and yellow tones evokes dryness and a lone tractor raises a column of dust into the sky. The sense of visual expansiveness, and the low velocity of the tractor's 'solemn procession' (van Leeuwen, 2021: 107), are scored with a sustained chord on an organ, lending the scene a sacred, churchy atmosphere (see also Pauw, 2019). The scene then cuts to a slow pan over a concrete farm dam and windpump [00:06] key elements of the vocabulary of white settler mythmaking about their 'soul country' (Burnett, 2019). Flares caused by the camera being directed at the sun combine with the colour palette to evoke dryness and heat. The camera then cuts to the stage, in darkness, where the five dark figures sit or stand, motionless. The artificiality of the staging, with its couches, hat rack and curtains draws attention to the roles of the singers as artists: not themselves directly involved in the rural scenes but its interpreters. While they remain motionless throughout the performance, the rural footage is projected onto a screen behind them, as if to articulate the passions hidden behind their serious and still expressions. Spotlights light up one singer after another: First Bok van Blerk and then Ruhan du Toit sing V1, before the whole stage is again sunk into darkness, and the sun sets in the image behind the singers. The darkness is then broken [00:41] by a spotlight on the seated figure of Steve Hofmeyr in centre stage (the other two singers, Bobby van Jaarsveld and Jay du Plessis, are revealed later). The contrast between light and dark, and his central position on stage, make the figure of Hofmeyr a key organising visual signifier in the video as a whole, linking the video and song ideologically to his politics.

The fact that all five singers are white Afrikaans men articulates generational continuity and belonging as an ethnic and masculine concern. In the rural

1.2 '*Die Land*', father and son share an affectionate moment as they tend cattle

scenes interspersed in the narrative all of the farmers are white men, and the only child explicitly connected to a future in farming is one of their sons (Figure 1.2, [02:23]). The loving moment between father and son is filmed from a horizontal angle, leaving sufficient distance between the viewer and the pair to create a sense of appropriate privacy. A contrasting moment of intimacy (between husband and wife, Figure 1.3) which I analyse below is filmed very differently, with less anxiety about same-sex masculine physical tenderness.

In the scenes where Black people appear, they do so in specific roles. In one scene [01:23], the white farmer's son races wire cars with a Black playmate; in a later scene [02:50], we see them running together to a Black woman dressed in a typical servant's uniform: a pink cloak with a white headwrap. The trope of interracial childhood friendships is a very common one in the white South African imaginary (Jenkins, 2006: 89). Rather than working to undermine the racial order, these intimate bonds are structured around hierarchical labour relationships (where a Black 'nanny' must care both for her own children and those of her white employers) and as instrumentally valuable for the white child's future role as the manager of Black labour, whom he will understand better due to his early friendships and basic vocabulary (Shefer, 2019). This future labour relationship is in fact powerfully visualised when a Black farm labourer in typical blue overalls is pictured with a modestly downcast gaze standing behind his boss, the white farmer, in a typical khaki suit, who raises his gaze to meet the camera [02:09]. While the viewer is at the same horizontal level as the farmer and his worker, it is only the farmer we encounter as having the agency to engage us directly (van Leeuwen, 2008: 141)

A contrast of movement is created between the high-velocity energy of the boys as they run with their wire car and the slow shift in gaze directed gradually upwards by the farmer. The raising of the gaze in this scene echoes similar gestures at other points in the narrative, where one of the white farmers (there are at least three) seems despairing, his face downcast, and then raises his eyes as the music surges up climactically. This parallel movement – swelling music, raised gaze – is associated with aid on its way, with something that will change. Looking to the horizon signals hope; a decisive turn of events that is signified by a line of people walking over the fields. The figures on the horizon in 'Die Land' are never seen in any great detail, but in their formation and movement they are similar to the image of the prepper commando used as a Twitter banner picture for *Suidlanders* (Figure 1.1): shot from afar to show them in formation; camouflaged against the dry veld looking for all the world like a rebel Boer army (as Marx Knoetze, 2020: 63 has suggested). The long shots of the commando figures [repeated between 01:31 and 02:05] are interlaced with close-ups of people holding hands to form a human chain, one of whom is clearly a little girl. This is not to discount the martial interpretation (the horizon figures are not close enough to hold hands) but rather to suggest that different dynamics of strength in unity are invoked.

If a hope–despair dynamic creates the dramatic tension of the song's text and the performance of looking to the horizon, the semiotisation of changes in the weather and its effect on the land work powerfully to structure the narrative of the video. The first scene of a white farmer raising his eyes to the horizon comes directly after he has lifted a fistful of dry sand which he lets fall through his fingers, as sweat rolls down his brow [01:18]. The dust that is raised by the tractor in the opening scene and later on by a utility vehicle on a dirt road evoke a sense of thirst, of drought. This drought is climactically broken at the conclusion of the song's bridge with a succession of movements. The music falls nearly silent, and the praying hands of a child, fingers splayed, are pictured against a candlelit background [03:03]. As the words of the final refrain start again, there is a sense of hushed expectation created by the slightly muted arrangement, before a crescendo is reached as the camera cuts to images of clouds swiftly expanding towards the viewer from over the mountain, as the farmer's tractor works the fields. On close shots of the parched ground, we see dark blotches form as the rain finally begins to fall [03:19]. From the front door of a sandstone farmhouse, as the chorus builds and an extra electric guitar is added to the instrumentation, a young boy in an orange T-shirt runs into the rain towards the camera [03:22]. We see his family join him from the vantage point of the farmstead, creating the sense that we as viewers are involved in this climactic rush out of the house to dance in the rain. Their father (whose

1.3 '*Die Land*', kissing in the rain

utility vehicle we had seen arriving in a previous shot) joins his family on the lawn, lifting his arms to the heavens as if in praise [03:39]. He picks up his children and embraces his wife, and she leans in to kiss him while the rain falls, to the accompaniment of the final bars of the song (Figure 1.3). Once the music has faded out, all that is left on the audio track is the sound of wind blowing. Once again, a drone shot sweeps over the figures on the still-brown landscape, as if to remind the viewer that rural idyll they have just witnessed is always threatened and requires unity and the threat of a violence from a Boer commando on the horizon to keep it secure.

There are a number of points at which the text accords in relations of synonymy with the images: a sunset is shown when mentioned, the farmer is in his field when 'seeds' are to be sown; the relationship between father(s) and son(s) plays a key role in both text and video. Rain/drought is, however, not textually thematised, serving instead as the organising dramatic dynamic of the visual narrative, while providing a powerful symbolic structure which resonates with the text. It is hard to overstate the affective power of rain after a drought, especially in the semi-arid regions of much of South (and southern) Africa. Rain restores non-human nature while also bringing a profound sense of relief, and even catharsis, to the people who had been longing for it. Rain makes the brown land green and restores that which seemed dead to life; it signifies hope and rebirth.

Rain is especially 'affective' in the sense of being a bodily experience in the South African context. In times of drought, our bodies long for the rain. The rush of the clouds over the mountain and the first sight of rain on the ground are visualised movements which are profoundly moving. These movements, however, are restricted in the social body whose skins they are felt on, which is here visually represented as that of the heterosexual, patriarchal, white Afrikaans family. The video thus represents a multimodal rhetorical argument for adopting specific emotional orientations that together carve out the social space that fits an Afrikaner ethnonationalist positionality (see Ahmed, 2004b for how affect shapes space). The sensational signs are articulated into a narrative structure that tells a causal story (see Forchtner, 2021) about threat and defence, strung between past and future. The argument shares some elements (such as the white farmer; the white farmer's child; the Black farm worker; the casting of Steve Hofmeyr; sweeping Edenic landscapes; the farmhouse as the scene for blissful family life) in common with *Treurgrond* (2015), but differs remarkably in eschewing the visual representation of violence (Titlestad, 2016) to focus powerfully instead on upliftment, reinvigoration and renewal. It achieves these effects through mobilising the affective power of water and dust, where rain restores life to the land. The land itself is pictured both as a beautiful natural landscape, with bushes dotting the side of a mountain, and an agricultural idyll evoking the ethnoscape. The song's text about leaving the land, the sea and the sun to one's children, and its assertion that the land 'belongs' to the child, is also an assertion of white futurity on the South African landscape, as secured in the patriarchal, heterosexual, nuclear family on its farm. The agricultural landscape is connected to sweat, in the face of a hardworking farmer who leads his labourers and guides his son. Belonging on the land/the land belonging to you is thus connected directly to honest toil. Hope is tied up in two powerful images: the unity and strength of the cordon of the commando on the horizon, who the sweating farmer looks to as his protection against an unnamed, advancing threat, and the blessing which comes from the heavens, in the form of the falling rain. The rain brings together the god-fearing family as the ground where the seeds of coming generations grow, projecting white security and belonging into the future.

Given the rigidity of the social order represented in the video, where the white landowner and patriarch is unapologetically presented as the centre of symbolic value, with women confined to the home sphere and Black people restricted to manual labour, it is reasonable to compare this articulation to other white supremacist and heteropatriarchal orders which are organised around the 'reproductive futurity' of white populations (Burnett and Richardson, 2022). It is highly significant that so many far-right movements have adopted the '14 Words'[8] as a slogan which centre on the future of the white child, and on securing 'the existence of our people' without any explicit reference to how this future is antagonised, or by whom. The rules of pop music, which relies on catchy tunes and broad appeal, rule out the overt visual thematisation of farm murders and white genocide, but provide a generative context for positive articulations of white racial imaginaries.

These are strategic both because of the structures of feeling they appeal to – rural nostalgia, happy families, childhood memories and the enjoyment of life outdoors – and because critique of this dream landscape of the future can easily be dismissed by its adherents as unfair, elite hostility to a harmless and 'threatened' minority.

Conclusion: the power in a drop of water

At the start of this chapter I identified a shift from swastikas and other ethnonationalist symbolism to (at first glance) neutral, natural symbols such as the droplet used by *Die Suidlanders*. This may be part of the broader 'rebranding' process associated internationally with the far right, which has increasingly tended to focus on building more consumer-friendly identities for the digital age. While just as steeped in hatred as their fascistic forebears, these groupings market themselves as rooted in reclaiming pride in your 'own' group in the face of victimisation by others. All of these meanings can be seen in the droplet of water: It can signify flowing together, tears of sorrow, or clean water; but also the rebirth and renewal of a fall of rain after a long drought. While the far right in South Africa are far from a cohesive political formation, and there are many points of disagreement between the actors mentioned here, a unifying sense of a dislocated post-apartheid Afrikaner identity is clearly being articulated in popular culture, finding powerful new symbols around which to coalesce.

Notes

1 See http://awb.co.za/ (accessed 30 November 2021).
2 See www.youtube.com/watch?v=BUecXQfdJ7U (accessed 8 October 2021).
3 See www.freelanced.com/nukedoor (accessed 4 October 2021).
4 Such as in Simon Roche's presentation to the Conservatives and Reformist Group in the European Parliament, www.youtube.com/watch?v=ppFfvL66AIw (accessed 8 October 2021).
5 See https://maroelamedia.co.za/debat/meningsvormers/afriforum-verklaar-n-dispuut-met-multichoice/ (accessed 2 December 2021).
6 See https://gildes.solidariteit.co.za/en/die-land-the-country-is-gone/ (accessed 2 December 2021).
7 See www.youtube.com/watch?v=Kf_BIm2SndE (accessed 3 December 2021). Original Afrikaans. All translations from Afrikaans to English by the author.
8 See www.adl.org/education/references/hate-symbols/14-words?fbclid=IwAR2 b2UUrcLM55yEEG5z4fY5jJpDDOESBOFyDE9_RYLdw1LfLdMm0-svBVGU (accessed 4 December 2021).

References

Ahmed, S. (2004a): *The Cultural Politics of Emotion*. Edinburgh: Edinburgh University Press.

Ahmed, S. (2004b): Affective economies, *Social Text*, 22(2): 117–139.

Baines, G. (2013): Lionising De la Rey: Afrikaner identity politics and performative nostalgia in post-apartheid South Africa, *African Identities*, 11(3): 249–259. https://doi.org/10.1080/14725843.2013.838895

Blair, J. A. (2012): The rhetoric of visual arguments. In: J. A. Blair and C. W. Tindale (eds), *Groundwork in the Theory of Argumentation: Selected Papers of J. Anthony Blair*. Dordrecht: Springer, 261–279.

Blaser, T. M. and van der Westhuizen, C. (2012): Introduction: The paradox of post-apartheid 'Afrikaner' identity – Deployments of ethnicity and neo-liberalism, *African Studies*, 71(3): 380–390. https://doi.org/10.1080/00020184.2012.740882

Boersema, J. R. (2012): Between recognition and resentment: An Afrikaner trade union's brand of post-nationalism, *African Studies*, 71(3): 408–425. https://doi.org/10.1080/00020184.2012.740884

Brodie, N. (2013): Are SA whites really being killed 'like Flies'? Why Steve Hofmeyr is wrong', *Africa Check*, 24 June 2013. http://africacheck.org/fact-checks/reports/are-sa-whites-really-being-killed-flies-why-steve-hofmeyr-wrong (accessed 11 February 2022).

Broodryk, C. (2016): Ons Sal Antwoord Op Jou Roepstem: Steve Hofmeyr and Afrikaner identity in post-apartheid Afrikaans cinema, *Communicare: Journal for Communication Sciences in Southern Africa*, 35(1): 59–76.

Bueckert, M. (2018): The post Trump fortunes of South Africa's White Nationalists, *Africa Is a Country*, 9 October 2018. https://africasacountry.com/2018/09/the-fortunes-of-south-africas-white-nationalists (accessed 11 February 2022).

Burnett, S. (2019): Constructing white autochthony in South Africa's 'Soul Country': Intersections of race and land, *Discourse, Context & Media*, 30, 1–11. https://doi.org/10.1016/j.dcm.2018.12.002

Burnett, S. (2022): Ethnoscaping Green resistance: Heritage and the fight against fracking. In: E. Uzer and F. Hamami (eds), *Heritage and Resistance*. London: Palgrave Macmillan.

Burnett, S. and Richardson, J. E. (2022): 'Breeders for race and nation': Gender, sexuality, and fecundity in post-war British fascist discourse, *Patterns of Prejudice*, 55(4): 331–356.

Coetzee, J. M. (1988): *White Writing: On the Culture of Letters in South Africa*. New Haven: Yale University Press.

de Greef, K. and Karasz, P. (2018): Trump cites false claims of widespread attacks on white farmers in South Africa, *New York Times*, 23 August 2018. www.nytimes.com/2018/08/23/world/africa/trump-south-africa-white-farmers.html (accessed 11 February 2022).

Deumert, A. (2019): Sensational signs, authority and the public sphere: Settler colonial rhetoric in times of change, *Journal of Sociolinguistics*, 23(5): 467–484. https://doi.org/10.1111/josl.12377

Forchtner, B. (ed.) (2019): *The Far Right and the Environment: Politics, Discourse and Communication*. London: Routledge.

Forchtner, B. (2021): Introducing 'Narrative in Critical Discourse Studies', *Critical Discourse Studies* 18(3): 304–313. https://doi.org/10.1080/17405904.2020.1802765

Forchtner, B. and Christoffer K. (2017): Extreme right images of radical authenticity: Multimodal aesthetics of history, nature, and gender roles in social media, *European Journal of Cultural and Political Sociology*, 4(3): 252–281. https://doi.org/10.1080/23254823.2017.1322910

Foster, J. A. (2008): *Washed with Sun: Landscape and the Making of White South Africa*. Pittsburgh, PA: University of Pittsburgh Press.

Friedman, S. (2021): *Prisoners of the Past: South African Democracy and the Legacy of Minority Rule*. Johannesburg: Wits University Press.

Gedye, L. (2018): White genocide: How the big lie spread to the US and beyond, *The M&G Online*, 23 March 2018. https://mg.co.za/article/2018-2003-23-00-radical-right-plugs-swart-gevaar/ (accessed 11 February 2022).

Hermansson, P., Lawrence, D., Mulhall, J. and Murdoch, S. (eds) (2020): *The International Alt-Right: Fascism for the 21st Century?* London: Routledge.

Holmes, C. E. (2019): The politics of 'non-political' activism in democratic South Africa, *Comparative Politics*, 51(4): 561–580. https://doi.org/10.5129/001041519X15647434970081

Holmes, C. E. (2020): Victimhood gone viral: Portrayals of extra-lethal violence and the solidarity of victims in the case of South African farm violence activists, *Politics, Groups, and Identities*, https://doi.org/10.1080/21565503.2020.1838303.

Hyslop, J. (2020): Anti-fascism in South Africa 1933–1945, and its legacies. In: K. Braskén, N. Copsey and D. Featherstone (eds), *Anti-Fascism in a Global Perspective*. London: Routledge, 77–95.

Jenkins, E. (2006): *National Character in South African English Children's Literature*. New York: Routledge.

Kleynhans, E. (2021): *Hitler's South African Spies: Secrets Agents and the Intelligence War in South Africa*. Johannesburg: Jonathan Ball.

Lambrechts, L. and Visagie, J. (2009): De la Rey, De la Rey, sal jy die Boere kom lei? *LiNet Akademies* 6(2): 75–105.

Lee, M. A. (2000): *The Beast Reawakens: Fascism's Resurgence from Hitler's Spymasters to Today's Neo-Nazi Groups and Right-Wing Extremists*. New York: Routledge.

Macklin, G. (2010): The British far right's South African connection: A. K. Chesterton, Hendrik van Den Bergh, and the South African Intelligence Services, *Intelligence and National Security*, 25(6): 823–842. https://doi.org/10.1080/02684527.2010.537879

Martin, J. (2014): *Politics and Rhetoric: A Critical Introduction*. New York: Routledge.

Marx Knoetze, H. (2020): Romanticising the '*Boer*': Narratives of white victimhood in South African popular culture, *Journal of Literary Studies*, 36(4): 48–69. https://doi.org/10.1080/02564718.2020.1822601

McMichael, C. (2021): A history of South African Nazis, *New Frame*, 20 July 2021. www.newframe.com/a-history-of-south-african-nazis/ (accessed 11 February 2022).

Milani, T. M. and Richardson, J. E. (2020): Discourse and affect, *Social Semiotics*, 31(5): 671–675. https://doi.org/10.1080/10350330.2020.1810553

Norval, A. J. (1996): *Deconstructing Apartheid Discourse.* New York: Verso.

O'Shaughnessy, N. (2017): *Marketing the Third Reich: Persuasion, Packaging and Propaganda.* London: Routledge.

Papacharissi, Z. (2015): *Affective Publics: Sentiment, Technology, and Politics.* Oxford: Oxford University Press.

Pauw, M. (2019): Die 'Die Land'-musiekvideo, mites en nostalgie, *LitNet*, 30 April 2019. www.litnet.co.za/litnet-akademies-weerdink-die-die-land-musiekvideo-mites-en-nostalgie/ (accessed 11 February 2022).

Richardson, J. E. (2017): *British Fascism: A Discourse-Historical Analysis.* Stuttgart: ibidem.

Shefer, T. (2019): 'Troubling' stories: Thoughts on the making of meaning of shame/ful memory narratives in (post)apartheid South Africa, *Social Dynamics*, 45(3): 365–381. https://doi.org/10.1080/02533952.2019.1668620

Smith, A. D. (1999): *Myths and Memories of the Nation.* Oxford: Oxford University Press.

Steyn, A. S. (2019): Story of a South African farm attack, *Africa Today*, 66(2): 55–81. https://doi.org/10.2979/africatoday.66.2.04

Steyn, M. E. (2001): *Whiteness Just Isn't What It Used to Be: White Identity in a Changing South Africa.* Albany: State University of New York Press.

Theweleit, K. (1987): *Male Fantasies*, Vol. 1, *Women, Floods, Bodies, History.* Minneapolis: University of Minnesota Press.

Titlestad, M. (2016): Nostalgia and apocalypticism in two post-apartheid films, *English in Africa*, 43(3). https://doi.org/10.4314/eia.v43i3.4

van der Waal, K. and Robins, S. (2011): 'De la Rey' and the revival of 'Boer Heritage': Nostalgia in the post-apartheid Afrikaner culture industry, *Journal of Southern African Studies*, 37(4): 763–779. https://doi.org/10.1080/03057070.2011.617219

van der Westhuizen, C. (2016): Afrikaners in post-apartheid South Africa: Inward migration and enclave nationalism, *HTS Teologiese Studies/Theological Studies*, 72(4): 9. https://doi.org/10.4102/hts.v72i4.3351

van der Westhuizen, C. (2018): South Africa's white right, the alt-right and the alternative, *The Conversation UK*, 4 October 2018. http://theconversation.com/south-africas-white-right-the-alt-right-and-the-alternative-103544 (accessed 11 February 2022).

van Leeuwen, T. (2008): *Discourse and Practice: New Tools for Critical Discourse Analysis.* New York: Oxford University Press.

van Leeuwen, T. (2021): The semiotics of movement and mobility, *Multimodality & Society*, 1(1): 97–118. https://doi.org/10.1177/2634979521992733

van Zyl, D. (2008): 'O, Boereplaas, Geboortegrond!' Afrikaner nostalgia and the romanticisation of the Platteland in post-1994 South Africa, *South African Journal of Cultural History*, 22(2): 126–148.

van Zyl-Hermann, D. (2018): Make Afrikaners great again! National populism, democracy and the new white minority politics in post-apartheid South Africa, *Ethnic and Racial Studies*, 41(15): 2673–2692. https://doi.org/10.1080/01419870.2017.1413202

Weys, D. (2016): (On-)Verantwoordelike rolprentvervaardiging: Die voorstelling van plaasmoorde in Darrell Roodt se Treurgrond (2015), *LitNet Akademies*, 13(1): 161–184.

Winter, A. (2019): Online hate: From the far-right to the 'alt-right' and from the margins to the mainstream. In: K. Lumsden and E. Harmer (eds), *Online Othering*. Cham: Springer, 39–63.

2

The exclusivist claims of Pacific ecofascists: visual environmental communication by far-right groups in Australia and New Zealand

Kristy Campion and Justin Phillips

There is no Conservatism without nature, there is no nationalism without environmentalism, the natural environment shaped us just as we shaped it. We were born from our lands and our own culture was molded by these same lands. The protection and preservation of our own ideals and beliefs.

For too long we have allowed the left to co-opt the environmentalist movement to serve their own needs,

(Tarrant, 2019: 38)

Introduction

The 15 March 2019 terrorist attack on two New Zealand mosques by an Australian citizen claimed the lives of fifty-one people and injured forty-nine more. In his manifesto *The Great Replacement*, the terrorist claimed to be motivated by a number of concerns. The most well-known justification was replacement theory, a demographic conspiracy theory concerning the supposed 'overpopulation' of other ethnicities in white-majority nations. One less examined justification in the manifesto, though, is expressed above: the environment. In Australia and New Zealand, and beyond, environmental concern is commonly connoted with the political left, but the rise of the far right in both countries now challenges such assertions.

Against this background, our chapter examines the presence and purpose of environmental visual communication of the far right in Pacific contexts through the lens of ecofascism. Ecofascism can be broadly understood as a reactionary and revolutionary ideology which champions a return to a romanticised 'natural order', which far-right adherents believe will regenerate their (often racially) imagined communities to a state of harmony and 'natural' dominance. We explore this via qualitative content analyses of two publicly accessible far-right websites in these countries. In so doing, we expose the presence and sophistication of environmental themes while interrogating ideological expressions and strategic communication.

We found in both case studies that a 'return to nature' aesthetic was visually communicated through outdoor activities such as hiking and camping, which provided opportunities for the expression of authentic identity within a 'natural order' and a cultural landscape. This permitted entitative demonstrations of nativity and racial homogeneity in nature – despite the genuine nativity held by Māori and Aboriginal nations. Actual concern for the environment was not based in scientific environmental considerations; instead, concern for the environment was local, geographically bounded, and ethnically particularistic, with an implied unity of people and place. Images of members in natural settings in both countries were leveraged to reinforce claims of white exclusivity and nativity to settler landscapes. This may serve the polysemic ends of conveying an ideological position while also contributing towards a strategic message.

In this chapter, we first position our study between three distinct areas of academic literature: namely, studies of the far right, their strategic communication, and broader environmental communication. We then lay out our methodology, including the theoretical approach and research method. Next, we turn to our two case studies, starting with the Nationalist Socialist Network in Australia before proceeding to Action Zealandia in New Zealand. The chapter concludes with a discussion of the two far-right groups within the Pacific context.

Interlinking the contexts

This study is uniquely located in a juncture: first, between studies on the far right in Australia, and New Zealand; second, strategic communication by extremist and terrorist organisations; and, third, environmental communication. To scaffold this three-way juncture, our definition of the far right relies on Bjørgo and Ravndal's (2019: 3) 'family tree of the far right', referring to a category of beliefs where the people and the state are one, and the presence of foreigners is a threat to this community. In more extreme iterations of this 'family', adherents position democracy as the obstacle to destroying their enemies. Ecofascism connects the triangle by expressing the same concerns and solutions through the lens of the environment (for example, metaphorically depicting 'invasive' species as an existential threat). Ecofascism conceptualised in this manner is therefore a reactionary ideology, spurning industrialisation, urbanisation and immigration; and a revolutionary ideology, with its idealised bucolic utopia which can only be achieved through a return to nature which will foster the complete rebirth of their (often racially) imagined community (Campion, 2021). As was found in Campion's study, ecofascist interpretations can vary, but many align with either deep or shallow ecology, reflecting either the ideological centrality of the 'race' or the centrality of nature. Yet in some cases, representations of saving nature and saving the race were almost indistinguishable. Having defined this three-way juncture, we are now in a position to explore each body of literature within the context of this study, starting with the far right in Australia.

Understandably, research into far-right threats in both national contexts have substantially increased since the Christchurch terrorist attack. However, Australia, much like New Zealand (discussed shortly), has long hosted far-right subcultures and groupuscules (Ray, 1973; Perkins, 1991; Moore, 2005; Evans, 2008). Contemporary research galvanised with the formation of far-right grassroots movements, such as Reclaim Australia and the United Patriots Front, which, after multiple reformations, became the Nationalist Socialist Network (NSN) (Mondon, 2012; Dean et al., 2016; Fleming and Mondon, 2018; Campion, 2019a). While such studies contribute to a growing body of work, they rarely examine how the far right in Australia conceptualised or communicated about the environment. Where the environment is considered, it is often only of passing academic interest. Campion's (2019b) study on extreme-right ideology represents one such example, which indicated the presence of cohesive narratives regarding the 'natural order'. Nature has long been a feature in the 'nationalist imaginary' (Forchtner, 2019a: 4), and Campion (2019b: 214) found the Australian narratives specifically position 'the white Australian as a harmonious and native figure in the spiritual and physical landscape'. Narratives around the natural order, much like the nationalist imaginary elsewhere, therefore indicated the presence of a territorially specific 'ethno-scape' (Forchtner, 2019a: 4–6).

Despite receiving limited attention, we know that New Zealand has also seen a growth in the far right over the last century. As Crosby (2017) shows, for example, far-right movements have persisted since the 1940s in New Zealand, largely drawn from fringe subcultures that identified with the British Commonwealth and white minority governments. In the two decades prior the Christchurch attack, much of the far-right context was dominated by skinhead gangs (Battersby and Ball, 2019: 197), and rare indications of Odinists (for example, New Zealander's feature in the commendable *Gods of the Blood* by Gardell, 2003). While notable historic academic explorations of New Zealand's far right exist (for example, Spoonley 1981), the field nevertheless remained under-researched until recently.

One of the more recent national concerns in the New Zealand context is that domestic security agencies also overlooked far-right threats, focusing too heavily on Islamic extremism post-September 11 – a critiqued echoed in the Royal Commission findings (part 8, chapter 16, 1–2). However, officials in this field contest such accusations (for example, Battersby and Ball, 2019). There are more regional concerns as well, with Ford's (2020) mapping of the New Zealand far right pointing geographically at the city of Christchurch as a hub for the organisation and activism of extreme-right groups. In the last decade or so, New Zealand has seen several groups emerge (and vanish), including the Right Wing Resistance, the Western Guard and the Dominion Movement. The more recent emergence of the last of these (2018) is particularly important, given its explicit focus on nature and the environment, and its ultimate splintering into Action Zealandia (AZ) (one of the case studies focused on below). In short, while research on the New Zealand and the Australian far right exists, and indeed both are growing fields, there is yet to be an examination of how these milieus conceive and communicate on environmental matters.

Our efforts here address this gap by assessing how the Australian and New Zealand far right communicate about the environment and its implications. Yet it is worth noting that these two contexts do not exist in vacuums. Instead, there is an observed level of transnational connectivity. By way of example, the Australian far-right leader from the National Action group, Jim Saleam, was known to travel to New Zealand to hold talks. Similarly, members of AZ's leadership have more recently attempted to travel to Australia to strengthen trans-Tasman connections with potential ideological partners, including with the NSN's own Thomas Sewell (Weir, 2021). Such connections continue, as evidenced in 2018, when the New Zealand Dominion Movement appeared on a far-right Australian podcast (Ford, 2020), and Sewell's more recent feature in a never-released AZ podcast (Weir, 2021). This alleged exchange further validates our combined examination of these groups, rather than looking at them in isolation. Beyond such explicit coordination, we should also expect to see some level of ideological commonalities between the groups, given the obvious and overlapping trans-Tasman context.

While research on environmental communication in both Pacific countries exists (for example, Bührs and Christoff, 2006), none, to our knowledge, examines the far right. Instead, this body of work is largely concerned with mainstream political parties or national politics, rather than examinations of the far-right fringe (for example, Craig, 2009; Lester, 2015) Despite their marginalised position within society, far-right fringe groups are indeed now one of those environmental voices. Understandably, far-right environmental communication is therefore an emerging research focus for scholars in European contexts, with key studies on, for example, Germany (Forchtner and Özvatan, 2019), Sweden (Westberg and Årman, 2019) and Denmark (Kølvraa, 2019).

Investigation of far-right visual (environmental) communication also remains to be undertaken in Pacific contexts. This is despite the fact that visual research in comparative contexts has established its value. For example, Fahmy (2020) examined the visual communication of Islamic State in 2014, finding that visuals were able to provide and reinforce distinct framing for accompanying narratives. Nor does Fahmy's study stand alone in noting the significance of visual communication. Other studies such as Herfroy-Mischler (2018) and Abdelrahim (2019) conducted a visual analysis of Islamic State's propaganda spanning *Dabiq* and *Rumiyah*, and importantly highlighted the role of imagery in magnifying the persuasive element within the propaganda. Gunther and Pfeifer (2020) expanded this to include soundscapes including *nasheeds*. Indeed, drawing on these studies yields valuable insights for the analysis of visual environmental communication by the far right – an area of study which is still in its infancy (but see, for example, the aforementioned Westberg and Årman, 2019; for initial comments and a review, see also the Introduction to this volume). There are, therefore, real gains to be made by applying the tools of visual communication to the (new) context of the far right in general and the environment in particular. This only further emphasises the need for a combined edition on the visual communication of the far right, and the relevance of a Pacific context within it.

Approaching the study

The role of nature and the environment in far-right cultural imaginaries lends itself to a constructivist approach, within the confines of subjective realities (Coghlan and Brydon-Miller, 2014). Like in other contexts, far-right visual communication can be understood as an expression of knowledge construction by recognising the role of human agency in communication. This approach reveals the visual communication of the far right as a deliberate expression of their constructed reality and cultural imaginary – particularly as a form of resistance to more dominant constructed realities, providing important space for visual content analysis to occur. The visual medium is well understood in its ability to convey meaning both literally and connotatively. As established by Forchtner and Kølvraa (2017: 252), 'the traditional note of ideological authority is established through visuals'. In an era where the far right is under increasing scrutiny both on and offline, the need for more subtle communication is all the more important. Thus, to study far-right visuals should yield important insight into cultural ideologies and meanings of ecofascists, while further enriching our understanding of the visual communication of the far right (Smith et al., 2005: 231).

For this study, we selected the two most visible far-right groups in Australia and New Zealand at the time of writing. From Australia, we examined the website created by the NSN (2021a). We have selected this particular group because its combined website and affiliated Telegram channels (which are publicly and externally viewable) offered rich visual data, especially in comparison to contemporaries such as Ironbark Resources (Guild, 2009), and because of its connections to AZ. Due to the high volume of Telegram posts, we focused on those produced (rather than just shared) on the channels, and we applied a timeframe of January 2021 to July 2021 specifically to the Telegram channels. The choice for our New Zealand sample – AZ – was quite straightforward. As previously discussed, this particular group emerged in the aftermath of the Christchurch attack, and is considered by one well-established New Zealand-based identitarian as the 'real' start of the far right in New Zealand (see Bolton's comments in AZ, 2020a). Given its prominence, public activities and the attention it received in New Zealand's first public counter-terrorism conference (He Whenua Taurikura, 2021), the group represents the ideal source for study.

For both, we surveyed the visual medium in conjunction with the accompanying text, looking for environmental or ideological themes, which were then critically analysed. In the case of NSN, this spanned the entire website and an additional sixteen images produced by the organisation and shared on Telegram channels within the specific timeframes. This is not the entirety of imagery shared, as the channels tend to reshare a vast amount of material. Hence, only that allegedly created by NSN was captured. In the case of AZ, this spanned the entire website as cached and an additional seven images apparently produced by the organisation and shared via the channels in the specific timeframe. From there, we undertook conventional content analysis, allowing themes to emerge from the visuals through open coding. This enabled the distinguishing of key or prominent themes in the images, which were analysed in conjunction to the text.

Welcome to Australia: the NSN

The Australian far right – much like the far right elsewhere – has the tendency to fragment and reform. One of the more recent reformations is NSN. Its members are likely drawn from former Lads Society/United Patriots Front and Antipodean Resistance. Their website went live in 2019, only to be removed months later for promoting discrimination. The website was later relaunched with a modified domain and membership criterion. The criterion mandates that prospective members must be white Australians of European descent, not Jewish, living in Australia, active and fit, mentally healthy, and

2.1 Screenshot of the NSN webpage, 'Australia for the white man'

live according to NSN values. These values represent a 'life of virtue', where members withhold from drug use, degenerate behaviour, 'sexual perversion' and mixed-ethnic sexual relationships and follow a desired way of life (NSN, 2021a). This represents a desired and collective identity in a landscape contained within bounded cultural imaginaries.

Prominent on the NSN website is the group's emblem (Figure 2.1), which features two bladed *fasces* on either side of the slogan 'Australia for the white man'. This clearly aligns the group with international fascist, white supremacist subcultures, and emphasises the ideological centrality of 'race'. Such visual expressions inform how we understand their cultural landscape, or more specifically who is entitled to be there. The website itself has a black background with dark grey runes. The runes may indicate Odinist belief, especially as NSN once held a memorial at the grave of Alexander Rud Mills, a prominent Australian Odinist. Racialist Odinists oppose the three major Abrahamic religions, especially Judaism, with anti-Semitic narratives in addition to those which depict immigrants as a foreign and disruptive species. Such narratives are frequently found in ecofascist expressions.

Ecofascist sentiment is also embedded in NSN's writings, and this provides a foundation for contextualising their complementary visual communication. In one article, 'This Country Is a Sinking Ship', NSN write of how sexual practices, immigration and low white birth rates were leading to the death of their civilisation as '[t]he natural laws of the universe are being transgressed' (NSN, 2021a). This focus on the decay of a racially imagined people in breach of 'nature's laws' is a common feature in ecofascism, elsewhere known as the 'myth of decadence' (Griffin, 1994: 201). In another article, they identify individualism as a further cause for their looming 'racial extinction' (NSN, 2021a). A third article, 'Why National Socialism?', establishes the revolutionary intent of ecofascism: an all-white nation, supposedly living in alignment with the natural order, which 'can be clearly seen among the vast majority of the animal kingdom'. Such ecofascist positions tend to reach the same conclusion: 'We must have exclusive possession of this country, in order to preserve, propagate and advance our nation' (NSN, 2021a).

In their written communication, NSN claim ownership over Australia, seeking to establish their exclusive claims of place often through reference to a 'natural order' as a matter of survival. Such statements on the NSN website are, however, rarely accompanied by visual aesthetics beyond singular stock images and their flag. But despite these simplicities, the group's visual communications nevertheless add nuance to these arguments.

The NSN flag, for example, represents one of the group's important visual artefacts. The flag has the same colours as the Australian flag (and that of the United Kingdom, New Zealand, and the United States, among others). It has a field of blue, and in the centre there is a white diamond, within which four large red arrows converge. As Australia has had the same flag since 1901, colour choice could indicate an attempt to leverage the patriotism that the Australian flag evokes – a similar effort that is apparent in AZ material to come. This may also be an attempt by NSN, like others, to step away from overtly Nazi symbols (Campion, 2019b). The flag also establishes a cultural symbol expressive of self-image, linked both to Australia and potentially beyond. The converging arrow emblem is reminiscent of that propagated by Italian fascist group Casapound Italia, whose ensign contains four black converging arrows. In this iteration, it is said to promote 'unity and order' (Bulli, 2019) and it is potentially co-opted in that way here.

Beyond the flag and the emblem, the bulk of NSN's visual communication is found on Telegram. NSN's (2021b) Telegram presence involves individual and group channels such as the National Socialist Network channel and the Converging Arrows Network. The visual content shared by support-ers is split between NSN members holding the converging arrow flag in natural landscapes, NSN members holding the converging arrow flag in cityscapes, NSN propaganda (stickers, posters) featured in natural landscapes or cityscapes and NSN members standing in front of NSN graffiti in the cityscapes. In many of these images, members are clad in black with their faces obscured, often prominently performing the *Sieg Heil* salute. Across these images, both cityscapes and natural landscapes are viable backdrops.

Despite this variety, photos shared by NSN generally involve members holding the converging arrow flag in rural bushland and natural landscapes. Given the current ideological predisposition of the group to claim exclusive entitlement to Australia, this close engagement with bush landscapes is important. The prominence of the natural Australian landscape is central to their claims of exclusivity: They are not simply finding a pleasing visual

2.2 Screenshot from Telegram, 'Planting the Flag on the Hill'

backdrop but establishing their claim. One image of NSN members quite literally planting the converging arrow flag atop a hill overlooking the Australian bush effectively says as much (Figure 2.2). Visual communication in this sense is not expressly concerned with caring for the environment but with claiming it.

The group's outdoors activities combine apparent concern for the environment with other motivations. The NSN trip to the Grampians National Park on Australia Day in January 2021 represents one such example. The NSN group were heard chanting '*Heil Hitler*', 'white power' and 'Ku Klux

Klan'. In one photo, the NSN members flew two converging arrow flags alongside the Australian flag in front of a natural bushland accompanied by Nazi salutes. Despite – or perhaps due to – the subsequent media uproar, NSN and its precursor organisations such an Antipodean Resistance have frequently engaged in bushwalks, hikes and other athletic activities in the Australian bush. As others have demonstrated (Westberg and Årman, 2019), physical training helps form the 'organisational core' of far-right groups, preparing them for (potentially violent) group operations while simultaneously expressing ideology.

There may be multiple explanations behind the centrality of the Australian bush in this communication. Australian history is rife with settler myths: brave pioneers battling the unpredictable and dangerous Australian bush. The Australian natural landscape was imagined as a vast and terrible place, resisting settler attempts to civilise it in the image of England (Dunlap, 1993). While this 'civilising' ambition quickly dissipated, the stories of pioneers taming the land and bushrangers charging through the wilderness and challenging colonial authorities endured. The Australian far right have long co-opted such settlement stories and myths. Therefore, we may observe some small parallel: an attempt, though perhaps subtle, to arrogate to themselves the grandeur of historical settler tales set in natural landscapes (for other cases of settler colonialism and far-right visual environmental communication, see Chapters 1 and 3 in this volume).

It may also be a self-expression in a culturally imagined landscape. Engaging with nature may have become part of NSN's representation of a desired ethnoscape to communicate their presumed heritage and exclusive claim to Australia. This is part of an overall communicative mechanism in which written and visual works serve both strategic communication goals (some more explicitly than others). This also appears in suspension with elements of ecofascist ideology, an ideology which rejects the presence of immigrants, opposes individualism, decries certain behaviours as degenerate and idealises a natural order. The reactionary elements of ecofascism can be identified, alongside the revolutionary ambition to return to an imagined natural order. This natural order itself becomes an artefact of the cultural imaginary.

However, we can also interpret more from the nature-focused activities of NSN. In pursuing healthy and athletically lifestyles, and in engaging with nature in group settings, the NSN are not simply building health and fitness or training for operations. These activities allow them to perceive themselves as part of the 'natural order': of people against (and within) nature. It becomes an expression of identity in a cultural imaginary but also of authenticity – the ideological enactment of how they believe *they* should be. In planting themselves seemingly as fixtures in the Australian landscape, they may also be projecting their belief in their native authenticity to the land. Such activities therefore demonstrate expressions of entitativity on the one hand, and exclusive claims on place on the other. This anthropocentric form of ecofascism highlights the centrality of 'the people' and the necessity of securing the place for the people to thrive, rather than being anchored in ecocentric concerns.

While the experience of nature is offline, it is then circulated online via social media. Even since the arrest and imprisonment of an NSN leader, fellow members and relatives continue to share content through his Telegram account. One such post of significance was a painting titled *Dandenong Ranges from Beleura*, attributed to an Austrian Romanticist painter. As the painting depicts an untouched and unspoiled Australian landscape, it would appear that the arrogation of natural landscapes continues. Of course, NSN channels also share the content of the European Australia Movement, the Pioneer group, Tasman Forth and others. But more importantly here, on 10 August 2021, a prominent NSN Telegram channel also shared and supported a post by AZ, reinforcing the relevance of a comparative approach between the two.

Aotearoa New Zealand: AZ

Like Australia and elsewhere, New Zealand's far-right groups seek to advance and normalise their ideological perspective in the public discourse (AZ, 2020b). The major challenge towards public acceptance in the New Zealand setting – according to the movement's advocates – has been one of membership and leadership. One New Zealand-based individual with decades of organisational involvement in this space perhaps best explains this obstacle, describing Kyle Chapman's National Front as being dominated by 'stupid' skinheads who effectively held the cause back through undisciplined public behaviour (see Bolton's comments in AZ, 2020a). In response to these perceived shortcomings, new 'promising' groups emerged which sought to advance their ideology in more approachable, disciplined and sophisticated ways. Such efforts unquestionably convey carefully curated ecofascist views, similar to what has occurred in Australia.

One of these new, ecofascist-inspired groups was the Dominion Movement, which emerged in 2018 using the slogan 'revolt against the modern world', drawn from the Italian fascist Julius Evola and since adopted by (eco)fascists internationally. The group prioritised the conservation and appreciation of nature, and even engaged in beach cleans (Ford, 2020; for similar examples of far-right eco-action, see, for example, Tarant, 2019 and Chapter 3 in this volume), demonstrating perhaps more conviction for environmental concerns than observed by NSN.

Though a contested point among some authorities (for example, Battersby and Ball, 2019), the Christchurch mosque attacks brought a great deal more attention to New Zealand-based right-wing extremists than they had previously experienced. According to members of the movement, Dominion's leadership crumbled in the face of this increased scrutiny (AZ, 2020a). AZ emerged as a direct response to this failed leadership, with the purpose of growing the public face of the identitarian cause with the slogan 'Building a community for European New Zealanders' (AZ, 2021a).

To build this community in New Zealand, AZ's leadership holds strict membership criteria: male only, reasonable weight and fitness, drug use is banned and appearance/presentability requirements. Members are encouraged to bushwalk, read, write and abstain from certain forms of deviancy. Ideologically, AZ opposes consumerism and materialism, immigration, unsustainable economic growth, drug-taking and vices, sexual deviancy and corporatism. They instead champion a racially homogenous (white) community which abides by their behavioural mandates and is economically and environmentally sustainable (AZ, 2021a). These positions would appear to indicate the adoption of select ecofascist positions.

The group also infuses environmental concepts into their public appeals and their internal activities, though there is some question regarding how important – and how genuine – such conceptualisations are to the group. Take the background image on their website, a vista of Queenstown's misty Remarkables mountain range (Figure 2.3). The snow-covered peaks of Kawarau overlook a stunning valley of farmland and river streams, with a hint of Queenstown's more populated areas on the horizon. The photo, apparently taken by an obscure Melbourne-based photographer on a recent visit (Smalls, 2018), represents how AZ sometimes crudely co-opts environmental communication to advance their cause.

To celebrate the launch of AZ, their website published three articles related to the movement's ideals. None of these articles discuss the environment explicitly, though the reference to identitarian ecofascist conceptualisations are quite clear. For example, one of these first articles, titled 'Ancient Aryans?', argues that Māori are potentially not the true indigenous people of New Zealand. Instead, as the author claims, Aryan people were perhaps the first to arrive on these islands. The physical evidence of this pre-Polynesian settlement is 'hushed up and hidden'; the genetic evidence can no longer be found, having been 'bred out' passively or violently' with Māori since that time. Nevertheless, by claiming the existence of such evidence, and a New Zealand-wide conspiracy to conceal the historical record, the author provides

2.3 Screenshot of part of the home page of Action Zealandia website

the very foundation from which the group can subtly claim indigeneity in this context. The white misty mountains of New Zealand, according to this view, historically belong to 'the people of the soil' of AZ's members (AZ, 2021c). It is language such as this that hints at a deeper historical connection with the New Zealand landscape.

Given New Zealand's existing indigenous population, membership sometimes seeks to redefine and resist constructions of indigeneity by either explicitly celebrating its own people as indigenous to Europe, or to run 'white lives matter!' campaigns on Indigenous Peoples' Day. The very name of the group represents a similar form of resistance and identity, while clearly being designed to shield AZ's entitlement to this landscape. The second article published on their website makes only a passing reference to Zealandia, but it is an instructive link nevertheless.

This second article on AZ's website laments the defacement of statues that celebrate colonialism in Aotearoa. One such defacement involves Zealandia, a nineteenth-century European adorned in a toga, representing the 'personification of our country' much like her mother: Britannia. The statue shows Zealandia laying a palm frond on a monument to the 'colonial forces and the friendly Māoris' in the New Zealand Wars. The Auckland statue has been defaced several times, though this time protestors had glued an axe to Zealandia's head leaving the note: 'fascism and white supremacy are not welcome here'.

AZ interprets this defacement as 'killing off the personification of White New Zealand, and by extension White New Zealanders'. In their view, the activists '[know] nothing of true New Zealand history, [thinking] that the New Zealand Wars were a simple white versus Māori affair. Evil white supremacist colonists fascistically genociding the poor innocent natives who were completely peaceful and certainly would never do anything to deserve even a bit of punishment.' Much like the Dominion Movement before it, AZ reimagines New Zealand's colonial history as a litany of abuses that Europeans suffered at the hands of Māori. According to this conceptualisation, the birth of the New Zealand Dominion brought civilisation to an uncivilised land: An attack on the personification of this land is a direct threat to membership's perceived culture, history, connection with the country, and its entitlement to these islands.

Since its inception, environmental activities feature as a major component of AZ's public face and their internal group-building exercises. Tree planting and beach clean-up operations, for example, represent the group's attempts to connect with the environment, both as its (exclusive) protectors and as a means of advertising the just nature of their cause. These outdoor activities are designed to be less confrontational to the public, though the leadership acknowledges that the deliberate use of balaclavas counteract that effort to some degree (AZ, 2020b).

The AZ flag is prominently represented in these events, often proudly displayed at the top of a group climb – much like the NSN example (Figure 2.1). Sitting at the centre of this blue and white flag is the symbol of AZ: a mountain – presumably Kawarau or Aoraki – decorated by the stars of the Southern Cross. The flag in this manner is seemingly distinctly New Zealand but, like the background image on AZ's website, hints at a more superficial and unoriginal meaning: The mountain itself bears a stark resemblance to the *lambda* in identitarian flags used by various movements across the globe to express opposition to immigration and Islam. The Anti-Defamation League (ADL, 2021) further suggests that the symbol is also seen to personify the defence of Europe from the Middle East, perhaps localised here to suggest the defence of European New Zealand.

AZ's Telegram channel (AZ, 2021b) reveals environmental communication less about ecocentrism and more about embedding themselves in natural landscapes as part of the anthropocentric ecofascism described by Campion (2021). Much like NSN channels, AZ shares visual content of propaganda materials (for example, stickers) affixed to poles and bins, but most content involves AZ members wearing black balaclavas and holding signs in natural settings with messages such as 'White lives matter! AZ' and 'Boer Lives

Matter' (on the South African case, see Chapter 1 in this volume). One image depicts AZ members holding paintball guns and wearing gas masks in the forest, while others show flag-draped members looking over New Zealand forests, Christchurch members exploring Maukatere and photos of natural landscapes (Figure 2.4). Like their website, by and large, this commentary on social channels does not discuss the environment but instead promotes ideological positions on the current government, anti-Semitism, AZ-authored articles, race and other topics.

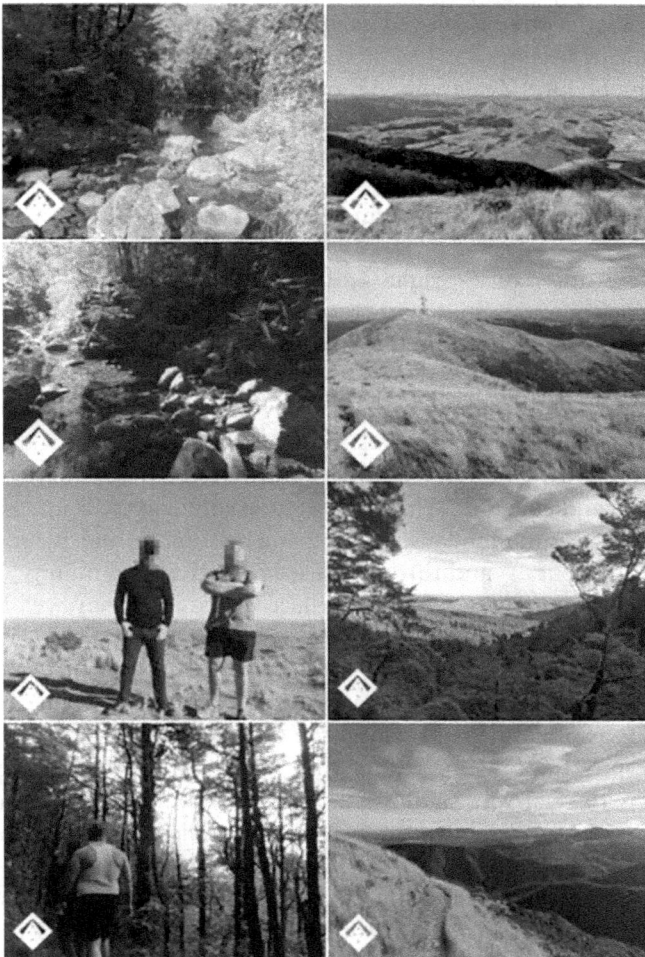

2.4 Screenshot from Telegram, AZ members exploring Maukatere

Herein lies the most important point. On its surface, the group seems to exhibit an environmental focus: Mission statements cite sustainability as a primary drive for the group, and bushwalks, beach clean-ups and tree plantings all point to a similar conclusion. While there is a clear ideological subtext, the strategic elements are more overt, in a context similar to what Kyriazi (2019) observes in Hungary. Viewed through this lens, AZ's operations may be strategically designed to help build internal coherence and construct an entitlement to the land, while offering a more attractive and welcoming face to the public. One needs only to peruse the Voice of Zealandia podcasts and their writings to see that ideological concern for the environment, though certainly present, infrequently features as a central cause. Where it does emerge, it is often deployed as merely a symptom of a wider problem: corruption, globalisation, neoliberalism, corporatism, communism or whatever other enemy pollutes Zealandia. AZ positions itself as the solution necessary to cleanse the country of these ills.

Conclusion: comparing Pacific far-right contexts

These case studies of far-right groups in Australia and New Zealand demonstrate commonalities with respect to serving both ideological and strategic ends: the projection and enactment of a desired identity features across both contexts. Both groups encourage environmental activities that no doubt support ambitions to be healthy and physically fit. On the one hand, membership likely perceives these activities as a return to an imagined 'natural order', or more crudely contribute to racial survivability. By experiencing and engaging with their natural landscapes, it is possible that both groups are simultaneously expressing self-image and identity within a cultural imaginary – and through this, ideological community. Although these are community activities, and collective activities may well be an end in themselves, it also becomes an avenue for expressing entitativity as a cohesive and homogenous group.

The visual environmental communication of Pacific far-right groups also buttress claims of entitlement within the cultural – but also natural – landscapes. Despite the obvious reality that neither group are native to their landscape with relatively shallow historical connections to the land, both nevertheless seek to establish exclusive and nativist claims. Some may see engagement with nature as an extension of nationalism. Some may leverage historical settlement narratives and create visual artefacts that seemingly promote their native authenticity in natural landscapes. This may be an attempt to arrogate to themselves exclusive entitlement to a bounded space – a discourse observed by Turner and Bailey (2021) who speak of 'ecobordering'. They suggest that ecobordering positions migrants as environmental vandals unlike the 'native' custodians of the land. The placement of NSN and AZ members in natural landscapes is therefore not without greater meaning: Above all else, they seek to communicate their exclusive and privileged claims to that space despite actual native populations (the Māori and Aboriginal nations). This further local and bounded concern for cultural landscapes is reminiscent of actors elsewhere, such as the German quarterly *Umwelt & Aktiv* (Forchtner, 2019b).

When we consider the written communication in addition to the visual communication, another commonality emerges. Despite professions to ownership and entitlement to space, and environmental concerns, neither group actually centralises environmental narratives. This leads us to question the sincerity of expressed environmental concern, which appear to be more culturally constructed than scientifically based or informed by empirical research on, for example, the climate crisis. Their concern for the environment appears to be both particular and bounded. Neither group propagates strong narratives concerning the global environment, nor does either group demonstrate consistent and comprehensive opposition to major polluters or destructive environmental practices. Seen though this perspective, operations such as rubbish clean-ups appear to be more marketing opportunities than attempts to redress major environmental concerns. Therefore, environmental representations seem bounded by their self-perceived entitlements, and become a bordering mechanism used to rationalise the 'keeping out' of immigrants deemed to be environmentally damaging or irresponsible.

To conclude, then, we suggest that ecofascist expressions in Pacific contexts are both ideological and strategic. Both of our case studies exploited the natural landscape as an artefact of their constructed cultural imaginaries. While this is clearly ideological, it also serves strategic ends by making exclusive and implicit claims on place which supplemented other narrative positions. Therefore, visual communication of the environment can be leveraged as a backdrop for identity performance, articulating who belongs and who does not, seeking to arrogate nativity and express entitativity. This perceived nativity of a select people in a geographically bounded place becomes an expression quite separate from scientifically based concerns for the environment. Instead, far-right groups in Australia and New Zealand appear to be particularistic in their communication, focused much more on emphasising their privilege and ownership than actually conserving the environment.

References

Abdelrahim, Y. A. A. (2019): Visual analysis of ISIS discourse strategies and types in Dabiq and Rumiyah online magazines, *Visual Communication Quarterly*, 26(2): 63–78. https://doi.org/10.1080/15551393.2019.1586546

ADL (2021): Identitarian Lambda: General hate symbols. www.adl.org/education/references/hate-symbols/identitarian-lambda (accessed 11 February 2022).

AZ (2020a): Conversation with Dr. Kerry Bolton, *Voice of Zealandia: Episode 9*.

AZ (2020b): Conversation with JChannel, *Voice of Zealandia: Episode 15* (removed c. November 2021).

AZ (2021a): Assorted articles, *Action Zealandia*, https://action-zealandia.com/.

AZ (2021b): Assorted posts, t.me/s/ActionZealandia.

AZ (2021c): We were interviewed by TVNZ One, *Voice of Zealandia*.

Battersby, J. and Ball, R. (2019): Christchurch in the context of New Zealand terrorism and right wing extremism, *Journal of Policing, Intelligence and Counter Terrorism*, 14(3): 191–207. https://doi.org/10.1080/18335330.2019.1662077

Bjørgo, T. and Ravndal, J. A. (2019): Extreme-right violence and terrorism: Concepts, patterns and responses, *ICCT Policy Brief*. https://icct.nl/publication/extreme-right-violence-and-terrorism-concepts-patterns-and-responses/ (accessed 11 February 2022).

Bührs, T. and Christoff, P. (2006): 'Greening the Antipodes'? Environmental policy and politics in Australia and New Zealand, *Australian Journal of Political Science*, 41(2): 225–240. https://doi.org/10.1080/10361140600672444

Bulli, G. (2019): CasaPound Italia's cultural imaginary, *Patterns of Prejudice*, 53(3): 253–269. https://doi.org/10.1080/0031322X.2019.1595465

Campion, K. (2019a): A 'lunatic fringe'? The persistence of right wing extremism in Australia, *Perspectives on Terrorism*, 13(2): 2–20.

Campion, K. (2019b): Australian right wing extremist ideology: Naratives of nemesis and nostalgia, *Journal of Policing, Intelligence and Counter Terrorism*, 14(3): 208–226. https://doi.org/10.1080/18335330.2019.1667013

Campion, K. (2021): Defining ecofascism: Historical foundations and contemporary interpretations in the extreme right, *Terrorism and Political Violence*, 1–20. https://doi.org/10.1080/09546553.2021.1987895.

Coghlan, D. and Brydon-Miller, M. (eds) (2014). *Constructivism*. London: Sage.

Craig, G. (2009): Aotearoa/New Zealand television news and current affairs representations of the environment, *Australian Journal of Communication*, 36: 55–71.

Crosby, H. (2017): *Right-Wing Extremism in New Zealand: Dialogues with those who Left*. Master of Arts, University of Auckland, New Zealand. www.researchgate.net/profile/Hayden-Crosby-2/publication/339300381_Right-wing_Extremism_in_New_Zealand_Dialogues_with_those_who_left/links/5e49e024458515072da45647/Right-wing-Extremism-in-New-Zealand-Dialogues-with-those-who-left.pdf (accessed 11 February 2022).

Dean, G. Bell, P. and Vakhitova, Z. (2016): Right-wing extremism in Australia: The rise of the new radical right, *Journal of Policing, Intelligence and Counter Terrorism*, 11(2): 121–142. https://doi.org/10.1080/18335330.2019.1667013

Dunlap, T. (1993): Australian nature, European culture: Anglo settlers in Australia, *Environmental History Review*, 17(1): 1–24. https://doi.org/10.2307/3984889

Evans, R. (2008): 'A menace to this realm': The New Guard and the New South Wales Police, 1931–1932, *History Australia*, 5(3): 76.1–76.20. https://doi.org/10.2104/ha080076

Fahmy, S. (2020): The age of terrorism media: The visual narratives of the Islamic State Group's Dabiq magazine, *The International Communication Gazette*, 82(3): 260–288.

Fleming, A. and Mondon, A. (2018): The radical right in Australia. In: J. Rydgren (ed.), *The Oxford Handbook of the Radical Right*. Oxford: Oxford University Press, 650–666. https://doi.org/10.1177%2F1748048519843412

Forchtner, B. (2019a): Introduction. In: B. Forchtner (ed.), *The Far Right and the Environment: Politics, Discourse and Communication*. London: Routledge, 1–17.

Forchtner, B. (2019b): Nation, nature, purity: Extreme-right biodiversity in Germany, *Patterns of Prejudice*, 53(3): 285–301. https://doi.org/10.1080/0031322X.2019.1592303

Forchtner, B. and Kølvraa, C. (2017): Extreme right images of radical authenticity: Multimodal aesthetics of history, nature, and gender roles in social media, *European Journal of Cultural and Political Sociology*, 4(3): 252–281. https://doi.org/10.1080/23254823.2017.1322910

Forchtner, B. and Özvatan, Ö. (2019): Beyond the 'German Forest': Environmental communication by the far right in Germany. In: B. Forchtner (ed.), *The Far Right and the Environment*. London: Routledge, 216–236.

Ford, K. (2020): Mapping the New Zealand far-right, *Peace Review*, 32(4): 504–511. https://doi.org/10.1080/10402659.2020.1921412

Gardell, M. (2003): *Gods of the Blood: The Pagan Revival and White Seperatism*. Durham, NC: Duke University Press.

Griffin, R. (1994): *The Nature of Fascism*. London: Routledge.

Guild, A. (2009): Defending our National Identity. www.ironbarkresources.com/nationalidentity/index.html (accessed 11 February 2022).

Gunther, C. and Pfeifer, S. (eds) (2020): *Jihadi Auidovisuality and Its Entanglments: Meanings, Aesthetics, Apropriations*. Edinburgh: Edinburgh University Press.

He Whenua Taurikura (2021): *New Zealand's Hui on Countering Terrorism and Violent Extremism*. Christchurch Town Hall, 15–16 June. New Zealand Government.

Herfroy-Mischler, A. (2018): Jihadist visual communication strategy: ISIL's hostage executions video production, *Visual Communication*, 18(4): 519–548. https://doi.org/10.1177%2F1470357218803396

Kølvraa, C. (2019): Wolves in sheep's clothing? The Danish far right and 'wild nature'. In: B. Forchtner (ed.), *The Far Right and the Environment*. London: Routledge, 107–120.

Kyriazi, A. (2019): The environmental communication of Jobbik: Between strategy and ideology. In: B. Forchtner (ed.), *The Far Right and the Environment*. London: Routledge, 184–200.

Lester, L. (2015): Containment and reach: The changing ecology of environmental communication. In: A. Hansen and R. Cox (eds), *The Routledge Handbook of Environment and Communication*. London: Routledge, 232–241.

Mondon, A. (2012): An Australian immunisation to the extreme right? *Social Identities*, 18(3), 355–372. https://doi.org/10.1080/13504630.2012.662001

Moore, A. (2005): The New Guard and the Labour Movement, 1931–1935, *Labour History*, 89: 55–72. https://doi.org/10.2307/27508249

NSN (2021a): Assorted articles, *National Socialist Network*. https://national-socialist-network.info/join/ (accessed 11 February 2022).

NSN (2021b): Assorted posts, *National Socialist Network*. Across two primary channels likely hosted by t.me/s/nationalsocialistnetwork, t.me/s/thomassewell, and t.me/s/convergingarrowsnetwork.

Perkins, J. (1991): Swastikas down under: Nazi activities in Australia, 1933–1939, *Journal of Contemporary History*, 26: 111–129. https://doi.org/10.1177%2F002200949102600106

Ray, J. (1973): Anti-Semitic types in Australia, *Patterns of Prejudice*, 7(1): 6–16.

Smalls, T. (2018): Shooting New Zealand's landscapes for a week with only a 50mm lens, *PetaPixel*. https://petapixel.com/2018/06/05/shooting-new-zealands-landscapes-for-a-week-with-only-a-50mm-lens/ (accessed 11 February 2022).

Smith, K. L., Moriarty, S., Kenney, K. and Barbatsis, G. (2005): *Handbook of Visual Communication: Theory, Methods, and Media*. London: Routledge.

Spoonley, P. (1981): New Zealand First! The extreme right and politics in New Zealand, 1961–1981, *Political Science*, 33(2): 99–126. https://doi.org/10.1177/003231878103300201

Tarant, Z. (2019): Is Brown the new Green? The environmental discourse of the Czech far right. In: B. Forchtner (ed.), *The Far Right and the Environment*. London: Routledge, 201–215.

Tarrant, B. (2019): *The Great Replacement*. Circulated online on 15 March 2019.

Turner, J. and Bailey, D. (2021): 'Ecobordering': Casting immigration control as environmental protection, *Environmental Politics*, 31(1): 110–131. https://doi.org/10.1080/09644016.2021.1916197

Weir, E. (2021): Action Zealandia, NZ's largest neo-Nazi group, on the hunt for new recruits, *New Zealand Herald*. www.nzherald.co.nz/nz/action-zealandia-nzs-largest-neo-nazi-group-on-the-hunt-for-new-recruits/BK56VEKDR5AJE2CMBVNAX2DKRA/ (accessed 11 February 2022).

Westberg, G. and Årman, H. (2019): Common sense as extremism: The multi-semiotics of contemporary national socialism, *Critical Discourse Studies*, 16(5): 549–568. https://doi.org/10.1080/17405904.2019.1624183

3

The National Socialist Movement of the United States and the turn to environmentalism: greenfingers or brownshirts?

Daniel Jones

Introduction

While the Nazi phrase *Blut und Ehre* (Blood and Honour) is one many are familiar with due to its continuing legacy, in neo-Nazi music in particular and in the eponymously named international music network, there was another, similar phrase: *Blut und Boden* (Blood and Soil). Originating in nineteenth-century nationalist thought, this phrase connected the concept of a people, the blood, with a specific land or place, the soil. More than this, it highlighted those unconnected to the land and its cultivation as a threatening corruption (Kiernan, 2007: 2–9). Within Nazi Germany, the concept championed rural living and outdoor pursuits, and contrasted this with what they argued were the unconnected and transitive natures of their identified racial enemies, in particular the Jewish and Roma diasporas. As Uekoetter (2006) explores in *The Green and the Brown*, this appeal to environmentalism and the use of its language helped sections of the environmentalist movement more easily cooperate with the Nazi regime.

Blood and Soil linked Nazi and fascist ideals around the strength and purity of their people to concepts of the natural environment and the preservation of an idealised rural landscape. Dixon and Wallwork (2004), though focusing on the British nationalist milieu, also identified the natural geographical landscape as one area developed by nationalisms in support of identity politics. The natural landscape and its boundaries became a way of dividing those within from those without; an opportunity for the creation of a motivating threat through the depiction of an imagined, idealised natural heritage under pressure. Often, fascist movements discursively constructed such threat and pressure by claiming that existing power structures fail to address an issue of concern due to some form of corruption or subversive influence, and that only the fascist leadership, representing the true voice of the people, could prevent disaster (Griffin, 1993: 41–43). Furthermore, this environment is an imagined space with an idealised landscape – freeing the far right from often problematic narratives of the land the groups occupied (Boggs, 2019). Indeed, such a settler colonialist attitude, of an imagined *terra nullius* waiting for the imprint of white Europeans, has also played an important role in the development of the American identity (Glenn, 2015).

Against this background, this chapter examines, first, the extent to which this connection with the physical environment, and its custodianship, is present within a leading actor of the contemporary American neo-Nazi movement. Second, it investigates to what extent these expressions of concern over the environment are recognisable offshoots of mainstream environmentalism or whether they are a novel reframing of traditional fascist tropes. That is, it considers how far environmental concern, for a real or an imagined landscape, has been retained as a key part of at least some of these continuing fascist legacies – in essence examining whether environmentalism still burns within what Macklin (2007: 15) referred to as fascism's 'Sacred Flame'.

To do so, this chapter analyses the National Socialist Movement (NSM), one of the most prominent and largest of the American neo-Nazi movements, which was founded in 1974. More specifically, the chapter considers their main propaganda outputs: specifically their website, the *NSM Magazine*, the precursor magazine *Stormtrooper* and flyers distributed to local chapters for them to reprint and use (*NSM Main Page*, n.d.):. The chapter examines content available on their website, from the time of the Charlottesville protests of August 2017, where the NSM gathered in support of the Unite the Right rally, up until August of 2020. In analysing environmental activism and communication over this three-year period, this chapter focuses on what can be identified as three crucial campaigns by the NSM: from a classic case of eco-action around the Adopt-a-Highway programme that saw the NSM take responsibility for keeping a stretch of roadway clean, to campaigns to protect the Mexican border and the promotion of outdoor activities.

The primary focus is on their use of the environment and environmentalism within their visual outputs – 278 images in total – and how these are presented alongside textual material. This draws on Wozniak et al. (2015), who highlighted the need to consider the visual alongside its corresponding text in a multimodal fashion. This was built upon by Hansen (2017), who argued that textual context plays an important role in influencing how that environmental imagery is then understood. The chapter also draws upon understandings of the far right organisations as cultural movements, seeking to carefully cultivate and craft their own internal milieu as highlighted by the work of Copsey (Copsey, 2004; Copsey and Richardson, 2015: 1). Visual references have also long played a part in cultural propagation among the far right, but have found new utility in the Internet era where the far right have begun to use websites, YouTube, static meme images and social media to engage new audiences with images that can often reference or evoke earlier periods of strength such as the Third Reich (Klein, 2020; Rodríguez-Serrano et al., 2021).

Within these outputs, the NSM transmitted their cultural ideals to their members, but also sought to motivate them to act against what the NSM presented as threats to the nation and its environment. These messages often encourage members to take action despite the cost to themselves, and through a romanticised concept of the natural environment that offers an opportunity to revitalise the country – what Zimmerman (1995; see also Taylor, 2019) and others have called ecofascism. This particular fusing of fascist and environmental concepts is concerned with the impact the degeneration of nature has on the nation, as a society and in the conceived strength of the individuals within it. Rather than arguing for action to defend nature for nature's sake, it instead seeks to readdress the balance between man and nature for the continued moral and physical health of man, and by restoring that balance undo the decline and degeneration fascists see in modern society. In identifying the renewed relevance of ecofascism, Campion (2021) also highlights how the ecological harmony sought within ecofascism acts in effect as a call for racial segregation, but racial segregation that very much identifies races and peoples with the land and sense of place; with their home environment. As such, it is also important to note that this chapter deals with the extreme-right section of the far right which rejects democracy, is often seen as violent and views the broader political establishment (including right and even other far right actors) as somehow corrupted or weak (Mudde, 2019: 30–31).

In what follows, this chapter first examines the campaigns around the Adopt-a-Highway programme before turning to campaigns to protect the Mexican border. It then considers the ways in which environmental imagery was used as part of an appeal to return to outdoor activities, with the creation of sacred spaces within NSM camps and activities, and the ways this represented the ecofascist notion of a restoration of moral and national health.

Neo-Nazism and the United States environment

As well as understanding and considering the ideological context, it is important to remember the historical context in which these movements exist. In the post-war period, Stone argued that Europe had settled into an anti-fascist consensus: that the experience of the Second World War had entrenched a passive cultural aversion to open fascism (Stone, 2014: 10). As Jackson (2014) observes, this discreditation of open fascism and Nazism went beyond the European continent and impacted in America as well, with openly fascist movements forced to seek connections internationally between one another rather than with a public that eschewed them as an undesirable fringe. However, compared to Europe, there were also reasons that America in particular saw such open Nazism and neo-Nazism continue to exist even in the hostile cultural environment, in particular the broad American approach to freedom of speech (Mudde, 2018: 4–8). To survive in these hostile cultural environments, the fascist movements stripped away parts of fascist ideology as part of an adaptation that would ensure they could survive either in their own right or as a groupuscule within larger organisations. This reduced fascist ideological core, Macklin's aforementioned 'Sacred Flame', was more transmissible, thus enabling its survival and its spread, often by the adaptation of other ideas that were still acceptable to wider society. Concern for the environment and increased activism for ecological causes can be argued to be one of these tropes, as it is increasingly important to mainstream society and offered a rich language of counterculture that they could seek to infiltrate.

It must also be considered that within American mainstream society there has been an idealisation of rural communities and an imagined landscape. Goddard (2011) explored how Virginia Lee Burton's *Little House on the Prairie*, first published in 1940, created a strong sense of anti-urbanism among the increasingly urban post-war American public. It also engendered a conservationism and environmental concern, linking the simplicity of this preserved rural idyll with a moral purity or simpleness that was attractive to a nation undergoing the upheavals of the early post-war years. These ideas fit well alongside the concepts of rebirth and renewal that nationalisms, including fascism, sought to evoke, where a decadent or decaying contemporary society is swept away in pursuit of the moral strength and purity of an earlier idealised age as the launching point for a new fascist future (Griffin, 1993: 32–36).

The most influential strand of post-war national socialism in America was George Lincoln Rockwell's American Nazi Party, who espoused a blend of open Nazism with classical American tropes – Rockwell himself was often pictured with a corn cob pipe and a Winchester repeating rifle. Following Rockwell's assassination in 1967, several offshoots were founded by members seeking to continue this legacy (Clark, 2006). The NSM, founded in 1974 by Robert Brannen and Cliff Herrington, is one of these offshoots and its legacy very clearly follows the avowedly Nazi political culture. By 1994, leadership had passed to Jeff Schoep under whom the NSM became the largest of the American neo-Nazi organisations by 2009, active across the country (Balleck, 2018: 242–243, 324–325; Southern Poverty Law Centre, n.d.). Charlottesville, which descended into violence and where anti-fascist activist Heather Heyer was killed, represented a key point of breakthrough of the NSM into the public consciousness, where their material came to a wider audience. Their presence at protests, with their familiar shields, became a regular fixture after Charlottesville. This success came as the NSM faced civil lawsuits related to Charlottesville and Schoep left the group, with control of the movement briefly passing to a Black activist intent on destroying the movement. In response, Schoep took back control to organise a more orderly transition before attempting to decouple himself from the extreme right (Lapin, 2020). To understand how the NSM's website reflected its campaigning around the environment, this study begins with the earliest campaigns still recorded on the website during this period: the Adopt-a-Highway campaign.

Adopt-a-Highway and litter: early claims to be custodians of the environment

Taylor (2019) highlighted how the American far right utilises classic tropes of revolutionary anti-modernism to engage in ecological discourse, but it is also important to note that this includes physical campaigning. For example, an ecological activist under the pseudonym 'Problem Animal' highlighted (and rejected) such intrusions in the magazine *Earth First* in 2005 ('Problem Animal', 2005), pointing to two initiatives in particular: the NSM's use of the Adopt-a-Highway programme and the campaigns by White Aryan Resistance against the environmental cost of disposable chopsticks. While the linking of chopsticks to environmental damage in the form of deforestation of the Pacific Northwest has obvious xenophobic connotations, the NSM's call to volunteer and pick litter to keep a stretch of public road clean seems a relatively uncontroversial affair with little obvious malice.

Indeed, the *Stormtrooper* (#19) highlights the use of the Adopt-a-Highway programme by an anti-immigration group near to the border with Mexico in California, and the subsequent removal of that group from the programme (*Stormtrooper* #19, 2008: 5). This appears again a year later in issue 32, where the NSM chapter in Missouri adopted a highway near Springfield (*Stormtrooper* #32, 2009: 7). Three photos are used to highlight this activity, showing members beside an open road, walking on the grass and with trees behind them (for example, Figure 3.1). In the photos the volunteers are carrying identical bags and male members wear coordinated clothing. These photos are clearly curated images designed to convey the aesthetic of responsible guardians. Though the written text speaks of needles and drug material found, the images present a clean environment: no litter is visible, and judging from the full bag of one volunteer, these photos were staged after the event, thus highlighting their achievement. These photos – all shot

3.1 Neo-Nazis picking litter

from a lower angle, ensuring a more open view with plenty of sky – present the NSM as curators of this space, as dutiful custodians of the natural environment.

Where the images take on additional meaning is in their contrast with the other activities of the group in the same report. The photos of the cleaning are contrasted with two photos of the NSM attending an LGBT event, where members 'showed their discussed [*sic*] and contempt for the parade' (*Stormtrooper* #32, 2009: 7). An image of the NSM group is labelled 'Unity' – a concept shown visually as it is taken at a distance and from a lower angle, allowing the NSM cadre to take on more heroic proportions, and emphasising their shared aesthetic of black uniforms and shields as it frames them against the sky and trees. This echoes what Yanay (2008) explored around the use of low-angle perspectives as a common technique in evoking a sense of heroic nationalism. This claim of unity is contrasted against a close-up image of an NSM member, with SS tattoo, being confronted by angry counter-protestors described as 'street filth' (*Stormtrooper* #32, 2009: 7). Taken from a higher angle that removes any sense of a wider environment, the close-up nature of the image creates a sense of crowdedness and disconnects the protestors from the space they occupy. The caption given to the photo also directly draws a parallel between this confrontation and the ways in which the NSM activists had cleaned the streets of literal filth. Their propaganda seeks to represent the NSM as guardians of the environment and its natural landscapes, and from this argue for the NSM as ideal guardians of American society's moral and political future, and its careful curation into the idealised fascist state.

Border campaigns: putting 'Boots on the Border' and claiming landscape

As Hultgren (2015) observes, within the United States the issue of the environment was increasingly being employed to support anti-immigrant narratives. This was part of a wider and long-term anti-immigrant discourse in the United States, involving the creation of fears and anxieties among the population towards migrants that culminated in the election of President Donald Trump in 2016 (Finley and Esposito, 2019). Trump's campaign about the border coalesced around the threat that these immigrants posed to American society and the failure of existing political structures to tackle this problem. It is important to understand how the NSM adapted their propaganda to fit in with this broader background, and how their campaigning shifted in order to maintain their claimed position as the guardians of white America and its environment.

The discussion mentioned in the previous section around roadway litter clearing quickly faded from the NSM's national narrative as it transitioned to its new *NSM Magazine* production from 2010. Littering only appears again in textual form for things like warnings against leaving literature in yards for fear of citation by law enforcement (*NSM Magazine* Summer/Fall, 2016: 48). Instead, just as their work with Adopt-a-Highway had followed efforts from other anti-immigration groups as identified in *Stormtrooper* #19, the NSM also copied anti-migration groups in establishing vigilante border patrols (*Stormtrooper* #19, 2008: 5).

Building on existing, more mainstream anti-immigrant discourses, the environment and its preservation are continuously linked to migration in the NSM's outputs. As early as 2009, *Stormtrooper* reports NSM chapters being active at the border to monitor it for illegal crossings (*Stormtrooper* #26, 2009: 6). This is accompanied by three small images: one of an NSM activist brandishing a movement flag in front of the border wall, another with a figure with binoculars and finally an image of the remote landscape with large rock formations and arid scrubland. Again, this evokes a sense of guardianship or custodianship over the land and physical space, expressing that the NSM – and not the government – are keeping people safe. To emphasise this, the pictures are captioned in red to one side: 'It's our members that are protecting our borders' (*Stormtrooper* #26, 2009: 6). As Wodak and Forchtner (2014) suggest, red is used to highlight danger or threats, but also to show passionate and warm speech, helping emphasise the point and showing the NSM's desire to counter this threat.

The border issue has become a frequent topic in *NSM Magazine*, one often accompanied with visual images of members at the border and in nature. Just as with litter picking, the guardianship of the border is linked to street activity against anti-fascist protestors, proclaiming that 'not only did the NSM put boots on the ground on our streets, but we placed boots on the border, too' (*NSM Magazine* Spring/Summer, 2017: 35). This was repeated in Schoep's speech to a rally in April 2015, stating that: 'We've put people on the borders where this government, the United States government refuses to do so' (*NSM Magazine* Winter/Spring, 2015: 6).

The documenting of this activity with photography continues with pictures of nature and of NSM figures using the land for their patrols (*NSM Magazine* Summer/Fall, 2010: 1–2). This early use also shows an interesting other side to these patrols, with pictures of the rubbish – backpacks and even a dead horse – that they claim was left by illegal migrants (*NSM Magazine* Summer/Fall, 2010: 3–5). This particular theme of litter and the intrusion into the natural environment of the migrants is picked up again in mid to late 2012 in a report entitled 'National Socialist Movement Border Operations' accompanied by photography (*NSM Magazine* Summer/Fall, 2012: 4–7) emphasising NSM activists' connection to and native status in the land. This is contrasted with images of litter (water bottles, jugs of suspicious brown water and discarded tents) left behind by migrants. In this way the migration they campaign against is also presented as a threat to the environment and, by extension, to the United States itself. These arguments were not new and drew again upon existing concerns, as Hultgren (2015: 42) describes how parts of the environmental movement in the 1960s expressed concerns about natural resources and social resources alike being drained by population growth. This understanding is based on the ideas of eighteenth-century British philosopher Thomas Malthus, who was concerned with the inability of food supply to match population growth. This included the national environmental organisation the Sierra Club, a group that first adopted a motion against overpopulation in 1959 (Hultgren 2015: 44–45). The moral decay the NSM argues is occurring in society is matched, in their visual propaganda, by the destruction of the natural environment and the litter left behind. This is juxtaposed against the image of the NSM as active guardians of the land and large sweeping imagery of the open landscape (Figure 3.2).

3.2 NSM photo of the Sonoran Desert

This link implied by the images, between the environment and its guardian-ship and government's failure leading to decay, is made clear when they declare that the issues around 'Border Control is a sign of US lack of self-control and an indulgence problem' (*NSM Magazine* Winter/Spring, 2016: 38).

This imagery combination – of wide-open landscape contrasted against pollution or crowding of land – has an older pedigree. In his examination of American imagery around environmentalism and the Cold War, Robertson (2008) critiques how images of the American Wilderness are used to raise awareness of threats to the landscape but were mixed with images of crowds of Hindus bathing in the Ganges. In this case, *This Is the American Earth*, a publication by the Sierra Club from 1960, made the contrast between famine in India, described as a rich land wasted by poor guardianship, and America. It went so far as to warn that such a future would face America if it did not protect its environment. It was, in this, the encroachment of the 'Non-American Earth' into the 'American Earth' and shows the historic importance of discourse around population within consideration of environmental issues.

These border campaigns and the images that convey them also emphasise the imagined nature of the landscape and its history within NSM rhetoric. Equally, the sense of ownership of these stretches of the southern deserts and borderlands of America ignored the Native American past of the land. In part this can be explained by a traditional view that has come through some conservative groups in America that presented a narrative of Native Americans, along with other non-white groups, as being unfit or unworthy of the land due to imagined laziness or other moral and intellectual failings (Blee and Yates, 2015: 129–130). Within *Stormtrooper*, images of tools and stone-age finds are argued to prove that European-heritage prehistoric humans first settled in America, promoting the notion that the white European is in fact the true owner of America as its 'original settlers' (*Stormtrooper* #28, 2009: 1).

With the government presented as corrupt, unwilling or unable to protect the community from the threat of migration on the southern border, the NSM articulates a classic aspect of fascism: an elite no longer representing the true values of the nation while a fascist movement finally acts in the interests of the populace. In this, the fascists come to occupy an elite position in society as genuine interlocutors of public needs and desires, with the nation understood in monist terms by the populist far right (Griffin 1993: 41–43; Mudde 2021). So, through claims around the environment and environmental guardianship, combined with the border issue, the NSM was able to transmit fascist thoughts without having to be overt about it.

The images of the border, with the NSM flags next to it and with NSM members patrolling, then stake a claim to this space as firmly – and arguably exclusively – theirs. In the text surrounding these images, they offered the opportunity to experience the reality of the border by joining the patrols and used it as a broader recruitment line, asking: 'Have you had it with illegal aliens streaming over the southwestern borders of this country and have been considering joining the NSM, find out more now' (*NSM Magazine* Summer/Fall, 2015: 45).

Though in a limited fashion, this can be seen as an offer into a hidden or sacred truth: the attempt to draw people into the movement by offering knowledge of the hidden threat of migration, to both the nation as a body of people and the nation as a physical space. This offer is a typical recruitment tool which, furthermore, provides a small window into the cultic milieu that these groups cultivated. This milieu was the creation of a space and community through the offer of a sacred truth that helps establish 'in' and 'out' identities to encourage the valuing of information from within the group and therefore help conspiratorial ideologies held by groups like the

NSM to take hold (Campbell, 2002: 14–15). Jackson (2017: 27–29) made a similar point with regard to how these movements are able to sustain imagined and conspiratorial narratives despite external societal pressures, and how movements continue to sustain themselves, drawing new recruits into the sacred space. Similarly, Kaplan (2001) observed that American Nazism exists within a sacred space and has an occult nature to its internal cultures, driven by a search for hidden or sacred truths. This is why the images of ownership, of showing largely empty natural spaces – in this case the border – with solely NSM authority is important, giving credibility to their claim to be the sole authority for understanding the truth of the migrant threat within.

Outdoor pursuits: the creation of the sacred space with the environment

The ways in which the environment, and the presence of the NSM within it, are imagined, are visible in their photo album webpage. This page contains an abundance of photos from various events, including camping events, showing NSM members (alongside Ku Klux Klan members) in various rural and natural locations, with group pictures occurring in front of swathes of green trees. Other images show the burning of swastikas and of crosses, proudly declaring the connection of the movement with the land it was on: the link between the blood and the soil (*NSM Mississippi Meet & Greet*, 2016). In contrast to the images spoken of previously, these tended to be less staged, lending them to not just an air of authenticity but also suggesting, again, that the viewer was given a glimpse into the private world of the NSM. They also present the NSM as existing within an open and healthy space, a pure National Socialist space, contrasted against a diseased and crowded space occupied by their opponents – something Westberg and Årman (2019) identify within European Nazi movements. This connection of a return to nature and outdoor pursuits to the revival of the nation's moral and physical health again draws on ecofascist ideas, and shows how these environmental concerns are understand through a fascist lens.

Outdoor pursuits are even emphasised in the NSM's *25 Point Plan*: a series of broad policy statements. These state a desire to create new green spaces using government grants, favouring natural space over development, and also to encourage children to learn survival skills and agriculture, with an emphasis on outdoor events. There is promotion of rural homestead living, offering grants to homesteaders as well as protection against fore-closures (*25 Point Plan*, n.d.). Green policies are placed alongside policies that promote a return to an idealised romantic rural past, restoring a connection between the next generation and the land in an effort to improve the nation.

As mentioned previously, this return to an imagined rural idyll plays on existing tropes within American post-war culture, such as the nostalgia for a simpler and seemingly more morally pure way of living, played upon – as mentioned earlier by Goddard (2011) – in popular culture through, for example, *Little House on the Prairie*. Environmentalism in this representation becomes not just about conserving existing resources but about pushing society back to that morally sound past while eschewing the existing society. A glimpse into this is given by the photo galleries highlighting their After Action Reports and rallies focused on more martial presentations. One such example is a photo of the Harrisburg Rally on 5 November 2016, which presents the NSM lined up with Klan and NSM flags behind an NSM banner and in black uniforms with shields (*NSM News Archives*, n.d.)

The other style of imagery offered are family-friendly events and meetups, which show the NSM in, as mentioned, wooded locations (*NSM Grassroots Action Gallery*, n.d.). In images depicting events in Michigan from 2015, from a Summer Solstice event in June and a meeting from May, the NSM flags are still present behind the group but in a far less martial atmosphere. While men are still largely wearing similar black outfits, there are women, children, babies and dogs (Figure 3.3) in various outfits. As can also be seen from Figure 3.3, these were relaxed affairs, with the flags used to create a boundary of their space within the environment. There are even blends of these two styles, such as where meetings and rallies coincide (*NSM News Archives*, n.d.). The rural environment in these images presents a safe and entirely National Socialist space.

Examining the wider galleries shows many more images, including dogs and barbeques, which give the impression – save for the swastikas and Klan outfits – of what might be described as a welcoming, family weekend (for example, *NSM GA, NSM TX Meeting*, 2016). Though they were removed from the website in late 2019, these images illustrate how the environment, and the appeal of the rural idyll, is used to draw people into the NSM and its milieu, where environmentalist terms are used – such as concern over water rights or talk of mass transit – but where the space remains, and visually so, a fascist one.

This attempt to appeal is also notable when the NSM's imagery is contextualised by considering the written text and the reasons given for these environmental policies. In their *25 Point Plan* they propose a focus on homogenous communities, connected by mass transit for environmental benefit, with green jobs, green energy and secure water rights (*25 Point*

3.3 Neo-Nazis with their flags and dogs

Plan, n.d.). This was repeated in direct appeals to the electorate, where points on water rights and green jobs are once again emphasised, such as their open letter to voters in Riverside (Hall, 2010). Indeed, exploring the *25 Point Plan* and the reasons it provides for their environmentalist policies reveals the links to the wider world view of the NSM. Green jobs and green energy are, the NSM says, to be brought in not just for their own sake but to end dependence on foreign energy supplies. Importantly, anthropogenic climate change is accepted by the NSM, but blamed on corporatisation and used as a justification for rapid revolutionary change to avoid ecocide. In other words, an urgent threat calls for their green agenda which, in turn, justifies even violent action.

Even green spaces in cities are to promote close-knit 'organic' communities, which are to be based on racial purity, dividing the desired white communities from the non-white or blended ethnic communities (*25 Point Plan*, n.d.). The position of the NSM, supporting the idea of action against the threat of climate change, is not unique to the far right. In their exploration of the German far right and climate change, Forchtner et al. (2018) identified that some actors were willing to accept climate change as real to some degree. Interestingly, this also found that rhetoric around green issues was often refocused onto nativist policies, highlighting critiques of buying green cars from foreign manufacturers as bearing hidden climate costs and thus it was better to support native conventional cars due to the lower cost in manufacture and transport despite ongoing costs in terms of petrol consumption.

This presentation of the NSM in green spaces and concern over urban environments are also shown in their use of images of opposition protests or of non-American spaces. In images from a Georgia anti-fascist protest in 2013, they frame Antifa against brown backgrounds and the road surface, with the images taken from above and cropped in tightly to exaggerate the crowded nature (*NSM Magazine* Summer/Fall, 2012: 17; *NSM Magazine* Spring/Summer, 2013: 8). By contrast, the NSM within these urban spaces are – as discussed previously in relation to Yanay (2008) – photographed from below to give them a heroic presence, also ensuring they are framed against the sky and the large white civic buildings that give a more open, airy and, from an ecofascist standpoint, healthy symbolism (*NSM Magazine* Spring/Summer, 2013: 6–10). Such scapegoating of non-white populations and overcrowding for environmental issues is identified by Dyett and Thomas (2019) as common within certain parts of Western discourse, and represents an opportunity for the penetration of ecofascist views into broader right-wing environmental discourse as it is a shared reference point.

It is especially telling that this emphasis on the environment in the *25 Point Plan* and the softer tone taken on communities, suggesting coexistence of the idealised white community with other communities that are homogenously non-white or are mixed race, is located in the front-facing portions of the website. The *25 Point Plan* is intended as an introduction to their policies, while Schoep's successor, Burt Colucci, had explicitly rejected terrorism and emphasised the legality of the movement (Colucci, c. 2019). Yet a small amount of searching on the website reveals less tolerant voices. For example, *NSM Magazine* uses meme-like images to attack anti-fascists and the LGBT+ community, and presents racial supremacist arguments (*NSM Magazine* Spring/Summer, 2017: 10–11).

Conclusion

When the NSM represented themselves as the true guardians of America – both the physical space and the people – they did so using written text and images regarding the environment and its stewardship. Indeed, the use of multimodal analysis allows for a deeper understanding of how the NSM's visual communication not just reinforced but at times led the way in presenting these ideas to their audience, especially in the online space. The call of the NSM, represented in their visual media and supported by textual propaganda, is to protect the landscape and environment of the United States by rejecting communities they see as foreign to their idealised, imagined white nationalist community. This is to be achieved through various modes of engagement with nature to, ultimately, restore the moral purity of earlier periods and use it as a springboard for a new future.

These proposed white communities would be connected through green travel networks, supported by green jobs and provided with clean water, and this would facilitate isolation from outsiders and remove dependence on foreign energy reserves. The necessity of such revolutionary steps is argued by the NSM to stem from the environmental threat facing America and the inability of the government to act decisively, which is part of their ecofascist appeal to disregard potential cost and instead to take action in defence of the physical environment of the nation so it can be reforged. This has forced the NSM to take on roles as genuine representatives of the American public through the provision of litter clean-ups, control of border areas as it patrols natural landscapes and outdoor pursuits.

Though wrapped up in a language of environmentalism as justification, the NSM's populist form of ultranationalism based around a palingenetic mythos (Griffin, 1993: 32) represents the classic fascist minimum. Environmentalism presents a language that is acceptable and even appealing in mainstream discourse, which allows the NSM to engage with a broader audience before unpacking how their particular use of these terms carries deeper and more ideological meanings. This is shown by the more public-facing material containing more moderate language, as well as through the representation of their meetings as family-friendly affairs with images of dogs and children. Indeed, the NSM is building on the notions described by Cook and Kelly (1999: 241) in their studies of the rise of violent extremism in America, who spoke of how 'the country has bred its own desperate groups who see themselves as victims of political forces that are in profound conflict with traditional cultures and values of rural America'. If the NSM does not see itself as one of these desperate groups, it certainly seeks to ally with those trends. In doing so, the NSM is not novel. For example, the Hungarian organisation Jobbik has engaged substantially with environmental issues since its inception to reinforce rather than dilute their nationalist message (Kyriazi, 2019: 184–189; see Forchtner, 2019 for further contemporary cases).

It could be tempting then to think that their expressions of support for the environment and their carefully staged photographs were simply a manipulative tool designed to attract and radicalise recruits. In fact, Griffin (1993: 167–171) even highlights environmentalism as an ideal 'Trojan Horse' to inject crypto-fascist discourse into the political mainstream. However, this would not be the whole story. While mainstream environmentalists may not recognise the motivations of the NSM, they would recognise large parts of the discourse (see also Chapter 9 in this volume for such overlaps) – even though for the NSM these terms held different meaning. Built on those ideas of Blood and Soil, in the National Socialist world view the people and the land are one and the same (Kiernan, 2007: 2–3). Out of this a disturbing, profound, ecological stance that represents a serious, not just calculated, concern for 'our natural environment' can grow. While mainstream environmentalism is willing to accept compromise and the deprioritisation of human desires or even needs in pursuit of the greater overwhelming need of environmental survival, for the NSM and their ecofascist vision the welfare of the land and of the people are intrinsically linked: two halves of an important whole. The preservation of the environment is a route to a revitalisation of American society, and the threat against it is a motivating tool that allows the NSM to draw individuals into active participation, even when that participation risks legal or social consequences. This romanticised environment, its landscape and its history – including those historical questions of ownership – are an imagined place that makes sense for those within its cultic milieu but confusing to those outside.

Understanding of this propaganda plays an important role in understanding that the NSM adapted classic National Socialism for a modern audience, and how we might see them continue into an age that is likely to see both an accelerating climate crisis and increasing awareness of environmental despoliation more broadly.

References

'Problem Animal' (2005): The peace that must end: White Supremacy and ecology, *Earth First!*, 25(3): 38.

25 Point Plan (n.d.): National Socialist Movement Website. http://web.archive.org/web/20200803083214/www.nsm88.org/25points/25PontsComplete.html (accessed 29 September 2021).

Balleck, B. J. (2018): *Modern American Extremism and Domestic Terrorism: An Encyclopedia of Extremists and Extremist Groups*. Santa Barbara, CA: ABC-CLIO.

Blee, K. M. and Yates, E. A. (2015): The place of race in conservative and far-right movements, *Sociology of Race and Ethnicity*, 1(1): 127–136. https://doi.org/10.1177%2F2332649214555031

Boggs, K. (2019): The rhetorical landscapes of the 'Alt Right' and the Patriot Movements: Settler entitlement to Native land. In: B. Forchtner (ed.), *The Far Right and the Environment*. London: Routledge, 293–309.

Campbell, C. (2002): The cult, the Cultic Milieu and secularization. In: J. Kaplan and H. Lööw (eds), *The Cultic Milieu: Oppositional Subcultures in an Age of Globalization*. Walnut Creek, CA: AltaMira, 12–25.

Campion, K. (2021): Defining ecofascism: Historical foundations and contemporary interpretations in the extreme right, *Terrorism and Political Violence*. https://doi.org/10.1080/09546553.2021.1987895

Clark, C. S. (2006): An American Nazi's rise and fall, *American History*, 40(6): 60.

Colucci, B. (c. 2019): *Welcome to the Commander's Desk: Commander Burt Colucci's blog*. http://web.archive.org/web/20200803084207/https://nsm88.org/commandersdesk/ (accessed 29 September 2021).

Cook Jr., W. and Kelly, R. J. (1999): The dispossessed: Domestic terror and political extremism in the American heartland, *International Journal of Comparative and Applied Criminal Justice*, 23(2): 241–256. https://doi.org/10.1080/01924036.1999.9678642

Copsey, N. (2004): *Contemporary British Fascism: The British National Party and the Quest for Legitimacy*. Basingstoke: Palgrave Macmillan.

Copsey, N. and Richardson, J. (2015): Introduction. In: N. Copsey and J. Richardson (eds), *Cultures of Post-War British Fascism*. London: Routledge, 1–7.

Dixon, J. and Wallwork, J. (2004): Foxes, green fields and Britishness: On the rhetorical construction of place and national identity, *British Journal of Social Psychology*, 43(1): 21–39. https://doi.org/10.1348/014466604322915962

Dyett, J. and Thomas, C. (2019): Overpopulation discourse: Patriarchy, racism and the specter of ecofascism, *Perspectives on Global Development and Technology*, 18(1–2): 205–224.

Finley, L. and Esposito, L. (2019): The immigrant as bogeyman: Examining Donald Trump and the right's anti-immigrant, anti-PC rhetoric, *Humanity and Society*, 44(2): 178–197.

Forchtner, B. (ed.) (2019), *The Far Right and the Environment*. London: Routledge. https://doi.org/10.1177%2F0160597619832627

Forchtner, B., Kroneder, A. and Wetzel. D. (2018): Being skeptical? Exploring far-right climate-change communication in Germany, *Environmental Communication*, 12(5): 589–604. https://doi.org/10.1080/17524032.2018.1470546

Glenn, E. N. (2015): Settler colonialism as structure: A framework for comparative studies of U.S. race and gender formation, *Sociology of Race and Ethnicity*, 1(1): 54–74. https://doi.org/10.1177%2F2332649214560440

Goddard, J. (2011): Virginia Lee Burton's *Little House* in popular consciousness: Fuelling postwar environmentalism and antiurbanism, *Journal of Urban History*, 37(4): 562–582. https://doi.org/10.1177%2F0096144211403087

Griffin, R. (1993): *The Nature of Fascism*. London: Routledge.

Hall, J. (2010): *To the Registered Voters of Riverside*. http://web.archive.org/web/20200811215329/https://nsm88.org/elections/jhgreenjobs10182010.htm (accessed 29 September 2021).

Hansen, A. (2017): Methods for assessing visual images and depictions of Climate Change. In: M. Nisbet (ed.), *Oxford Research Encyclopedia of Climate Science*. Oxford: Oxford University Press. https://doi.org/10.1093/acrefore/9780190228620.013.491

Hultgren, J. (2015): *Border Walls Gone Green: Nature and Anti-immigrant Politics in America*. Minneapolis: University of Minnesota Press.

Jackson, P. (2014): Accumulative extremism: The post-war tradition of Anglo-American neo-Nazi activism. In: P. Jackson and A. Shekhovtsov (eds), *The Post-War Anglo-American Far Right: A Special Relationship of Hate*. Basingstoke: Palgrave Macmillan, 2–37.

Jackson, P. (2017): *Colin Jordan and Britain's Neo-Nazi Movement: Hitler's Echo*. London: Bloomsbury.

Kaplan, J. (2001): The post-war paths of occult national socialism: From Rockwell and Madole to Manson, *Patterns of Prejudice*, 35(3): 41–67. https://doi.org/10.1080/003132201128811214

Kiernan, B. (2007): *Blood and Soil: A World History of Genocide and Extermination from Sparta to Darfur*. New Haven: Yale University Press.

Klein, O. (2020): Misleading memes: The effects of deceptive visuals of the British National Party, *Partecipazione E Conflitto*, 13(1): 154–179.

Kyriazi, A. (2019): The environmental communication of Jobbik: Between strategy and ideology. In: B. Forchtner (ed.), *The Far Right and the Environment*. London: Routledge, 184–200.

Lapin, A. (2020): The ex-Nazi next door, *The Detroit Jewish News*, 21 May 2021. https://thejewishnews.com/2020/05/21/the-ex-nazi-next-door/ (accessed 29 September 2021).

Macklin, G. (2007): *Very Deeply Dyed in Black: Sir Oswald Mosley and the Resurrection of British Fascism after 1945*. London: I. B. Taurus.

Mudde, C. (2018): *The Far Right in America*. Abingdon: Routledge.

Mudde, C. (2019): *The Far Right Today*. Cambridge: Polity.

Mudde, C. (2021): Populism in Europe: An illiberal democratic response to undemocratic liberalism, *Government and Opposition*, 56(4): 577–597. https://doi.org/10.1017/gov.2021.15

NSM GA, NSM TX Meeting (2016): June 11, 2016 http://web.archive.org/web/20190608021711/http://gallery.nsm88.org/thumbnails.php?album=68 (accessed 29 September 2021).

NSM Grassroots Action Gallery (n.d.): http://web.archive.org/web/20190608021724/http://gallery.nsm88.org/index.php?cat=3 (accessed 29 September 2021).

NSM Magazine Spring/Summer (2013): http://web.archive.org/web/20190608022422/www.nsm88.org/stormtrooper/nsm-magazine-spring-summer-2013-issue.pdf (accessed 29 September 2021).

NSM Magazine Spring/Summer (2017): http://web.archive.org/web/20190608022422/www.nsm88.org/stormtrooper/NSM%20Magazine%20Spring%20Summer%202017%20%2041617.pdf (accessed 29 September 2021).

NSM Magazine Summer/Fall (2010): http://web.archive.org/web/20190908231750/www.nsm88.org/stormtrooper/NSMMagazineApril2011.pdf (accessed 29 September 2021).

NSM Magazine Summer/Fall (2012): http://web.archive.org/web/20190608022416/www.nsm88.org/stormtrooper/NSMMAGAZINESUMMERFALL2012.pdf (accessed 29 September 2021).

NSM Magazine Summer/Fall (2015): http://web.archive.org/web/20190608022524/www.nsm88.org/stormtrooper/NSMMagazineSummerFall2015.pdf (accessed 29 September 2021).

NSM Magazine Summer/Fall (2016): http://web.archive.org/web/20190608022458/www.nsm88.org/stormtrooper/NSMMagazineSummerFall2016.pdf (accessed 29 September 2021).

NSM Magazine Winter/Spring (2015): http://web.archive.org/web/20190608022459/www.nsm88.org/stormtrooper/NSM_Magazine_WinterSpring2015_Issue.pdf (accessed 29 September 2021).

NSM Magazine Winter/Spring (2016): http://web.archive.org/web/20190608022601/www.nsm88.org/stormtrooper/NSMMagazineWinterSpring2016_.pdf (accessed 29 September 2021).

NSM Main Page (n.d.): http://web.archive.org/web/20200823094841/www.nsm88.org/ (accessed 29 September 2021).

NSM Mississippi Meet & Greet (2016): 20 August 2016. http://web.archive.org/web/20190809013854/http://gallery.nsm88.org/thumbnails.php?album=70 (accessed 29 September 2021).

NSM News Archives (n.d.): http://web.archive.org/web/20200803095214/https://nsm88.org/news_archives.htm (accessed 29 September 2021).

Robertson, T. (2008): 'This is the American Earth': American Empire, the Cold War, and American environmentalism, *Diplomatic History*, 32(4): 561–584.

Rodríguez-Serrano, A., García-Catalán, S. and Martín-Núñez, M. (2021): Audiovisual production by the contemporary European extreme right: Filmic inheritances and intertexts to spread the hate, *Communication & Society*, 34(2): 231–246. https://doi.org/10.15581/003.34.2.231-246

Southern Poverty Law Centre (n.d.): *SPLC – National Socialist Movement*. www.splcenter.org/fighting-hate/extremist-files/group/national-socialist-movement (accessed 29 September 2021).

Stone, D. (2014): *Goodbye to All That? The Story of Europe since 1945*. Oxford: Oxford University Press.

Stormtrooper #19 (2008): http://web.archive.org/web/20190608023251/www.nsm88.org/stormtrooper/the%20stormtrooper%20019.pdf (accessed 29 September 2021).

Stormtrooper #26 (2009): http://web.archive.org/web/20190608023253/www.nsm88.org/stormtrooper/ST%2026.pdf (accessed 29 September 2021).

Stormtrooper #28 (2009): http://web.archive.org/web/20190608023244/www.nsm88.org/stormtrooper/ST%2028.pdf (accessed 29 September 2021).

Stormtrooper #32 (2009): http://web.archive.org/web/20190608023243/www.nsm88. org/stormtrooper/ST%2032.pdf (accessed 29 September 2021).

Taylor, B. (2019): Alt-right ecology: Ecofascism and far-right environmentalism in the United States. In: B. Forchtner (ed.), *The Far Right and the Environment*. London: Routledge. 275–292.

Uekoetter, F. (2006): *The Green and the Brown: A History of Conservation in Nazi Germany*. Cambridge: Cambridge University Press.

Westberg, G. and Årman, H. (2019): Common sense as extremism: The multi-semiotics of contemporary national socialism, *Critical Discourse Studies*, 16(5): 549–568. https://doi.org/10.1080/17405904.2019.1624183

Wodak, R. and Forchtner, B. (2014): Embattled Vienna 1683/2010: Right-wing populism, collective memory and the fictionalisation of politics, *Visual Communication*, 13(2): 231–255. https://doi.org/10.1177%2F1470357213516720

Wozniak, A., Lück, J. and Wessler, H. (2015): Frames, stories and images: The advantages of a multimodal approach in comparative media content research on Climate Change, *Environmental Communication*, 9(4): 469–490. https://doi.org/10.1080/17524032.2014.981559

Yanay, N. (2008): Violence unseen: Activating national icons, *Cultural Studies*, 22(1): 134–158. https://doi.org/10.1080/09502380701480683

Zimmerman, M. E. (1995): The threat of ecofascism, *Social Theory and Practice*, 21(2): 207–238.

4

The environmental semiotics of Spanish far-right populism: Vox's visual rhetoric strategies online

Carmen Aguilera-Carnerero

Introduction: the (former) Spanish exception

On 10 November 2019, Vox set a landmark in its young life as a political force by entering the Spanish Parliament. Until very recently, the prevailing view among academics and experts in the field (Alonso and Rovira Kaltwasser, 2014; González Enríquez, 2017) was that Spain – together with Portugal – was an outlier case in the far-right scenario that other European countries, such as Austria, France, Italy and the Netherlands, were experiencing. The Spanish exception started to be challenged in December 2018, when Vox made a breakthrough in Andalusia's regional elections. That rise escalated, culminating in the fifty-two seats the party, led by Santiago Abascal, got in the general elections of November 2019. In just eleven months, Abascal's party had passed from having no presence in official institutions to being the key to forming conservative coalition governments in many parts of Spain. In the words of the leader of the French radical-right party National Rally, Marine Le Pen, Vox's extraordinary electoral success was a 'stunning progression' (see La Vanguardia, 2019).

For Cas Mudde, a scholar of the far right, both Vox and National Rally belong to the radical right rather than the extreme right. He (Mudde, 2007: 24) sets the main difference in that whereas the extreme right confronts democracy and tries to abolish it (for example, Golden Dawn in Greece), the radical right accepts it but challenges both the institutions and values typical of liberal democracy, including minority rights or the separation of powers. Vox's development mirrors what Mudde (2019: 4) calls 'the fourth wave of the post-war far right' in which the previously marginal rhetoric, which builds upon the far right's core ideological pillars – authoritarianism and nativism – has permeated into the 'mainstream', becoming normalised with the complicity of so-called mainstream media and moderate parties.

The unique political landscape of Spain until Vox's outburst has been explained as logical, considering the country's fascist past; indeed, no far-right party had entered the Parliament since the death of dictator Francisco Franco in 1975 with the exception of a marginal seat obtained by *Fuerza Nueva* (New Force), an ultra-Catholic and Francoist party (Xidias, 2020) in 1979. However, and as Mudde (2019) explains, Vox's unprecedented success depends on four main factors: first, the fact that most voters have not lived under Franco's dictatorship; second, the Spanish economic crisis (2008–2014) that opened new sociocultural spaces which became the breeding ground for populisms on both the left and right; third, the management of such a crisis, the policies of conservative Prime Minister Mariano Rajoy, and the manifold cases of corruption within *Partido Popular* (People's Party, PP); and above all, fourth, the independentist threat of Catalonia.

Two facts seem to be undeniable in Vox's ascension. On the one hand, no other far-right force had such an official status and weight in Spain's political landscape until the breakthrough of Abascal's party. On the other hand, and although immersed in a global wave of far-right populism, scholars and analysts link Vox's success to a unique Spanish reality (see Applebaum, 2019). Thus, Spain is no longer a political exception, and neither is Portugal, which has seen how Vox's counterpart, Chega, is experiencing a similar rise that has made Abascal call for 'an alliance against communism in the Iberosphere' (see voxespana.es, n.d.). However, unlike in other European countries (Forchtner, 2019; Westberg and Årman, 2019; Lubarda, 2020), ecological issues are not central in Vox's policy and iconography. Indeed, this too can (partly) be understood within a particular Spanish context. Despite the existence of a Ministry of Environment, environmental issues are hardly discussed in Parliament. Although Spanish society has remarkably increased its ecological awareness in recent years, Spain is still behind other European countries regarding environmental measures adopted at a political level.[1] As such, the role of nature and ecology, as presented in Vox's party programme and beyond, mainly highlights the countryside as the backbone of the nation and their workers as the epitome of the 'common man' they aim to represent. This contrasts sharply with the supposedly urban, progressive intellectuals and artists they radically oppose. Rural Spain is thus the ultimate keeper of Spanish identity and traditions such as hunting and bullfighting.

Based upon the above introduction, this chapter raises the following research questions: first, can any visual discursive axes in Vox's narrative on social media be identified?; and second, what is the role of environmental images in framing Vox's concept of 'Spanish identity'?

The structure of this chapter is as follows. First, I present Vox's political trajectory and its relationship with environmental policies before explaining the main features of far-right populism. I then introduce the corpus data and the methodology used in the analysis, and, finally, I analyse Vox's visual online strategies, particularly concerning how they tackle nature and ecology within their extensive online propaganda.

Vox: origins and history

Vox is a young party founded in December 2013 by some who had left the most successful conservative party at that time, the PP. They abandoned the PP as, on the one hand, they did not identify with the corruption scandals the party was involved in. On the other hand, they felt disappointed with a leadership they considered to be 'too moderate' on critical political issues, such as Catalonian independence. In particular, they accused Rajoy of not altering or even blocking some of the political measures that former Prime Minister José Luis Rodríguez Zapatero had adopted, such as legislation on abortion and the express divorce law, the allowance of same-sex marriages and the controversial Critical Historical Memory law.

During the second decade of the century, the Spanish political scene was not very stable, witnessing the abdication of King Juan Carlos I, his son Philip VI taking his place in 2014 and the foundation of the far-left political party *Podemos* (We Can), born in the aftermath of the socio-political movement of 15-M, popularly known as *Los Indignados* (The Outraged).

Two further facts decisively affected Vox's launch. One was the so-called Islamic State's terrorist attack in Barcelona in August 2017, and the other was the non-binding vote on the independence of Catalonia. As Ariza (2020: 180) contends, 'the issue of Catalonia's independence meant doubling down on a nationalist discourse and calls to centralise power, including getting rid of all the 17 autonomous communities'. Finally, Vox's birth is intricately connected with the Spanish inflammatory socio-political context of the time, when unemployment and youth unemployment rates were 27 per cent and 57 per cent, respectively.[2]

In this setting, Vox named former PP Member of Parliament in the Basque country, Santiago Abascal, as the party leader, following the resignation of Aleix Vidal-Quadras, the first party leader and one of the founders of the political organisation. Iván Espinosa de Los Monteros, a well-known name among the most prominent socio-economic circles of the country, was appointed as the general secretary. As such, Abascal and Espinosa de los Monteros represent what Xidias (2020) calls the 'Vox' nexus between authoritarian conservatism and neoliberalism.

Building on its unexpected electoral breakthrough in Andalucía in December 2018, Vox increased its national vote by about 2.6 million in the April 2019 general elections, winning 24 seats in Parliament. Since general elections had to be held again in November 2019, as the Socialist Party failed to form a coalition government, Vox subsequently increased its support by winning 3.6 million votes, accounting for 15 per cent of the national popular vote and fifty-two seats in Parliament. Since then, Vox has been the third political force in the country. As indicated, it seems like Spain's far-right voters were quietly camouflaged within the PP for four decades but found a voice in Vox.

From the moment it got into Parliament, Vox's presence has been remarkable. They have been a very active opposition, suing the government on many different occasions, requesting the illegality of the imposed lockdown in March 2020 and even putting forward a failed no-confidence vote to oust President Sánchez for his management of the COVID-19 crisis.

Although Vox's political agenda is in line with most elements of the European far right, their approach to environmental issues differs slightly from some of the views on nature and ecology adopted by far-right European actors, such as the non-party Greenline Front or the Italian *Lega* (Lubarda, 2020). While they distance themselves from, for example veganism or anti-specism, they adopt a pastoral view deeply rooted in their defence of farmers and cattle breeders as the epitome of 'good Spaniards' betrayed by the so-called socio-communist government as well as of rural Spain for being the cradle of genuine Spanish heritage and traditions. It is this identitarian concern for the natural environment which I unpack further below – though before doing so, the following section further clarifies Vox's core ideology.

Vox's radical-right populism

The labelling of Vox's ideology has been at the centre of the discussion by scholars and journalists regarding how to classify their political agenda, which has been described as 'far-right', 'radical right' or even 'extreme right'.[3] As mentioned above, this chapter follows Mudde (2019) in categorising Vox as embodying 'radical right populism', a type of ideology based on three main principles: nativism (rejection of those considered to be non-native), authoritarianism (affirming a strong state to prevent chaos) and populism. However, Vox itself has continuously rejected the definition of 'far right', underlining they are not a party of 'extreme right' but of 'extreme need' (see Applebaum, (2019).

Whatever category is chosen to describe Abascal's party, the tag 'populism' (from Latin *populus*, the people) seems recurrent. The term populism is problematic too since, as Hidalgo-Tenorio et al. (2019) argue, it is a global phenomenon mainly characterised by its ambiguity. Along the same lines, Mudde and Rovira Kaltwasser (2012: 153) underline the chameleonic character of populism: it can be adopted by both left and right and displays different but sometimes opposing features, such as being leader-dependent or leaderless. The study of populism can embrace many different perspectives, although Hidalgo-Tenorio et al. (2019) underline three main approaches to the phenomenon: strategy, ideology and discursive style. In contrast to Mudde, this study considers populism as a rhetorical style, a linguistic code in itself, to avoid understanding the phenomenon as binary but gradual (Laclau, 2005; Moffitt, 2016). What these diverse approaches have in common, however, is that they all share an understanding of populism as emphasising an antagonism between 'the people' (to whom positive values are ascribed, for example, purity) and 'the elite' (associated with negative values, such as corruption) along with the crucial role of concepts such as crisis and threat.

The discursive strategies present in far-right populism have been described among others by Canovan (1999) and Wodak (2015). The latter (2015: 7, 21–22), speaking of right-wing populism, enumerates nine tenets that describe different aspects:

- A generalised claim to represent '*THE* people' (Wodak 2015: 21) as a homogenised entity based on nativist ideologies. This view goes hand in hand with a revisionist view of history which involves a rhetoric of exclusion. Central to this principle is the self-construction of both the party and its leader(s) as the saviours of the country, defending the 'man in the street' from all the external threats that surround him.
- A political style related to diverse ideologies (right wing and left wing) that differs from the political imaginaries and the parties' recruitment and structures.
- It overcomes the traditional opposition of left–right and constructs 'new social divides' usually related to fears about globalisation, nationalism or a socio-economic crisis, among others.
- Success relies on performance strategies in modern media democracies, which implies extensive use of the media, mainly social media.
- A focus on charismatic leaders due to the personalisation and com-modification of politics. Usually, right-wing parties have very hierarchical structures and masculine leaders (although recently female leaders have become prominent, for example in Denmark, Norway, the US and France).
- Front-stage performance techniques linked to popular celebrity culture. These performances and discourses are heavily context-dependent.
- A proud display of anti-intellectualism or 'arrogance of ignorance'. Far-right populism calls to common sense and the traditional values linked to an aggressive and exclusivist rhetoric.
- Anti-Muslim rhetoric and a contradictory pseudo-emancipatory gender policy (right-wing feminism) link feminism to traditional family values and active campaigns against pro-choice movements.

- Differences between populist rhetoric and style with politicians in government or the opposition.

The analysis of Vox's online visual rhetoric presented below mirrors all these features to a certain extent and there is frequent overlap.

Theoretical framework and methodology

The theoretical framework used to analyse images in this chapter was a combination of two main models: multimodal critical discourse analysis (Kress and van Leeuwen, 1996, 2001) and visual framing (Rodríguez and Dimitrova, 2011). Multimodal critical discourse analysis is firmly based on social semiotics (Hodge and Kress, 1988) as the theoretical approach which studies how sign systems are used to create meaning in a given context. It is built upon core principles that focus on human signifying practices in specific social and cultural circumstances and explain meaning-making as a social practice (Kress and van Leeuwen, 1996; van Leeuwen, 2005).

In this approach, both the choices of visual constituents made out of a set of alternatives and the process of meaning-making are central, always being aware that 'visual and linguistic semiotic resources have different affordances' (Machin and Mayr, 2012: 31) that make, for example, images more suitable than words to fulfil specific functions. Indeed, the rhetorical significance of images has long been highlighted (see the Introduction to this volume). The specific toolkit used in this chapter was provided by Kress and van Leeuwen (1996) (for example, information value, salience and framing), together with aspects such as gaze, posing, distance, angle, and/ or light, taken from Machin and Mayr (2012). Furthermore, the work by Peeples (2013) and Rebich-Hespanha et al. (2015) on the process of visual meaning-making and the identification of visual frames and Forchtner and Kølvraa (2017) and Westberg and Årman (2019) on the visual articulation of closeness, intimacy and common sense were inspiring as practical examples of how to analyse visual environmental communication and visual environmental communication by the far right. For the analysis of the videos, I used van Leeuwen's work (2021), which focuses on the features of movement, direction, expansiveness, velocity, force, angularity, fluidity, directedness and regularity.

The second theoretical reference used for the analysis is visual framing, developed by Rodríguez and Dimitrova (2011). This four-tiered model takes as its point of departure the concept of 'framing' formulated by Goffman (1974) and, later, Entman (1991, 1993), who defined frames as calling 'attention to some aspects of reality while obscuring other elements, which might lead audiences to have different reactions' (Entman, 1993: 55). Rodríguez and Dimitrova (2011: 52) propose a model to study visual framing that consists of four levels that 'can be applied to whether the unit of analysis is any media material (media frames) or audiences' individual perception of the overarching message of a visual (audience frames)'. These levels include visuals as denotative (frames are identified by the enumeration of the objects and discrete elements that are actually shown in the visuals), social semiotics (the stylistic conventions and the technical transformations involved in the representation of visuals) and connotative systems (this level moves from the persons, objects and places shown in the visual to the ideas or concepts attached to them) as well as ideological representations. This last tier is related to Barthes' (1977) concept of 'iconographical symbolism' (drawing together an image's symbols and stylistic features into a coherent interpretation that provides the 'why' behind the representations) and ideological meaning and tackles how news images are employed as instruments of power in shaping public consciousness.

In times of digital political communication primacy, political parties are highly aware of mainstream and new media's key role in electoral success. Social media are excellent channels for parties to disseminate their political programmes, recruit new followers and reinforce ideological bonds with their supporters. This is partly a consequence of a change in the communicative paradigm (from verticality to horizontality), underlining bidirectionality and symmetry (Alonso, 2015). In the field of so-called cyberpolitics (Cotarelo, 2013), social media enable political parties to put forward their political agenda (agenda setting) (Martín et al., 2020). As such, populism and social media seem to be closely interrelated, and populist politicians have used digital platforms and applications particularly successfully to interact directly with the people through a more personal and informal language (Kreis, 2017).

In this new political communicative style, memes are highly relevant. Memes – 'tokens of postmodern culture' (Shifman, 2014: 15) and multimodal artefacts in essence – are not frequently used by parties as discursive tools despite their popularity among young voters and followers. As highly medium-dependent constructions of discourse, memes are multimodal in essence, combining image and text, usually with humoristic purposes (Milner, 2012). However, the very notion of humour is problematic, and memes have evolved towards other communicative functions, some of which may be closer to extreme speech and radicalisation (Bogerts and Fielitz, 2019), allowing 'extreme message to masquerade as a medium specific parody' (Crawford, 2020).

Considering Vox in particular, the latter's relationship with the media, both traditional and new, has always been a complicated one, alternating between love and hate. During the last national election campaigns in 2019, the radical-right party evaded the mainstream media in Spain and gave very few interviews, an attitude that paradoxically guaranteed their constant presence in the press. On social media (mainly on Twitter, Instagram and YouTube), where the party is very active, Vox has also experienced problems, and their accounts have been banned (and quickly restored afterwards) several times (see PRESS, R. es / E., 2021). However, the presence of Vox on social media is outstanding, specially on Instagram, where it has the highest number of followers among Spanish parties (641,000; in comparison, *Podemos* has 264,000) (see El Plural, 2019).

Turning now to data, the corpus analysed in this study comprises the visual material published from October 2017 (when the non-binding vote for the Catalan independence was held) to November 2021 right after the celebration of the UN Climate Change Conference by the party's official accounts on Instagram (@vox_es) and Twitter (@vox_es). The former is a photo and video-sharing social platform launched in 2010 and preferred by millennials and generation Z, while Twitter is a microblogging social networking service often frequented by professionals created in 2006.

Once the corpus was compiled, I discarded material shared by both accounts (although taking note of the different hashtags) and tweets that did not contain any image. A total number of 1,777 posts (1,110 from Instagram and 367 from Twitter) were collected, out of which twenty-seven were devoted explicitly to aspects related to the environment. Twelve of these posts were videos in which several aspects of Vox's approach to the environment were tackled (from bullfighting to Spanish produce) and in which the theatrical component dominated. In line with the comparably weak status of the environmental movement in Spain and while this relatively low number suggests that environmental aspects are not prioritised by the party, it does enable an analysis of their complete visual environmental communication and, thus, a view on the totality of how Vox imagines the natural environment and Spaniards' relation to it. The next stage was to classify these images according to their content: first, checking if they were representational or symbolic, before, in a second stage, applying a more fine-grained codification which included the presence of the members of the party (even as part of memes), other people (for example, armed forces, the king or political opponents) and/or historical symbols and their relationship with environmental issues.

The visual construction of 'made in Spain' radical-right populism

In this chapter, radical-right populism is considered to be a rhetorical style (Hidalgo-Tenorio et al., 2019), and as such I analyse Vox's visual linguistic choices to spread and shape their political agenda on social media. Following Chilton (2004), political discourse operates indexically – different language choices imply political distinctions – as an interaction and functions to negotiate representations or conceptualisations of the world. Accordingly, my analysis focuses on the three main visual discursive frames around which Vox organises its arguments to see how they interrelate with the party's environmental policies. Vox's stance on ecology issues, such as global warming, departed from a negationist view and gradually changed towards more moderate positions. However, they were the only political force to vote against the resolution of the European Parliament to declare a 'climate emergency' and did not support any of the Spanish government's bills on energy and environment (see Vozpópuli, 2019). Still, their discourse remains constant in their fierce confrontation with what they consider the imposition of a green agenda by the left.

Lubarda (2020) distinguishes eight ideological elements prevailing in what he calls far-right ecologism: naturalism, spirituality, mysticism, authority, organicism, autarky, nostalgia and Manichaeism. Vox's three main visual rhetorical environmental themes – the defence of the average man's (represented by farmers and cattle breeders) rights, the importance of symbols in constructing the Spanish identity and the party's ideological commitment illustrated by their political activities – speak mainly to nostalgia and Manichaeism. Although Turner and Bailey (2021) have identified traces of ecobordering in Vox's discourse, I have not found any explicit visual communicative strategies to construct such a border in the corpus. However, what is clearly identifiable are three broad areas of visual communication, to which I now turn.

#theSpainthatwakesupwearly

The pillar of any populist movement is their defence of 'the people', mainly due to the alleged disappointment provoked by the government's inability to solve the socio-economic crisis and to provide them with a sense of security and stability (Betz, 1994). This 'man in the street' that Vox refers to – abandoned, disappointed and in danger – is epitomised through the hashtag #theSpainthatwakesupearly (*La España que madruga*) that Vox recurrently uses. That hashtag articulates the division of Spain into two groups of social actors: on the one hand, ordinary workers whom their government neglects, and, on the other hand, what they see as the socio-economic looters of the country, mainly illegal immigrants and independentists, along with the socio-communist government and friends.

This is closely connected to Vox's main environmental concern: the defence of rural Spain, mainly of their workforce – the backbone of the country

– and the Spanish produce, which they feel is disdained and discriminated against by the European Union. Indeed, the blue-collar workforce, mainly farmers and cattle breeders, is what Abascal's party calls '*la España que madruga*'. As such, Vox's approach to environmentalism is mainly anthropocentric, which is in line with an argument by Lubarda (2020: 722), who states that the 'alleged eco-centrism of ecofascism is hardly applicable to nationalist, even less populist anthropocentric postulates: the "people" are the ones in danger, the ones that are given priority'.

This polarised discourse – farmers/cattle breeders versus the elite – offers no alternative to the citizens, forcing them to choose either the first or the second group and thus creating the dichotomy 'patriots vs. traitors', as can be seen in Figure 4.1.

Figure 4.1 illustrates the far-right division between us (the people) and them (the elite). For Vox, the notion of 'them' comprises what they consider to be the enemies of the country (the ones who want to destroy the unity of the nation), which includes, in the most classical populist tradition, the artists who have publicly shown their support to the left – whom Vox pejoratively calls 'puppeteers'. Shots of Oscar-awarded and internationally acclaimed actor Javier Bardem (left), director Pedro Almodóvar (centre) and popular actor Eduardo Casanova (right), are juxtaposed with a farmer. The post, published in the middle of the first lockdown in March 2020, contains a straight message ('Perhaps now Spaniards realise we can live without puppeteers but not without farmers and cattle breeders'), which provoked the artist's outrage and led to claims that Vox should be prosecuted for hate crimes (see abc, 2020).

In multimodal critical discourse analysis terms, Figure 4.1 depicts the divisive discourse spread by the party. Regarding framing, artists and farmers are opposites (up and down) and visually disconnected through a central line that sets them as belonging to different worlds. Concerning information value (Kress and van Leeuwen, 1996: 177), the upper part represents 'the ideal' versus the bottom area referring to 'the real'. Farmers are portrayed as working and placed in the middle of the photo, making them salient, whereas artists are represented while attending social events and located in a triptych in which Almodóvar remains central. Targeting left-wing artists matches what Wodak (2015: 2) calls 'the arrogance of ignorance' and draws on connecting Vox to 'the common sense' (see #Voxsentidocomún (#Voxcommonsense)) in opposition to the elites' intellectualism (what Abascal's party calls 'the dictadura progre', the progre(ssist) dictatorship): 'those who are rooted in the soil are more self-dependent, but also more cognizant of the profoundness of the relation between a man and the land, as opposed to nomadic-incivilized, feral, or cosmopolitan lifestyles' (Lubarda, 2020: 724). Essential to Vox's narrative is the co-articulation of 'common sense', linked

4.1 'Perhaps now Spaniards realise we can live without puppeteers but not without farmers and cattle breeders'

to the notion of 'authenticity' and, in line with this, real patriots are located in the countryside, whereas artists are found in the city. This is in line with the glorification of nature that prevailed during Franco's regime as the 'embodiment of the essences of true Spain' (Del Arco Blanco and Gorostiza, 2021: 81). As Westberg and Årman (2019: 563) state: 'naturalness and authenticity are core values'. Following the party's uncomplicated and straightforward lexicon and syntax, Vox's visual narrative perpetuates that type of written discourse to the point that they offer elementary solutions to highly complex problems. Their minimalist images on display, mostly isolated landscapes or farmers and cattle breeders with their problems, focus more on exposing the rural world's difficulties than on enhancing the idyllic side of nature or offering specific solutions.

The key role of symbols and traditions

This section analyses two of the most frequently used semiotic resources in Vox's discourse: first, the crucial role of national symbols (flag, anthem, Crown); and second, their revisionist view of history, that is, the commemoration of outstanding events and historical figures of Spain's glorious past.

Concerning the flag, the anthem and the Crown, it is worth clarifying that Vox's content is always linked to the backbone of their 100-point political programme, whose first block is entitled: 'Spain, Unity, and sovereignty' (see España, Unidad y Soberanía, n.d.). Point 3 in the programme refers to the legal protection of the nation's symbols, especially the flag, the anthem and the Crown. In Vox's eyes, any insult to these national symbols should not be restricted from the full force of the law. The party feels the nation's enemies have continually attacked these emblems that create a solid and robust nation and reinforce in-group solidarity.

The Spanish flag is the predominant sign in all the electoral and propaganda events held by Abascal's party. It is also one of the most recognisable cultural artefacts that identify any community since they confer social cohesion to the group. Firth (1973) argues that flags are primary symbols for conveying attitudes or expressing emotions as simple actions such as waving them arise feelings of loyalty and belonging. In the same line, Smith (1969) legitimises the study of flags as central political symbols at the core of political life, as an instrument of control and an effective tool for propaganda. From the perspective of visual framing theory, flags are tokens of iconographic symbolism (Barthes, 1977) as they are fully charged with ideology and used as an instrument of power. For Vox, love and respect for the flag (hence its continuous visual presence) distinguishes real patriots from traitors to the nation.

With regard to Vox's revisionist view of history, I depart from Wodak (2015: 21), who argues that far-right populisms specifically construe a revisionist view of history, a history which involves a 'rhetoric of exclusion'. This happens to be the case with Vox too, a party that enhances past, epic narratives in which Spaniards fight 'an Other' but, guided by Christian principles and Western values, always arise triumphantly out of bravery and loyalty to their country. Historical characters (the Catholic kings, Hernán Cortés or Blas de Leza, to name a few) are portrayed as legendary heroes and role models who accomplished the epic task of saving, setting the standard for similar contemporary enterprises.

Vox recontextualises past events in present times in order to 'make Spain great again' (#hacerEspañagrandeotravez), a calque of Trump's 'make America great again'.[4] In up-to-date mythological recreations, Santiago Abascal is framed as a post-modern populist hero offering a new historical reinterpretation of Spanish history, the only one capable of being the saviour of a country whose identity and values are fading due to the disastrous administration of former governments.

The primary historical episode upon which Vox builds its narrative is 'the Reconquista' (the Reconquest), the motto of their 2019 national campaign. The Reconquista is a historical event that comprised a set of military campaigns from the late ninth century which attracted Christian knights from all over Europe and ended on 2 January 1492, with the surrender of Granada's Emirate to the Catholic kings. In Vox's rhetoric, the Reconquista is again taking place today, implying that the country needs to be 'reconquered' from its enemies (Figure 4.2) who, they claim, have again overtaken the country. Crucially, this hero mythology, that is, the projection of Vox's struggles in contemporary Spain, is at times embedded in 'the land'. Figure

4.2 Shot from the promotional video for the 2018 Andalusian elections 'Andalucía por España' (Andalusia for Spain)

4.2 shows a still caption from a video of the 2018 Andalusian campaign in which Abascal rides across the Andalusian countryside surrounded by a group of men while *The Lord of the Rings* soundtrack can be heard. The connotative system comes into play since the clip ends with the motto *Andalucía por España* (Andalusia for Spain), proclaiming the Reconquista of Spain would start in Andalusia. In the video, Abascal is foregrounded either in the centre or in close shots and surrounded by an all-male group of 'knights', among which the most recognisable face is the acclaimed bullfighter Morante de la Puebla, who has campaigned for Vox since the very beginning. Following Sheets-Johnstone (2013), the movement in this video is symbolically expressive since they are firmly advancing or reconquering the Andalusian land as an advance for their subsequent plan. Most of the time, they move from left to right, suggesting goal-directedness (van Leeuwen, 2021: 107), while regular trotting suggests control and discipline (van Leeuwen, 2021: 109). Horses can also be interpreted as twofold iconographic symbols that are reminiscent of the past (Reconquista) as well as icons of loyalty and nobility, qualities that Vox ascribes to rural life.

For Abascal's party, bullfighting along with hunting are essential pillars of Spanish identity, and proposals number 67 and 68 of their 2019 100-point electoral programme explicitly called for the protection of both practices. Following traditional justifications used by the far right, they framed it as a valuable wildlife management tool and 'a traditional activity of the rural world'. Departing from vegan, ecofascist actors, Vox thus strongly encourages meat consumption – opposing the advice of the so-called socio-communist government to reduce the ecological impact of the meat industry, an opposition even linked to conspiracy theories connected to Bill Gates' businesses. Interestingly, Vox's attitude seems to be discontinuing the line of ideological predecessors since, as Camus and Lebourg (2017: 86) state: 'in the late 1970s, the Spanish radical far right made a speciality of setting up environmental and anti-speciesist associations'. Vox's visual narrative conveys the fusion of nativism and nature, which 'cast[s] pastoral labour and agrarianism as exemplary of rooted national character' (Turner and Bailey, 2021: 5). Nature is identified with the homeland where natives (Spanish farmers and cattle breeders) are custodians.

A proactive team with a clear leader

Wodak (2015: 21) mentions the focus on charismatic leaders as one of the distinctive features of right-wing populisms. It happens to be the case with most radical-right populist parties, such as Salvini (the *Lega* in Italy), Trump (the Republican Party in the United States) and Modi (the Bharatiya Janata in India), although the presence of women leading the radical right is increasing, such as Marine Le Pen and the National Rally in France. Vox follows Wodak's principle of leadership, and their digital communication strategies indeed mostly revolve around Abascal's mega-supremacy (Aladro and Requeijo 2020; Castro and Díaz, 2021). However, this analysis offers nuances to this claim as, visually at least, Vox is not exclusively constructed as a leader-dependent but instead as a hierarchical team-driven force.

Although Santiago Abascal is the head of the party and the one who has been holding the reins throughout its political rise, the idea of a team is continuously alluded to. Most images in which the party is portrayed display Vox's backbone and are organised symmetrically around the leader. Following Kress and van Leeuwen's (1996: 176) notion of composition, that is, 'how they [the representational and interactive elements] are integrated into a meaningful whole', we can distinguish the presence of the three interrelated systems. In terms of *information value*, all Vox's members are placed around the central figure of Abascal, portrayed as the undeniable leader of the group, with women placed in the margins. Regarding *salience* (Kress and van Leeuwen, 1996: 177), or how elements are made to attract the viewer's attention, the party's president is much more prominent in size and is foregrounded but supported by his band in the background, a visual 'having one's back' philosophy. In this way, Vox puts forward the message of being a team (visual elements are not disconnected) but hierarchically organised with members clearly signified as central or peripheral. In visual *framing* (Rodríguez and Dimitrova, 2011), medium shots (as is the case in most photos of Vox's members) mean close relationships, although they are never looking directly at the camera. They are usually portrayed dynamically (mostly publicly speaking) and looking slightly to one side, usually towards the right that is associated with the future, according to Kress and van Leeuwen (1996). The closeness of elements reinforces the idea of a cohesive group, being perceived as a totality (Rodríguez and Dimitrova, 2011).

This pattern is also reproduced in Vox's videos on environmental issues. Abascal is the undisputed leader in those videos uploaded during electoral campaigns, but on certain occasions, several members of the party – mainly Secretary General Javier Ortega Smith – visit farmers and rural areas to experience their problems first hand. In Figure 4.3, a still image is taken from a promotional video interview made with Abascal in the mountains in which he explains Vox's plan for Spain. He is the video's prime protagonist, and rarely can another man be seen walking and talking to him. Vox's leader is smartly dressed in a khaki outfit and occasionally takes his professional photo camera out to take shots of the breathtaking scenery. That is, the beauties of 'our homeland' act as a banal background for Abascal's performance, they are drawn closer to the saviour and the audience through his photographing, and they are signified as the prize worth fighting for

la izquierda totalitaria y el separatismo no avanzan más.

4.3 Shot taken from Vox's video with the caption reading '[thanks to the presence of Vox in the Parliament], the totalitarian left and separatism do not advance more'

(against 'the totalitarian left and separatism'). The whole video conveys the idea of intimacy and closeness (Forchtner and Kølvraa, 2017), showing, at a connotation level, an approachable and down-to-earth leader who offers solutions (Vox's plan for Spain) rather than demanding them from the viewer (Kress and van Leeuwen, 1996).

Conclusion

Drawing on multimodal critical discourse analysis and visual framing theory, this chapter has provided answers to two research questions: Can any visual discursive axes in Vox's narrative on social media be identified? And what is the role of environmental images in framing Vox's concept of 'Spanish identity'?

Coexisting with the general tenets of radical-right populism, Vox's discourse also shapes a unique 'made in Spain' political style. Regarding the first question on discursive axes, this chapter points to Vox's rhetoric revolving around three main lines intertwined with the political force's stance towards the environment. First, the party's nativist and populist approach results in the defence of the man of the street, represented by farmers and cattle breeders, who have allegedly been abandoned and betrayed by the socio-communist government. The second research question focuses on the construction of a Spanish identity built upon a modern reinterpretation of history and traditions as well as on the symbols that represent the unity of the nation (flag, anthem and Crown). These represent a revisionist revival of the traditional and moral values they want to return to (mainly bravery and Spanish pride), along with the reinforcement of Spanish emblems as agglutinating motifs that assemble an impervious nation. Nature and homeland are interchangeable concepts. Heritage and belonging are epitomised by bullfighting and hunting and tightly linked to nostalgia for a world they perceive to be endangered by the pressure exerted by progressive values, such as veganism and anti-speciesism. In that post-modern mythological reinterpretation of an epic Spain, Santiago Abascal is framed as the country's hero – specially of a rural Spain – while the party, a cohesive team, is constantly represented as fighting to protect the nation.

The role of images has proven to be essential for constructing Vox's concept of 'Spanish identity'. The party's visual rhetoric echoes its textual discourse, relying on uncomplicated, straightforward lexico-grammar to trigger emotions and reach their target (the trust of the average Spaniard). This deliberate simplicity simultaneously distances them from what they see as the sophisticated and convoluted narratives of the (left-wing) elite.

Vox's divisive rhetoric cleaves the population into 'patriots' (farmers, cattle breeders, custodians of the traditions) and 'traitors', compelling the audience to take a side. Multimodal strategies self-portray the party as the only possible protector of rural Spain, articulating a concept of Spanish identity that excludes those who, from the perspective of their rigid principles, jeopardise it, imperilling the unity of the country in different ways.

Notes

1 For more information on Spain, check Ipsos. (n.d.).
2 See 'Euro Area Unemployment Rate at 12.2%'. https://ec.europa.eu/eurostat/documents/2995521/5164586/3-31102013-BP-EN.PDF/ac1c16fc-35ba-4d32-a0a0-91e9409eda8f (accessed 11 February 2022).
3 For some examples of the different labels attached by the media and experts to Vox's ideology see Santana et al. (n.d.) and Amón (2018).
4 Along the same lines, see also Wodak and Forchtner (2014) for the vindication of an imperial past by the Freedom Party of Austria.

References

abc (2020): Paco León denuncia 'un delito de odio' de Vox por un tuit en el que llama 'titiriteros' al cine español. www.abc.es/play/cine/noticias/abci-paco-leon-denuncia-delito-odio-tuit-llama-titiriteros-cine-espanol-202003231930_noticia.html (accessed 11 February 2022).

Aladro Vico, E. and Requeijo Rey, P. (2020): Discurso, estrategias e interacciones de Vox en su cuenta de Instagram en las elecciones del 28-A. Derecha radical y redes sociales, *Revista Latina de Comunicación Social*, 77: 203–229. https://doi.org/10.4185/RLCS-2020-1455

Alonso, M. (2015): Podemos: el ciberactivismo ciudadano llega a la política europea, *Dígitos. Revista de Comunicación Digital*, 1: 91–110. https://revistadigitos.com/index.php/ígitos/article/view/5 (accessed 11 August 2021).

Alonso, S. and Rovira Kaltwasser, C. (2014): Spain: No country for the populist radical right?, *South European Society and Politics*, 20(1): 21–45.

Amón, R. (2018): Por qué Vox es un partido de ultraderecha, *El País*, 4 December 2018. https://elpais.com/elpais/2018/12/03/opinion/1543827038_058171.html (accessed 11 February 2022).

Applebaum, A. (2019). Los secretos de la estrategia de Vox, *El País*, 12 May 2019. https://elpais.com/elpais/2019/05/10/ideas/1557485729_129647.html (accessed 10 March 2020).

Ariza, C. (2020): The end of Spanish exceptionalism. In E. Leidig (ed.), *Mainstreaming the Global Radical Right: CARR Yearbook*. Stuttgart: ibidem, 177–181.

Barthes, R. (1977): *Image, Music, Text*. London: Fontana.

Betz, H. G. (1994): *Radical Right-Wing Populism in Western Europe*. New York: St. Martins' Press.

Bogerts, L. and Fielitz, M. (2019): 'Do you want Meme war?': Understanding the visual memes of the German far right. In M. Fielitz and N. Thurston (eds), *Post-digital Cultures of the Far-Right: Online Actors and Offline Consequences in Europe and the US*. Bielefeld: transcript, 137–153.

Camus, J.-Y. and Lebourg, N. (2017): *Far-Right Politics in Europe*. Cambridge, MA: Harvard University Press.

Canovan, M. (1999): 'Trust the people!': Populism and the two faces of democracy, *Political Studies*, 47(1): 2–16.

Castro Martínez, A. and Díaz Morilla, P. (2021): La comunicación política de la derecha radical en redes sociales: De Instagram a TikTok y Gab, la estrategia digital de Vox, *Dígitos: Revista de Comunicación Digital*, 7: 67–89. http://dx.doi.org/10.7203/rd.v1i7.210

Chilton, P. (2004): *Analysing Political Discourse. Theory and Practice*. London: Routledge.

Cotarelo, R. (ed.) (2013): *Ciberpolítica: Las nuevas formas de acción y comunicación políticas*. Valencia: Tirant Humanidades.

Crawford, B. (2020): The influence of memes on far-right radicalisation, *Centre of the Analysis of the Radical Right*. www.radicalrightanalysis.com/2020/06/09/the-influence-of-memes-on-far-right-radicalisation/ (accessed 10 August 2021).

Del Arco Blanco, M. A. and Gorostiza, S. (2021): 'Facing the sun': Nature and nation in Franco's 'New Spain' (1936–1951), *Journal of Historical Geography*, 71: 73–82.

El Plural (2019): No solo en las encuestas: Vox ya es el partido con mayor proyección en redes sociales. www.elplural.com/politica/no-solo-en-las-encuestas-vox-ya-es-el-partido-con-mayor-proyeccion-en-redes-sociales_227143102 (accessed 11 February 2022).

Entman, R. M. (1991): Framing US coverage of international news: Contrasts in narratives of the KAL and Iran air incidents, *Journal of Communication*, 41(4): 6–27.

Entman, R. M. (1993): Framing: Towards clarification of a fractured paradigm, *Journal of Communication*, 43(4): 51–58.

España, Unidad y Soberanía (n.d.): www.voxespana.es/biblioteca/espana/2018m/gal_c2d72e181103013447.pdf. (accessed 11 February 2022).

Firth, R. (1973): *Symbols: Public and Private*. Ithaca, NY and London: Cornell University Press.

Forchtner, B. (ed.) (2019): *The Far Right and the Environment*. London: Routledge.

Forchtner, B. and Kølvraa, C. (2017): Extreme right images of radical authenticity: Multimodal aesthetics of history, nature, and gender roles in social media, *European Journal of Cultural and Political Sociology*, 4(3): 252–281. https://doi.org/10.108 0/23254823.2017.1322910

Goffman, E. (1974): *Frame Analysis: An Essay on the Organization of Experience*. Cambridge: Harvard University Press.

González Enríquez, C. (2017): *La excepción española: el fracaso de los grupos de derecha populista pese al paro, la desigualdad y la inmigración*. Madrid: Real Instituto Elcano.

Hidalgo-Tenorio, E., Benítez-Castro, M. A. and De Cesare, F. (2019): Introduction: Unravelling populist discourse. In: E. Hidalgo-Tenorio, M. A. Benítez-Castro and F. De Cesare (eds), *Populist Discourse: Critical Approaches to Contemporary Politics*. London: Routledge, 1–13.

Hodge, R. and Kress, G. (1988): *Social Semiotics*. Cambridge: Polity.

Ipsos (n.d.): Despite the increase in extreme climate events, citizen mobilisation for climate change is not growing. www.ipsos.com/en-be/international-observatory-climate-and-public-opinion (accessed 11 February 2022).

Kreis, R. (2017): The 'Tweet politics' of President Trump, *Journal of Language and Politics*, 16(4): 607–618. https://www.jbe-platform.com/content/journals/10.1075/jlp.17032.kre

Kress, G. and van Leeuwen, T. (1996): *Reading Images: A Grammar of Visual Design*. London: Routledge.

Kress, G. and van Leeuwen, T. (2001): *Multimodal Discourse: The Modes and Media of Contemporary Communication*. London: Bloomsbury.

La Vanguardia (2019): Vox: La extrema derecha europea celebra el auge del partido de Abascal. www.lavanguardia.com/politica/20191110/471503757346/extrema-derecha-europa-celebra-vox-santiago-abascal-elecciones-generales-2019-10n-espana.html (accessed 19 March 2023).

Laclau, E. (2005): *On Populist Reason*. New York: Verso.

Lubarda, B. (2020): Beyond ecofascim? Far-right ecologism (FRE) as a framework for future enquiries, *Environmental Values*, 29(6): 713–732. https://doi.org/10.319 7/096327120x15752810323922

Machin, D. and Mayr, A. (2012): *How to do Critical Discourse Analysis: A Multimodal Introduction*. London: Sage.

Martín Cubas, J., Soria-Olivas, E., Llosa Guillén, Á. and Buendía Ramón, V. (2020): La agenda building de los partidos políticos españoles en las redes sociales: Un análisis de Big data, *Dígitos*, 1(6): 253–274.

Milner, R. M. (2012): *The World Made Meme: Discourse and Identity in Participatory Media*. PhD thesis. Lawrence: University of Kansas.

Moffitt, B. (2016): *The Global Rise of Populism. Performance, Political Style, and Representation*. Stanford: Stanford University Press.

Mudde, C. (2007): *Populist Radical Right Parties in Europe*. Cambridge: Cambridge University Press.

Mudde, C. (2019): *The Far Right Today*. Cambridge: Polity Press.

Mudde, C. and Rovira Kaltwasser, C. (2012): Exclusionary vs. inclusionary populism: Comparing contemporary Europe and Latin America, *Government and Opposition*, 48(2): 147–174.

Peeples, J. A. (2013): Imaging toxins, *Environmental Communication*, 7(2): 191–210.

PRESS, R. es / E (2021): Twitter suspende la cuenta de Vox por 'incitar al odio' contra los musulmanes, *RTVE.es*. www.rtve.es/noticias/20210128/twitter-vuelve-suspender-cuenta-vox-incitar-odio-contra-musulmanes/2070480.shtml (accessed 11 February 2022).

Rebich-Hespanha, S., Rice, R. E., Montello, D. R., Retzloff, S., Tien S. and Hespanha, J. P. (2015): Image themes and frames in US print news stories about climate change, *Environmental Communication*, 9(4): 491–519. https://doi.org/10.108 0/17524032.2014.983534

Rodríguez, L. and Dimitrova, D. V. (2011): The levels of visual framing, *Journal of Visual Literacy*, 30(1): 48–65.

Santana, A., Rama, J., Zanotti, L. and Turnbull-Dugarte, S. J. (n.d.). VOX: La emergencia de la derecha radical populista y el fin del excepcionalismo español. *The Conversation*. https://theconversation.com/vox-la-emergencia-de-la-derecha-radical-populista-y-el-fin-del-excepcionalismo-espanol-164129 (accessed 11 February 2022).

Sheets-Johnstone, M. (2013): *The Primacy of Movement*. Amsterdam: John Benjamins.

Shifman, L. (2014): *Memes in Digital Culture*. Cambridge, MA: MIT Press.

Smith, W. (1969): *Prolegomena to the Study of Political Symbols*. Boston: Boston University.

Turner, J. and Bailey D. (2021): 'Ecobordering': Casting immigration control as environmental protection, *Environmental Politics*, https://doi.org/10.108 0/09644016.2021.1916197.

van Leeuwen, T. (2005): *Introducing Social Semiotics*. London: Routledge.

van Leeuwen, T. (2021): The semiotics of movement and mobility, *Multimodality & Society*, 1(1): 97–118.

voxespana.es (n.d.). *StackPath.* www.voxespana.es/actualidad/abascal-es-un-honor-sumar-a-andre-ventura-a-esta-alianza-frente-al-comunismo-en-la-iberosfera-20210925 (accessed 9 May 2021).

Vozpópuli (2019): Vox en terreno enemigo: Niega la 'emergencia climática', pero se apunta a la Cumbre del Clima. www.vozpopuli.com/espana/politica/vox-territorio-emergencia-cumbre-clima_0_1304869898.html (accessed 11 February 2022).

Westberg, G. and Årman, H. (2019): Common sense as extremism: the multi-semiotics of contemporary national-socialism, *Critical Discourse Studies*, 16(5): 549–568. https://doi.org/10.1080/17405904.2019.1624183

Wodak, R. and Forchtner, B. (2014): Embattled Vienna 1683/2010: Right-wing populism, collective memory and the fictionalization of politics, *Visual Communication*, 13(2): 231–255. https://doi.org/10.1177%2F1470357213516720

Wodak, R. (2015): *The Politics of Fear: What Right-wing Populist Discourses Means.* London: Sage.

Xidias, J. (2020): *Vox: The Revival of the Far Right in Spain: CARR Research Insight.* London: Centre for Analysis of the Radical Right.

5

Purity and control: gender and visual environmental communication by the extreme right in Cyprus

Miranda Christou

ELAM proves once again its sensitivity to environmental issues; without too many words but with meaningful action. (ELAM, 2021a)

When our motherland needs us, we rush! We are never inactive! (ELAM, 2021b)

Introduction

In the first week of July 2021, Cyprus registered its dark presence in the Pyrocene (Pyne, 2019). Just like the Australian 'Black Summer' (2019–2020), the 2020 catastrophic fires in Brazil, Argentina and Siberia, and the annual fire season in California, the fires raging in Cyprus were the most devastating since the 1960 establishment of the Republic of Cyprus. During that period, the extreme-right party *Ethniko Laiko Metopo* (National Popular Front, ELAM) reported that its volunteers were on the front lines. Following a steady line of blogs and images related to their environmental 'sensitivities', ELAM kept sharing its presence alongside fire service personnel. Often, there were dramatic action photos, such as showing the back of a male figure in a black ELAM T-shirt holding a fire hose or fighting the blaze with digging tools. While the motherland (*patrida*) was burning, ELAM was there to save it. A few weeks later, when the government of Turkey announced its decision to open the fenced-off, abandoned city of Famagusta (also called Ammochostos or Varoshia) in the occupied area, ELAM posted land images of barbed wire around the beautiful, pristine beaches of the seafront city. In this case, the enslaved *patrida* calls for its liberation, with ELAM declaring its readiness to fight.

This chapter explores how ELAM's visual environmental communication involves positioning the party as liberators of a sacred national territory by showcasing the masculine, self-described ELAMite (ELAM member) as the saviour of the (female) enslaved and endangered land. Despite increasing attention to the complexities of far-right environmental ideology (Forchtner and Kølvraa, 2015; Lockwood, 2018; Forchtner, 2019a, 2019b), their visual communication has been mostly overlooked (see the Introduction to this volume). Little research has systematically considered how ideologies of pure and pristine national land or proclamations of territorial sovereignty are visually represented and symbolised by groups that promote environmentalism through a nativist lens. In this chapter, I take on the mandate of the 'visual turn' (Hall, 1997; Rose, 2007) to examine ELAM's representation of nature and land. By analysing 109 website images (2016–2021), three major thematic categories were identified in the party's visual environmental communication: the barbed wire in occupied Cyprus (twenty-five images), the protection of natural gas resources (twenty-two images) and saving the land from fires (sixty-two images). These themes were then analysed based on Barthes' (1972, 1977) levels of meaning in visual analysis (denotation, connotation, mythology) where myth illustrated Ortner's (1972) analogy which posited that female is to male what nature is to culture. I argue that these images represent gendered codes of purity and control which are shared concepts both in nationalist ideologies and performances of hegemonic masculinities (Connell and Messerschmidt, 2005).

The chapter begins by connecting environmental ideology to gender, both as a variable and at the level of symbolism (Ortner, 1972). This is followed by an introduction to ELAM and an account of how ELAM's approach to the environment relates to current manifestations of 'far-right ecologism' (Lubarda, 2020). The next section presents the methodology of categorising and analysing the 109 images followed by the three major themes that arose from the analysis: 'enslaved and pure motherland', 'our land must be protected' and 'ELAM as saviour'. The chapter concludes with a discussion on how ELAM's visual communication of environmental action conveys a mythological version of militarised masculinity that is seen as endangered.

Gender, nature and ideology

My starting point is that an analysis of how far-right ideology adopts, appropriates and communicates varieties of environmental thinking can be crystallised through the lens of gender. According to Forchtner and Kølvraa (2015), far-right ideology is connected to the environment in different dimensions: the land is the *aesthetic* pride of the nation, a *material* resource for its survival and a *symbol* of cultural hygiene. Thus, the nation endures when its territorial integrity is preserved and its purity defended. An examination of ELAM's visual environmental communication shows that the concepts of *purity* and *control* are central both in nationalist ideology and patriarchal relations which, in turn, are symbolically demonstrated in representations of the natural environment. I echo here Douglas' (2003 [1966]) powerful thesis in *Purity and Danger* where she argues that rituals of removing pollution (dirt, dust, harmful substances) are investments both in cleanliness and in communal formations of social boundaries. Indeed, as Forchtner (2019c) has argued, the far right's quest for land purity uses, among others, the language of 'invasive species' in the natural world as a metaphor to describe the presence of migrants in the territory of the endangered national group.

The gender symbolism of the natural environment has been meticulously explored in Ortner's (1972) classic essay 'Is Female to Male as Nature Is to Culture?', where she attempts to explain the question of women's universal devaluation. Ortner argues that beyond the easily identifiable practices of calling women inferior or assigning them to marginal positions in society, there must be other symbolic ways through which these practices are legitimised. She finds the answer in another universal phenomenon: the relationship between nature and culture which is a relationship of control. Thus, she points out: 'the pan-cultural devaluation of woman could be accounted for, quite simply, by postulating that woman is being identified with, or symbolically associated with, nature, as opposed to man, who is identified with culture' (Ortner, 1972: 11–12).

Ortner argues that women's identification with nature begins with her body and its reproductive function, is extended into the social roles that reproduction entails (raising children, preparing food, sustaining life) and ends with the belief that women are 'like nature' because they are the key to procreation. Thus, women's physiology becomes their destiny, and their mothering function reflects 'women's psyche'. In contrast, men occupy the higher domain of culture and are seen as too sophisticated to be tending to the needs of animal-like small species. For Ortner, men are tasked with developing culture, which oftentimes involves regulating and controlling nature (hunting, mining, drilling, exploring). As women are, thus, seen as being closer to nature than men, they are often portrayed as driven by emotional, almost 'animalistic' instincts, while the cool, calm, collected figure of the man is the rational voice in the room.

Beyond symbolism, connections between gender and the environment can be traced on different levels. As a variable, gender determines differences in attitudes between men and women, with women exhibiting greater concern for environmental degradation (Joireman and Liu; 2014) even at a young age (Zelezny et al., 2000). Interestingly, there are indications that women's greater political participation in a country is linked to the country's lower carbon dioxide emissions (Ergas and York, 2012). Other studies have shown that gender effects are minimal compared to the explanatory power of political affiliation and political ideology in accounting for beliefs in climate change (Hornsey et al., 2016). Women also seem to know more about climate change compared to men, although they tend to underestimate the breadth of their knowledge (McCright, 2010). Men's lack of urgency for the environment has been dubbed the 'cool dude' effect (McCright and Dunlap, 2011), which is partially explained by the type of white conservative male who overrates his understanding of global warming while endorsing denialist views. Some of this variability can be accounted for by differential gendered vulnerabilities in relation to the immediate and long-term impact of climate change (Pearse, 2017). Feminist perspectives emphasise that this is a direct result of structural constraints in the social positioning of men and women and note that these constraints are even more pronounced for women in the Global South (Roy, 2018).

This is where the space of ecofeminist thought has expanded the gender–environment connection beyond mainstream approaches. Despite essentialist undertones associated with its rise in the 1970s, ecofeminism is not about women who believe they can save the earth simply because they are women. Gaard (2015), for example, steers away from approaches where women are called to 'mother the Earth' or are constructed as victims of environmental destruction. Instead, she proposes an ecofeminist, intersectional approach and argues that:

[C]limate change and first world overconsumption are produced by masculinist ideology, and will not be solved by masculinist techno-science approaches. Instead, I propose, queer feminist posthumanist climate justice perspectives at the local, national, and global levels are needed to intervene and transform both our analyses and our solutions to climate change. (Gaard, 2015: 20–21)

The contribution of feminist theory to radicalising environmental thought lies in critiquing both masculine ideals and the patriarchal practices that underpin the destruction of the environment (Warren, 2000; Plumwood, 2002) while, at the same time, opening up the debate to other intersections of dominance and exploitation. This has extended feminist theoretical explorations of care into the animal world and our relations with other non-human species (Kheel, 2008; Adams and Gruen, 2014). Kheel (2008), for example, develops Carol Gilligan's 'ethic of care' into the idea of 'contextualized care', that is, employing empathy in our relations with the living world and avoiding harm and exploitation. Thus, ecofeminism shifts ecological debates to questions of control, oppression and domination that run as key themes in both gender relations and relations between humans and the environment.

Building on these foundations is the notion of 'ecological masculinities' (Hultman and Pulé, 2018; Pulé and Hultman, 2021), which embraces the feminist critique of domination of nature and argues that a critical examination of industrial masculinities needs to be part of these debates. Indeed, hegemonic versions of masculinity have been at the forefront of encounters with nature given that hunting, colonial conquest and oil rigging have not only been means of accumulating economic wealth or developing innovative science but also domains of masculine validation (Pulé et al., 2021). Thus, any effort to address the current climate crisis or humanity's relationship with the environment must resist those instances where a camouflaged ecological masculinity mimics ecological thinking. As I show, the parochial environmental agenda of ELAM in Cyprus belongs in this category as it serves narrow populist interests. More importantly, I argue that they do not adopt an ecological approach to climate change but see this as an opportunity to restore hegemonic masculinity through the brawny male performance of saving the burning land and liberating occupied areas.

The extreme right in Cyprus: introducing ELAM

The rise of the far-right in Cyprus has, until recently, remained under the radar compared to the well-documented case of Golden Dawn in Greece (Ellinas, 2013; Vasilopoulou and Halikiopoulou, 2015). A 'Golden Dawn, Cyprus Branch' unsuccessfully attempted to register as a political party in 2008 under the leadership of Christos Christou, a Greek Cypriot who served for many years at the side of Nikos Michaloliakos, the now imprisoned leader of Golden Dawn. Eventually, ELAM was founded in 2011 and has since grown its numbers: from a meagre 0.88 per cent in the national elections of 2013, to 3.71 per cent in 2016, resulting in two Members of Parliament (MPs), and 6.78 per cent or four MPs in 2021.

Although ELAM's image does not yet resemble the violent outbursts of Golden Dawn, it is important to note the historical links in right-wing extremism between Greece and Cyprus (Katsourides, 2013). The Republic of Cyprus became independent in 1960, following a period of British rule (1878–1960) and Ottoman control (1570–1878). The constitution, drafted by Greece, Turkey and the UK, aimed at maintaining a delicate balance of political control between the two main communities: Greek Cypriots (77 per cent) and Turkish Cypriots (17 per cent) with the remaining percentage of Armenians, Maronites and Latins. The tumultuous 1960s culminated in 1974 when a Greek junta-led coup ousted the Greek Cypriot president and Turkey invaded five days later, claiming to protect Turkish Cypriots. The northern part of the island declared itself the Turkish Republic of Northern

Cyprus in 1983. However, it remains unrecognised internationally. Cyprus is currently separated by the ceasefire line (Green Line), which was a closed border until 2003 when the Turkish Cypriot side allowed a partial Green Line opening. In 2004, the Republic of Cyprus officially became part of the European Union, although the accession of the northern part of the island is suspended until a resolution between the two communities is reached. ELAM is the only political party in Cyprus that actively opposes the bizonal, bicommunal federation as a solution to the division of Cyprus despite this being the official negotiating framework since the 1970s.

ELAM's success has partially been attributed to the dire economic situation on the island which led to a controversial Eurogroup bailout deal for Cyprus' banks, along with an influx of migrants (Katsourides, 2013). However, it is also true that the ultra-nationalist, nativist and anti-immigrant ELAM has taken a conservative approach by avoiding the flamboyant neo-Nazi symbolism of Golden Dawn. Instead, it focused on emulating its food and clothing drives by putting women on the front lines of charity work (Félix, 2015; Christou, 2019). Thus, by holding its extremist side in abeyance and by employing populist rhetoric (Charalambous and Christoforou, 2018), ELAM attempts to blur the line between radical-right and extreme-right parties. As Mudde (2019) explains, while the radical right subscribes to the legitimacy of democratic procedures but challenges liberal democratic values, the extreme right is anti-democratic and actively undermines both values and procedures. In the case of ELAM, its leader has not been shy about reminding people of ELAM's potential for violence. Indeed, ELAM has been linked to incidents of violence against migrants at various points since 2011, though the party claims that these individuals were deceptively acting in their name. More importantly, after the Greek Supreme Court decision which upheld that Golden Dawn is a criminal organisation, ELAM announced that it had long since cut ties with them.

ELAM's far-right 'environmentalism'

This 'serious' Golden Dawn of Cyprus (Kapsalis, 2021) has also been mimicking its Greek neo-Nazi relative on their approach to environmental crises. ELAM has created 'volunteer groups' in various communities around the island and activates these groups to dash to the front lines in case of fire emergencies. ELAM also donated 'fire systems' to at least two villages in 2017 and 2020, that is, modified pick-up trucks which carry a water tank and high-pressure hoses to act as fire extinguishers. On both occasions, the media covered the event with the village leader posing next to ELAM members in front of the truck that features ELAM's oversized logo and the fact that it was donated by them. Golden Dawn had utilised similar tactics of volunteering at fire emergencies and, in one case, even went as far as to claim that their presence had been requested by the authorities – something that was officially refuted.

ELAM's environmental approach has two main characteristics. First, it isolates natural disasters (such as fires) from the larger global discourse on climate change and environmental devastation by focusing only on local events. Second, it spotlights their image as saviours of the land. As I show, ELAM's visual environmental communication does not prioritise science-based nature protection but embraces a far-right view on the nation's territory through nostalgia for militarised hegemonic masculinity. Indeed, the environmental manifesto of ELAM is particularly brief, and it is designed to address the narrow interests of hunters and their dissatisfaction with environmental protection laws. Beyond some general and vaguely communicated priorities, such as 'protection of sea habitats', 'better waste management' and 'planting of trees', they lack an overall ecological perspective. As Dobson (1999) has argued, it is important to distinguish between ecologism – which demands a radical dismantling of industrialisation and anthropocentrism in approaches to nature – and environmentalism, which aims at more conservative 'green' policy reforms. ELAM's environmentalism comprises thin ideology and even thinner policy perspectives while, as I show, it maintains a performative activism of caring about the land. For example, there are references in support of hunters and their 'rights' and condemnations of climate 'activists' (which they refer to in quotation marks, see ELAM, 2021c).

The subtext in these declarations by ELAM is the issue of trapping rare migratory birds. Jonathan Franzen, the highly acclaimed American author and avid bird watcher, visited Cyprus, Malta and Italy in 2010 and wrote a *New Yorker* article about 'the most intensive songbird-killing operations in the European Union' (Franzen, 2010). Franzen met up with CABS (Committee Against Bird Slaughter) activists in Cyprus and followed their attempts to save birds by entering fields and breaking up stick glue traps that capture not only the coveted *ambelopoulia* (blackcaps, a type of warbler), but a range of other, rare species of songbirds that are being driven to extinction.

According to some 2017 media reports, ELAM members have been among those attacking CABS activists when debates were taking place regarding the government's plan to relax the ban on capturing *ambelopoulia*. Linos Papayiannis, an ELAM MP, addressed a big protest by hunters demanding lower penalties for violating the law and told them: 'I am one of you and you know it.' ELAM's environmental decree is fully devoted to maintaining the tradition of the burly nature predator who has invested his masculinity in hunting. Even new generations seem to have revived this tradition with a populist, anti-authority, anti-elitist slant. As a member of Bird Life told Franzen: 'Now, for eighteen- and nineteen-year-olds, there's a kind of patriotic machismo to poaching. It's a symbol of resistance to Big Brother E.U.' (Franzen, 2010).

ELAM's approach exemplifies how far-right parties at times strive to maintain a delicate balance between demonstrating concern for the environment without sounding like the (stereo)typical 'green' parties they detest. There are different variations of these approaches. On the one hand, right-wing populist parties tend to be sceptical towards climate change policies (Tranter, 2013; Lockwood, 2018; Huber et al., 2021). In the European context, analysis of public attitudes has shown that nationalist ideology is linked to denial of climate change and opposition to fossil fuel taxes, as well as a higher likelihood to vote for right-wing parties (Kulin et al., 2021). This scepticism can be about the actual evidence on the phenomenon of climate change (especially anthropogenic) or about the policies for rectifying the situation (Forchtner, 2019b). Groups have also used climate change agony to serve far-right politics in relation to their moral panics regarding migration. The rhetoric of safeguarding the nation's natural treasures conveniently merges with the far right's anti-immigration rhetoric to create the discourse of 'ecobordering' (Turner and Bailey, 2022) where environmental degradation is blamed on immigration. The Nazi 'green wing' projected a similar logic when Heinrich Himmler declared that removing Jews and Slavs from Germany was helping the environment (Staudenmaier, 2004). This is a type of 'green patriotism' (Schaller and Carius, 2019) which resembles ELAM's narrow approach to the environment.

On the other hand, some populist radical right parties have strategically supported climate change initiatives in the name of national sovereignty and sustainability. There have been indications that far-right parties have begun to move away from denial of anthropogenic climate change and into more comprehensive ecological frameworks which reflect the original ecofascist identification of nature with nation (Voss, 2014). Couched in the ideology of the *völkisch* movement, which drew inspiration from German romanticism, ecofascism is not simply the love of nature but a nationalist embrace of the environment that relies on a mythic revival of the past. This backwards-looking frame is essential both in the 'palingenetic' theme that fascism is grounded on (Griffin, 2012) and the ecological approaches that do not propose future solutions for environmental problems but are interested instead in harking back to a time when unpolluted land symbolised the purity of the people (Campion, 2021). For example, Vihma et al. (2020) analysed the radical-right Danish People's Party, Finns Party and Sweden

Democrats to conclude that denialism is no longer the defining feature of these parties. Rather, they have sought to capitalise on the climate change momentum to increase their popularity while obstructing European Union initiatives. These different climate agendas are often limited in scope and oppose any obligation to coordinate actions on an international, multilateral level (Schaller and Carius, 2019).

More recently, Lubarda (2020) introduced the term 'far-right ecologism' (FRE) which attempts to capture this wide ideological range without limiting the frame through the widely used term of 'ecofascism'. FRE is a framework that addresses the foundational elements of ecologism (spirituality and mysticism, organicism and naturalism) and the 'green perimeter' of far-right ideology (autarky, authority, nostalgia and the Manichean worldview) which informs their environmental approaches. Indeed, far-right ecologism may resemble ELAM, which is more invested in proving masculine control over nature through performative acts of eco-nationalism while not necessarily committing to the mystical aspects of ecologism. As I demonstrate, these ambiguities are registered in the elevation of a mythological militaristic masculinity that protects, controls and dominates the victimised land.

Visual analysis of ELAM's environmental communication

The process of collecting data on ELAM's visual environmental communication is challenging given extensive deplatforming on social networking sited over recent years. Leading up to their first success in the 2016 parliamentary elections and a few years after that, ELAM had fully embraced Facebook and even created its own free Android/iOS app which is still available. However, a few months after Golden Dawn was expelled from Facebook in 2019, ELAM was banned as well. During the 2021 elections, the party managed to create a Facebook page titled 'Cyprus First' (their official motto), but the page no longer exists. One Twitter account under ELAM's name is not officially linked on their website, although it is used to tweet articles that appear on the website. Thus, data for this chapter were collected in 2021 from ELAM's official website (www.elamcy.com). The criterion for their selection was any images that represented nature and/or land. In total, the corpus comprises 109 images, which included a representation of the natural environment in articles and press releases between 2016 and 2021 in two categories: 'environment' and 'politics'. Three themes emerged inductively from these images and each image was then categorised in one of the following categories: first, the barbed wire in occupied Cyprus (twenty-five images); second, the protection of natural gas resources (twenty-two images); and third, saving the land from fires (sixty-two images).

Adopting a semiotic approach means starting from an understanding of images as cultural products that have meaning, and that this meaning is made possible by the use of signs. Thus, the question is: what signs are used in these images and what type of meaning do they convey about ELAM, their ideology and their relation to nature? In 'Rhetoric of the Image', Barthes (1977) distinguished between the purely descriptive reading of signs (*denotation*), where the task of analysis is to record the content of the image, and the interpretive reading (*connotation*), which registers how these elements make meaning in a specific context. In *Mythologies*, Barthes (1972) further added the level of *myth*, pointing to the larger ideology that holds together all these meanings. This last stage is crucial as it allows the analysis to highlight 'ideological values that are assumed or normalized by an image' (Culloty et al., 2019: 184).

For Barthes (1972: 114), *myth* is 'a second-order semiological system' where the sign (formed by the signifier and the signified) becomes the signifier or form for another signified or concept. For example, in the most prevalent motif of men putting out fires the *denotation* of strong, muscular men leads to the interpretation/*connotation* that ELAMites care abut nature and are ready to sacrifice themselves to protect it. This latter interpretation becomes itself the sign of another concept: the idea of men controlling nature. In Ortner's (1972) analogy – female to male is nature to culture – this relationship of control informs both dimensions so that men's control over nature and over women is *natural*. As Barthes (1972: 129) remarks: '[w]e reach here the very principle of myth: it transforms history into nature'.

Table 5.1 demonstrates how the coding proceeded in each theme: the subgrouping at the descriptive level (*denotation*), interpretation of the images in the context of Cyprus (*connotation*) and the ideological discussion (*mythology*).

Theme 1: enslaved and pure motherland

ELAM's visual environmental communication tells a story: that the earth/ Cyprus is pure and rich, that earth/Cyprus is in danger (due to fires, occupation and Turkey) and that the strong masculine ELAMite is here to save/liberate earth/Cyprus. This story is told through various images: first, photographs of Ammochostos are presented in at least ten different variations. Ammochostos means 'buried in the sand' and it used to be the island's most prime and iconic seaside city which was evacuated in 1974 when the Turkish army invaded. Since then, it has been fenced off and remains a ghost-like, abandoned

Table 5.1 Three themes in ELAM's visual communication of the environment

Theme 1: Barbed wire/border (25 images)

Denotation	Connotation	Mythology
Occupied area behind barbed wire (21) Border image (2) Politicians superimposed on land image (2)	Our land is beautiful, our land is enslaved/ occupied, our land is restricted, we cannot get to our beautiful land	Motherland is enslaved, waiting for someone to liberate her

Theme 2: Protection of natural gas resources (22 images)

Denotation	Connotation	Mythology
Political map of eastern Mediterranean sea/ gas exploration (15) Politicians superimposed on map of Cyprus (3) Turkish ships at sea (4)	Cyprus is in danger, Turkey poses immanent threat to the natural riches of Cyprus, drilling for natural gas is not a problem	Turkey is the eternal/ perpetual enemy of the island, our land and its resources must be saved

Theme 3: Saving the Earth (62 images)

Denotation	Connotation	Mythology
Man/men putting out fires (49) Men posing in front of fire equipment (5) Men picking up trash (8)	ELAM saves the land from fire, ELAM is active in putting out fires, ELAM provides material help in putting out the fires, ELAM cares about the environment	Strong, heroic men saving mother earth from fire, nature as a victim

city. It is an 'object of desire' for Greek Cypriots, one symbolising the issue of returning home and one which has become a bargaining point in peace negotiations. It is commonplace, as well, to hear Greek Cypriot refugees talk about the occupied areas as 'the most beautiful parts of the island' (Dikomitis, 2004; Roudometof and Christou, 2015), which is something that illustrates the far right's aesthetic engagement with nature (Forchtner and Kølvraa, 2015). The unspoiled beaches and the intense blue of the sea

5.1 Ammochostos, the 'ghost city,' buried in the sand

(*denotation*) in these images point to the purity of the land that is also symbolic of the people's virtues (Figure 5.1; ELAM, 2020a).

Furthermore, in nine of these ten variations, Ammochostos is presented behind barbed wire or some type of fencing. Nothing signifies nature's intersection with politics better than this invention that has not become outdated despite technological achievements (Razac, 2000). This twisted, spiked piece of metal is pivotal in marking territorial borders and controlling the movement of both human and non-human animals. The constant depiction of Ammochostos behind barbed wire is intended to operate as a reminder that land is territory that is limited and contested; there is still some of 'our land' out there – and there is thus a national duty to liberate it (*connotation*). In most of these images, the run-down, makeshift bordering matches the derelict buildings of the 'ghost city' in the background. In one case, when an aerial view of the beach does not feature barbed wire or a fence, it is used with the image of the party's MP Papayiannis superimposed on the photo of the city, indicating him as an emancipator. Thus, the occupied areas become symbols of both purity and agony through their natural beauty that is contradicted by the ugliness of the barbed wire. Both beauty and purity are signals of innocence as the national land expects the ultimate sacrifice from us to be liberated (*mythology*).

Theme 2: our land must be protected

The story of exploring and exploiting gas reserves in the area adds to the narrative of the national land as material resource (Forchtner and Kølvraa, 2015; for more on land, masculinity and resources, see Chapter 6 in this volume) and the urgent need to protect these assets. During the past twenty years, the Republic of Cyprus proceeded with exploring its 'Exclusive Economic Zone', which refers to thirteen maritime blocks south of the island that are internationally recognised as areas of exploration and economic exploitation. The presence of gas drilling companies in 2018 led to a diplomatic escalation in the relations between Cyprus and Turkey (Kontos and Bitsis, 2018) and it features prominently on ELAM's website, although it is evident that their perspective is more political and less about the environmental impact of drilling for gas and/or oil. Visually, this is represented with a political map of the eastern Mediterranean sea that features the thirteen 'blocks', often with menacing Turkish ships approaching dangerously (*denotation*) (Figure 5.2). In one of these photos, the image of the Turkish President Recep Tayyip Erdoğan is pasted on the forefront or the map and in another case

5.2 Cyprus with the thirteen blocks of Exclusive Economic Zone, surrounded by Turkish ships

his open arms are holding a Photoshopped map of Cyprus with his open mouth seemingly ready to devour the whole island (*connotation*).

In these images, nature is the playground of geopolitics and it exists only as a resource. As Anderson (2006 [1983]) pointed out, maps are abstracted realities of the land that were instrumental in establishing colonial control through the representation of territories but also in providing perceptible evidence to the 'imagined community'. In this case, the reproduction of the map of Cyprus with the charting of marine waters as sovereign spaces expands the national imagination. This chessboard in a game of domination is ELAM's way of representing nature through a story of victimisation and injustice: the land is beautiful but in danger, it is rich and threatened (*mythology*). ELAM's visual communication fetishises the land but only to emphasise its victimisation; it represents an island in a perennial state of distress. This visual rhetoric generates the need for a saviour and this is where ELAM fills the gap with the images of muscular ELAMites putting out fires.

Theme 3: ELAM as saviour

The largest category of images related to the representation of the land, nature and the environment were the images in the theme 'saving the earth' and, more specifically, the images of ELAM members putting out fires (49 out of 109 images). There are several characteristics in these images. First, they showcase strong, muscular bodies in a wide stance, often holding a water hose or a digging tool (*denotation*) (Figure 5.3; ELAM, 2020b). In many cases they are photographed from behind so that the ELAM name is visible in the back of their signature black T-shirt. Finally, these photographs function as representations of reality by furnishing evidence that something really happened (Sontag, 2001) in an unplanned, un-staged and natural manner. There are several obvious interpretations (*connotation*) of these images: that ELAM is active in putting out the fires, that they save the land from fire and that ELAM cares about the environment. This is confirmed by another group of photographs (eight images) which show ELAM volunteers picking up trash from parks. The focus on fires, however, as the almost exclusive area of ELAM's environmental care, also works at a *mythological* dimension to elevate them as saviours. These action images confirm their quotes at the beginning of the chapter ('we are never inactive!') as they capture bodies in motion, responding to the urgency of the situation. It is clear that the fires are dangerous and that putting them out is a risky operation which requires the presence of brave and fearless men. More importantly, these photographs are reminiscent of the genre of action or

5.3 ELAM volunteer putting out a fire

war films which fetishise the spectacle of masculinity through toughness and being in control (Neale, 1983).

Conclusion

In this chapter, I have outlined how the parochial environmental agenda of ELAM in Cyprus is not designed as a response to climate change but represents an opportunity to stage ecological gestures in order to restore a vision of masculinity through the brawny performance of saving the burning land. Taking as a starting point the idea of images as political artefacts, I use Barthes' (1972, 1977) three levels of analysis (*denotation, connotation, mythology*) to examine ELAM's visual environmental communication in 109 images collected from their website and organised in three themes: the barbed wire in occupied Cyprus, the protection of natural gas resources and saving the land from fires. Reading the images through the lens of *mythology* shows ELAM's commitment to natural purity and control of the national territorial with 'the land' being presented as beautiful and helpless, as rich and threatened. The defenceless occupied areas, the threatened surrounding sea and the burning land function as opportunities for the emergence of ELAM as saviour. In this mythology, Ortner's (1972) analogy of the female–nature under the control of the male–culture is on full display through the images of strong men saving the earth and struggling for its liberation through any means necessary.

ELAM's admittedly brave actions and the party's members being photographed next to real fire personnel is the projection of a mythical hegemonic masculinity. Connell and Messerschmidt (2005) have maintained that hegemonic forms of masculinity are not 'normal' because they do not represent most men, but are normalising because they project the type of man everyone should aspire to become. Thus, their far-right imaginaries of the relationship between 'the land' and 'the people' (see the Introduction to this volume) are saturated by the imaginary of a male hero who saves both the land and the people. Efthymiou (2019) has argued that the post-war (post-1974) Greek Cypriot masculinity has faced a major challenge. The old prototype of a militarised hegemonic masculinity that invested in heroic, nationalist discourse is being replaced by the 'Euro-Cypriot' male: the neoliberal negotiator who is armed with decrees, declarations and denunciations rather than guns. The undermining of this muscular, nationalist masculinity has opened up the space for groups such as ELAM to provide the 'palingenetic' (Griffin, 2012) option of restoring the militarised male. Indeed, ELAM is fully invested in this masculinity through their recurrent hero memorials and the military-style demonstrations where they chant about 'liberation' as the only solution to the division of the island. ELAM resents the idea of negotiations, they are against reconciliation with Turkish Cypriots and they provide a vision of 'return' to the occupied areas. The story of these images is a story of a land that is endangered and enslaved with the brave, masculine ELAMite as the saviour and liberator.

These gendered nuances of country, land and nature have been illustrated by a methodology of analysing visual communication able to capture the ideological metaphors of nationalism in a multimodal symbolic interplay. ELAM's willingness to act and to work with their hands is also a signal to the lost virtue of the breadwinner, working-class masculinity as they are literally down-to-earth, saving the land (Loomis, 2021). ELAM's visual environmental communication of volunteer fire extinguishing is the performance of a nostalgic militarised masculinity and the opportunity to restore the epic visual of a male hero. Therefore, analysis of these images reveals that what is seen by ELAM as endangered is not primarily nature but the nationalist masculinity that has lost its currency. The mythology of ELAM as saviour requires the romanticisation of both history and nature: the idea that there was a time when the nation was whole and complete and when we could all enjoy its natural, unblemished beauty. More importantly, it was a time of heroic men.

Analysis of ELAM's 'myopic environmentalism' (Darwish, 2021) and their visual communication of nature shows why it is difficult to assume any kind of ideological coherence under the banner of ecological thought. The focus on climate change, especially since the rise of global youth protests in 2019, means that we need to attend to instances of 'green' thought by far-right actors (Szenes, 2021). The challenge is not simply to tease out the contradictions of far-right ecologism or gendered performances but to understand how their ideological commitments result in an exclusionary, particularistic concern for the natural environment that is markedly different from today's often rather egalitarian and universalist green movements.

References

Adams, C. J. and Gruen, L. (eds) (2014): *Ecofeminism: Feminist Intersections with Other Animals and the Earth*. New York: Bloomsbury.

Anderson, B. (2006 [1983]): *Imagined Communities: Reflections on the Origin and Spread of Nationalism*. London: Verso.

Barthes, R. (1972): *Mythologies*. London: Vintage.

Barthes, R. (1977): Rhetoric of the image. In: R. Barthes (ed.), *Image–Music–Text*. London: Fontana, 32–51.

Campion, K. (2021): Defining ecofascism: Historical foundations and contemporary interpretations in the extreme right, *Terrorism and Political Violence*, 1–19. https://doi.org/10.1080/09546553.2021.1987895

Charalambous, G. and Christoforou, P. (2018): Far-right extremism and populist rhetoric: Greece and Cyprus during an era of crisis, *South European Society and Politics*, 23(4): 451–477. https://doi.org/10.1080/13608746.2018.1555957

Christou, M. (2019): The benign feminism of an extreme right-wing party. Presentation at the CARR Inaugural Conference 'A Century of Radical Right Extremism: New Approaches Centre for Analysis of the Radical Right', London, 15–17 May 2019.

Connell, R. W. and Messerschmidt, J. W. (2005): Hegemonic masculinity: Rethinking the concept, *Gender & Society*, 19(6): 829–859. https://doi.org/10.1177%2F0891243205278639

Culloty, E., Padraig, M., Brereton, P., Suiter, J., Smeaton, A. F. and Zhang, D. (2019): Researching visual representations of climate change, *Environmental Communication*, 13(2): 179–191. https://doi.org/10.1080/17524032.2018.1533877

Darwish, M. (2021): Nature, masculinities, care and the far-right. In: M. Hultman and P. Pulé (eds), *Men, Masculinities, and Earth Contending with the (m)Anthropocene*. Cham: Palgrave Macmillan, 183–206.

Dikomitis, L. (2004): A moving field: Greek Cypriot refugees returning 'home', *Durham Anthropology Journal*, 12(1): 7–20.

Dobson, A. (1999): Ecologism. In: R. Eatwell and A. Wright (eds), *Contemporary Political Ideologies*. London: Pinter, 231–254.

Douglas, M. (2003 [1996]): *Purity and Danger: An Analysis of Concepts of Pollution and Taboo*. London: Routledge.

Efthymiou, S. A. (2019): *Nationalism, Militarism and Masculinity in Post-conflict Cyprus*. Cham: Palgrave Macmillan.

ELAM (2020a): Η Κυβέρνηση ανοίγει τα οδοφράγματα και οι κατακτητές «'ευχαρ ιστούν'» με άνοιγμα της περίκλειστης πόλης!, 9 June, 2020. https://elamcy.com/i-kyvernisi-anoigei-ta-odofragmata-kai-oi-kataktites-efcharistoun-me-anoigma-tis-perikleistis-polis/ (accessed 31 August 2021).

ELAM (2020b): Συμβαίνει ΤΩΡΑ: Εθελοντές του ΕΛΑΜ στην κατάσβεση των πυρκαγιών στην Αγία Νάπα, 17 May, 2020. https://elamcy.com/symvainei-tora-ethelontes-tou-elam-stin-katasvesi-ton-pyrkagion-stin-agia-napa/ (accessed 31 August 2021).

ELAM (2021a): Οι εθελοντές του ΕΛΑΜ και πάλι στην πρώτη γραμμή κατάσβεσης των πυρκαγιών, 28 June 2021. https://elamcy.com/oi-ethelontes-tou-elam-kai-pali-stin-proti-grammi-katasvesis-ton-pyrkagion/ (accessed 31 August 2021).

ELAM (2021b): Τα παιδιά του ΕΛΑΜ στην πρώτη γραμμή κατάσβεσης των πυρκαγιών, 5 July 2021. https://elamcy.com/ta-paidia-tou-elam-stin-proti-grammi-katasvesis-ton-pyrkagion/ (accessed 31 August 2021).

ELAM (2021c): Οι θέσεις μας. https://elamcy.com/theseis/ (accessed 15 October 2021).

Ellinas, A. A. (2013): The rise of Golden Dawn: The new face of the far right in Greece, *South European Society and Politics*, 18(4): 543–565. https://doi.org/10.108 0/13608746.2013.782838

Ergas, C. and York, R. (2012): Women's status and carbon dioxide emissions: A quantitative cross-national analysis, *Social Science Research*, 41(4): 965–976. https://doi.org/10.1016/j.ssresearch.2012.03.008

Félix, A. (2015): Old missions in new clothes, *Intersections. East European Journal of Society and Politics*, 1(1): 166–182.

Forchtner, B. (ed.) (2019a): *The Far Right and the Environment: Politics, Discourse and Communication*. London: Routledge.

Forchtner, B. (2019b): Climate change and the far right, *WIREs Climate Change*, 10(5). https://doi.org/10.1002/WCC.604

Forchtner, B. (2019c): Nation, nature, purity: Extreme-right biodiversity in Germany, *Patterns of Prejudice*, 53(3): 285–301. https://doi.org/10.1080/0031322X.2019. 1592303

Forchtner, B. and Christoffer K. (2015): The nature of nationalism: Populist radical right parties on countryside and climate, *Nature and Culture*, 10(2): 199–224. https://doi.org/10.3167/nc.2015.100204

Franzen, J. (2010): Emptying the skies: In the Mediterranean, songbirds are being decimated for fun and profit – and in open defiance of law, *New Yorker*, 26 July 2010. www.newyorker.com/magazine/2010/07/26/emptying-the-skies (accessed June 2021).

Gaard, G. (2015): Ecofeminism and climate change, *Women's Studies International Forum*, 49: 20–33.

Griffin, R. (2012): Studying fascism in a postfascist age: From new consensus to new wave? *Fascism*, 1(1): 1–17.

Hall, S. (1997): *Representation: Cultural Representations and Signifying Practices.* London: Sage.

Hornsey, M. J., Harris, E. A., Bain, P. G. and Fielding, K. S. (2016): Meta-analyses of the determinants and outcomes of belief in climate change, *Nature Climate Change*, 6(6): 622–626. http://dx.doi.org/10.1038/nclimate2943

Huber, R. A., Maltby, T., Szulecki, K. and Ćetković, S. (2021): Is populism a challenge to European energy and climate policy? Empirical evidence across varieties of populism, *Journal of European Public Policy*, 28(7): 998–1017. https://doi.org/10.1080/13501763.2021.1918214

Hultman, M. and Pulé, P. M. (2018): *Ecological Masculinities: Theoretical Foundations and Practical Guidance.* London: Routledge.

Joireman, J. and Liu, R. L. (2014): Future-oriented women will pay to reduce global warming: Mediation via political orientation, environmental values, and belief in global warming, *Journal of Environmental Psychology*, 40: 391–400. https://doi.org/10.1016/j.jenvp. 2014.09.005

Kapsalis, N. (2021): Η 'σοβαρή' Χρυσή Αυγή στην Κύπρο, *Imerodromos*, 19 July 2021. www.imerodromos.gr/elam-i-sovari-chrysi-aygi-stin-kypro/ (accessed 4 October 2021).

Katsourides, Y. (2013): Determinants of extreme right reappearance in Cyprus: The National Popular Front (ELAM), Golden Dawn's sister party, *South European Society and Politics*, 18(4): 567–589. https://doi.org/10.1080/13608746.2013.798893

Kheel, M. (2008): *Nature Ethics: An Ecofeminist Perspective.* Lanham, MD: Rowman & Littlefield.

Kontos, M. and Bitsis, G. (2018): Power games in the Exclusive Economic Zone of the Republic of Cyprus: The trouble with Turkey's coercive diplomacy, *The Cyprus Review*, 30(1): 51–70.

Kulin, J., Johansson Sevä, I. and Dunlap, R. E. (2021): Nationalist ideology, rightwing populism, and public views about climate change in Europe, *Environmental Politics*, 1–24. https://doi.org/10.1080/09644016.2021.1898879.

Lockwood, M. (2018): Right-wing populism and the climate change agenda: Exploring the linkages, *Environmental Politics*, 27(4): 712–732. http://dx.doi.org/10.1080/09644016.2018.1458411

Loomis, E. (2021): Masculinity, work, and the industrial forest in the United States Pacific Northwest. In: P. M. Pulé and M. Hultman (eds), *Men, Masculinities, and Earth: Contending with the (m)Anthropocene.* Cham: Palgrave Macmillan, 269–287.

Lubarda, B. (2020): Beyond ecofascism? Far-right ecologism (FRE) as a framework for future inquiries, *Environmental Values*, 29(6): 713–732. http://dx.doi.org/10.3197/096327120X15752810323922

McCright, A. M. (2010): The effects of gender on climate change knowledge and concern in the American public, *Population and Environment*, 32(1): 66–87. https://doi.org/10.1016/j.gloenvcha.2011.06.003

McCright, A. M. and Dunlap, R. E. (2011): Cool dudes: The denial of climate change among conservative white males in the United States, *Global Environmental Change*, 21(4): 1163–1172.

Mudde, C. (2019): *The Far Right Today*. Oxford: Polity Press.

Neale, S. (1983): Masculinity as spectacle, *Screen*, 24(6): 2–17.

Ortner, S. B. (1972): Is female to male as nature is to culture? *Feminist studies*, 1(2): 5–31. https://doi.org/10.1093/screen/24.6.2

Pearse, R. (2017): Gender and climate change, *WIRES Climate Change*, 8(2). https://doi.org/10.1002/wcc.451

Plumwood, V. (2002): *Feminism and the Mastery of Nature*. London: Routledge.

Pulé, P. M. and Hultman, M. (eds) (2021): *Men, Masculinities, and Earth: Contending with the (m)Anthropocene*. Cham: Palgrave Macmillan.

Pulé, P. M., Hultman, M. and Wågström, A. (2021): Discussions at the table. In: P. M. Pulé and M. Hultman (eds), *Men, Masculinities, and Earth: Contending with the (m)Anthropocene*. Cham: Palgrave Macmillan, 17–101.

Pyne, S. (2019): *Fire: A Brief History*. Seattle: University of Washington Press.

Razac, O. (2000): *Barbed Wire: A Political History*, trans. Jonathan Kneight, New York: New Press.

Rose, G. (2007): *Visual Methodologies: An Introduction to Researching with Visual Materials*. London: Sage.

Roudometof, V. and Christou, M. (2015): 1974 and Greek Cypriot identity. In: R. Eyerman, J. C. Alexander and E. Butler Breese (eds), *Narrating Trauma: On the Impact of Collective Suffering*. Boulder, CO: Paradigm Publishers, 163–187.

Roy, S. S. (2018): *Linking Gender to Climate Change Impacts in the Global South*. Cham: Springer.

Schaller, S. and Carius, A. (2019): *Convenient Truths: Mapping Climate Agendas of Right-Wing Populist Parties in Europe*. Berlin: adelphi.

Sontag, S. (2001 [1973]): *On Photography*. New York: Farrar, Straus and Giroux.

Staudenmaier, P. (2004): Fascism. In: S. Krech III, J. McNeill and C. Merchant (eds), *Encyclopedia of World Environmental History*. London: Routledge, 517–521.

Szenes, E. (2021): Neo-Nazi environmentalism: The linguistic construction of ecofascism in a Nordic Resistance Movement manifesto, *Journal for Deradicalization*, 27: 146–192.

Tranter, B. (2013): The great divide: Political candidate and voter polarisation over global warming in Australia, *Australian Journal of Politics & History*, 59(3): 397–413.

Turner, J. and Bailey, D. (2022): 'Ecobordering': Casting immigration control as environmental protection, *Environmental Politics*, 31(1): 110–131.

Vasilopoulou, S. and Halikiopoulou, D. (2015): *The Golden Dawn's 'Nationalist Solution': Explaining the Rise of the Far Right in Greece*. New York: Palgrave Macmillan.

Vihma, A., Reischl, G. and Andersen, A. (2021): A climate backlash: Comparing populist parties' climate policies in Denmark, Finland, and Sweden, *The Journal of Environment & Development*, 30(3): 219–239.

Voss, K. (2014): *Nature and Nation in Harmony: The Ecological Component of Far Right Ideology*. EUI PhD theses. Florence: European University Institute. http://hdl.handle.net/1814/32125 (accessed 12 February 2022).

Warren, K. (2000): *Ecofeminist Philosophy: A Western Perspective on What It Is and Why It Matters*. Lanham, MD: Rowman & Littlefield.

Zelezny, L. C., Chua, P.-P. and Aldrich, C. (2000): Elaborating on gender differences in environmentalism, *Journal of Social Issues*, 56(3): 443–458.

6

The new Russian civilisation: Arctic fossil fuels, white masculinity and the neo-fascist visual politics of the Izborskii Club

Sonja Pietiläinen

Introduction

Due to its political and material consequences, the representation of geo-graphical spaces, with their natures and peoples, 'is of immense moral and political significance' (Livingstone, 2010: 8). Images – one form of representing – are never innocent (Rose, 2012) but play an important role in producing human–nature relationships (Hansen, 2018) and social identities (Foxall, 2013; Clark et al., 2020; Doerr, 2021), and in maintaining ideologies and power relations (Roberts, 2012). Drawing on work on political and visual geographies, this chapter investigates the relationship between natural resources and national identity in the context of far-right politics in Russia. More notably, this chapter investigates how the far right's visual politics regarding Arctic fossil fuels produce white masculine notions of national identity and, reciprocally, how ideas of white masculine national identity justify fossil fuel extraction.

The Russian Arctic has long been a site for nationalist and authoritarian politics centred around the control of territories and natural resources, especially oil and gas, which play a crucial role in the Russian political economy. Visuals have traditionally played an important role in Arctic politics: while most Russian have never travelled to the Arctic, widely circulating images in popular media, such as the Russian flag being deposited on the floor of the Arctic Ocean in 2007, have stirred nationalist sentiments in Russia and geopolitical concerns outside Russia (Dodds and Rowe, 2021). Indeed, representations of the Arctic have functioned as an important form of nationalist performativity, as the Arctic has been visualised as a site of various heroic, scientific and nationalist deeds (Dodds and Rowe, 2021). Furthermore, in more radical discourses in Russia, the Arctic is also a frontier for imperialist conquest and 'the homeland' of the white Russian race.

While the nationalist politics of the Russian Arctic have been extensively studied, little is known about what the Russian far right has to say about (Arctic) natural resources. Indeed, while contemporary research on the far right has shed light on the far right's affinity to fossil fuels and technology (for example, Malm and The Zetkin Collective, 2021) and on the greenwashing of anti-immigration discourses (for example, Forchtner and Kølvraa, 2015; Forchtner, 2019a), the perception of nature among the Russian far right is largely an unstudied field. Investigating the far right–nature nexus in the context of Russia is thus important, especially since the Russian context is indicative of the wider global rise of the far right (Arnold and Umland, 2018).

Against the background of the climate emergency and abundant hydrocarbon resources in the Arctic, the intertwining of nature and national identities on different material, symbolic and emotional levels becomes important. The relationship between nature and the social world is reciprocal. 'Natural resources' do not simply exist, waiting to be used, but are defined 'in relationship to the mode of production which seeks to make use of them and which simultaneously "produces" them through both the physical and mental activity of the users' (Harvey, 1974: 265). Fossil fuels play a special role in modernity because the continuous flow of cheap fossil fuels forms the basis of fossil capitalism. However, fossil fuels not only provide profits and power, but also contribute to making identities and political subjectivities (Daggett, 2018) and, consequently, also stir emotions (Kangasluoma, 2021).

In nationalist politics the interlinkages between fossil fuels and national identity can manifest as resource nationalism, which concerns 'how a state and its population should manage and distribute profits derived from natural resources' and also refers to expressions of national identity in which collective national belonging is 'expressed through the idiom of natural resources' (Koch and Perrault, 2019: 611–612). However, as scholars of nation and nationalism have long emphasised, national belonging is a socially produced category. Nations are not 'naturally' occurring social entities but are 'imagined' political communities (Anderson, 2006) that are produced through discourses and practices (Paasi, 2000; Anderson, 2006). Indeed, in producing national identity, 'individual and collective forms of identity become fused in time and space-specific ways' (Paasi, 2000: 4). Although often conceptualised as gender neutral, gendered visions play a crucial role in producing and reproducing a nation, mutually constructing gendered norms (Sharp, 1996). Stereotypical male citizens are often portrayed in the role of saviours of the nation while the nation is presented as figuratively female, as in, for example, the case of 'Mother Russia' (Sharp, 1996; Werbner and Yuval-Davis, 1999).

Against the background of research illustrating the important role that visual elements play in far-right politics for promoting traditional gender roles (see, for example, Forchtner and Kølvraa, 2017) and racially exclusive ideologies (for example, Doerr, 2021), this chapter analyses how gendered and racialised notions of national identities are produced in relation to the far right's visual politics regarding Arctic space and fossil fuels. That is, I examine how masculinity features in the production of white national identity. By masculinity I refer to socially produced identity that is constructed within a gender order that defines masculinity in opposition to femininity. There are various kinds of masculinities; importantly here, the far right advances a particular kind of hypermasculinity which is intertwined with the far right's authoritarian and illiberal aspirations (Daggett, 2018).

As such, my chapter asks three interrelated questions: What themes do the Izborskii Club's Arctic images portray and in what ways are these themes connected? How is a gendered and racialised notion of national identity produced in references to Arctic nature and hydrocarbons? How are ideas of white masculine national identity used to justify fossil fuel extraction? To answer these questions, I utilise a two-phase method in the analysis of the written material produced by the Izborskii Club: first, I conduct quantitative visual content analysis where I analyse all images regarding the Arctic (N = 57) to identify relevant themes. Second, I conduct qualitative iconographical interpretation of three images, analysing the production of national identity and its gendered and racialised dimensions.

The structure of this chapter is as follows. First, I discuss the Izborskii Club in the context of Russia's political sphere before next presenting a brief overview of the role of the Arctic in Russian nationalist politics. Third, the two-phase methodology is introduced. Fourth, the results are presented and discussed, and fifth, in conclusion, I summarise the key points of the chapter.

The Izborskii Club in Russian politics

I use the term 'far right' to refer to actors ranging from radical right to neo-fascist. The far right is not a homogenous movement (for example, Rydgren, 2018). However, what unites far-right individuals and collectives is authoritarianism and the political ambition to create an ethnically homogenous nation (for example, Copsey, 2018) that is often 'represented through the territorial state' (Ince, 2019: 2). The far right's politics furthermore revolve around ultranationalism and the idea of national rebirth (Griffin, 2013), imagining national 'revival' after a phase of degradation. This is evident in slogans such as 'Make America Great Again' or 'Restore Finland!' and based on the idea that, for example, multiculturalism and 'weak borders' are the cause of national degradation. It is via purifying the nation of unwanted 'others' and by restoring social hierarchies (for example, patriarchy) that the nation will return to its old 'glory'.

In Russia, the dividing line between far-right and mainstream politics is vaguer than in many other countries due to the authoritarian politics exercised by the cabinet of President–Prime Minister–President Vladimir Putin (Umland, 2007). Although the processes of racialisation existed already in Imperial Russia and the Soviet Union (Zakharov, 2015), the modern Russian state has undergone new ethnic and authoritarian developments over recent decades. If during President Boris Yeltsin's administration (1991–1999) Russian nationalism relied on the non-ethnic statist view of *rossiiskii narod* (Russian people as a political entity), the ethnically charged concept of *russkie narod* (Russian people as an ethnic entity) has been more commonly used since Putin's second presidential term (2004–2008) (Kolstø, 2016). *Russkie narod* as an ethnic entity refers above all to white Russians. Indeed, as argued by Zakharov (2015: 20), in Putin's contemporary nationalist politics the Russian nation is being reconstructed as the 'true civilizational centre [...] that will boldly dare to carry the white man's burden' and is 'determined to become as white as possible' (Zakharov 2015: 2). This idea of nation is widely circulated in Putin's public speeches, which represent Russian culture and identity as great and distinctive – interpellating ethnic Russians as being involved in the 'great mission' to 'unite and bind together the civilization' (Putin, 2012).

Since the beginning of the 2000s, Russia has started to build up different resources to challenge Western influence (Lutsevych, 2016). For instance, it has refined a policy of publicly funding nationalist actors that promote patriotic civil society (Laruelle, 2019). One of these organisations is the Izborskii Club, founded in the city of Izborsk in 2012 (Arnold and Umland, 2018; Bacon, 2018), a neo-fascist club which has become one of the most prominent far-right actors in Russia (Laruelle, 2019). The club was brought together by one of the most influential actors in Russian right-wing extremism, Alexandr Prokhanov, who gathered well-known politicians, thinkers and public figures that shared anti-liberal and extreme nationalist views, with the goal of influencing Russian politics (Laruelle, 2019). Although the club's members are not homogenous in their political views, they share extreme nationalistic and Eurasianist stances, thus 'idealizing the vision of a powerful imperialist Russia, the vision of imposing a Russian empire over the Euro-Asian continent' (Eberhardt, 2018: 134). While some of the club's members promote an imperialist view that recognises and allows multiple ethnicities, many of the key members 'have long been known for their efforts to introduce neo-fascist language, and even Nazi symbolism, to the Russian nationalist landscape' (Laruelle, 2019: 45).

Arctic fossil fuels in Russian national politics

By Arctic I refer to the region within the Arctic Circle north of latitude 60°N. Eight states have territory in the Arctic region, with approximately 10 per cent of the region's inhabitants belonging to Indigenous groups. Due to fossil fuel capitalism, climate change warms polar regions at three times the rate of global warming elsewhere, leading to disastrous impacts on local ecosystems and the cultural survival of Indigenous peoples. In global politics, the Arctic has moved to the centre of debates over climate change and geopolitical competition (Dittmer et al., 2011), as an increase in global consumption and demand for natural resources, as well as melting ice and new possibilities for transit routes, has sped up Arctic states' zeal to secure their shares of Artic resources.

The Arctic and its hydrocarbons have played an important yet contradictory role in the nationalist politics of Russia. During the times of the Russian Empire, the first steps towards modernising Arctic space were undertaken, including systematic colonisation of Indigenous lands. During this period, the interest in Arctic lands was driven by the desire to modernise the northern territories, which offered vast resources that would strengthen the empire (Klapuri, 2021). In the early twenty-first century, the Arctic re-emerged in Russia as a 'flagship for nationhood', becoming a key element in nationalist politics (Laruelle, 2011; Tynkkynen and Gritsenko, 2016). Although the Soviet Union did not have an official strategy for the Arctic (Tynkkynen and Gritsenko, 2016), the modern Russian state launched a series of strategies to transform the Arctic into a 'leading strategic resource base' (Ministry for the Development of the Russian Far East and Arctic, 2021).

Russia's political economy and geopolitical power is highly dependent on fossil fuels, which has also impacted how Russian society 'is governed and ruled' (Tynkkynen, 2019: 4). In 2019 the fossil fuel industry amounted to 14.2 per cent of Russia's gross domestic product and 59.9 per cent of its export earnings, making Russia the world's largest fossil fuel exporter (Makarov, 2021). Russia's political elite is organised around the fossil fuel industry and approximately 75 per cent of the country's wealth is owned by 1 per cent of the population (Tynkkynen, 2019). As such, the Russian government's current interest in the Arctic and its active role in the region's geopolitics can be explained by the strategic importance of the northern sea route and its desire for Arctic fossil fuels. The Arctic is one of the world's most important untapped hydrocarbon resources and even tighter control over Arctic resources would mean a continuity of fossil fuel flows and therefore the political economy and power relations they sustain. In 2016, the Arctic region was the source of approximately 20 per cent of Russia's crude oil and 80 per cent of its natural gas (Simola and Solanko, 2017). New Russian strategies aim at increasing this share significantly (Ministry for the Development of the Russian Far East and Arctic, 2021).

To ensure continued access and demand for oil and gas, Russia's government has strengthened authoritarian politics and practices, such as supporting far-right actors with fossil fuel money (Tynkkynen, 2022). Furthermore, the government has also had to justify to its citizens hydrocarbon's central role in the Russian economy and politics, 'turning the focus from systemic economic and societal problems caused by the fossil energy dependence to producing conflicts on the international arena in hopes that the construction of an outside threat will unite the Russian people' (Tynkkynen, 2019: 5). Indeed, as argued by Rutland (2015: 67), fossil fuels play a contradictory role in Russian national identity because Russians widely reject the notion of Russia as merely a producer of raw materials and do not include them into the national narrative.

In the light of the far right's affinity with fossil fuels (Malm and The Zetkin Collective, 2021), it is thus no surprise that some of the most prominent neo-fascists in Russia have mobilised a slew of different methods to legitimatise the burning of fossil fuels. In these discourses, the Arctic is 'the promised land, the source of Russian myth and spirit' where, with the help of oil and gas, a new 'Arctic civilisation' will be created (Moskovskij Komsomolets, 2016). Neo-fascists have also evoked the Aryan myth that perceives the Russian Arctic, or 'Hyperborea', as a homeland of Aryan, white Russians, who are 'the forefathers of the White Race, and all the other "white people"' (Shnirelman, 2014: 127). One active defender of the Aryan myth is the aforementioned Alexandr Dugin. Dugin legitimatises the dreams of imperialist territorial expansion by presenting the Arctic as 'the original lands of human history' (Dugin, 1993: 3). These racist and imperialist ideas are widely circulated in public and, in the context of mainstreamed ethnonationalism, positively received in Russia. Thus, they shape public opinion about the Arctic (and its hydrocarbons) as being Russia's destiny, both in material but also spiritual ways (Laruelle, 2019).

Analysing the conflation of nature and identity: data and methods

The analysis presented below draws on photographic images, maps and written texts published in the Izborskii Club's journal *Russkie strategii* (Russian strategy). The journal has been published monthly since 2013, the year the club was founded, and belongs to the Russian tradition of 'thick journals', as each journal is approximately 140 pages long. The journal is the primary channel for the club to spread its political messages and it is publicly available on the club's website.[1] It includes policy recommendations and political analyses for the political elite of Russia, reflecting the policy-oriented nature of the club, and is well designed.

The image corpus was built by searching seventy-nine issues of the journal for the terms 'Arctic' (*Arktika* (noun), *arkticheskaya/arkticheskiy* (adjective)) 'Polar' (*Polyarnaya/polyarnoy*) and 'North' (*Sever*). In so doing, I analyse all issues published to date – from the first published article in 2013 to the time of the analysis in June 2021. I selected articles that mentioned the terms in the headline or lead paragraph to ensure that the article's focus is on the analysed subject. This resulted in a corpus comprising sixteen articles and fifty-seven images.

The analysis was conducted in two phases. First, a quantitative content analysis of the visual images attached to articles, policy reports and columns regarding the Arctic examined the dominant themes and how these themes are connected. I conducted content analysis by assigning at least one code to each image. The main categories (*people, nature, industry/technology*) were predefined, drawing on studies on depictions of the environment (Hansen, 2018) and the Arctic (Haines-Young and Potschin, 2012; Runge et al., 2020).

In the second phase, I drew on the method of visual iconography. Iconographic analysis is a qualitative method of interpretation that departs from the notion that images communicate by a logic of symbolic association (Müller and Özcan, 2007). The method explores the meanings of images by situating them in specific historical and geographical contexts and by identifying the intertextualities which grant the images their meanings (Müller and Özcan, 2007; Müller, 2011; Rose, 2012). The method has been applied in analysing socially produced identities that rely on gendered and racialised stereotypes (for example, Wonders, 2005). Thus, my aim was to locate what kinds of meanings the images produced regarding national identity, gender and race by examining the different associations that the images communicated. Following Müller (2011), the analysed images were selected based on their relevance to the research. Accordingly, I chose images that featured elements from the most prevalent subcategories (*ice, maritime transportation* and *science*). Since the images can communicate an enormous amount of politically and culturally specific information, the accompanying texts were used to help define the meaning of the analysed images. Drawing on the work of van Straten (2012), the analysis was conducted by first describing each image. Second, I situated each image in relation to other analysed images. Third, I conducted iconographic interpretation, aiming to explore the symbolic meanings by analysing the images in relation to their wider historical and cultural context.

A white nation's rebirth

Arctic nature in numbers

I initially approached the data via a quantitative content analysis which indicated how frequently certain visual themes occur. The category *nature* is the most frequent theme (present in forty-six out of fifty-seven images). Non-living environments dominate the pictures, as most images portray nature as abiotic (forty-four images) and only seven images feature biotic nature. The most significant subcategories within abiotic nature are *frozen water* and *water* (thirty-eight and nineteen images, respectively). The most significant subcategories in biotic nature are *wildlife* (five images) and *plants* (two). Of the fifty-seven images, forty-three feature *technology/industry*, the second most significant theme. In this theme, the subcategory of *maritime transportation* plays the most important role, as twenty-three images featured different maritime vessels, such as ice breakers. The second most significant subcategory is *fossil fuel industry* (twelve images), which contains images of, for instance, oil platforms. The third most significant theme is *people* (twenty-nine images). More specifically, the portrayed people are not 'ordinary'; rather, the most numerous subcategories are scientist/explorer (eleven images) and politician (six images).

Non-living nature, such as soil, bedrock and frozen water, play the most important role in the images – even though the Arctic also consists of various living elements, such as tundra plants and wildlife. Non-living nature is rarely portrayed alone but instead as a background for technology and industry. As O'Lear (2020: 196) argues, the elements of the Arctic environment that are or are not shown in different contexts depend on political motives. Indeed, 'different perspectives may focus on particular elements of these larger, interconnected processes depending on the argument'. The prevalence of non-living nature, maritime transportation and the fossil fuel industry indicates that Arctic nature is represented in terms of its potentialities for the hydrocarbon industry. Non-living nature is emphasised to give the impression of an empty resource hinterland. Such depictions of the Arctic as frozen and 'dead' are not new but have been used throughout history to justify territorial expansion, natural resource exploitation and colonialism (Bloom et al., 2008). For example, content analyses of tourist's social media images of Arctic nature show a predominance of images that reflect the large diversity of nature (mammals, birds, fish, plants) (Runge et al., 2020), while in the context of politics that aim to advance natural resource extraction, Arctic nature is often visualised as dead and empty (Bloom et al., 2008).

Contrary to existing research, which illustrates that people are the most common elements in visuals of the natural environment (Hansen, 2018), the material analysed here features people less frequently than technology/ industry. The people that feature in the club's images of the Arctic are not 'ordinary' but scientists, explorers and politicians: people that occupy expert positions and/or are part of the political elite. The prevalence of the former illustrates that the analysed images present nature as an object for scientific and industrial interests, drawing on a modernist view of the human–nature relationship which views nature as a passive object to be studied, monitored and utilised for fossil fuel-dependent economic expansion that would benefit the Russian 'nation'.

Content analysis provided a 'background map' for the iconographic analysis and for the investigation of gendered and racialised notions of national identity. The next part of the analysis revolves around the three most important themes found in the content analysis: *ice*, *maritime transportation* and *scientists*.

Polar dream

The first analysed image (Figure 6.1) is selected from the category *ice*. It appears in an article titled 'People of the Polar Dream' (*Lyudi polyarnoy mechty*) written by Alexandr Prokhanov (2016a). It is the entrance image of an article regarding an Izborskii Club meeting devoted to 'the creation of a new Arctic civilisation to replace the Soviet one that has vanished' (Prokhanov 2016a: 3). The topics of the meeting included discussing the 'countless riches of the Arctic' and planning new infrastructure projects relating to the fossil fuel industry and the military (Prokhanov 2016a: 3).

The image portrays a Russian ballistic missile submarine breaking through thick ice in the Arctic Ocean. The frontal angle creates direct involvement between the viewer and the submarine (see van Leeuwen, 2011). Arctic nature is frozen and abiotic, and ice shimmers under the sun. Over half of the image depicts light blue sky. In Russian symbolism, light blue is associated with spirituality (Paramei, 2007) and with dreaming and hope. The image's symbolism partially contrasts with the message of the text: While the image signifies power and the advanced state of Russian technology, in the written text Prokhanov expresses his concerns over obstacles to Artic development, as new infrastructure projects require advanced technologies that are not yet developed or cannot be borrowed from the West because of sanctions. As such, the image supposedly serves as 'proof' that hope for the future is warranted, despite the challenges.

The image's colour symbolism is in line with the headline of the article that presents the Arctic as a dream of the *white* Russian nation. Narrating Arctic fossil fuels as a 'common' dream is a way to unite people around a historically and spatially specific identity: an imagined group of people

6.1 'People of the polar dream'

(nation) is told to have their own destiny which conquering the Arctic would fulfil. In the image, this dream Arctic future is portrayed in terms of potential conflict (military submarine breaking through the ice) and in terms of successful conquest (the soldier peeking from the submarine victoriously) of 'countless riches', in other words Arctic oil and gas. Furthermore, the image can be viewed as an act of territory-making, as spaces (and natural resources) are nationalised through national iconographies (submarine). The submarine symbolises not only national power but also imperialist pursuits, as Prokhanov (2016a: 2) explicitly argues that 'the Arctic is becoming a springboard for new Russian expansion. A Russian world, a new Arctic civilisation.'

In the image, the nation is gendered: the act of exploring and clearing the path for the new civilisation and securing Russian lands (against invaders) is presented as a masculine duty. Military troops symbolise masculinity and masculine power, as traditionally men occupy military services and are perceived as 'protectors' of the feminised nation and its non-male members. The soldier standing on top of the submarine in the cold and harsh (yet sunny) environment at the frontier of Arctic civilisational development symbolises masculine bravery, heroism and endurance.

Untapped Arctic oil and gas resources are framed as being the key for unlocking the new Arctic civilisation. According to Prokhanov (2016a: 5), without 'mastering' the riches of the Russian north, 'full development of Russia is impossible'. This becomes illustrated particularly well in his nostalgia:

> The drillers washed their happy faces with this oil, laughed, rejoiced, glorified the beginning of the great oil boom when Russian oil [...] pushed the entire Soviet civilisation forward. [...] And today the people take a new deep breath, filled with strength, full of great feelings, of the great Russian dream. This dream rushes to the Arctic. (Prokhanov 2016a: 5)

As such, utilisation of Arctic fossil fuels is justified by highlighting their importance for Arctic civilisation (that is, the white Russian nation), but also by emphasising the positive emotions that new fossil fuel sites would bring. Fossil fuels are presented as a necessity for achieving national rebirth and this rhetoric aims at uniting the imaginary group of people who, according to the text, share the same dream. Here, emotions play an important role, as the Russian people are presented as 'full of great feelings' about new oil and gas resources. That is, emotions are stirred when fossil fuels are framed as bringing positive impacts to the lives of Russians (see, Kangasluoma 2021).

Technology as the key for unlocking Russian civilisation

The second analysed image (Figure 6.2), this time from the category *maritime transportation*, appears in an article titled 'Arctic – The Izborskii Club's Philosophy of the Common Task' (*Arktika – Izborskiy klub filosofiya obshchego dela*), written, again, by Prokhanov (2016b). This is the last image in an article in which Artur Shilingarov, a famous Russian polar explorer and close associate of Putin, is interviewed. The article discusses Shilingarov's career and his perspectives on the future of the Arctic. The article presents the utilisation of the Arctic as a national duty, as 'the vital

6.2 '50 years of victory'

interests of Russia, [as] her future is inseparably linked with the Far North and the Arctic' (Prokhanov, 2016b).

The image depicts a nuclear icebreaker that moves in the open Arctic Ocean. Small clouds and the light portray the icebreaker almost as divine. Furthermore, the light blue sky occupies over half of the picture, and thus gives a heavenly impression. A calm sea gives the impression of easy accessibility. The angle of the image, a frog's-eye view, makes the icebreaker look even more powerful in relation to both the small snow-covered mountain in the background and the viewer. Indeed, depicting an object from below signifies that it has symbolic power over the viewer (Jewitt and Oyama, 2011). Although barely visible, two small figures, most likely members of the crew, stand on the deck of the icebreaker, alongside 'big' technology. Depicting humans from a long distance was also applied in Figure 6.1, which is a method for anonymising and for portraying humans 'as though they belong or should belong to "our group", and that the viewer is thereby addressed as a certain kind of person' (Jewitt and Oyama, 2011: 16). In the context of the analysed material, this emphasises togetherness and unity, and can foster a sense of national belonging.

Various national symbols, such as the double-headed imperial eagle and the text '50 years of victory' (*50 let pobedy*), link the icebreaker to the Russian nation. Furthermore, the image symbolises the opening of the sea and territory-making, as the state-owned icebreaker is designed for clearing paths and developing new energy projects in the Arctic. Both this and the previous image give an impression of easy accessibility and the advanced state of technology that can be utilised in developing the Arctic and utilising its oil and gas resources. A similar way of portraying the Arctic in terms of accessibility has been noted elsewhere. Dodds and Powell (2013: 2), for instance, argue that the growing interest in Arctic natural resources has created visualisations of the Arctic as 'a polar Mediterranean, with associated notions on accessibility and exploitation'.

Furthermore, and like the previous picture, this image of Arctic nature conveys a masculine frame, as technology is conventionally viewed as a masculine enterprise. As also noted by others (Bloom et al., 2008; Dittmer et al., 2011), the Arctic has historically been a site for performing and promoting certain kinds of masculinities as it is narrated in terms of exploration and adventure, and is presented as a site for manly duties associated with bravery and courage.

Arctic as scientific laboratory

The third analysed image (Figure 6.3) is from the category *science* and appears in an article titled 'Arctic – Laboratory of the Planet' (*Arktika – laboratoriya planety*) by Alexandr Peterman (2016), a known businessman and polar explorer, and the chairman of the club's Arctic branch. The image is situated within the context of *Nordic troopers*, an Izborskii Club project led by Peterman which brings together scientists and members of the military in order to explore the nature and people of the Arctic. According to Peterman (2016), the expeditions not only have a scientific purpose but also a military one as they conduct 'reconnaissance', 'patrol' and 'fight opponent groups'.

National iconography ties Nordic Troopers and Peterman to national pursuits, as Peterman's jacket is decorated with the logo 'Russia, Nordic Troopers, Expedition' (*Rossija Severnii desant, ekspeditsija*) and includes a Russian flag in the corner of the logo. In the picture, which looks edited,

6.3 'Arctic as scientific laboratory'

Peterman looks unnaturally large. He is depicted alone and close up, which is a method to highlight his individuality (contrary to showing him as a member of a group) (van Leeuwen, 2011). Peterman's size and gestures reflect masculine authority, rationality and expertise with respect to knowing and defending the Arctic; the frontal angle presents him as an object to identify with. Peterman is presented as an active actor who is heroically exploring new territories at the Arctic frontier. His scrutinising eyes and serious face give the impression of an observant and cautious person who is facing the future (the right). His bare head and open jacket in the cold Arctic represent masculine endurance, and consequently, the image represents Russian nation-building as a masculine act.

While the two previous images were dominated by blue light, this one features peach/light yellow. The colours used when visualising the Arctic have differed over time, depending on the purpose. For example, during the Russian Empire, the Arctic was pictured as grey and static, as a means to compare Russia to more modernised Europe and, thus, to justify the modernisation of Arctic spaces (Klapuri, 2021). In contrast, this image's dreamy lighting constructs a positive notion of Arctic territories as easily exploitable and stirs positive emotions which, in turn, frame fossil fuel as having positive impacts on human lives.

The image also points to territorial expansionism and colonialism, as the returning expedition group (four snowmobiles) is portrayed in contrast with the wide horizon of vast and 'empty' space (although the Arctic has historically been inhabited by numerous Indigenous groups). In its wider political context, the image represents the frontier of Russia, the site where civilisation expands. The new Arctic civilisation is built around racial lines, as the space is presented as empty and as a destiny for ethnic Russians. Drawing on Frederic Jackson Turner's frontier thesis, which argues that the western frontier of the United States produced American identity around the ideas of civilisation and 'American Spirit' (Turner, 1921), the construction of the Russian Arctic frontier too can be viewed as a site of nation-building and the reproduction of Russian national identity around spatial and racial lines. Russian civilisation is thus expanding: a reborn, fossil fuel-powered, white masculine nation.

To summarise, the club's representations of nature as frozen and dead, yet in harmony with technology and human activity, functions as a means to frame Arctic fossil fuels as accessible and easily exploitable by masculine, white nationalist men. The Arctic was represented as a resource hinterland and its hydrocarbon resources were presented as being the material entitlement of the Russian nation and thus rightfully belonging to white Russians. The exploitation of Arctic fossil fuels was justified because it is the 'destiny' of the Russian nation, which was further emphasised by highlighting fossil fuels' symbolic and emotional value. Arctic oil and gas were framed as the means to fulfil Russian destiny and thus to achieve national rebirth. Exploration of Arctic territories and resources was also justified by drawing on positive emotions, such as joy and hope, while rationality was emphasised by highlighting technological and scientific progress. That is, the images draw on the viewer's positive feelings of the Arctic as an easily exploitable and open space where the dreams of the Russian national community will come true.

Although the images and the text attempted to mobilise sentiments of national unity, the nation was defined in exclusive forms, as the members of the nation were defined based on class, race and gender lines. In the analysed materials, women, Indigenous people, non-white Russians and workers (for instance, those who operate the oil platforms) were absent or presented only from a long distance (Figure 6.2). A white male was the protagonist of the Russian Arctic story and, as such, hydrocarbon extraction and nation-building were presented as a gendered social practice. Soldier (Figure 6.1), worker (Figure 6.2) and scientist/explorer (Figure 6.3), traditionally masculine roles, contributed to nation-building through searching for new fossil fuels: he penetrated (Figure 6.1, 6.2 and 6.3), monitored (Figure 6.3) and protected (Figure 6.1) Arctic territories and their resources. These figures were narrated as knowledgeable, rational and brave; in turn, these traits award them with the authority that legitimatises their subjectivities. While the Russian state is not an exception in colonising Indigenous peoples' lands, the situation of Indigenous peoples and other minorities is particularly constrained in contemporary Russia, where authoritarian policies have reduced political freedoms, repressed dissent and made social justice extremely difficult. For instance, due to the new 'foreign agent' law, several non-governmental organisations working on civil rights or Indigenous issues have ceased operations.

The rebirth of the white nation is the underlying goal of the Izborskii Club and, accordingly, this can only be achieved by exploiting Arctic fossil fuels. Fossil fuels are important for the far right because fossil fuels have ensured the prosperity and power of white nation-states. As argued by Daggett (2018: 2), 'leaving fossil fuels in the ground likely means leaving trillions of dollars of profit in the ground' and it also threatens 'vast networks of privilege' sustained by fossil fuel economies. This is why the fossil fuel economy has historically relied on authoritarianism to ensure its continuity.

Conclusion

Because it operates in tandem with the state, the Izborskii Club plays an influential role in defining the far right and national imaginary in Russia (Eberhardt, 2018). In light of the new Russian Arctic strategy, Russia will continue expanding fossil fuel activity and developing the northern sea route. As such, dreaming about untapped fossil fuels is not new in the Russian political context (Tynkkynen, 2019) and, thus, cannot be reduced to the Izborskii Club. However, by framing this in specific symbolic and emotional ways, the Izborskii Club presents fossil fuels as the means to build the new Arctic civilisation.

Nationalism that was expressed with reference to Arctic natural resources was exclusionary and based on ethnic and gendered hierarchies. The club's ethnic notions of national identity and masculinity are not unusual in the context of contemporary Russian ethnic nationalism. This further confirms the claim that the dividing line between the far-right and 'mainstream' political discourse is not clear. However, what separates the club's communication from 'mainstream' nationalism is the dream of territorial expansion and national rebirth that was also used to justify the utilisation of Arctic fossil fuels.

Some scholars of the environmental politics of the far right conceptualise 'far-right ecologism' as a distinctive environmental view where 'respect for everything "natural" arises from instinct qualities of nature' (Lubarda, 2019: 13). A similar line of argument is also presented by Forchtner (2019b), who argues in the context of research on extreme-right communication in Germany that the far right shows signs of a special kind of ecological sensitivity that sees humans as embedded in their ecosystems (see also Olsen, 1999). The analysed material of the Izborskii Club's Arctic visualisations shows, however, a different picture. Contrary to some far-right parties and movements (see Forchtner, 2019a), the Izborskii Club does not romanticise nature, for instance, by presenting it as wild, untouched and atemporal. Instead, the club presents (Arctic) nature in the context of rationality, technology and progress, though not in universal terms but as a bounded (national) space. The Arctic is a site for the development of new technologies and the accumulation of primitive fossil fuel capital – a space that turns nature into white masculine power.

Notes

1 See https://izborsk-club.ru (accessed on 3 February 2022).

References

Anderson, B. (2006): *Imagined Communities: Reflections on the Origin and Spread of Nationalism.* London: Verso.

Arnold, R. and Umland, A. (2018): The radical right in post-Soviet Russia. In: J. Rydgren (ed.), *The Oxford Handbook of the Radical Right.* Oxford: Oxford University Press, 582–607.

Bacon, E. (2018): Policy change and the narratives of Russia's think tanks, *Palgrave Communications*, 4(1): 1–12. https://doi.org/10.1057/s41599-018-0148-y

Bloom, L., Glasberg, E. and Kay, L. (2008): Gender on ice: Introduction. http://sfonline.barnard.edu/ice/intro_01.htm (accessed 1 February 2022).

Clark, K., Hawkins, R. and Silver, J. J. (2020): Gender, nature and nation: Resource nationalism on primary sector reality TV, *Environment and Planning E: Nature and Space*, 3(4): 1196–1214.

Copsey, N. (2018): The radical right and fascism. In: J. Rydgren (ed.), *The Oxford Handbook of the Radical Right.* Oxford: Oxford University Press, 105–121. https://doi.org/10.1177%2F2514848619899785

Daggett, C. (2018): Petro-masculinity: Fossil fuels and authoritarian desire, *Millennium: Journal of International Studies*, 47(1): 25–44. https://doi.org/10.1177 %2F0305829818775817

Dittmer, J., Moisio, S., Ingram, A. and Dodds, K. (2011): Have you heard the one about the disappearing ice? Recasting Arctic geopolitics, *Political Geography*, 30(4): 202–214.

Dodds, K. and Powell, R. (2013): Polar geopolitics: New researchers on the Polar regions, *The Polar Journal*, 3(1): 1–8. https://doi.org/10.1016/j.polgeo.2011.04.002

Dodds, K. and Rowe Wilson, E. (2021): Red Arctic? Affective geopolitics and the 2007 Russian flag-planting incident in the central Arctic Ocean. In: M. Lehtimäki, A. Rosenholm and V. Strukov (eds), *Visual Representations of the Arctic*. Abingdon: Routledge, 178–195.

Doerr, N. (2021): The visual politics of the Alternative for Germany (AfD): Anti-Islam, ethno-nationalism, and gendered images, *Social Sciences*, 10(1). https://doi.org/10.3390/socsci10010020

Dugin, A. (1993): *Giperboreyskaya teoriya: Opyt ariosofskogo issledovaniya*. Moscow: Arktogeia.

Eberhardt, P. (2018): The Izborsk Club and their geopolitical phantasmagorias, *Studia Polityczne*, 46(3): 129–144.

Forchtner, B. (ed.) (2019a): *The Far Right and the Environment*. London: Routledge.

Forchtner, B. (2019b): Nation, nature, purity: extreme-right biodiversity in Germany, *Patterns of Prejudice*, 53(3): 285–301. https://doi.org/10.1080/0031322X.2019.1592303

Forchtner, B. and Kølvraa, C. (2015): The nature of nationalism, *Nature and Culture*, 10(2): 199–224. https://doi.org/10.3167/nc.2015.100204

Forchtner, B. and Kølvraa, C. (2017): Extreme right images of radical authenticity: Multimodal aesthetics of history, nature, and gender roles in social media, *European Journal of Cultural and Political Sociology*, 4(3): 252–281. https://doi.org/10.108 0/23254823.2017.1322910

Foxall, A. (2013): Photographing Vladimir Putin: Masculinity, nationalism and visuality in Russian political culture, *Geopolitics*, 18(1): 132–156. https://doi.org/10.108 0/14650045.2012.713245

Griffin, R. (2013): *The Nature of Fascism*. London: Routledge.

Haines-Young, R. and Potschin, M. (2012): Common international classification of ecosystem services (CICES, Version 4.1), *European Environment Agency*, 33. https://cices.eu/.

Hansen, A. (2018): Using visual images to show environmental problems. In: A. F. Fill and H. Penz (eds), *The Routledge Handbook of Ecolinguistics*. New York: Routledge, 179–195.

Harvey, D. (1974): Population, resources and the ideology of science, *Economic Geography*, 50(3): 256–277.

Ince, A. (2019): Fragments of an anti-fascist geography: Interrogating racism, nationalism, and state power, *Geography Compass*, 13(3). https://doi.org/10.1111/gec3.12420

Jewitt, C. and Rumiko, O. (2011): Visual meaning: A social semiotic approach. In: T. van Leeuwen and C. Jewitt (eds), *The Handbook of Visual Analysis*. London: Sage, 134–156.

Kangasluoma, S. (2021): Experiencing (in)securities in northern Norway: Narratives of emotion and extractivism, *The Extractive Industries and Society*, 8: 1–8.

Klapuri, T. (2021): The winners of the globe? The Russian imperial gaze at the north in late nineteenth-century travelogues. In: M. Lehtimäki, A. Rosenholm and V. Strukov (eds), *Visual Representations of the Arctic*. Abingdon: Routledge, 81–98.

Koch, N. and Perreault, T. (2019): Resource nationalism, *Progress in Human Geography*, 43(4): 611–631. https://doi.org/10.1177%2F0309132518781497

Kolstø, P. (2016): *The Ethnification of Russian Nationalism*. Edinburgh: Edinburgh University Press.

Laruelle, M. (2011): Russia's narrative on the Arctic: From patriotic rhetoric to the Arctic 'brand', *Baltic Rim Economies*, 4: 5–6.

Laruelle, M. (2019): *Russian Nationalism: Imaginaries, Doctrines, and Political Battlefields*. Abingdon: Routledge.

Livingstone, D. N. (2010): *Putting Science in Its Place*. Chicago: University of Chicago Press.

Lubarda, B. (2019): Beyond ecofascism? Far-right ecologism (FRE) as a framework for future inquiries, *Environmental Values*, 29(6): 713–732. https://doi.org/10.319 7/096327120X15752810323922

Lutsevych, O. (2016): Agents of the Russian world: Proxy groups in the contested neighbourhood. *Chatham House Research Paper*. www.chathamhouse.org/sites/default/files/publications/research/2016-2004-2014-agents-russian-world-lutsevych.pdf (accessed 2 February 2021).

Makarov, I. (2021): Does resource abundance require special approaches to climate policies? The case of Russia, *Climatic Change*, 170(3). https://doi.org/10.1007/s10584-021-03280-0.

Malm, A. and The Zetkin Collective (2021): *White Skin, Black Fuel: On the Danger of Fossil Fascism*. London: Verso.

Ministry for the Development of the Russian Far East and Arctic (2021): Strategiya razvitiya Arktiki do 2035 goda utverzhdena! www.arctic2035.ru/ (accessed 11 November 2021).

Moskovskij Komsomolets (2016): Bogatstvo Rossii prirastat' budet Arktikoy. https://ugra.mk.ru/articles/2016/06/28/bogatstvo-rossii-prirastat-budet-arktikoy.html (accessed 15 October 2021).

Müller, M. G. (2011): Iconography and iconology as a visual method and approach. In: E. Margolis and L. Pauwels (eds), *The SAGE Handbook of Visual Research Methods*. London: Sage, 283–297.

Müller, M. G. and Özcan, E. (2007): The political iconography of Muhammad cartoons: Understanding cultural conflict and political action, *PS: Political Science & Politics*, 40(2): 287–291. https://doi.org/10.1017/S104909650707045X

O'Lear, S. (2020): Environmental geopolitics. In: A. Kobayashi (ed.), *International Encyclopedia of Human Geography*. Amsterdam: Elsevier, 193–200.

Olsen, J. (1999): *Nature and Nationalism: Right-Wing Ecology and the Politics of Identity in Contemporary Germany*. Basingstoke: Macmillan.

Paasi, A. (2000): Territorial identities as social constructs, *Hagar: International Social Science Review*, 1(2): 91–113.

Paramei, G. V. (2007): Russian 'blues'. In: R. E. MacLaury, G. V. Paramei and D. Dedrick (eds), *Anthropology of Color: Interdisciplinary Multilevel Modelling*. Amsterdam: John Benjamins, 75–106.

Peterman, A. (2016): Arktika: laboratoriya planet, *Izborskii Club: Russkiye Strategii*, 8–9(44–45): 58–63.

Prokhanov, A. (2016a): Lyudi polyarnoy mechty, *Izborskii Club: Russkiye Strategii*, 8–9(44–45): 2–5.

Prokhanov, A. (2016b): Arktika: Izborskiy klub filosofiya obshchego dela, *Izborskii Club: Russkiye Strategii*, 8–9(44–45): 6–17.

Roberts, E. (2012): Geography and the visual image: A hauntological approach, *Progress in Human Geography*, 37(3): 386–402.

Rose, G. (2012): *Visual Methodologies: An Introduction to Researching with Visual Materials*. London: Sage.

Runge, C. A., Hausner, V. H., Daigle, R. M. and Monz, C. A. (2020): Pan-Arctic analysis of cultural ecosystem services using social media and automated content analysis, *Environmental Research Communications*, 2(7). https://doi.org/10.1088/2515-7620/ab9c33

Rutland, P. (2015): Petronation? Oil, gas, and national identity in Russia, *Post-Soviet Affairs*, 31(1): 66–89. https://doi.org/10.1080/1060586X.2014.952537

Rydgren, J. (2018): *The Oxford Handbook of the Radical Right*. Oxford: Oxford University Press.

Sharp, J. (1996): A feminist engagement with national identity. In: N. Duncan (ed.), *Bodyspace: Destabilizing Geographies of Gender and Sexuality*. London: Routledge, 97–107.

Shnirelman, V. (2014): Hyperborea: The arctic myth of contemporary Russian radical nationalists, *Journal of Ethnology and Folkloristics*, 8(2): 121–138.

Simola, H. and Solanko, L. (2017): Overview of Russia's oil and gas sector, *BOFIT Policy Brief*, 5.

Turner, F. J. (1921): *The Frontier in American History*. New York: Henry Holt.

Tynkkynen, V.-P. (2019): *The Energy of Russia: Hydrocarbon Culture and Climate Change*. Cheltenham: Edward Elgar Publishing.

Tynkkynen, V.-P. and Gritsenko, D. (2016): Arktinen Venäjän poliittisessa viestinnässä, *Idäntutkimus*, 23(4): 3–18.

Tynkkynen, V.-P. (2022): Valtapolitiikkaa öljyn jälkeen: Miten vihreä energiasiirtymä muokkaa Euroopan ja Venäjän välejä? Webinar held by *Finnish Journal of Foreign Affairs*, 17 January 2022.

Umland, A. (2007): *Post-Soviet 'Uncivil Society' and the Rise of Aleksandr Dugin: A Case Study of the Extraparliamentary Radical Right in Contemporary Russia*. https://ssrn.com/abstract=2892325 (accessible 12 February 2022).

van Leeuwen, T. (2011): *The Language of Colour: An Introduction*. London: Routledge.

van Straten, R. (2012): *An Introduction to Iconography: Symbols, Allusions and Meaning in the Visual Arts*. London: Routledge.

Werbner, P. and Yuval-Davis, N. (ed.) (1999): *Women, Citizenship and Difference*. London: Zed Books.

Wonders, K. (2005): Hunting narratives of the Age of Empire: A gender reading of their iconography, *Environment and History*, 11(3): 269–291. http://dx.doi.org/10.3197/096734005774434511

Zakharov, N. (2015): *Race and Racism in Russia*. Hampshire: Palgrave Macmillan.

7

Not so green after all: visual representation of green issues by the far-right Kotlebovci – People's Party Our Slovakia

Radka Vicenová, Veronika Oravcová and Matúš Mišík

Introduction

The Slovak far right comes in many shapes, ranging from civic associations, such as *Slovenská pospolitosť* (the Slovak Togetherness Party) and *Slovenské hnutie obrody* (the Slovak Revival Movement), to paramilitary groups engaged in combat and military training and vigilance activities, including *Slovenskí Branci* (the Slovak Conscripts) and *Akčná Skupina Vzdor Kysuce* (the Action Group Resistance Kysuce). However, a substantial segment of far-right supporters gathers around what has so far been the most successful far-right political project of the Slovak Republic (that is, since 1993, when the country gained independence): *Kotlebovci – Ľudová strana Naše Slovensko* (Kotlebovci – People's Party Our Slovakia, ĽSNS). Differing in terms of political strategy, forms of communication and degree of radicalism, all of the above-mentioned groups have a common ideological origin and belong to the far right – a term used in this chapter for political actors situated at the far-right end of the right-wing political spectrum, characterised by aggressive nationalism, myth of the homogeneity of the nation, xenophobic and chauvinist views towards minorities and opposition to the principles of liberal and pluralist democracy, or even democracy as such (Mudde, 2002, 2019). With its neo-Nazi background (Mareš, 2018), ĽSNS revolves around nationalist and anti-minority attitudes, revisionism and glorification of the clerical fascist Second World War Slovak state, and idealised views of the nation and its history. The latter refers to Slavic tradition, including the connection to nature, the country's natural beauty, rural people, traditional values and natural resources providing wealth for the country.

While the party's communication has been dominated by anti-minority rhetoric, especially in its depiction of the Roma minority and immigration as security threats (Kluknavská, 2013; Kluknavská and Smolík, 2016), it also includes the natural environment as a symbol and national treasure.

As such, ĽSNS's protectionist attitude is reflected in regular calls to protect (Slovak) nature – for example, in its electoral manifestos (called the Ten Party Commandments; ĽSNS, 2016) – as well as the imagery featured in the party's promotional materials. Although an increasing volume of literature deals with environmental issues in relation to far-right narratives, it has been illustrated that far-right stances vis-à-vis environmental aspects are not always in line with their stances towards climate (Lockwood, 2018). Therefore, in this chapter, we examine how ĽSNS addresses what we call green issues, a term which encompasses both environmental and climate issues, to offer a broad perspective.

ĽSNS uses both online and offline communication with its voters and sympathisers. To understand the party's visual presence, one cannot rely on an analysis of electronic channels, such as social media, since they have been seriously disrupted in recent years. After both the party's and the party leader's official Facebook pages were blocked in April 2017 (as part of a massive drive which took down numerous ĽSNS-related channels, some of them with tens of thousands of followers), ĽSNS has been without an official Facebook presence. Since then, the party has relied on a few remaining unofficial Facebook pages, closed Facebook groups and the marginal Facebook pages of regional branches.[1] Moreover, the availability of (visual) content of the ĽSNS official web page is limited. The web page containing the history of articles and materials published since the foundation of the party in 2010 was taken down by the party itself in early 2020, presumably as a precaution following a lawsuit against the ĽSNS leader for supporting and promoting groups aimed at suppressing fundamental rights and freedoms. An alternative version of the web page has since been introduced but offers only very limited content. Therefore, our analysis focuses on the party's newspaper, *Naše Slovensko* (*Our Slovakia*). Although political parties are increasingly turning their attention towards online communication, a party's newspaper is still an important instrument for spreading its vision and ideology (Santo and Costa, 2016).

The aim of this chapter is threefold. First, to map the visualisation of green issues by ĽSNS as presented in its newspaper; second, to compare this visualisation with the written presentation in the same medium; and third, to examine whether there is an emotional charge or rational argumenta-tion prevalence among green (and non-green) issues. This chapter examines a case from Slovakia, a country outside of western Europe – the region that has enjoyed the most academic attention with regard to the study of the far right and the environment. Our analysis is based on an examination of 6,002 sentences and 339 images collected from thirty-eight issues of the newspaper published by ĽSNS between January 2013 and March 2021. The analysis shows that green issues are only marginally discussed in the party newspaper. However, compared to non-green issues (which are dominated by hatred and anger emotions), newspaper texts dedicated to green issues present their arguments mostly by asserting ĽSNS's competence in this area and pride in Slovak nature.

The chapter proceeds as follows. The next section offers a general overview of ĽSNS, its ideological background, political development and position within Slovak politics. The third part provides a brief overview of the theoretical assumption the chapter is built on, while the fourth part presents its methodology. The final sections discuss our results. The conclusion summarises the main findings and offers avenues for future research.

The Slovak far-right political party ĽSNS

ĽSNS was founded in 2010 by Marian Kotleba, who took control of the Party of the Friends of Wine (*Strana priateľov vína*) and renamed it the People's Party Our Slovakia (later Kotleba – People's Party Our Slovakia). ĽSNS leaders thus bypassed the rule requiring them to collect at least 10,000 citizen signatures to register a new political party with the Ministry of the Interior of the Slovak Republic. The party leaders have a background in the 2000s extreme-right scene, some of them even being associated with the 1990s neo-Nazi scene (Mareš, 2018). The first attempt by ĽSNS leaders, in particular the long-term chairman Marian Kotleba, to enter politics was linked to the extreme-right civic association Slovak Togetherness and its associated political party *Slovenská pospolitosť – Národná strana* (Slovak Togetherness – National Party). This party was active for only one year before being dissolved by the Supreme Court of the Slovak Republic in 2006.

After marginal gains in the 2010 and 2012 parliamentary elections (1.33 per cent and 1.58 per cent, respectively), ĽSNS gained victory in the 2013 regional elections as Kotleba was elected governor of the Banská Bystrica region (in office between 2013 and 2017). The regional success of the party was soon followed by nationwide success in the 2016 parliamentary elections, in which ĽSNS became the fifth strongest political party with 8.04 per cent of votes and fourteen Members of Parliament (MPs), marking the first time a far-right political party was elected to the Slovak National Parliament since the Second World War. The party repeated its electoral success in the 2019 European Parliament elections, gaining 12.07 per cent of the vote and two seats. ĽSNS was again successful in the 2020 parliamentary elections, this time coming in fourth with 7.97 per cent of the vote and seventeen MPs. Soon after the elections, in early 2021, a group of ĽSNS MPs led by Milan Uhrík, the then speaker of the party and elected member of the European Parliament, left ĽSNS and established a new political party,

Republika (The Republic), which has a similar agenda and ideological background to ĽSNS.

ĽSNS has been the strongest far-right political actor in Slovakia and is considered to be nationalist, anti-minority, anti-immigrant, anti-European and anti-liberal democracy by official authorities (Ministry of Interior of the SR, 2015). Anti-minority and nationalist attitudes have been an essential part of ĽSNS's political identity. While topics on its agenda have stayed the same over the course of the party's political history, its political presentation has gradually developed. Violent and aggressive anti-minority – mostly anti-Roma – attacks by members of neo-Nazi movements were frequent in the past (Struhár, 2016). They were later followed by a series of demonstrations led by Slovak far-right movements in 2008 and 2009, then grouped under Slovak Togetherness. Recent strategies have mostly been limited to verbal assaults, hostile claims and 'othering', taking place predominantly through social media (Kluknavská and Hruška, 2018; Kluknavská and Smolík, 2016).

Nationalist sentiments and pride in Slovakia as the homeland of the nation have been reflected in a variety of ĽSNS's political activities. Its public self-presentation is based on identification with the legacy of historical figures associated with national independence, with an emphasis on national and territorial integrity (Mesežnikov and Gyárfášová, 2016). The party's romantic ideas about the Slovak nation, reflected (among other things) in its stance towards nature and natural resources, are especially prominent in ĽSNS's use of its associated youth organisation *Ľudová mládež* (The People's Youth) to stress the importance of 'educating the young generation of the Slovak nation in the spirit of patriotic and Christian values', while also 'protecting nature from pollution and devastation in order to preserve the untouched beauty of the Slovak land for future generations' (People's Youth, 2021). Moreover, the topic of aggressive nationalism and protectionism is also reflected in militant and vigilante activities which demand that the homeland be protected against foreign elements, as well as in calls to protect the territorial integrity of the country (Mesežnikov and Bránik, 2017; Vicenová, 2020).

ĽSNS has built its ideological profile by openly praising the legacy of the Slovak State (1939–1945), a client state of National Socialist Germany, and its dominant party, *Hlinkova slovenská ľudová strana* (Hlinka's Slovak People's Party). This includes not only aggressive anti-minority positions (often accompanied by Holocaust denialism; the previously dominant anti-Semitism has recently been replaced by anti-Roma and anti-immigrant sentiments), but also exclusionary nationalist sentiments. The Slovak state is celebrated by members of Slovak far-right movements as the first success of the nation's independence, while its clerical fascist government led by

Jozef Tiso (later executed as a war criminal) is seen as the first milestone and significant symbol of Slovak nationalist identity.

The independence of the Slovak nation is therefore closely connected to the concept of 'homeland', defined by its political borders but also by well-known natural symbols, such as rivers or mountains. Its romantic perceptions can also be traced back to nationalist efforts of nineteenth-century historical figures engaged in political, social and cultural activities, including the creation and development of the Slovak language. The tradition of the national climb to the Kriváň peak (often used as a national symbol by the far right), recently revitalised by ĽSNS, has its origins in the nineteenth century and was started by a national group of literates, linguists and cultural personalities called *Štúrovci* (named after its most prominent member, Ľudovít Štúr). These historically grounded and symbolic ties to Slovak territory are in line with theoretical understandings of the role of nature in far-right ideology. Moreover, it provides a background for the current positions of far-right parties regarding the treatment of nature, natural resources and green issues in general.

Establishing the link between the far right, environmental issues, visual communication and emotional charges

Recent research has argued that the natural environment serves strong symbolic functions for the far right and is closely connected to the nationalist element of far-right ideology, as it imagines an idealised homeland: a territory with its resources that is exclusively 'ours' (Forchtner and Kølvraa, 2015; Forchtner, 2020). The literature on nationalism explains the importance of nature and environmental protection in the wider ideology of the far right on different levels. Ideologically, nature as part of the homeland has a strong symbolic function in terms of emphasising the ties between nation and territory (Smith, 1999), as well as other members of the nation whose shared identity is strongly tied to the territorial environment. In this way, nature serves as an idealised and romantic symbol of the nation (Forchtner and Kølvraa, 2015), or embodies the mysticism and spirituality that ties the nation to the land (Lubarda, 2020). This provides the basis for support for environmental protection or even for arguments related to natural resources which are seen as the nation's property and right (Forchtner and Kølvraa, 2015). By this means, environmental issues on the agenda of the far right reinforce nativist and anti-establishment narratives (Tosun and Debus, 2021). However, it is not uncommon for far-right actors to deny aspects of the environmental protection agenda – particularly climate change – since, as research suggests, climate is less likely to be part of the national identity in the same way as the natural environment and landscape (Forchtner, 2019). Indeed, sceptical positions towards climate change and policy responses, often presented as being connected to the agenda of cosmopolitan elites (Lockwood, 2018), are common.

A rise in public interest in green issues in the previous decade (von Zabern and Tulloch, 2021) brought about an increase in scholarly interest in their visualisations (Duan et al., 2017; Hansen, 2018), even though, according to Niemelä-Nyrhinen and Uusitalo (2021), these visual representations are often stereotypical and focused on several major themes. The literature has also examined visual art (for a review, see Rice et al., 2019) and the reception of visual messages (for a review, see Wang et al., 2018), be they in the form of film (Manzo, 2017), or popular science magazines (Born, 2020). When it comes to the far right, research claims that visual depictions of nature, outdoor life, and harmony help recontextualise these parties within mainstream politics (Westberg and Årman, 2019), which is also closely connected to emotions such as fear regarding the security of the people and territory, or nostalgia for an idealised past (Hurd and Werther, 2016). Emotions are considered to play a crucial role in far-right ideology as they are intertwined (Virchow, 2007) with the emotional component powerfully affecting voters by helping to mediate the feelings of pride and enthusiasm related to the in-group, but also the feelings of fear and alienation related to the out-group (Rivera Otero et al., 2021). Most importantly, emotions reinforce a sense of shared identity and belonging (Hokka and Nelimarkka, 2019). As such, they are key aspects to be considered when engaging with political communication and meaning-making, although, to the best of our knowledge, research on whether or not emotional charges of far-right narratives are balanced by rational argumentation has not been properly conducted.

Dissecting ĽSNS: the what and the how

To address the visual depiction of green issues in ĽSNS's communication we analysed thirty-eight issues of the party newspaper, each ranging between four and twelve pages and published between January 2013 and March 2021. The newspaper, *Naše Slovensko*, offers comprehensive sources of information on the party's political views and reflects its authentic positions (Santo and Costa, 2016), unmodified by external editors, as is the case with statements published in the media. The newspaper reflects ĽSNS's political priorities at a given time, providing researchers with an opportunity to study party positions and their prioritisation over time.

Each sentence and image – our units of analysis – in the thirty-three issues that constitute our corpus was coded and analysed separately (excluding the elements of standardised newspaper layout such as header and footer, which recur in each issue). This approach enabled us to track the diversity of topics covered in greater detail and record instances in which different topics appeared within one article. Moreover, the approach helped us record all comments on green topics, even those included within discussions on other topics, and enabled a detailed analysis of emotional charge.

The analysis captures almost a decade of the party's political development, even though it should be noted that the distribution of issues over time is irregular. In 2013, the newspaper was published on a monthly basis, but only occasionally during other periods (but in regional variations, as in 2018) or not at all (as in 2015). For 2021, only pre-September issues were included in our research due to the finalisation of the data collection for this chapter. In total, the dataset contains 6,002 sentences and 339 images spanning 337 articles (Figure 7.1). These were written by thirty-one different authors, with more than half of the articles (220) written by an anonym. The majority of articles with named authors were written by high-ranking ĽSNS members who were also MPs during the 2016–2020 election period, including the chairman of the party, Marian Kotleba, who wrote forty articles. The highest number of sentences (1,478) appears in the 2013 issues, while most images (eighty-nine) were identified in the 2019 issues. Indeed, since 2013, the party has increased the amount of visual content in its newspaper.

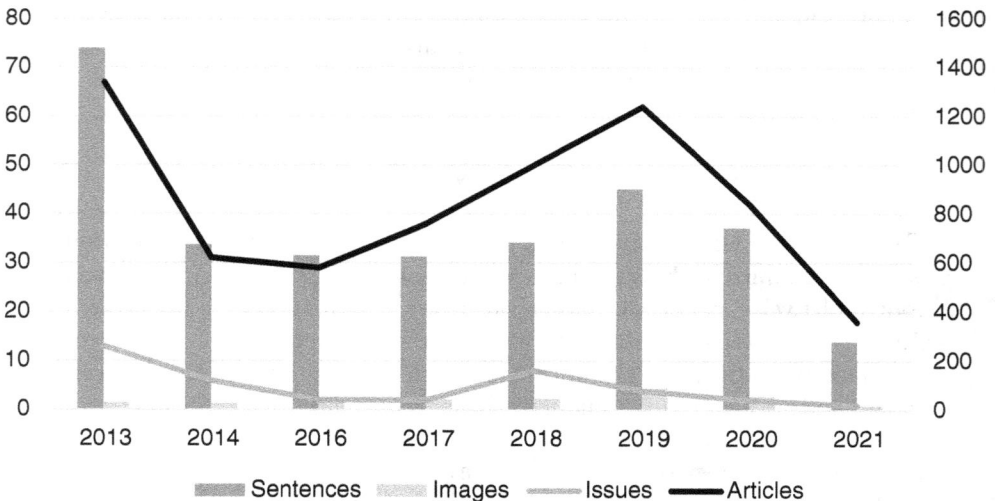

7.1 Distribution of issues, articles (left axis), sentences and images (right axis) by year; no newspapers were published in 2015

We analysed our dataset in two steps. First, each researcher coded one-third of the newspaper issues, while discussing the progress and nuances with the other researchers. The codebook has two parts. The first part contains basic information about each unit (main topic and object of the sentence or image), as well as information on whether a given sentence is related to green topics and whether it is emotionally (Amusement–Feeling good–Enthusiasm; Empathy–Compassion–Solidarity; Pride–Membership–Ambition; Fear–Threat–Insecurity; Anger–Disgust–Hate; Justice–Honesty) or rationally (Competence–Knowledge–Reliability; Concrete data–Statistics) charged (EEMC, 2019). This allowed us to examine the role of emotions and their prevalence with respect to individual topics, particularly green issues, and to assess the extent to which the party uses data or rational arguments to support its claims. The second part of the codebook focuses on visual aspects of the ĽSNS newspaper. We coded whether the analysed units are images, headlines, subheadings or standard sentences, and whether the sentences are in any way highlighted (for instance, bold, underlined, written in colour, or with a highlighted background; Kress and van Leeuwen, 1996).

In the second step of our analysis, individual sentences and images coded as relevant for green issues were analysed qualitatively. The visual analysis of the images was based on the key assumption that visual communication is emotive, engages audiences and enforces written narratives (Di Francesco and Young, 2011), while significantly contributing to the way in which issues are framed and depicted in the public debate (Chouliaraki and Stolić, 2019). Although low in number, the examined images present the entirety (rather than a sample) of the party's visual communication within this newspaper and thus provide a comprehensive insight into how green topics are visually depicted and communicated in this medium.

Green (and non-green) issues in numbers: energy autarky, nature protection and absence of climate change

Of the overall number of sentences coded (6,002), only 188 (approximately 3.1 per cent) were coded as being connected to green issues, with eleven out of 339 images related to these topics (approximately 3.2 per cent). Green issues are mentioned in forty-two articles, three of which are exclusively dedicated to these topics. These numbers can be considered rather low, especially as two of ĽSNS's political priorities are connected to promoting ecological and sustainable solutions; specifically, the party's goal is 'to build and deepen a truly social, market- and ecologically-oriented economy, based on private ownership and the support of a broad business class', as well as

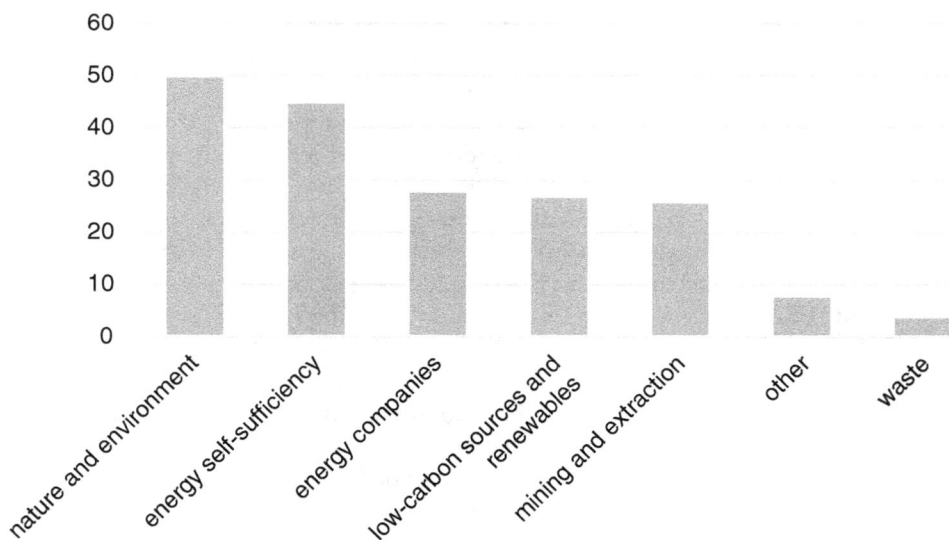

7.2 Number of sentences on green issues in ĽSNS newspaper

'to promote sustainable life on Earth, thus preserving it for future generations' (Kotlebovci, 2021).

Taking note of this discrepancy, the findings of our content analysis of the textual representation of green issues are presented in Figure 7.2. The largest group, with fifty sentences (28 per cent), falls within the nature and environment category (including topics such as nature protection, logging, nature wealth and environmental quality), followed by arguments on energy self-sufficiency, mentioned in forty-five sentences (25 per cent). Energy companies are mentioned in twenty-eight sentences (15 per cent), low-carbon and renewable energy sources in twenty-seven (15 per cent), and mining and extraction in twenty-six sentences (14 per cent). Waste is the main subject four times, while eight sentences fall within the category of 'other' (miscellaneous). Sentences in the last category are not primarily concerned with green issues, although they contain arguments related to nature and the environment. For example, one article supports a strongly pro-life position by making a comparison between environmental protection on the one hand and abortion rights on the other: 'It is absurd that in the civilised society of the twenty-first century the rights of trees, forests, dogs, and cats should be protected more than the rights of unborn children' (Our Slovakia, 2019a).

When it comes to green topics, ĽSNS devotes its attention to conservation and the environment but not climate: We found only one mention of 'climate' in the whole dataset. The newspaper often declares that nature is valuable and should be protected; however, no specific environmental agenda was identified, apart from calls to protect Slovak forests in the context of criticising companies for their excessive logging and selling unprocessed wood abroad, which is in line with anti-globalist and protections framing typical of the far right.

ĽSNS demands energy self-sufficiency for Slovakia, but it does not provide details. Specific measures and solutions are offered in only one article, which calls for increased utilisation of nuclear energy and promotion of thorium-based nuclear power (Mészáros, 2013). When it comes to renewable sources of energy, the party acknowledges their potential only once without being specific, when it claims that: '[w]e see the future of Slovakia in the use of alternative and renewable resources that save nature and money' (Schlosár, 2016). Moreover, ĽSNS strongly supports alternative fuels in the transport sector, and discusses the advantages of liquefied petroleum gas and compressed natural gas in fourteen articles. The party even prepared a bill developing a subsidy scheme for rebuilding vehicles with internal combustion engines to enable them to use these types of fuels (National Council of the SR, 2018).

ĽSNS is critical of the privatisation of energy companies which leads to high energy prices and profit for foreign companies, while at the same time condemning corruption in state-owned energy companies. The negative stance of a far-right party towards private energy companies is not surprising (Dinc and Erel, 2013). ĽSNS emphasised the need to nationalise energy companies so as to prevent foreign owners from exporting profits outside of Slovakia. When the party protested against fracking and mining in the Banská Bystrica region, it argued that 'we will not allow our nature to be irretrievably destroyed by the ruthless profiteering of the owners of mining companies' (Schlosár, 2016). Its anti-mining activities were especially intensified during the period when Kotleba was the governor of this region (2013–2017).

The emotional and rational charges of the analysed sentences are presented in Figure 7.3. Differentiating between the emotional and the rational allowed us to look at the way in which ĽSNS communicates various topics and identify differences between green and non-green issues. When it comes to green issues, the largest group of sentences (fifty-six) falls within the Pride–Membership–Ambition category, which comprises emotional statements presenting ambitious goals without specifically indicating how to achieve them; for example, 'We value Slovak nature more than a gold chandelier!' (Our Slovakia, 2016) or 'We will return the water, electricity, gas or land owned by foreigners to the nation!' (Schlosár, 2016). Competence–Knowledge–Reliability is the second-largest category with fifty-four sentences. It is relatively

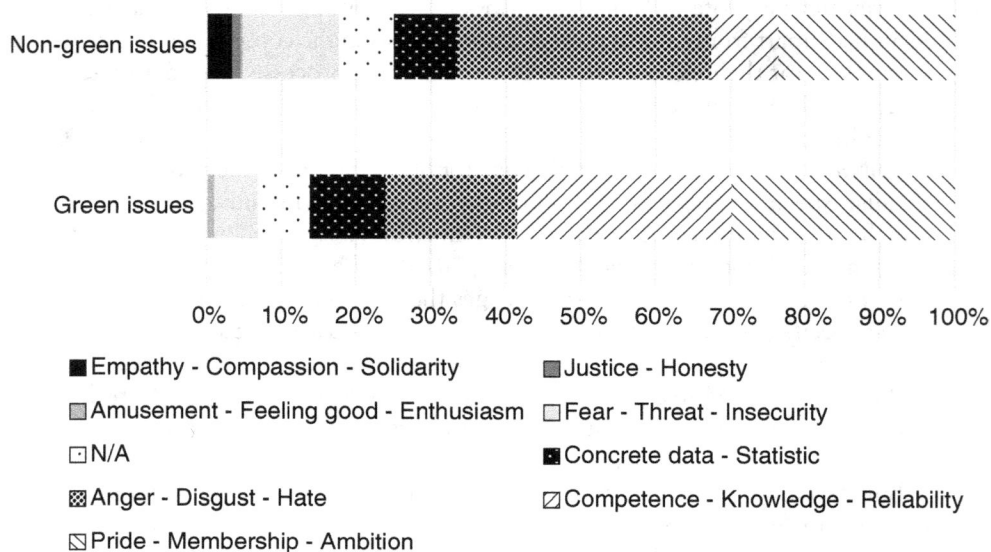

7.3 Emotional versus rational charges

larger compared to its non-green counterpart, which indicates that the party tries to use specific arguments and facts when debating green issues. This approach is most visible in discussions on alternative fuels and energy self-sufficiency. However, only nineteen sentences were identified within the Concrete data–Statistics category – that is, rational argumentation instead of emotional appeal – indicating that the party does not emphasise facts and numbers in its argumentation related to green topics.

Anger–Disgust–Hate was identified in thirty-three green issues-related sentences, with anger towards politicians and (foreign) energy companies gaining profit being especially prominent: 'The Germans, Italians, and French are constantly raising the prices of electricity, water, and gas, just to make as much profit on us as possible' (Our Slovakia, 2019b). This category is the largest within the non-green group, expressing attitudes towards other politicians, the Roma minority, the European Union and Western values and institutions. The Fear–Threat–Insecurity category was identified in eleven green sentences, which is relatively less compared to the non-green group. A category with marginal occurrence is Amusement–Feeling good–Enthusiasm (two sentences). Thirteen sentences do not fit any of the categories and were therefore coded as N/A. These are neutral statements, such as the occupation of the party's candidate for elections.

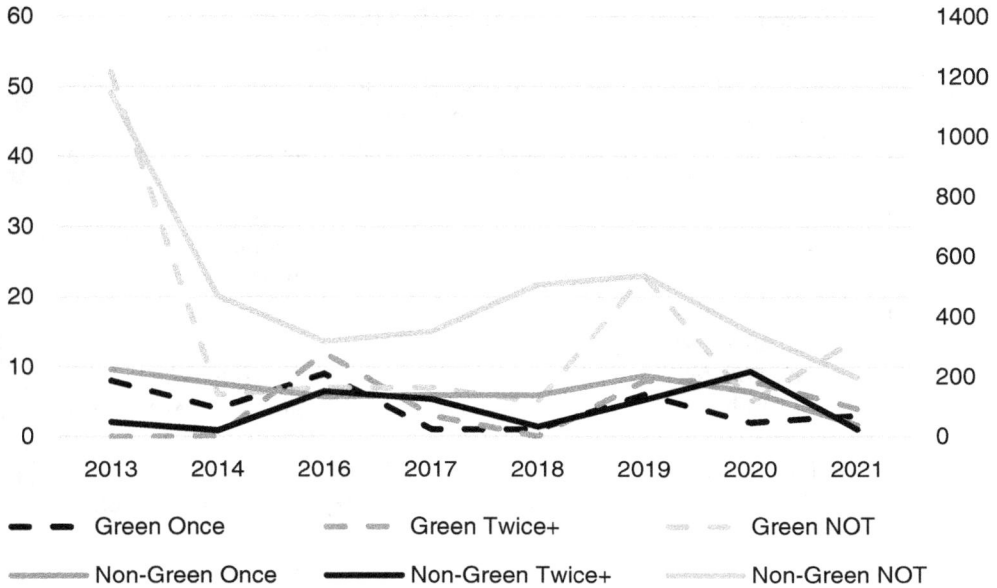

7.4 Visual highlighting of the text (green issues: left axis, non-green: right axis)

Lastly, we looked at the visual highlighting (bold, colour, underlined or with a coloured background) of the analysed texts (Figure 7.4). Green issues are not highlighted at all in 119 cases, which is more than 63 per cent (this is similar to the results for non-green-issue sentences: 66 per cent). Green sentences are highlighted with one feature in 18 per cent of cases (for example, bold); non-green sentences are highlighted in 21 per cent of cases. Two and more highlights were identified in almost 19 per cent of cases within green and almost 13 per cent within non-green issues. Green issues are therefore not visually prioritised over other topics on the ĽSNS agenda.

However, we see differences over time. At the beginning of the examined period (2013 and 2014), sentences are highlighted only rarely. Subsequently, the party begins to increasingly highlight its content, especially by using colours and bold type, presumably to boost the accessibility and appeal of its communication. The majority of highlighted sentences appear in 2020, when most of the content is visually emphasised. In 2021, the text is not highlighted as much, but the party starts to use large images. When it comes to green topics, highlighting is most prevalent in 2016 and 2020 (years of parliamentary elections) in the context of the party's critique of corruption in energy companies, mining activities and calls for the nationalisation of energy companies.

Green issues on the ĽSNS agenda: what does it mean?

Despite being a small corpus, our dataset offers a complete look at ĽSNS's green communication. A qualitative consideration of the 11 images and 188 sentences helps us further explore the core message of the party's environmental communication. Looking at the content of the sentences, the text directly proclaims ĽSNS's admiration for Slovak nature ('God has given us the most beautiful land in the world' (Schlosár, 2016)); criticises established methods of extraction, production or consumption from the perspective of their consequences for the environment ('We will defend Slovak nature from mining companies' (Schlosár, 2016)); or calls for food, economic and energy self-sufficiency of the Slovak Republic, referring to the Second World War Slovak state ('Industry prospered, we produced quality goods, we were food and energy self-sufficient' (Our Slovakia, 2014)).

When looking at the wider context of individual sentences on green topics, three prevailing messages were identified. The most frequent message identified is *stopping the destruction of nature*, which emphasises the negative impacts of industrial production on the environment or other activities directly destroying nature, such as logging and mining ('We will tighten penalties for environmental devastation' (Schlosár, 2016)). The second most visible message is *appealing to self-sufficiency*, especially in the energy sector ('Energy self-sufficiency at a reasonable price is worthwhile for the state to start investing in modern and ecological technologies instead of thieves and parasites!' (Mészáros, 2013)). Finally, the text presents green issues in relation to the *fight against corruption and foreign companies*, which is another type of protectionist view on green issues, this time from an economic perspective ('We will not allow foreigners to buy Slovak land and water, or mine its mineral wealth!' (Our Slovakia, 2020)). Protectionist attitudes accompanied by an emphasis of the importance of land, nature and its resources further underline the nationalist charge of ĽSNS's environmental positions: calling for nature protection not for nature itself but because it is important for the nation.

A detailed analysis of images related to green issues provided further information on how these issues relate to nationalism as a core element of ĽSNS's far-right ideology and, at the same time, how this is consistent with Pride–Membership–Ambition, identified as the emotion most often associated with green issues. Five images present landscapes and mountains, mostly partial views of well-known peaks; for instance, a picture of Kriváň peak in High Tatras, identified as a symbol of Slovakia through the accompanying phrase 'For Our Slovakia. National, Christian, and socially just!', and mountains and landscapes serving as a background in photos of ĽSNS members and supporters. Four images show forests, such as a photo of logging and activities taking place in forests, including a series of photos showing ĽSNS members collecting garbage. Finally, flowers and plants appear as dominant features in two images, in both cases as illustrative elements within drawings with nationalist and traditional (religious) undertones. The content of these pictures underlines the importance of territory as well the symbolic value of natural monuments for the Slovak nation and its (both territorial and metaphorical) independence. This is constantly emphasised and serves as the basis for protectionist sentiments, as well as appeals for renewing Slovakia's self-sufficiency.

In terms of topics with which the analysed images are associated, tourism and nature is the umbrella topic in four pictures, including those depicting hiking trails and mountains, but also those showing supporters and sympathisers participating in ĽSNS activities in nature. Three pictures show predominantly nationalist and traditional content, for example, collage artwork depicting Christian symbols, Slovak national symbols and historical figures associated with the ideas of Slovak independence and sovereignty. Two pictures refer to the topic of nature protection and garbage collection, both depicting ĽSNS members taking part in cleaning the forest. Certain variations can also be observed when looking at who is depicted. Apart from four cases in which people are not depicted, the images show either groups of ĽSNS members and sympathisers (including images of a children's summer camp organised by the party) or drawn characters – symbolic depictions of Slovak people or historical figures (representatives of different sections of society, including a priest, a soldier, a worker and a mother with a child). These depictions of 'ideal Slovak subjects' are articulated against the symbolic background of Slovak nature.

Contrary to the messages identified within sentences, images tend to be framed rather positively. Here, we also identified three key messages (based on the wider context of the published images, including their accompanying text). *Pride and protection* refers to images emphasising nature and natural elements as nationalist symbols of the Slovak nation, as well as symbols of the Christian religion, an idealist vision of Slovakia and its people. These images are set in the context of the necessity to strengthen national pride and enhance the protection of the symbols and traditions they depict. *Getting to know Slovak nature* brings together images which also contain elements of pride in Slovak nature, but its message primarily revolves around actions and initiatives aimed at learning about and exploring Slovak nature. Such images often accompany reports on the specific actions and initiatives organised by ĽSNS and led by its members, targeting the public and youth with educational and awareness-raising activities. Images conveying *care for Slovak nature and landscape* either depict the actions of forest cleaning and garbage collection and warn about the potential consequences of neglected nature protection, or are attached to articles reporting on concerns regarding soil cultivation and food self-sufficiency.

Conclusion

This chapter examined the visual representation of green issues in the party newspaper of ĽSNS, the dominant far-right political party in Slovakia. The study of the visual aspects of the newspaper was complemented with an analysis of the content of the written text. In total, we examined thirty-eight issues of the ĽSNS newspaper published between 2013 and 2021, and collected 6,002 sentences and 339 images. Of these, only 188 sentences and 11 images were connected to green issues, responding to our question regarding the extent to which ĽSNS, as a representative of the Slovak far right, visualises green issues. Despite the party's proclaimed interest in green issues, as described in their manifestos, there is not much actual presentation of such topics in its primary medium of communication.

When it comes to green issues, more than half of them (53 per cent) are connected to energy and confirm protectionist and anti-globalist attitudes typical of the far right. These range from energy sufficiency and support for renewable sources of energy to criticism of the privatisation of energy companies and foreign investors. Support for renewables is in contrast with the position of the German *Alternative für Deutschland*, which uses economic disappointment with green transition to mobilise its supporters (Brock et al., 2021), as well as the findings by Hess and Renner (2019) on the negative stance taken by right-wing parties towards renewables being expensive and cost prohibitive.

The party's position on energy self-sufficiency is not surprising as self-sufficiency is a key nationalist goal connected to agriculture and other economic sectors (Forchtner and Kølvraa, 2015; Lubarda, 2020). The discussion on climate change in the newspaper is almost non-existent: The issue is addressed in only one sentence (out of 6,002). This does not correspond to the findings of previous research focused on climate change stances within the far right, which emphasises its rather sceptical positions towards the issue (Forchtner, 2019; Jylhä and Hellmer, 2020).

Concerning our second research aim regarding how and in what context green issues are communicated in written and visual form, our analysis showed that when presenting its position on green issues, ĽSNS tends to promote ambitious goals without specifying how to meet them. Even in situations when the party wants to highlight its competence, the newspaper does not offer specific solutions. With regard to differences in how green and non-green issues are depicted, we could not identify any major difference concerning highlighting the text covering green and non-green issues, with minor differences found only within individual publication years.

When looking at the emotional versus rational charge of the claims (the third research aim of this chapter), pride and competence regarding green issues are in stark contrast to anger and hatred, which dominate non-green issues. The prevalence of pride as the key emotion connected to environmental issues is in line with existing research on this topic, which highlights the relevance of emotions such as pride or belonging to the in-group (in this case, the nation) within far-right ideology (Hokka and Nelimarkka, 2019; Rivera Otero et al., 2021). Moreover, we identified efforts to use specific arguments and facts within sentences related to green issues (as opposed to non-green issues), mostly visible when discussing alternative fuels and energy self-sufficiency. Nevertheless, ĽSNS's use of specific data in relation to green topics was not recorded to a significant extent. A more detailed explanation of these observations should be the subject of further research.

Looking at the content of the images depicting green topics, we found that they mostly present a positive message regarding the beauty of Slovak nature and the need to protect and get to know it better. Through the images, ĽSNS mostly aims to highlight the frame of pride and protection, ambitions to get to know Slovak nature or even activities aimed at taking care of nature and the landscape, such as forest cleaning and garbage collection (see also Chapter 3 in this volume). This finding further confirms theoretical assumptions about the importance of nature and natural landscape in the ideology of the far right, particularly in relation to these parties' nationalist attitudes.

Against this background, interesting tendencies are observable in the way ĽSNS approaches green issues. Emphasising nature as a powerful symbol of an idealised homeland for a nationalist ideology, which represents the territorial integrity of the nation, ĽSNS uses images to present nature as a romantic symbol of the nation and its roots. This is more visible in older issues of the ĽSNS newspaper, while images in more recent issues depict elements of nature in connection to topics of nature and environmental protection, although the element of pride in nature as a national treasure is still observable. Moreover, the lack of climate-related discussions within ĽSNS's newspaper is rather puzzling, as is the party's support for alternative fuels for vehicles (liquefied petroleum gas and compressed natural gas). Future research should focus on explaining these findings.

Notes

This work was supported by the Slovak Research and Development Agency under the contract No. APVV-20–0012. The authors would like to thank Michaela Hrabušajová for her research assistance, the civic initiative Not in Our Town from Banská Bystrica for their help with data collection, the European Election Monitoring Center led by Roma Tre University for helping with the codebook and Nada Kujundžić for language editing.

1 In Slovakia, Facebook has long been the major social network and is considered to have greater significance than Twitter or Instagram. For this reason, political actors focus primarily on Facebook when developing their online presence, so by disrupting the ĽSNS Facebook pages, the direct link between the party and its voters/sympathisers has been significantly weakened.

References

Born, D. (2020): Visual climate communication: Making facts and concerns in popular science magazines. In: U. Felt and S. R. Davies (eds), *Exploring Science Communication: A Science and Technology Studies Approach*. London: Sage, 109–130.

Brock, A., Sovacool, B. K. and Hook, A. (2021): Volatile photovoltaics: Green industrialization, sacrifice zones, and the political ecology of solar energy in Germany, *Annals of the American Association of Geographers*, 111(6): 1756–1778. https://doi.org/10.1080/24694452.2020.1856638

Chouliaraki, L. and Stolić, T. (2019): Photojournalism as political encounter: Western news photography in the 2015 migration 'crisis', *Visual Communication*, 18(3): 311–331. https://doi.org/10.1177%2F1470357219846381

Di Francesco, A. D. and Young, N. (2011): Seeing climate change: The visual construction of global warming in Canadian national print media, *Cultural Geographies*, 18(4): 517–536. https://doi.org/10.1177%2F1474474010382072

Dinc, I. S. and Erel, I. (2013): Economic nationalism in mergers and acquisitions, *The Journal of Finance*, 68(6): 2471–2514.

Duan, R., Zwickle, A. and Takahashi, B. (2017): A construal-level perspective of climate change images in US newspapers, *Climatic Change*, 142: 345–360.

EEMC (2019): European Election Monitoring Center. www.electionsmonitoringcenter.eu/ (accessed 30 November 2021).

Forchtner, B. (2019): Climate change and the far right: *WIREs Climate Change*, 10(5). https://doi.org/10.1002/wcc.604.

Forchtner, B. (2020): Far-right articulations of the natural environment: An introduction. In: B. Forchtner (ed.), *The Far Right and the Environment: Politics, Discourse, and Communication*. London: Routledge, 15–27.

Forchtner, B. and Kølvraa, C. (2015): The nature of nationalism: Populist radical right parties on countryside and climate, *Nature and Culture*, 10(2): 199–224. https://doi.org/10.3167/nc.2015.100204

Hansen, A. (2018): Using visual images to show environmental problems. In: A. Fill and H. Penz (eds), *The Routledge Handbook of Ecolinguistics*. London: Routledge, 179–195.

Hess, D. J. and Renner, M. (2019): Conservative political parties and energy transitions in Europe: Opposition to climate mitigation policies, *Renewable and Sustainable Energy Reviews*, 104: 419–428. https://doi.org/10.1016/j.rser.2019.01.019

Hokka, J. and Nelimarkka, M. (2019): Affective economy of national-populist images: Investigating national and transnational online networks through visual big data, *New Media & Society*, 22(5): 770–792. https://doi.org/10.1177%2F1461444819868686

Hurd, M. and Werther, S. (2016): The militant media of neo-Nazi environmentalism. In: H. Graf (ed.), *The Environment in the Age of the Internet: Activists, Communication, and the Digital Landscape*. Cambridge: Open Book Publishers, 137–170.

Jylhä, K. M. and Hellmer, K. (2020): Right-wing populism and climate change denial: The roles of exclusionary and anti-egalitarian preferences, conservative ideology, and anti-establishment attitudes, *Analyses of Social Issues and Public Policy*, 20(1): 315–335. https://doi.org/10.1111/asap.12203

Kluknavská, A. (2013): Od Štúra k parazitom: Tematická adaptácia krajnej pravice v parlamentných voľbách na Slovensku, *Politologický časopis*, 14(3): 258–281.

Kluknavská, A. and Hruška, M. (2019): We talk about the 'others' and you listen closely, *Problems of Post-Communism*, 66(1): 59–70. http://dx.doi.org/10.1080/10758216.2018.1500861

Kluknavská, A. and Smolík, J. (2016): We hate them all? Issue adaptation of extreme right parties in Slovakia 1993–2016, *Communist and Post-Communist Studies*, 49(4): 335–344. https://doi.org/10.1016/j.postcomstud.2016.09.002

Kotlebovci (2021): Kto sme a čo chceme. http://kotlebovci.sk/kto-sme-a-co-chceme/ (accessed 11 October 2021).

Kress, G. and van Leeuwen, T. (1996): *Reading Images: The Grammar of Visual Design*. New York: Routledge.

Lockwood, M. (2018): Right-wing populism and the climate change agenda: Exploring the linkages, *Environmental Politics*, 27(4), 712–732. http://dx.doi.org/10.1080/09644016.2018.1458411

ĽSNS (2016): *10 points for our Slovakia! Election program of the political party Ľudová strana Naše Slovensko*. Banská Bystrica: ĽSNS.

Lubarda, B. (2020): Beyond ecofascism? Far-right ecologism (FRE) as a framework for future inquiries, *Environmental Values*, 29(6): 713–732. http://dx.doi.org/10.3197/096327120X15752810323922.

Manzo, K. (2017): The usefulness of climate change films, *Geoforum*, 84: 88–94. https://doi.org/10.1016/j.geoforum.2017.06.006

Mareš, M. (2018): How does militant democracy function in combating right-wing extremism? A case study of Slovakian militant democracy and the rise of Kotleba – People's Party Our Slovakia. In: A. Ellian and B. Rijpkema (eds), *Militant Democracy: Political Science, Law and Philosophy*. Cham: Springer, 61–76.

Mesežnikov, G. and Bránik, R. (2017): *Hatred, Violence and Comprehensive Military Training: The Violent Radicalisation and Kremlin Connections of Slovak Paramilitary, Extremist and neo-Nazi Groups*. Budapest: Political Capital.

Mesežnikov, G. and Gyárfášová, O. (2016): *Súčasný pravicový extrémizmus a ultranacionalizmus na Slovensku: Stav, trendy, podpora*. Bratislava: Inštitút pre verejné otázky.

Mészáros, M. (2013): Slovensko a energetická nezávislosť, *Our Slovakia*, 7: 3.

Ministry of Interior of the SR (2015): *Koncepcia boja proti extrémizmu na roky 2015–2019*. Bratislava: Ministry of Interior of the Slovak Republic.

Mudde, C. (2002): *The Ideology of the Extreme Right*. New York: Manchester University Press.

Mudde, C. (2019): *The Far Right Today*. Cambridge: Polity.

National Council of the SR (2018): Návrh poslancov Národnej rady Slovenskej republiky. www.nrsr.sk/web/Default.aspx?sid=zakony/zakon&MasterID=6894 (accessed 17 November 2021).

Niemelä-Nyrhinen, J. and Uusitalo, N. (2021): Aesthetic practices in the climate crisis: Intervening in consensual frameworks of the sensible through images, *Nordic Journal of Media Studies*, 3(1): 164–183. http://dx.doi.org/10.2478/njms-2021-0009

Our Slovakia (2014): 14. marca sme oslávili 75. výročie štátnosti, 3:4. Banská Bystrica: ĽSNS.

Our Slovakia (2016): V kraji sme zastavili korupciu a rozkrádanie verejných financií – peňazí nás všetkých!, 2:3. Banská Bystrica: Kotleba-ĽSNS.

Our Slovakia (2019a): Za ochranu života bojujeme nielen pred voľbami, 2(3): 3. Banská Bystrica: Kotleba-ĽSNS.

Our Slovakia (2019b): Kam miznú miliardy zo štátu?, 2(4): 8. Banská Bystrica: Kotleba-ĽSNS.

Our Slovakia (2020): Pre obnovu poľnohospodárstva a ochranu životného prostredia, 2: 11. Banská Bystrica: Kotlebovci-ĽSNS.

People's Youth (2021): Naše ciele. http://ludovamladez.sk/ (accessed 14 October 2021).

Rice, R. E., Rebich-Hespanha, S. and Zhu, H. (2019): Communicating about climate change through art and Science. In: J. Pinto, R. E. Gutsche and P. Prado (ed.), *Climate Change, Media and Culture: Critical Issues in Global Environmental Communication*. Bingley: Emerald, 129–154.

Rivera Otero, J. M., Castro Martínez, P. and Mo Groba, D. (2021): Emotions and the far right: The case of VOX in Andalusia, Spain. *Revista Española de Investigaciones Sociológicas*, 176: 119–140. http://dx.doi.org/10.5477/cis/reis.176.119

Santo, P. E. and Costa, B. (2016): Party newspapers perspectives and choices: A comparative content analysis view, *SAGE Open*, 6(2). https://doi.org/10.1177%2F2158244016640859

Schlosár, R. (2016): 10 bodov za naše Slovensko! *Our Slovakia*, 2: 4–7. Banská Bystrica: Kotleba-ĽSNS.

Smith, A. D. (1999): *Myths and Memories of the Nation*. Oxford: Oxford University Press.

Struhár, P. (2016): Vývoj neoficiálnej pravicovo-extrémistickej scény na Slovensku od roku 1989, *Rexter – Časopis pro výzkum radikalismu, extremismu a terorismu*, 14(1): 1–43.

Tosun, J. and Debus, M. (2021): Right-wing populist parties and environmental politics: Insights from the Austrian Freedom Party's support for the glyphosate ban, *Environmental Politics*, 30(1–2): 224–244. http://dx.doi.org/10.1080/09644016.2020.1813997

Vicenová, R. (2020): The role of digital media in the strategies of far-right vigilante groups in Slovakia, *Global Crime*, 21(3–4): 242–261. http://dx.doi.org/10.1080/17440572.2019.1709171

Virchow, F. (2007): Performance, emotion, and ideology: On the creation of 'collectives of emotion' and worldview in the contemporary German far right, *Journal of Contemporary Ethnography*, 36(2): 147–164. https://doi.org/10.1177%2F 0891241606298822

von Zabern, L. and Tulloch, C. D. (2021): Rebel with a cause: The framing of climate change and intergenerational justice in the German press treatment of the Fridays for Future protests, *Media, Culture & Society*, 43(1): 23–47. https:// doi.org/10.1177%2F0163443720960923

Wang, S., Corner, A., Chapman, D. and Markowitz, E. (2018): Public engagement with climate imagery in a changing digital landscape, *WIREs Climate Change*, 9(2). https://doi.org/10.1002/wcc.509

Westberg, G. and Årman, H. (2019): Common sense as extremism: The multi-semiotics of contemporary national socialism, *Critical Discourse Studies*, 16(5): 549–568. http://dx.doi.org/10.1080/17405904.2019.1624183

8

From metapolitics to electoral communication: visualising 'nature' in the French far right

Zoé Carle

Introduction: the apparition of environmental issue in the French far right

September 2020. The far-right, Identitarian think tank *Institut Iliade* runs its annual conference, this time on the topic of 'Nature as our bedrock', featuring as its highpoint a panel discussion between Hervé Juvin, a key figure in the 'greening' of the *Rassemblement National* (National Rally) and Julien Langella from the self-styled Identitarian Catholics *Academia Christiana* under the title 'For a rooted ecology: Localism and Recognition of Local Soils' (Institut Iliade, 2020b).

These speakers, representing different political factions within the French far right, propose different stances on political ecology and economy which they implement via different strategies for action – and yet, they are united in attributing a significant role to environmental topics, a sign of the importance of the environment across the political spectrum (Carter, 2013) and for the far right in particular (Forchtner, 2020; Otteni and Weisskircher, 2021). This concern arises against the longstanding background of theoretical work on ecology, lead by Alain de Benoist (François, 2021: 81) among other activists of the French *Nouvelle Droite* (New Right).

After showing scepticism towards ecologists, accusing them of idealising nature (de Benoist, 1977), de Benoist evolved towards a syncretic ecologism, mixing references to the Conservative Revolution (Woods, 1996; François, 2021), criticism of capitalism and consumerism, and concepts coined by the degrowth movement (de Benoist, 1994, 2007). An heir to *völkisch* ecology, this neo-pagan ecology perceives nature as a sacred entity and a territory organically linked to its people. Its call for the preservation of living environments against disruptions of all kinds follows a holistic approach, placing natural aspects on a par with social phenomena. Those include threats posed to the climate and biodiversity by human activity, but also processes thought to threaten the balance of traditional communities, such as immigration and overpopulation. Books and magazines edited by the *Nouvelle Droite* have given voice to this neo-pagan brand of environmentalism which falls in line with a defence of European cultures informed by de Benoist's ethnopluralist approach, later articulated under the formula 'integral ecology' (de Benoist and Champetier, 2000). The significance of the *Nouvelle Droite* for the ideological and conceptual toolkit of the French far right (and beyond) cannot be doubted, with Tamir Bar-On (2013: 221) stating that the *Nouvelle Droite* 'provided the right with an aura of respectability and legitimacy by crafting a coherent worldview' thanks to their metapolitical activity. This is particularly true for ecology. The notion of 'integral ecology' has thus recently gained traction among the far right in France and is now championed by various actors (François, 2017; Malm and The Zetkin Collective, 2021: 138). Along with neo-pagans, the Identitarians began to promote localism, while anti-technicist arguments gained ground among traditionalist Catholics, following mobilisations against gay marriage and bioethics laws in France in 2013. As such, ecology appears as a new pillar in the metapolitical action of the radical margins of the far right (Lebourg, 2012; François, 2017).

'Metapolitics' (Venner, 1964; de Benoist, 1982; Faye, 2002) describes an ideological and cultural operation carried out prior to an effective rise to political power, consisting in the dissemination of political ideas and formulas to the wider public debate – like ethnopluralism, national preference and great replacement[1] – but also to promote a certain way of life. It relies on a variety of methods constantly reshaped by evolutions in communication technologies: Books, journals, conferences, flyers and stickers are now supplemented by videos, photos and content tailored for online communication. The strategy is based on intellectual and theoretical agitprop, but also by the promotion of a certain way of life. It is commonly associated with the *Nouvelle Droite* and its satellites, but also *Institut Iliad*, the above-mentioned Identitarian think tank launched on 20 June 2014 by Philippe Conrad, Bernard Lugan and Jean-Yves Le Gallou. Other movements such as the *Bloc identitaire* (Identitarian Block) and *Academia Christiana*, both emblematic of the renewal of communication strategies in the Identitarian scene (Cahuzac and François, 2013), champion a less theoretical approach and prefer direct action as part of the cultural and aesthetic war they are waging.

Beyond such groups, and prime among far-right actors in France, the *Rassemblement National* has also turned towards 'ecology' (Boukala and Tountasaki, 2020; Gautier, 2021). Far from the neo-pagan degrowth, the party remains dominated by productivist ideology and focuses on the defence of identity and sovereignty, applying 'national preference' to territorial issues. With the exception of one noticeable attempt to develop 'ecologist thinking',[2] it was not until 2016 and the aforementioned conservative thinker and geopolitical expert Hervé Juvin that the environmental issue appeared under the formula 'patriotic ecology'. Together with Andrea Kotarac, Juvin co-founded the satellite party to the *Rassemblement National*, *Les Localistes* (The Localists) and is the author of an essay which drew considerable attention among far-right circles, *The Great Separation: In Defence of a Civilizational Ecology* (Juvin, 2013), which develops an ethnopluralist, defence-oriented approach to ecology.

Despite theoretical differences, far-right actors constitute a political family connected by a set of shared core principles, a worldview rather than any sort of fixed doctrinal content (Lebourg, 2012). Its various branches share an organicist conception of societies united in the defence of cultures and identities, with both terms replacing the notion of 'race' in the conceptual and activist lexicon of the French far right (Taguieff, 1998; Bar-On, 2013). Ecological thinking has no trouble fitting into this ethnocentric worldview wherein society is thought to function as a living organism, an inegalitarian realm governed by the law of the strongest. While the environmental issue is also fraught with dissensions between far-right groups, an overarching common denominator unifies the various actors. That is, the notion of rootedness is celebrated in opposition to nomadism, which is thought to define modern life and is accused of demolishing traditional bonds and organic communities alike. The environment is thus primarily understood as 'the local': the natural and traditional landscape of organic communities (for a discussion of the role of 'the local', see also Chapter 11 in this volume). Their landscapes are 'ethnoscapes in which a people and its homeland become increasingly symbiotic' (Smith, 2009: 50), threatened by immigration and 'antinatural' elements, especially to do with gender roles and reproduction (Forchtner and Kølvraa, 2017). This 'civilisational ecology' relies on a strong criticism of technology and progress (both social and technological), the promotion of regional specificities, the preservation of a healthy body through topics such as food and health, and the praise of a rooted lifestyle wary of any kind of mixing. Addressing natural and environmental content helps to pursue respectability and normalisation (Bouron, 2014) and allows the far right to speak to aesthetic and symbolic concerns (Forchtner and Kølvraa, 2015). However, in speaking of 'natural environment', the far right appears to focus more on 'nature' than on 'environment', the former being a vaguer term permitting them to rhetorically bridge between 'environment' and 'identity'. Indeed, nature is at the same time home to its own laws which should guide humans, a pleasant and beautiful place to enjoy, a landscape invoked as the 'paradise lost' of rural communities, the sovereign territory of endangered autochthon peoples and the mould that gave birth to imperilled civilisations and identities.

Against this background, this chapter focuses on the visualisation of nature in far-right communication, from metapolitics to elections. Embracing a critical perspective on multimodal far-right interventions (Kress and van Leuween, 2001), and drawing on three cases, this chapter explores how a loosely shared ideological foundation is actualised through complementary communication strategies around the notions of 'localism' and 'rootedness', as the main conceptual and ideological propositions of the far-right environmental discourse. By analysing the visual communication of *Institut Iliade* and *Academia Christiana*, this chapter illustrates the implementation of metapolitical strategies by two far-right organisations: Whereas the neo-pagan think tank *Institut Iliade* has taken up a longstanding theoretical and activist tradition, the youth movement *Academia Christiana* utilises its familiarity with the codes of online communication in connection to their Catholic identity. In addition, the third empirical section examines how 'civilisational ecology' is framed in the context of local elections around the *persona* of Hervé Juvin.

Following this introduction to the French far right and its stance vis-à-vis the natural environment, I turn to a more specific introduction of data analysed in this chapter before presenting my analyses of the three afore-mentioned far-right actors.

Methodology

This chapter is based on the observation of online visual material dating from 5 September 2019 to 7 December 2021 and the collection of environment-themed visual material. In recent years, the European far right has actively turned to online communication, making extensive use of news sites, print and TV news, and social media (Albertini and Doucet, 2016). This has led to an increasing amount of visual and audio-visual content and has given rise to a multimodal communication strategy in tune with the requirements of online communication, revamping their outdated iconography and 'style' (Novak, 2011; Bouron, 2014). Content produced by the *Institut Iliade*, *Academia Christiana* and Hervé Juvin fashions a consistent visual identity which partakes of a concerted visual communication strategy. Organisations often tap into image banks and utilise material which can be used across different media and for various purposes. Those visuals are often reassembled on platforms such as Instagram that allow the publication of multimodal content: audio-visuals, visuals and written text. These platforms are thus key sources for my analysis. Although this content does not necessarily circulate widely,[3] is offers the advantage of concentrating visualised ideological content in one place. Therefore, I compared these multimodal products with theoretical texts, online and offline, produced by respective authors, activists and think tanks on the matter of political ecology.

I collected eighty-five visual and seven audio-visual productions for *Institut Iliade*, fifty visuals for *Academia Christiana* and 101 visual and audio-visual productions for Juvin, among which five videos are entirely dedicated to his 'patriotic ecology'. To delineate environmental-themed content among the other themes tackled by those actors, I used a core list of keywords: 'nature', 'environment', 'ecology', 'local', 'root' and their grammatical derivatives, to stick to their understanding of 'environmental' matters as expressed in theoretical texts. The keywords were thus defined according to each actor's understanding of 'ecology', with relevant themes added according to each context. That is, 'landscape', 'industrialization of the living' and 'degrowth' were added to the core list for *Institut Iliade* and 'localism', 'natural', 'earth' and 'organic food' in the case of *Academia Christiana*, due to their broader interest in localism in connection to food and reproduction issues. As for Juvin, the keywords 'energies', 'wind-turbines', 'agriculture', 'environment', 'organic', 'natural heritage' and 'landscape' were added for their relevance in the context of local elections and the focus on tangible issues for the region.

With regard to *Institut Iliade*, the collected material includes visuals produced in connection with the above-mentioned conference 'Nature as our bedrock', as well as the institute's official website and environment-themed visuals hosted on it. Of a total of 592 articles published on the website, eighty-five were environment-related, all of them containing the keyword 'nature', twenty-one were associated with the keyword 'ecology', fourteen with the keyword 'rooted' and six with the keyword 'localism'. Each one is illustrated by at least one visual (photography, drawing) and more rarely by audio-visual productions. The website hosts seven videos in total, out of which one is entirely about 'nature', the promotional video of the conference, which is at the centre of my analysis in the first empirical section.

This first section is followed by an analysis of online communication implemented by *Academia Christiana*. Research on *Academia Christiana* consisted in observing online content hosted on the organisation's website and on their social media accounts (Facebook, Instagram). Since they use the same bank of images, I collected the visuals on the Instagram account which was opened in January 2017, currently has 4,032 followers and hosts 603 posts of which 50 are related to 'ecology' in a broad sense. Noticeably, the word 'environment' is not used a single time in the texts nor in the keywords accompanying visuals, whereas the word 'localism' is a common keyword/hashtag (twenty-one posts) along with 'rooted' and its derivatives (thirty-three times). 'Environment-themed' concerns mainly the relocalisation of agriculture and production, while 'nature' and its derivate 'natural', frequently associated with the words 'tradition' and 'order', is a theme commonly associated with the main symptoms of the 'artificialisation' of the world the movement denounces (consumerism and gender/reproduction issues).

The same approach was applied to the visual and audio-visual content produced by Hervé Juvin, taken from his personal website and Instagram and Twitter accounts. His Instagram account hosts ninety-four videos out of which thirty-six were produced for the regional elections during which *Rassemblement National* experimented for the first time with an own 'ecological' approach. As a result, twenty-eight tackle ecological issues in a broad sense (keywords: 'nature', 'ecology', 'energies', 'agriculture', 'localism'), against thirteen for security issues (the party predilection topic) and sixteen for international policies and sovereignty issues (Juvin's original area of expertise). As for Twitter, I counted 1,848 posts, out of which 48 (accompanied by videos and photos) concern environmental issues, against 61 dedicated to security and immigration. This analysis includes visual and audio-visual material produced for the regional elections of 2021 and relates them to Juvin's books (Juvin, 2005, 2007, 2013) and programmatic texts (Juvin and Kotarac, 2020).

Following this introduction of data, I now turn to the findings of the three analysed actors.

Institut Iliade: the renewal of neo-pagan imagery

Institut Iliade aims to 'rouse the European conscience' and 'spread a worldview […] and attitude of dissent against mainstream thinking, through whatever means available (viral communication, books, press, training programmes, cultural activities and events, developing and sustaining networks …)' (Institut Iliade, 2014). The institute operates under the tutelary figure of Dominique Venner, a major strategic and theoretical reference for the French far right, who died by suicide in 2014 in Notre Dame de Paris. This think tank aims to establish the myth of the European roots of French identity (Camus, 2018). In so doing they spread a number of themes inherited from the New Right and other prevalent concepts among Identitarians such as the 'Great Replacement' theorised by Renaud Camus.

Two main instruments serve to circulate this ideology: the training institute and the annual conferences held at the Maison de la Chimie, in Paris, since 2015. Regular attendees include veterans of the *Nouvelle Droite*; the editors of their magazine *Éléments*, Alain de Benoist, François Bousquet and Fabien Niezgoda; far-right intellectual and academics such as Pascal Gauchon; and young activists from the Identitarian Block or from conservative 'alterfeminist' movements such as *Les Antigones*. These activists belong to movements with divergent political and tactical strategies, yet who agree on a set of core principles: localism and rootedness as a means of defending imperilled European civilisations, and an attitude of intellectual and political dissidence. This syncretic approach hinges on the personality of its initiator, Jean-Yves Le Gallou, a pioneer for issues of communication and agitprop in the French far right, who serves as a conduit among the groupuscule far right (Albertini and Doucet, 2016: 201; Lamy, 2016). One of *Institut Iliade*'s ambitions is to facilitate a conversation between different generations of activists. By catering to the younger generation through its training institute, it has also acquired new graphic and communication skills that are usefully employed to spruce up neo-pagan imagery handed down from the *Nouvelle Droite*. The audio-visual bites punctuating the conference, created by students of the institute or audio-visual companies, such as the promotional video for their sevents conference 'Nature as our bedrock',[4] are of remarkable aesthetic quality (Institut Iliade, 2020a).

In this video, running at four minutes and thirty-four seconds, a voice-over unfolds the typical themes of this ecology, displaying aesthetic pictures of wild landscapes while dramatic music plays in the background. As an introduction, it condemns the 'violent boarding of this world' – an expression regularly found in the writings of *Nouvelle Droite* – while the images lay out the various perils defacing the natural environment today, showing aerial views of landscapes mutilated by deforestation or rubbish tips. The dramatic depiction of a nature under threat ties back to a largely declinist narrative championed by Identitarianism. A defence of 'diversity' in all its meanings then follows: diversity of fauna and flora, diversity of sexes and eventually diversity of peoples and cultures. At this point, the visuals shift towards an agrarian vein, alternating between portraits of farmers at work and families playing in wheat fields, while the voice-over recalls the naturalness of the 'parentage laws'. These portraits highlight a certain relationship to nature and land: one that is symbiotic, traditional and under threat (Smith, 2009: 50).

While nature is feebly defined and contextualised, it is unquestionably rooted in that European landscape which allowed the European civilisation to blossom. The visual content is indeed all subtly evocative of 'European landscapes', with the wild scenery of mountains, forests and lakes conjuring up an Alpine geography. Other visuals display a handful of traits evocative of a European context – mushrooms, snowy mountains, rural villages and Greek colonnades – as many signs referring to those European cultures endangered by modernity. 'Nature' as an ethnoscape is the foremost model for human creation and culture, as the last section of the video recalls. As such, European nature only is to be preserved for its seminal role in the development of an endangered European civilisation.

Institut Iliade's depictions of the environment suggest a genuine mystique landscape. In 'We Are the Landscape of Europe', the authors describe 'experiencing beauty' on the pathways of Europe as formative of their feeling of belonging to a specific land and community (Institut Ililalde, 2021). These representations are shaped by the legacy of the *völkisch* movement and its singular cosmogony, which combines the return to Celtic and Germanic roots with a celebration of the sacred forces of nature, a prevalent theme of Identitarian ecology (Baillet, 2017). In neo-paganism's 'cosmic' worldview, man stands at the centre of the cosmos, and the contemplation of nature helps him reconnect with a spirit of sacredness lacking in the modern age. In an article referring to Venner's triad, an excerpt from Maurice Barrès' *La Colline inspirée* underlines this: 'How often, upon a profound and joyful day, have we come upon the edge of a wood, a summit, a source, a humble meadow, calling on us to silence our thoughts and lend an ear to depths beyond our hearts! Silence! The Gods are here' (Institut Iliade, 2018). The second part of the video illustrates this mystique of landscape, showing wild scenery and beautiful pictures of preserved natural spaces, while the voice-over glorifies the value of 'free man' as opposed to 'domesticated man'.

This aesthetic relationship to the environment transpires from audio-visual content such as in Figure 8.1, which is heavily inspired by the neo-pagan imagery prevalent among the *Nouvelle Droite* and its breakaway groups. The latter fluctuates between pre-Raphaelite depictions of women set amid aestheticised greenery, in a hospitable environment, to depictions of a wilderness against which man must prove himself. Women – as well as children – are shown in a symbiotic relationship with nature: long-haired, they often wear supposedly 'traditional' outfits, flowers, branches, sheaves of wheat, while dancing in bucolic landscapes. Those visuals are commonly accompanied by ethnopluralist speeches about the protection of diversity and the defence of tradition and 'parenting laws'.

In contrast to women, men are depicted in an antagonistic relationship to nature, which is shown as a site of initiation. The topic of man alone against the elements – elements that regenerate him, that testify to his worth and are constitutive of his might – looms large in written text and images alike. It harks back to a romantic and aristocratic conception of life, articulated by Venner (1964) as the basis of nationalism. This elitist conception runs through the *Nouvelle Droite* (François, 2021) and is also prevalent among its historical inspirers, authors from the Conservative Revolution and the likes of Friedrich Nietzsche. It allows the far right to reaffirm its posture of dissidence and rebellion against 'mainstream thinking', in a nod to Ernst Jünger's *Waldgänger*, at once figure of the 'forest-goer' and the rebel. The result can be incongruous, as when the promotional video encourages viewers

8.1 'Nature as our bedrock', promotional video by *Institut Iliade*, posted on 12 April 2020

to 'wash with cold water' or 'to prefer stairs to elevators', that is, to take up naturist notions of a healthy lifestyle, a direct relationship to nature and deliberate simplicity.

Overall, visuals stand on a crest line: While subtly quoting an ideological and iconographic background that owes much to the *völkisch* movements, they remain at the same time vague. *Nature* remains a polysemic goddess to be worshipped as natural nature and human nature, even if never defined, have an 'intrinsic value' (de Benoist, 1994b).

Academia Christiana: priests and peasants, mothers and fighters

The Catholic youth movement *Academia Christiana* was created in 2013 by a group of four students, including Julien Langella, a former activist of *Action Française* and one of the co-founders of *Génération Identitaire*. The movement's go-to text is Langella's *Refaire un peuple* (2021), which calls for a 'revolution of the local' against the global. Tangible proposals are few and are in keeping with the main lines of right-wing ecology: criticism of consumer society, nomadism and immigration, and the defence of rootedness as a way to preserve damaged traditional regional identities. 'Nature' in all its forms is at threat and localism is the solution.

The Internet and social media are central for the group, as is the case with other youth Identitarian movements in Europe (Forchtner and Kolvraa, 2017; Zúquete, 2018: 3). The slogan '*Catholiques et enracinés*' (Rooted Catholics) is present across *Academia Christiana*'s various online communication platform. *Academia Christiana*'s members appear at home with the codes of these platforms, putting out finely crafted pictures that promote an aesthetics of political struggle. In so doing, the movement aims to delineate a circumscribed and exclusive 'we', targeting an audience informed by the same values and possibly the same feeling of rejection (Wodak, 2020: 34). In the case of Identitarian Catholicism, this group-building effort draws at once on a strategy informed by ideas of 'resisting the system' and the global order, 'dissidence' and the search for a 'third way', and on their particular Catholic identity. The group has a taste for logos and stickers, insignia and symbols, which make use of an implicit and allusive language, and act as markers of shared identity (Novak, 2011).

Academia Christiana makes extensive use of visual media, both online and offline, which involves the use of those rallying signs. Significantly, they are the subject of a number of posts on the Instagram account: Activists' pictures show glimpses of discreet tattoos (twenty-four pictures) whereas others are only dedicated to t-shirts displaying those signs (twenty pictures). While tattoos and logos remain central to the movement's merchandizing strategies, the pictures show a departure from the distinguishing marks used by the groupuscule far right up to the early 2000s, with shaved heads, rangers and bomber jackets – elements which have given way to, for example, smiling young women in sportswear. On a visual level, this shift is evidenced by the use of dusty traditional content adjusted to the new requirements of online communication. As shown for other countries such as Germany and the United States, '[t]he extreme right, too, has undergone its moments of modernisation (or post-modernisation)' (Forchtner and Kolvraa, 2017: 253), through the appropriation of youth culture codes, actions and communication repertoires commonly associated with the left (Bouron, 2014; Pisoiu and Lang, 2015) and through the merchandizing of their struggles (Miller-Idriss, 2018).

Of the 604 posts on the account, the majority (348) are dedicated to the documentation of their annual spring universities and conference events, underlining the importance of those moments for the group. They show young militants listening to speakers, helping with the everyday life of the camp and attending mass or martial art trainings. The 'warlike' staging is of foremost importance and is built through the discourse about 'racial war' via pictures of activists practising martial arts or through religious/cultural representations, such as Saint George killing the dragon (seventy posts). The other categories of pictures show representations of natural or rural landscapes (thirty-five posts), religious topics (ninety-three posts) and, more generally, the framing of a dissenting lifestyle. A certain type of publication stands out: pictures representing text or quotes from *Academia Christiana*'s authors or reference authors from *Action Française*, displayed on landscapes, and still life visuals marked by their logo. In those publications, texts undergo a process of 'iconization' (Paveau, 2019) whereby text is treated as image and made to stand out from adjacent explanatory texts. This process is encouraged by the activists' taste for catchphrases such as this recurring quote from the Bible: 'Vita hominis super terra militia est' (Job 7:1).[5] Those prove to be particularly easy to crop and circulate on social media when defining a fighting style; all multimodal content incarnating this way of life promoted by *Academia Christiana* revolves around religious, familial and rooted values in which 'natural roles' are respected.

In *Academia Christiana*'s communication, the environmental issue is present but secondary (thirty-five posts address it, against ninety-three for religious subjects), most likely due to the limited theoretical conceptualisation of ecology. Nature has an ambiguous presence in these visuals: The hashtag is associated with pictures of wild animals – bears but mostly stags for its symbolic link to Christianity – still lifes and pictures of mountains but mostly rural landscapes. Nature is once again perceived as an 'ethnoscape', here suggestive of the 'French' countryside, and those rural landscapes are often visually equated with pictures of religious buildings or pieces of local heritage. This use of visual representation of 'nature' almost systematically illustrates written statements about rootedness and its reverse figure, uprooting, thus defined by Julien Langella: 'The great uprooting is the application of gender theory to all aspects of life: Each person could chose its sexual, cultural identity, or even its species since some people feel more like a goat than like a human being' (Academia Christiana, 2021). The phonetic likeness of the French words '*déracinement*' (uprooting) and '*remplacement*' (replacement) and the adjective 'great' immediately suggest Renaud Camus' the 'Great Replacement' to the reader. The sentence thus puts in equivalence rootedness, immigration and gender theory, suggesting the 'naturality' of gender roles as the main foundation of *Academia Christiana*'s thinking.

Academia Christiana repeatedly associates nature with female figures, driven by a communication strategy designed to stress the feminisation of its activist base. The presence of feminine subjects is indeed quite remarkable. Young women are widely represented, whether in photographs taken during workshops, in staged photographs (seventy-six posts) or in cultural representations through paintings or artistic photographs (thirty posts), meant to illustrate the dissident lifestyle championed by the organisation. They are portrayed as co-fighters (fourteen out of the forty pictures of activists in martial art training sessions) and seductive young women taking their share in the struggle. This dimension is echoed by cultural representations of medieval female fighters, reminiscent of Joan of Arc, a major reference for the French far right, with pictures of young women wearing helmets while smoking cigarettes or drinking beer.

The young women of the movement are caught in a semantic network polarised by two guiding mythological figures, the Christian Amazon and the glowing young mother. Significant figures include the ancient goddesses of fertility, though the main reference is, unsurprisingly, the Virgin Mary. Women are associated in these pictures with the fertility of nature, carrying sprays of flowers or strolling through wheat fields, young children sometimes tagging along. They are meant to embody the value of motherhood in a movement where the narrative of family and its values, reproduction and filiation, but also strength and youth is all-important.

Figure 8.2 exemplifies precisely that, showing a woman in old-fashioned outfit who carries a female baby, while contemplating a countryside landscape covered in flowers. The visuals insist on the fertility of nature and women who have a special connection to it, while the single word in white capitals insist on the notion of 'duty'. As Forchtner and Kolvraa underline with regard to the German extreme right: 'the theme of nature and gender is framed by an authoritative imaginary' (Forchtner and Kolvraa, 2017: 266), that is, demanding reproduction (and traditionality) from the onlooker. The comment that accompanies this picture is a quote of the Maurrassian writer Gustave Thibon, insisting on that dimension: 'Any happiness that does not give birth to a duty diminishes or corrupts.' While more savvy in the use of online communication tools than the older generation, *Academia Christiana*'s approach nevertheless seems to attest to a certain continuity with neo-pagan trend: Cosmos and Nietzschean supermen have given way to figures of young men and women respectful of their 'duties' towards the community, but the idea of 'sacred nature' is what must guide them.

Hervé Juvin: defending landscapes and individual mobility

A newcomer to the far right, Hervé Juvin gives an ecological endorsement to the *Rassemblement National*. However, the 'civilisational ecology' he promotes is centred on geopolitical issues: relocalisation of industry and defence of national territory, as well as sovereignty against globalisation and immigration at the same time. His writings express an ethnopluralist concern over the disappearance of first peoples and their civilisations, and a criticism levelled at 'the confusion of sameness', identified as an 'avatar of colonialism'.[6] His analyses are highly critical of the Americanisation of lifestyles and this denunciation is bolstered by Juvin's status as a geopolitical

8.2 'Duty', posted on 4 December 2019

expert, leading him to provide various analyses on matters of sovereignty. This resonates with his stances on reshoring and European competitiveness against the American superpower, as well as his neo-Malthusian beliefs.

The theme of the authenticity of land is present throughout Juvin's communication (Juvin, 2021a, 2021b), echoing the infamous Chief of State of Vichy France (1940–1944) Phillipe Petain's agrarian motto 'land does not lie' as a backwards-glancing praise of a lifestyle threatened by financial elites, technology and European environmental policies. Juvin's platform contained three 'environmental' planks: 'No to wind turbines and the destruction of our natural heritage', 'Young farmers for biodiversity' and 'Food and health education' meant to promote locally produced food in schools. Over recent years, wind turbines have been a central subject for the European far right (see Otteni and Weisskircher, 2021). In line with the defence of the 'local' environment, far-right opposition to wind turbines is consistent with the strategy of mobilising against global warming policies; they are also frequently associated with 'minarets', another cultural sign defacing the 'local' countryside. One of the main arguments at hand is the defence of the landscape as 'natural heritage', wherein the environment is once again primarily seen as a cultural signifier: 'The plan to set up tens of thousands of giant wind turbines throughout Europe is an insult to rural populations, whose landscapes are part of our heritage: Every corner of our land will be placed in sight of these aggressive wind mills that massacre migrating birds and bats' (Juvin, 2020). Beyond remarks on biodiversity, those arguments can largely be boiled down to aesthetic criticism, a classic dismissal of wind turbines in far-right discourse (Forchtner and Kolvraa, 2015).

Despite the campaign's slogan, 'A Region that Protects You', explicitly environmental proposals were stripped down to a bare minimum in the candidate's programme, foregrounding instead issues of security, economic policies for small and medium businesses, and matters of local governance. These proposals, which are typical of *Rassemblement National* candidates, go hand in hand with a certain candidate ethos and a provocative tone, relying on a classical reversal of shame in the face of moralising political elites (Wodak, 2020: 34). Far-right leaders seek to cast themselves as the true representatives of the people and the environmental streak that runs through Hervé Juvin's platform emphasises this aspect, as shown by formulas such as 'proximity ecology' as opposed to 'top-down ecology' (from Europe) and 'happy ecology' versus 'punitive ecology' that intends to push through reforms of the Western way of life (Juvin, 2020). That is, Juvin aims to articulate an 'authentic' environmentalism, not a moralising one. The result is a populist take on sometimes disconcerting environmental policies, as Juvin has proved by backing a plan to build Amazon warehouses on farmland or defending individual mobility.

In contrast to the two previous cases discussed, Juvin represents a very different approach. Beyond discreet signals sent out to the party's activist base, the purpose is one of broad appeal, with a view to electoral success. Personal branding emerges as a key aspect: With the need to appeal to voters, biographical storytelling become just as important, if not more so, as the policies themselves. In his video 'A Few Words about Me', Juvin (2020) casts himself as a 'native son', born into a family of farmers and small business owners in the French department of Loire-Atlantique. He typically casts himself as the candidate of the 'local folk' versus the 'cosmopolitan elite', as the 'common sense' candidate standing in contrast to modern hubris (Wodak, 2020: 35–36). Childhood as a paradise lost is another theme at play, as it is in the discourse of other *Rassemblement National* representatives, candidates or sympathisers. These communicators seize on feelings of nostalgia and loss in the face of the modern world (Forchtner, 2016), where damage to the environment and landscape is picking up pace and becoming visible. The virtual tour offered in the presentation video takes us through the candidate's childhood memories, charging the region's landscape with a specific meaning (Juvin, 2021a). The candidate's efforts to root himself in a given area involves practices of naming and cruising the land (Juvin, 2021a).

Indeed, exploring 'the land' contributes to building an ethos of *proximity* that conjures up a nostalgic aesthetics of country life. Pictures and videos show him paying visits to local small fishermen, farmers and tradesmen, dually affected by the race for financial profit and by the 'harassment' of moralising environmentalists (Juvin, 2020, 2021b). His trips during the electoral campaign, the national rallies of *Rassemblement National* or the sessions of the European Parliament are documented through visuals showing him, for example, driving his car (Figure 8.3) and running along the shore. This 'backstage' aesthetic enables this notion of proximity and is also frequently the occasion to record his 'environmental' stances, as in Figure 8.3, posted on Twitter after the elections with the comment: 'Back from RN [*Rassemblement National*] Congress: We are forced to notice the massive presence of wind-turbines in our beautiful Mediterranean landscapes.' The point of view places the viewer in the car, in the passenger position: The hands on the wheels and the windscreen anchor the point of view on 'disfigured' landscapes – disfigured by wind turbines but not by highway infrastructures.

More generally, the images circulating in this communication focused on electoral success are far less aestheticised but foreground the persona of the candidate. As such, classic ideological stances, such as the confrontation with natural elements, localism and the mystique of landscape, are reconfigured within the specific scope of building an ethos of proximity for a specific representative.

Conclusion

The present case studies demonstrate the pivotal role played by aesthetic and symbolic dimensions in far-right activists' visual communication about 'nature', in a 'metapolitical' perspective as well as in the prospect of electoral conquest. In both cases, visual communication is a constitutive part of strategies to achieve respectability and normalisation pursued by activists

Hervé Juvin @HerveJuvin · 4 juil.   ...

De retour du #CongresRN on ne peut que constater la présence massive d' #Eoliennes dans nos beaux paysages du midi
#StopEolien #Perpignan

💬 7   ⟲ 28   ♡ 86   ⬆

8.3 'Back from RN [*Rassemblement National*] Congress: We are forced to notice the massive presence of wind-turbines in our beautiful Mediterranean landscapes', tweeted on 4 July 2021

in their attempt to challenge classic assumptions about far-right militants. In this context, environmental issues mainly boil down to a few themes: the industrialisation of living things and particularly of agriculture, the question of alimentation and the defacement of rural landscapes. Those are particularly tackled in the electoral context, in connection with local and concrete subjects, whereas metapolitical communication can focus thoroughly on the aestheticisation of a dissident way of life. The visualisation of nature, understood as a quasi-synonym for environment, is designed to build up and solidify attractive activist communities, or aiming at wider audiences in the context of local elections. In both cases, the invocation of *nature* acts emotively vis-à-vis the audience.

As such, nature is above all summoned as an experience, individual or collective, capable of arousing feelings. The remnant *völkisch* heritage is certainly to be found in this definition of 'nature' as an experience, as well as in the insistence on the sacredness of this 'nature'. These representations are part of an intimate imaginary, worked by feelings of nostalgia (of lost landscapes and authenticity), of danger (of imminent loss) and of belonging (identity). Nature is what gives substance to the various moral panics of the far right, from immigration to 'gender theory', jeopardising tradition and identity. It is at this point that authoritarian imaginaries of nature make sense: To fight against the anomie of the contemporary liberal world, it is necessary and demanded to return to authority and to traditional 'natural' structures. Indeed, this is arguably the main common denominator between various trends within the French far right (beyond the conceptualisation of 'environment' as the territory and landscape of an endangered French or European civilisation): The defacement of nature is the main *sign* and symptom of a disaster caused by globalisation, world industrialisation and liberalism. Hence, and as Olsen (1999: 29) has argued, '[t]he politics of nature is at the same time a politics of identity'.

Notes

1 We owe the first concept to Alain de Benoist, the second to the *Club de l'Horloge*, of which Jean-Yves Le Gallou was a member (Lamy, 2016), and the third to Renaud Camus.
2 In January 2011, the far-right ecologist and activist Laurent Ozon, editor in chief of the magazine *Le Recours aux forets*, briefly joined the party executives of Front National at the invitation of Marine Le Pen. He was excluded in August 2011 for publicly supporting Anders Breivik.
3 Despite the effort to invest in recent communication tools, Hervé Juvin's Instagram account only has 781 subscribers. *Academia Christiana* has 4,032, while the videos on Juvin's YouTube channel rarely exceed a thousand views.
4 The phrase is taken from a text written by Dominique Venner (2009).
5 'The life of man upon earth is a warfare, and his days are like the days of a hireling' (Douay-Rheims Bible).
6 This denunciation of colonialism in the writings of the New Right goes back to the 1980s, as well as the denunciation of the 'ideology of sameness'. This anticolonialism acts as a way to denounce the 'inverse colonialism' within Europe, by the capitalist way of life and consumer society, but also by *no-borderism*, and 'the replacement' of indigenous populations by others.

References

Academia Christiana (2021): Instagram post. www.instagram.com/p/CWlmAqUo1nR/ (accessed 30 November 2021).
Albertini, D. and Doucet, D. (2016): *Fachosphère: Comme l'extrême-droite remporte la bataille du Net*. Paris: Flammarion.

Baillet, P. (2017): *Piété pour le cosmos*. Paris: Akribeia.

Bar-On, T. (2013): *Rethinking the French New Right: Alternatives to Modernity*. New York: Routledge.

Benoist de, A. (1977): Les équivoques de l'écologie, *Eléments*, 21/22: 2.

Benoist de, A. (1982): *Pour un 'gramscisme de droite': Acte du XVIe colloque national du GRECE Palais des congrès de Versailles 29 novembre 1981*. Paris: Le Labyrinthe.

Benoist de, A. (1994a): La fin de l'idéologie du progrès, *Eléments*, 79: 2.

Benoist de, A. (1994b): La valeur intrinsèque de la nature. http://alaindebenoist.s3.amazonaws.com/pdf/la_nature_et_sa_valeur_intrinseque.pdf (accessed 5 December 2021).

Benoist de, A. (2007): *Demain la décroissance! Penser l'écologie jusqu'au bout*. Paris: E-dite.

Benoist de, A. and Champetier C. (2000): *Manifeste pour une renaissance européenne: À la découverte du GRECE. Son histoire, ses idées, son organisation*. Paris: GRECE.

Boukala, S. and Tountasaki, E. (2020): From black to green: Analysing *Le Front National*'s 'patriotic ecology'. In: B. Forchtner (ed.), *The Far Right and the Environment: Politics, Discourse and Communication*. London: Routledge, 67–78.

Bouron, S. (2014): Un militantisme à deux faces: Stratégie de communication et politique de formation des Jeunesses identitaires, *Agone*, 54: 45–72.

Cahuzac, Y. and François, S. (2013): Les stratégies de communication de la mouvance identitaire, *Questions de communication*, 23: 275–292.

Camus, J.-Y. (2018): Le mouvement identitaire ou la construction d'un mythe des origines européennes, Fondation Jean Jaurès. www.jean-jaures.org/publication/le-mouvement-identitaire-ou-la-construction-dun-mythe-des-origines-europeennes/ (accessed 5 December 2021).

Carter, N. (2013): Greening the mainstream: Party politics and the environment, *Environmental Politics*, 22(1): 73– 94. https://doi.org/10.1080/09644016.2013.755391

Faye, G. (2002): *Pourquoi nous combattons: Manifeste de la Résistance européenne*. Paris: L'AEncre.

Forchtner, B. (2016): Longing for communal purity: Countryside (far-right) nationalism and the (im)possibility of progressive politics of nostalgia. In: C. Karner and B. Weicht (eds), *The Communalities of Global Crises*. Basingstoke: Palgrave, 271– 295.

Forchtner, B. (ed.) (2020): *The Far Right and the Environment: Politics, Discourse and Communication*. London: Routledge.

Forchtner, B. and Kølvraa, C. (2015): The nature of nationalism: Populist radical right parties on countryside and climate, *Nature and Culture*, 10(2): 199–224. https://doi.org/10.3167/nc.2015.100204

Forchtner, B. and Kølvraa, C. (2017): Extreme right images of radical authenticity: Multimodal aesthetics of history, nature, and gender roles in social media, *European Journal of Cultural and Political Sociology*, 4(3): 252–281. https://doi.org/10.108 0/23254823.2017.1322910

François, S. (2017): Comment l'écologie est-elle conçue à l'extrême droite, *Fragments du temps present*. https://tempspresents.com/2017/10/12/comment-lecologie-est-elle-concue-a-lextreme-droite/ (accessed 13 February 2022).

François, S. (2021): *La Nouvelle Droite et ses dissidences*. Lormont: Editions Le Bord de l'Eau.

Gautier, J.-P. (2021): De la haine de l'écologie au *greenwashing* nationaliste? Le RN et l'environnement, *Contretemps*. www.contretemps.eu/rassemblement-national-lepen-racisme-ecologie-nucleaire/ (accessed 15 December 2021).

Institut Iliade (2014): Présentation. https://institut-iliade.com/presentation/ (accessed 17 June 2021).

Institut Iliade (2018): Vivre en Européen: 'La nature comme socle, l'excellence comme but, la beauté comme horizon', 6 April 2018. https://institut-iliade.com/vivre-en-europeen-la-nature-comme-socle-lexcellence-comme-but-la-beaute-comme-horizon/_(accessed 17 June 2021).

Institut Iliade (2020a): La Nature comme socle. www.youtube.com/watch?v=WNTc JeYoIFs (accessed 23 September 2021).

Institut Iliade (2020b): Pour une écologie enracinée: localisme et mise en valeur des terroirs. https://institut-iliade.com/pour-une-ecologie-enracinee-localisme-et-mise-en-valeur-des-terroirs/ (accessed June 2021).

Institut Iliade (2021): Nous sommes le paysage de l'Europe, 27 July 2021. https://institut-iliade.com/nous-sommes-le-paysage-de-leurope/ (accessed 23 May 2021).

Juvin, H. (2005): *L'Avènement du corps*. Paris: Gallimard.

Juvin, H. (2007): *Produire le monde*. Paris: Gallimard.

Juvin, H. (2013): *La Grande Séparation: Pour une écologie des civilisations*. Paris: Gallimard.

Juvin, H. (2020): L'écologie contre l'écologisme. https://hervejuvin.com/ecologisme-escroquerie/ (accessed 13 February 2022).

Juvin, H. (2021a): Qui suis-je en quelques mots? Mieux me connaître. www.youtube.com/watch?v=n7MvoY02bgk (accessed 24 June 2021).

Juvin, H. (2021b): L'écologie heureuse contre l'écologie punitive. www.instagram.com/p/CPn407Qntdr/ (accessed 24 June 2021).

Juvin, H. and Kotarac, A. (2020): *Manifeste du Parti localiste*, 9 March 2020. www.leslocalistes.fr/manifeste-localiste/ (accessed 13 February 2022).

Kress, G. and van Leeuuwen, T. (2001): *Multimodal Discourse: The Modes and Media of Contemporary Communication*. Oxford: Oxford University Press.

Lamy, P. (2016): *Le Club de l'Horloge (1974–2002): évolution et mutation d'un laboratoire idéologique*, thèse sous la direction de Claude Dargent, Université Paris 8.

Langella, J. (2021): *Refaire un peuple*. Paris: La Nouvelle Librairie.

Lebourg, N. (2012): *Le Monde vu depuis la plus extrême droite*. Perpignan: Presses Universitaires de Perpignan.

Malm, A. and The Zetkin Collective (2021): *White Skin, Black Fuel: On the Danger of Fossil Fascism*. London: Verso.

Miller-Idriss, C. (2018): *The Extreme Gone Mainstream: Commercialization and Far Right Youth Culture in Germany*. Princeton: Princeton University Press.

Novak, Z. (2011): *Une histoire visuelle de la droite et de l'extrême droite*. Montreuil: L'Echappée.

Olsen, J. (1999): *Nature and Nationalism: Right-Wing Ecology and the Politics of Identity in Contemporary Germany*. New York: St. Martin's Press.

Otteni, C. and Weisskircher, M. (2021): Global warming and polarization: Wind turbines and the electoral success of the greens and the populist radical right, *European Journal of Political Research*. https://doi.org/10.1111/1475-6765.12487

Paveau, A.-M. (2019): Technographismes en ligne: Énonciation matérielle visuelle et iconisation du texte, *Corela*. https://doi.org/10.4000/corela.9185

Pisoiu, D. and Lang, F. (2015): The porous borders of extremism: Autonomous nationalists at the crossroad with the extreme left, *Behavioral Sciences of Terrorism and Political Aggression*, 7(1): 69–83. https://doi.org/10.1080/19434472.2014.977327

Smith, A. D. (2009): *Ethno-Symbolism and Nationalism*. Abingdon: Routledge.

Taguieff, P.-A. (1998): *Le Racisme*. Paris: Cahier du CEVIPOF.

Venner, D. (1964): *Pour une critique positive*. http://1000tempetes.free.fr/venner_critique_positive.pdf (accessed 23 September 2021).

Venner, D. (2009): La triade homérienne: L'avenir prend racine dans la mémoire du passé'. www.dominiquevenner.fr/2009/07/la-triade-homerienne-lavenir-prend-racine-dans-la-memoire-du-passe/ (accessed 23 September 2021).

Wodak, R. (2020): The trajectory of far-right populism: A discourse analytical perspective. In: B. Forchtner (ed.), *The Far Right and the Environment: Politics, Discourse and Communication*. London: Routledge, 21–37.

Woods, R. (1996): *The Conservative Revolution in the Weimar Republic*. London: Palgrave Macmillan.

Zúquete, J. (2018): *The Identitarians: The Movement against Globalism and Islam in Europe*. Notre Dame: University of Notre Dame Press.

9

The murky world of ideologies: the (un)troubling overlaps in visual communication between Hungarian greens and far-right ecologists

Balša Lubarda

Introduction

The times of multifaceted crisis that beset not only liberal democracy but the very planet we live on lend themselves to visualising dystopias through environmental communication. The culturally loaded act of articulating messages and arguments through 'seeing' can substantiate, if not replace, the semiotic complexity of written text (Sontag, 2004). Images appear 'natural' and seemingly purged of semiotic conventions and ideological intrusions, as opposed to the structured presentation of written text. Because of this, visuals are particularly enticing for those interested in political communication and the study of ideologies.

Yet visualising a crisis and responses to it presuppose the existence of a normative standard from which the troubling deviations and aberrations can be identified – as when distinguishing between desired and deviant behaviours in articulating the ideal polity. While ideologies that are considered 'radical', for example far right or green ideologies, seem more likely to resort to binary distinctions in constructing their political appeal, 'moderate' ideologies, such as liberalism and conservatism, are often imagined as defending the status quo. However, it is not always clear how such banal constructions of ideological differences play out in the visual environmental communication of different political parties. By looking at the case of Hungary, this chapter examines the semiotic decontestation of ideologies through visual environmental communication, discussing how political parties of different ideologies communicate the environmental crisis.

While definitions may vary, political ideologies present a deliberately incomplete map through which one makes sense of the social and political world. In that sense, ideology is a glue loosely holding together often disarrayed ideations and political concepts such as 'equality', 'liberty' and 'order'

(Freeden, 2006). In their portrayal of ideal and unwanted societies, better worlds and 'geographies of hope' (Hicks, 2014), ideologies benefit from visual communication. Visual communication also serves to strengthen and appeal to particular identities, marking emotional orientations (Fahlenbrach, 2008) and being unquestionably political in its conscious framing and semiotic strategies (O'Neill, 2013). This may lead to the (un)warranted conclusion that visual communication serves to temper ideology's internal inconsistencies or make its messages appear more mundane, sensible and 'untroubling'. However, this would result in ignoring the polysemic and often intentionally ambiguous nature of visuals and communication in general (Warlaumont, 1995). As noted above, visual communication is ideologically compelling, which is why the sign-making process is particularly valuable for analysis. This chapter asserts that ideologies are murky at best, which makes an ideological differentiation through visual communication, in this case far-right from green political appeals, particularly difficult. For this reason, the arising hybrids become valuable for the delicate task of ideological rendition.

Simultaneously, the current salience and the intersectional nature of environmental issues means that these topics are no longer (if they had ever been) reserved only for standalone 'green', left-leaning ideologies and politics. Even though a wide array of parties engages with environmental topics, from social democrats to pirate parties, it can no longer be argued that environmentalism is a valence-consensus issue (Mertig and Dunlap, 1995). Yet the intersection between the far right and environment is both historically and ideologically profound (Forchtner, 2019). This prompts an exploration into diverse ideal-types of ideological communication on the environment, such as eco-socialism or far-right ecologism (Lubarda, 2020a). For instance, the latter consists of ideologically decontested concepts such as Manichaeism (binary moral contrasts), naturalism (using nature as a blueprint for the human world), organicism (the nation being an indivisible whole; the organism), nostalgia (for the idyllic landscapes), spirituality (as derived from 'nature') and authority (environmental crises should be resolved through a clear chain of command). However, it remains unclear how these ideological varieties play out in visual environmental communication.

In order to address this gap, this chapter continues by offering contextual background to Hungarian (environmental) politics, mapping the two parties examined in the following: *Mi Hazánk* (Our Homeland Movement), a far-right party; and *Lehet Más a Politika – Magyarország Zöld Pártja* (LMP – Hungarian Green Party), a left-of-centre green party. Moreover, it provides a brief overview of the scholarship on visual environmental communication, before introducing the data and methods used in the analysis. The actual analysis focuses on the Facebook pages of the environmental sections of Our Homeland and LMP, consisting of a content analysis of the topics covered by the visual environmental communication, paired with the in-depth, semiotic analysis of selected images by the two parties.

Hungarian environmental politics: an expanding field?

Besides the historical and contextual embedding, any discussion on Hungarian politics needs to take into account the ruling Fidesz. Not only has the party, led by the current Prime Minister Viktor Orbán, been in uninterrupted power since 2010 (following a first spell in power in 1998–2002) but it has also been the beacon of right-wing populism and illiberal democracy in Europe (Wilkin, 2018). Even though this chapter points to the important ideological nuance between right-wing populism and the far right, particularly in relation to the latter's ethnonationalism and historical revisionism, Fidesz has contributed to the increasing political polarisation and radicalisation of right-wing politics in Hungary. Its institutional encroachments characterise an 'accumulative state' (Scheiring, 2020) and bode ill for future prospects for a democratic polity in Hungary (Buzogány, 2017). The lasting influence of Fidesz on the political economy of 'authoritarian neoliberalism' (Fabry, 2019) has not circumvented the environmental domain, where Fidesz's technocratic approach and eco-modernisation discourse have not made substantive inroads to mitigating the consequences of climate change or energy transition (Lubarda, 2023: 2, 38).

Equally important for understanding the context of Hungarian environmental politics, and consequently visual environmental communication, is the interpretation of the country's environmental history. While these accounts are usually convergent, they differ with respect to the role of nationalist sentiments in the late socialist and early post-socialist era. The partly clandestine organisations operating in the 1980s opened space for movement surrogacy, integrating the spectrum of environmental issues with civil rights and political independence from Moscow. However, such emancipatory 'eco-nationalism' (Dawson, 1996) mostly failed to assume its relevance in the post-socialist era (Harper, 2006). Nevertheless, at least two major breakthroughs, the Danube (late 1980s) and Zengő (early 2000s) movements, indicated the potential for mainstreaming environmental topics and creating a broad and ideologically eclectic environmental front (Kerényi and Szabó, 2006). Amid the lack of governmental support for environmental policies, the mainstreaming of the environment was sufficiently attained in the 2010s, partly through the emergence of a strong green party (LMP), but even more through the global recognition of the topic, epitomised in the looming danger of climate change and the 'Fridays for Future' movement. Because of this recognition of the global nature of the environmental threat, the interest of left-leaning political actors in this topic – for example *Párbeszéd Magyarországért* (Dialogue for Hungary), a breakaway party from LMP – is not particularly surprising. Moreover, the Hungarian environmental movement mirrored organisational strategies and ideological positioning characteristic of contemporary 'Western' environmentalisms (Mikecz, 2017).

However, in a country where almost two-thirds of the electorate votes for right-wing populist or far-right parties, and in which even green parties have at times had a considerable 'right-wing' and even far-right dimension (Lubarda, 2020b), ecologism coming from the right of the ideological spectrum needs to be taken into account. Although it is important not to overemphasise the nationalist bent of Hungarian environmental history, it is notable that Hungarian radical nationalism has set up its own, parallel environmental network. A significant part of this network is Our Homeland. The history of the latter is best understood through the ideological turn of Jobbik (*Jobbik Magyarországért Mozgalom* or The Movement for a Better Hungary). For long the dominant far-right party, Jobbik has moved towards the centre since around 2014, prompting a reshuffling on the whole far-right scene in Hungary (Polyakova and Shekhovtsov, 2016). Not only did it prove unacceptable to extreme-right movements previously affiliated with the party (*Hatvannégy Vármegye Ifjúsági Mozgalom, Betyársereg*), but also to some of Jobbik's members, who publicly discredited Jobbik's leadership for moving away from national radicalism. One of these factions was led by László Toroczkai and Dóra Dúró, who split from Jobbik to form Our Homeland in June 2018. Our Homeland claimed to have continued the tradition of right radicalism, calling for a 'radical change' in order to stop the ongoing decadence of the Hungarian nation (Mi Hazánk Mozgalom, 2018). In essence, the party took over most of the ideological positions of Jobbik from its most extreme era (2006–2014), including the environmental platform (Kyriazi, 2019). The environmental cabinet of Our Homeland, called *Zöld Hazánk* (Green Homeland), was established in 2019, accentuating the stewardship framing of responsibility not only 'for our fellow human beings, but also for the protection of our nature and wildlife' (Mi Hazánk, 2019). Yet electoral results have shown that Our Homeland has not been able to take over Jobbik's electorate, winning only 3.3 per cent of the votes in the 2019 European Parliament elections.

Against this far-right background, LMP has, for more than a decade, been the strongest green party in the country. It has been in Parliament since 2010, winning 7 per cent of the vote and five seats in the 2018 national elections. From its foundation in 2009 to the early 2010s, the party was on the (radical) left. Yet after several splits and electoral defeats, it gravitated towards the centre, making it no longer a clear party of the left in 2021. This journey has included serious political turmoil as frequent changes in leadership have induced major shifts in its ideological profile, to the extent that it has been claimed that the 'green' ideological background is now missing (Kovarek and Littvay, 2019). The change has also entailed cooperation with Jobbik on agricultural matters (Lubarda, 2020b) and, most recently, in announcing a joint opposition candidate for the national elections of 2022 (a coalition including Jobbik but excluding Our Homeland). In spite of these shifts towards the centre and some of its conservative membership, LMP remains an unambiguously green, left-of-centre party. This was also indicated by a name change in 2019 (from LMP – Politics Can Be Different, to LMP – Hungarian Green Party). These brief overviews of the two parties examined in this chapter serve to provide a contextual background against which the methods used in this study can now be situated.

Data and method: visual semiotics and Facebook

The focus of the analysis is on posts published on the official Facebook pages (constituting the communicative context in semiotics) of the two Hungarian parties (as the cultural context) under scrutiny. In the case of Our Homeland, this meant analysing Green Homeland, Our Homeland's environmental section, while LMP, for obvious reasons, did not have such a counterpart. Thus, all visuals at least tangentially referring to the wide spectrum of 'environmental topics' were taken into consideration (climate change; water, air, land and noise pollution; farming and land use; chemicals; environment and health; biodiversity; animal welfare; etc.). The posts considered in the analysis contained images generated by the page author. Videos have been excluded from the study, as have comments, likes and sites of further dissemination (for example, through the option 'share'). The timeframe of the analysis included the end of the last elections for the National Parliament (8 April 2018) until 1 March 2021. Overall, the empirical data include 278 images (Our Homeland: 170; LMP: 108).

In order to assess the visualisation of ideology, this chapter uses a mixed methods approach, pairing content analysis with visual semiotics. The former serves to identify the particular environmental issues the parties under scrutiny engage with. The latter provides an understanding of ideology working in this visual environmental communication by committing to a twofold task: assessing the visual environmental communication as a whole, that is, for the selected timeframe; and singling out images that represent dominant or particularly rich ideological content.

Drawing on Kress and van Leeuwen's (2006) work in conceptual visual representations, semiology is particularly useful for providing closer inspections or 'thick descriptions' of a selection of images (Rose, 2016: 73). More specifically, the analysis draws on Barthes' (1968) conceptualisation of the process of significations as entailing three orders: denotative (literal), connotative and myth (indicative of the ideological domain). Since semiologists aim to 'dissect the workings of ideology' (Rose, 2016: 71), this approach is particularly useful in identifying the underlying ideological moralities (Lakoff, 1996) conveyed through the visual form.

To do so, I analyse, first, the use of frames and angling: How was the image divided, from which angle were the images taken and what can the selection of frames or 'panels' (if the image is a comic) tell us about the whole? In relation to this, I focused on the symbolic processes (for example, embedding) and analytical processes, that is, the way in which the elements of the image are related to one another. For instance, the elements/objects in an image can be arranged in a 'part-to-whole' structure of 'the carrier' (the whole, for example the model) and 'the possessive attributes' (the parts, for example pieces of clothing worn by the model) (Kress and van Leeuwen, 2006: 87–88). Moreover, the analysis focuses on modality, the 'semiotics of colour' (van Leeuwen, 2008: 132–133), in particular the connotative meaning of texture and luminosity, saturation and modulation, but also the less technical aspects of identity and ideology (see Wodak, 2009 on the semiotics of racism). As there are no unambiguous signs (and consequently images), the focus was also on the relative degree of foreclosure, aiming to identify the space for developing a range of ideological connotations. Finally, the analysis also included the anchorage (Barthes, 1977), that is, the way in which the text implies denoted meanings in an attempt to exclude the 'unwanted' or 'wrong' interpretations of the image.

Our homeland: animals and far-right ecologism

Less than a year after being founded, Our Homeland decided to set up its 'green' cabinet, perhaps implicitly indicating willingness to continue the intention of the (Hungarian) far right to increase its influence by engaging with topics which lend themselves to symbolism (Forchtner and Kølvraa, 2015: 207). Similarly to how such a cabinet was set up in Jobbik, Green Homeland represents the party expertise in environmental issues. The cabinet also has its president and the leading figure, Krisztina Csereklye, although Erik Fülöp, upon deciding to leave Jobbik, became another party poster-person for environmental affairs (he also left Our Homeland in February 2021). Besides its authentic content branded with the logo of the organisation, Green Homeland's Facebook page (c. 3,800 likes in April 2021) reposts content from other (mostly Hungarian) websites, such as the non-nationalist *Sokszínű vidék* and *Turistamagazin*, but also nationalist outlets such as *Szent Korona Rádió* and *Zöld Ellenállás*.

A first glance at the results of the content analysis of 170 images posted on Green Homeland's Facebook page points to a single outlier: images related to animal welfare, coded a total of seventy times, or more than 40 per cent of the whole corpus (see Figure 9.1). The extensive focus on issues related to animal welfare may seem surprising, although this is less the case when one takes into account both the ideological predilection of far-right ecologism for animal welfare, the role of animals in political communication, that is, whitewashing the far-right, and the links between Our Homeland's politicians and animal rights activists. An example of these links includes *Szurkolók az Állatokért* (Sports Fans for Animals), which comprises Our Homeland supporters and whose leadership has a good relationship with Erik Fülöp. The appeal to animal sentience, constitutive of animal liberation movements (Singer, 2002), is also present in Green Homeland's imaginary, although it has never openly argued against hunting. The images referring to the issues of animal welfare rarely contained threatening or 'negative' images and anchorage, for example, depicting tortured or caged animals (although there are exceptions, such as a post from 3 September 2020), but instead resorted to images of affection (Halliday, 1985: 137).

Even though a lot of images refer to pets in the context of animal welfare but also animal cruelty, the overwhelming presence of these topics point to

Number of appearances

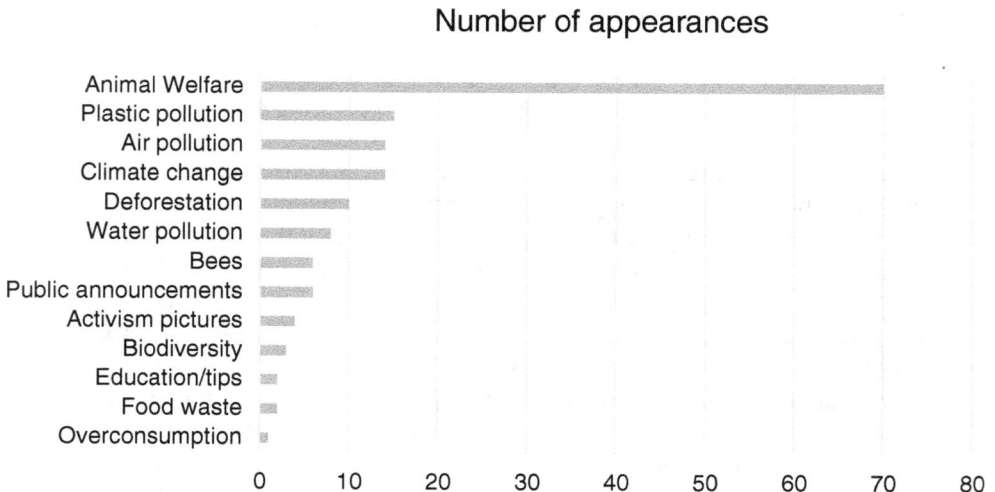

9.1 Overview of Themes/Images: Our Homeland

'charting a shifting line between us and them' (Kete, 2002: 20), where 'them', that is, the perpetrators of animal cruelty, are never explicitly represented through visual communication. This is not the case with Szurkolók, which aims most of its activism at/against the local Roma communities. Thus, while this activism is aimed at those who torture animals, it is also hinting at those who resemble cultural outsiders (such as immigrants) by engaging in practices such as ritual-religious slaughter. It is interesting that Green Homeland also paid particular attention to the protection of bees (six images, coded separately from 'animal welfare'), most often through the celebration of the World Bee Day and the relevance these species have for the food chain. Other topics include various forms of pollution, with a focus on plastic (fifteen images), air (fourteen) and water pollution (eight), as well as deforestation (ten). While most of the images point to common problems in relation to industrial pollution and inefficient heating systems, some of them are aimed at the pollution on the river Tisza, which originates in Ukraine. Green Homeland has openly blamed Ukraine for the extent of the pollution, claiming that 'the communal waste produced by Ukrainians is poisoning Hungarian people', thus highlighting the nationalist dimension of Our Homeland's environmental appeal (MTI, 2019).

Climate change action is also among the most frequent topics the page engages with (fourteen), going against the established scientific findings in relation to far-right climate denialism (Lockwood, 2018), let alone 'anti-environmentalism' (Gemenis et al., 2012). The images posted on the Green Homeland page indicate climate change acceptance, but the call for systematic or global action is deliberately avoided. Instead, the images referring to climate change often depict a two-framed composition, denoting a Manichean duality of a gloomy and apocalyptic scenario versus a positive, prosperous and polychrome visual of the globe or blooming trees. Indeed, contrasting luminosity and colours are often employed by Green Homeland in order to underpin the Manichean message of urgency.

Besides Manichaeism, another component of far-right ecologism that was conveyed through visual communication, albeit significantly less frequently, was naturalism, implying the unity of the natural and the social world and distinguishing in-species from out-species through the 'ethnic' principle (Olsen, 1999; Lubarda, 2020a). This was conducted most often through the anchorage referring to the 'protection of native species' in biodiversity. Less frequent are images concerning organic farming and food waste, which appear only once in the corpus. Images featuring their leading environmentalist, Csereklye, appear only once, using a slightly lowered vertical angle and a public distance shot presenting the whole figure, thus indicating (scientific) authority, with a quote calling for 'action and not only words' (15 February 2020). What is particularly interesting from the point of ideological idiosyncrasies is the scope of topics and posts, as some of them feature John Lennon quotes (12 April 2020) or emphasise the 'importance of global action on environmental protection' (17 June 2020), neither of which are particularly characteristic of far-right ecologists.

An example of this ideological murkiness in Green Homeland's visual environmental communication is the image-comic posted on 6 April 2020 (on the composition of comics, consisting of panels, a gutter, word balloons and the caption text, see Saraceni, 2003). The comic is a (unidirectional) transactional narrative process (see Figure 9.2) consisting of two separate frames-panels presented from the frontal, 'objective' and maximum-involvement angle, divided horizontally across the middle. The upper panel presents The Actor – a (white) male white-collar worker performing a transaction – tossing a phone in the rubbish bin in his office. The phone permeates to the bottom panel (divided by the brick-like gutter), which presents a dire image of 'the second participant': dark-skinned, poor children, possibly from the Global South or, closer to home, the Roma children performing hard labour at a grim, highly polluted trash heap. The racial component as a 'possessive attribute' at play is also amplified by an obvious colour contrast, both in luminosity and colour modulation and differentiation. The bottom image (presenting children) is darker, with reduced colour differentiation, whereas the top image (presenting the man in white collar and tie) is significantly brighter with increased colour differentiation. The contrast evokes the difference between *locus terribilis* (topos of terrible place, the bottom image, see Wodak, 1999: 38–39) and the less clear *locus amoenus* (topos of idyllic place, the upper image). The image itself contains a textual anchorage, 'People may live on different levels, but will drown in trash equally (GH)', and the logo of Green Homeland in the upper frame of the picture. The mention of 'levels' possibly alluding to racial qualities echoes a 'calculated ambivalence' (Engel and Wodak, 2012) with respect to the undergirding ideological message.

The presence of two panels-frames in an image, often used by Green Homeland, may hint at a Manichean, binary representation between 'good' and 'evil', but this is hardly the case in this picture. The image is symbolically representing the environmental degradation happening worldwide (but possibly also in Hungary), contextualising the intersectional, if not also global, nature of insatiable consumption. If a Manichean logic was to be pursued after all, it is more likely to point to the actor from the upper panel as the culprit rather than the 'good' actor. This is particularly surprising in light of what is known about the far right's lack of interest for 'the subaltern other', be it Global South workers or Roma, in realms conspicuously different from that of the ethnocracy purported by these political actors. The self-criticism rooted in the ideologically anti-consumerist positioning is also interesting, and

9.2 Our Homeland Facebook page: 'People may live on different levels, but will drown in trash equally'

is characteristic of both the (radical) left and right, as well as of ecologism. The less likely semiotic interpretation of the implicit 'white guilt' in this image could signal greenwashing Our Homeland's far-right reputation (or its tarnishing by the wider far-right community). Perhaps a more unsettling finding is that this attempt at greenwashing, epitomised in acknowledging guilt for both environmental degradation and global inequality, may indicate a broader issue: that the arguments associated with far-right ecologism are evidently coming closer to mainstream environmental politics.

LMP: a green party lamenting Trianon?

Unlike the case of Green Homeland, the visual environmental communication of LMP needs to be distinguished from the rest of the (also visual) content posted on the party's Facebook page (77,500 likes in April 2021). The analysis of a total of 108 images shows that climate change is the most dominant topic the party engages with (twenty-four images). Climate change images are usually denoted using a dark scenario, with the use of colours from the same spectrum, hence no visible contrast. Such use of the analytical process frequently entails an instrumental relation through the gesture of a hand: a carrier holding the planet and conveying a subtly anthropocentric undertone but also accentuating the extent of human responsibility for the ongoing changes. The anchorage for such apocalyptic images is often equally negative, such as the post referring to 'ecological catastrophe' (LMP Facebook, 2020b). Images against the presence of nuclear energy in the renewable energy mix appear twelve times, especially in relation to the construction of the Paks nuclear powerplant, which was, for a long time, one of the most important topics in Hungary due to its important geopolitical significance (Benazzo, 2017: 209). Much like the case of Green Homeland, issues related to different aspects of plastic (eight images), air (eight), water (four) and land (three) pollution are particularly noticeable in the party's visual communication (see Figure 9.3). Similar to climate change, images referring to (various types of) pollution are usually divided into two frames or present the 'negative' frame and dim lights, again evoking the Manichean urgency of the matter and the looming danger of the threat.

The majority of the content posted on the LMP website is aimed at antagonising the ruling Fidesz, which is not surprising given both the electoral dominance of Orbán's party and its results in the environmental arena. Examples include criticisms of the recent ideological turn of Fidesz, indicated in the 2020 New Year's address of Orbán (Kormány, 2019), such as the image pointing to the 'Fidesz's fake green' (23 February 2020). Likewise, some of the images are directly aimed at Orbán's allegedly deceiving care for animals, such as an image with the prime minister holding a puppy, followed by a caption: 'The majority of the Fidesz committee today swept away the LMP's proposal, which would have initiated a tightening of the Penal Code in the case of qualified animal torture' (3 February 2021). There are also frequent criticisms of Fidesz being inactive in the field of climate action.

The fight against smog is another prominent feature of LMP's visual environmental communication, which is mostly presented through black-and-white images of polluted areas (or sources of air pollution such as the Mátra Power Plant) and a binary representation of a carbon-intensive energy

Number of appearances

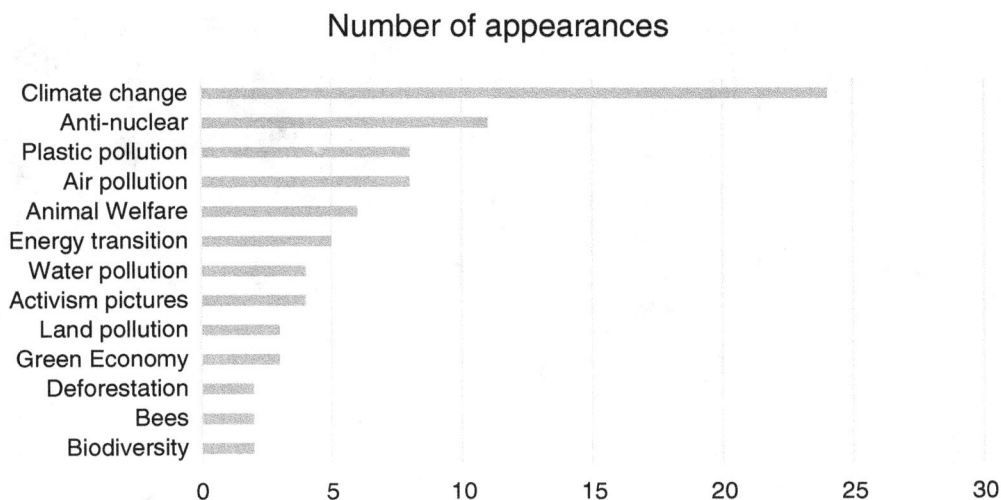

9.3 Overview of Themes/Images: LMP

juxtaposed with renewable sources of energy. An iconic sign often employed to accentuate the extent of the problem are smokestacks which, during the socialist era, often connoted progress (Harper, 2006), but which nowadays serve to signify outdatedness and decay (O'Neill and Smith, 2014). The campaign against smog features leading party members, such as Erzsébet Schmuck, the leader of the party's parliamentary group and a founding member of several green parties and political initiatives since the 1990s. Images which include prominent LMP politicians in 'far personal distance' (from the waist up, see Kress and van Leeuwen, 2006: 124–125) are frequent, and far more common compared to Our Homeland. This finding, however, needs to be contextualised, as the majority of environmental posts do not feature politicians (but use animals or images of natural environment instead).

However, not all of LMP's environmental communication points to 'green' topics the party has previously dealt with. An example is the post from 4 June 2020, marking a centenary since the Treaty of Trianon was signed in the aftermath of the First World War, signalling the end of the Austro-Hungarian empire, as well as the Kingdom of Hungary (see Figure 9.4). The Treaty of Trianon is the foundation of historical revisionism in Hungary, interpreted as an injustice committed to all Hungarians. It is for this reason that Trianon is a recurring theme even among Hungarian left-liberals (Ogris and Rathkolb, 2010: 88). What is particularly interesting, though, is the context in which this commemoration is situated among LMP: The above-mentioned post points to 'the ecological unity of the Carpathian Basin'[1]

9.4 LMP Facebook page: 'One Nation Trianon'

and the 'indivisibility of the Hungarian nation', calling for 'the preservation of the unique natural values [of the basin]' (LMP Facebook, 2020a). The idea that Trianon was an interruption to the perceived 'naturalness' of the organic and natural unity of the nation (Lubarda, 2020b) is one of the the building blocks of contemporary Hungarian nationalism. This image may also connote the idea of bioregionalism in which the world is/should be divided into regions representing authentic, 'naturally' defined ecosystems. Such a theory is principally anti-modernist (Olsen, 2000: 77), connoting environmental determinism (Frenkel, 1994): a belief that environmental conditions mould cultural values. Such a nexus seems to accentuate the alleged ideological emptiness of ecologism, which requires a host ideology to overcome its internal ambiguities (Humphrey, 2013).

In that sense, the image accompanying LMP's post is an ideologically dense example of the analytical process and a textbook example of the 'compounded exhaustive structure' (Kreuss and van Leeuwen, 2006: 97–98). The carrier (or 'whole') in this image is the map of Greater (pre-Trianon) Hungary, coloured in three shades of green and white (albeit not red, which is the third colour of the Hungarian flag). The possessive attributes, or 'parts', are the territories that today belong to surrounding Serbia, Slovakia and Romania. On this green and white canvas, the thick, black pattern, similar to bricks, symbolises the artificiality (but also strictness) of the green and white, pre-Trianon borders. Another symbol present in the image is the logo of LMP (a white silhouette of a man walking) inside the tri-coloured circle filled with green, white and red, that is, colours of the Hungarian flag. The central anchorage of the image is the capitalised text *Egy a Nemzet* (One Nation) paired with the hashtag #trianon100 (in smaller fonts) in the upper left-hand corner. Even though this image is an outlier in the sense of portending potentially nationalistic signs, it is of extraordinary importance for this analysis as it indicates the contextual susceptibility of ecologism towards national identity.

Instead of a conclusion: blurred lines of ideological allegiances?

The content analysis of visual environmental communication by Our Homeland and LMP points to a variety of similarities and differences. Notable similarities include the choice of topics, with the most salient being climate change and animal welfare, the latter particularly through the stereotypical choice of pets. The third type of issue comprises various sorts of pollution. Even though water and plastic-related pollution are most popular, air pollution is also an issue of high salience, being contextually bound because of the extent of the issue in Hungary (in relation to Mátra Power Plant). The emphasis on plastic pollution is linked to the pollution of water, hence it is partly related to the context: the extent to which these issues appear in the Danube and Tisza in particular, but also the global importance of the issue and its politically mobilising potential. Along similar lines is the celebration of World Environment Day, or days dedicated to the conservation of certain species (bees in particular), which are particularly prominent in visual communication of both GH and LMP.

The comparative analysis of the images also reveals notable, even if potentially troubling, commonalities with regard to ideological features.

The most visible feature is Manichaeism – the assertion of competing moral binaries of the 'good' and the 'evil' – which has long been considered a feature of right-wing populism (Mudde, 2004) and other radical and extremist ideologies (Backes, 2009: 184). The frequent juxtaposition of two frames-panels within the image indicate the antipodes of a negative, unwanted (most often current) outcome and an ideal, desired state. The selected images both point to a form of 'negative' communication, albeit denoting interconnectedness between the human beings and perhaps even connoting the necessity for a global response to environmental issues. While this can be explained through the fact that these are political parties, in particular parties in opposition, the Manichean form of communication seems to pervade what is likely an attempt to urge action on the array of environmental issues as opposed to the status quo position of Fidesz. Although this is not often the case, narrative structures and analytical processes (and even the compounded exhaustive structure) could be used to infer an 'either–or' choice, although the culprit is hardly ever explicitly denoted or even connoted. The totalism and polarisation of environmental discourse, also appearing as problematic in visual environmental communication, may actually signal an attempt to form a broad front (which LMP has already become a part of), but also acknowledging Manichean messages as the only way to stay afloat in Hungarian environmental politics.

The continuous emphasis on the people as protagonists of political (popular) sovereignty is another notable residue of the populist communicative context created by Fidesz. The increasing personalisation of politics, which is far from a new phenomenon (Garzia, 2014), is evident in both cases, since both LMP and Our Homeland feature their leading specialists in environmental politics. However, there is a difference in the use of frames, angles and representation: Whereas Our Homeland's leading environmentalist (ten images) is always presented from a public distance using a long shot or an oblique angle, and without a gaze, images containing messages of LMP politicians (thirteen) are always taken using a medium shot, far personal distance, looking directly at the viewer. Yet in both cases this personalisation can hardly be read as an attempt to pinpoint the charismatic or even potentially authoritarian figure behind the movement. It should thus not be read as confirming the 'authoritarian principle' characteristic of far-right parties, be it through the desire for an ecologically minded dictator (Olsen, 1999; Lubarda, 2020a) or a type of 'law-and-order' authoritarian polity.

Simultaneously, it is virtually impossible to distinguish opposing ideological moralities among the two parties, as similarities in form and content outshine the differences of the two parties (see Chapter 13 in this volume for a comparison which focuses on formal aspects of visual design). The images selected for the 'closer' analysis are not representative of the ideological content as they both potentiate a negative scenario: Trianon commemoration aside, the visual communication of LMP does not include even the faintest resonance to the idea of the nation. Our Homeland also does not seem to be a textbook case of far-right ecologism, judging by its emphasis on colourful presentation and animals without reference to the naturalist and nativist authoritarianism characteristic of this ideology. There was furthermore no mention of a religious sentiment, or even a remote reference to Christian ecologism (Bloomfield, 2019) which is, more often than not, present in far-right ecologism. However, scratching the surface reveals naturalistic references or the 'order of nature' which brings about misanthropic undertones.

Overall, this chapter has shown that boundaries between ideologies are hardly ever impermeable. In fact, ideologies are usually cobbled together from a variety of elements: concepts that are either original and indispensable or 'borrowed'. Through the use of an analytical process, the link between the denotative and connotative meaning of visuals is particularly strengthened, although even anchoring through the written mode failed to assist in the ideological positioning of an image. Moreover, while some of the visual communication of Green Homeland and LMP points to contextually specific features and topics, a lot of it is rather universal, pointing to the appropriation of strategies from green parties in western Europe and around the world. This 'universality' of visual environmental communication is profoundly disturbing, a finding more forcefully indicated than in previous studies (for example, Lubarda, 2020b). To summarise this finding, far-right ecologism uses, inter alia, visual communication to normalise and temper its ideological message, and the difference between far-right ecologism and green ideologies is murky at best.

Finally, it is important to indicate limitations and avenues for future research, such as the fact that this chapter focused mostly on the 'content' or supply side of visual environmental communication. As ideologies are not only produced and disseminated but also consumed in particular ways, the domains of 'reception' or 'demand' constitute important avenues for future research. Visual communication is 'made to mean' a particular way (Hansen, 2015: 387), but through its dissemination, the original message may become ideologically modulated, such that is bears a significantly different meaning. The process of sign-making in (visual) communication resembles ideology, in both its often unclear internal consistency and its external dissemination and appropriation. The attempt to foreground a political morality through visuals is highly unlikely to produce a standardised visual ideological grammar. In spite of their commonsensical and politically decontested nature in individual cases, ideologies as systems of political signs remain profoundly unclear.

Notes

1 The Carpathian Basin or Pannonian Plain is a large basin in Central Europe which, to some extent, geographically overlaps with the borders of Greater Hungary.

References

Backes, U. (2009): *Political Extremes: A Conceptual History from Antiquity to the Present.* Abingdon: Routledge.

Barthes, R. (1968): *Elements of Semiology.* London: Cape.

Barthes, R. (1977): Rhetoric of the image. In: S. Heath (ed.), *Image–Music–Text.* New York: Hill and Wang, 32–51.

Benazzo, S. (2017): Not all the past needs to be used: Features of Fidesz's politics of memory, *Journal of Nationalism, Memory and Language Politics*, 17(1): 198–221.

Bloomfield, E. (2019): *Communication Strategies for Engaging Climate Skeptics: Religion and the Environment.* London: Routledge.

Buzogány, A. (2017): Illiberal democracy in Hungary: Authoritarian diffusion or domestic causation?, *Democratization*, 24(7): 1307–1325.

Dawson, J. I. (1996): *Eco-nationalism: Anti-nuclear Activism and National Identity in Russia, Lithuania, and Ukraine.* Durham, NC: Duke University Press.

Engel, J. and Wodak, R. (2012): 'Calculated ambivalence' and Holocaust denial in Austria. In: R. Wodak and J. Richardson (ed.), *Analysing Fascist Discourse.* London: Routledge, 73–96.

Fabry, A. (2019): *The Political Economy of Hungary: From State Capitalism to Authoritarian Neoliberalism.* London: Palgrave.

Fahlenbrach, K. (2008): Emotions in sound: Audiovisual metaphors in the sound design of narrative films, *Projections*, 2(2): 85–103. http://dx.doi.org/10.3167/proj.2008.020206

Forchtner, B. (ed.) 2019: *Far Right and the Environment: Politics, Discourse, and Communication.* London: Routledge.

Forchtner, B. and Kølvraa, C. (2015): The nature of nationalism: Populist radical right parties on countryside and climate, *Nature and Culture*, 10(2): 199–224. https://doi.org/10.3167/nc.2015.100204

Freeden, M. (2006): Ideology and political theory, *Journal of Political Ideologies*, 11(1): 3–22.

Frenkel, S. (1994): Old theories in new places? Environmental determinism and bioregionalism, *The Professional Geographer*, 46(3): 31–41.

Garzia, D. (2014): *Personalization of Politics and Electoral Change.* London: Palgrave.

Gemenis, K., Katsanidou, A. and Vasilopoulou, S. (2012): The politics of anti-environmentalism: Positional issue framing by the European radical right. MPSA Annual Conference, Chicago, 12–15 April 2012.

Halliday, M. (1985): *An Introduction to Functional Grammar.* London: Edward Arnold.

Hansen, A. (2015): Promising directions for environmental communication research, *Environmental Communication*, 9(3): 384–391. https://doi.org/10.108 0/17524032.2015.1044047

Harper, K. (2006): *Wild Capitalism: Environmental Activists and Post-socialist Political Ecology in Hungary*. Washington, DC: East European Monographs.

Hicks, D. (2014): A geography of hope, *Geography*, 99(1): 5–12. http:// dx.doi.org/10.1080/00167487.2014.12094385

Humphrey, M. (2013): Green ideology. In: M. Freeden and M. Stears (eds), *The Oxford Handbook of Political Ideologies*. Oxford: Oxford University Press.

Kerényi, S. and Szabó, M. (2006): Transnational influences on patterns of mobilisation within environmental movements in Hungary, *Environmental Politics*, 15(5): 803–820. http://dx.doi.org/10.1080/09644010600937249

Kete, K. (2002): Animals and ideology: The politics of animal protection in Europe. In: N. Rothfels (ed.), *Representing Animals*. Bloomington: Indiana University Press, 19–34.

Kormány (2019): Prime Minister Viktor Orbán's New Year International Press Conference. https://2015-2019.kormany.hu/en/the-prime-minister/the-prime-minister-s-speeches/prime-minister-viktor-orban-s-new-year-international-press-conference (accessed 17 March 2023).

Kovarek, D. and Littvay, L. (2019): Where did all the environmentalism go? 'Politics can be different' (LMP) in the 2018 Hungarian parliamentary elections, *Environmental Politics*, 28(3): 574–582. https://doi.org/10.1080/09644016.2019.1567874

Kress, G. and van Leeuwen, T. (2006): *Reading Images: The Grammar of Visual Design*. London: Routledge.

Kyriazi, A. (2019): The environmental communication of Jobbik: Between strategy and ideology. In: B. Forchtner (ed.), *The Far Right and the Environment*. London: Routledge, 184–200.

Lakoff, G. (1996): *Moral Politics*. Chicago: University of Chicago Press.

LMP Facebook (2020a): 4 June 2020. www.facebook.com/lehetmas/photos/pb.100059329459909.-2207520000./10157636948287013/?type=3 (accessed 17 March 2023).

LMP Facebook (2020b): 10 October 2020. www.facebook.com/photo/?fbid=1015796 2071182013&set=pb.100059329459909.-2207520000 (accessed 17 March 2023).

Lockwood, M. (2018): Right-wing populism and the climate change agenda: Exploring the linkages, *Environmental Politics*, 27(4): 712–732.

Lubarda, B. (2020a): Beyond ecofascism? Far-right ecologism (FRE) as a framework for future inquiries, *Environmental Values*, 29(6):713–732. http://dx.doi.org/10.319 7/096327120X15752810323922

Lubarda, B. (2020b): 'Homeland farming' or 'rural emancipation'? The discursive overlap between populist and green parties in Hungary, *Sociologia Ruralis*, 60(4): 810–832.

Lubarda, B. (2023): *Far-Right Ecologism: Environmental Politics and the Far Right in Hungary and Poland*. London: Routledge.

Mertig, A. and Dunlap, R. (1995): Public approval of environmental protection and other new social movement goals in western Europe and the United States,

International Journal of Public Opinion Research, 7(1): 145–156. http://dx.doi. org/10.1093/ijpor/7.2.145

Mi Hazánk (2019): Megalakult a Zöld Hazánk, a Mi Hazánk Mozgalom természet-, környezet- és állatvédelmi kabinetje. https://mihazank.hu/megalakult-a-zold-hazank/ (accessed 20 April 2021).

Mi Hazánk Mozgalom (2018): Alapító Nyilatkozat [Founding Declaration]. https:// mihazank.hu/alapito-nyilatkozat/ (accessed 17 March 2023).

Mikecz, D. (2017): Environmentalism and civil activism in Hungary. In: M. Moskawicz and W. Przybylski (eds), *Understanding Central Europe*. London: Routledge, 127–134.

MTI (2019): Our Homeland Movement urges for a solution to stop waste pollution in Tisza [A Mi Hazánk Mozgalom megoldást sürget a Tisza hulladékszennyezésének felszámolására]. https://hirado.hu/belfold/belpolitika/cikk/2019/06/22/a-mi-hazank-mozgalom-megoldast-surget-a-tisza-hulladekszennyezesenek-felszamolasara (accessed 26 April 2021).

Mudde, C. (2004): The populist zeitgeist, *Government and Opposition*, 39(4): 542–563.

Ogris, G. and Rathkolb, O. (2010): *Authoritarianism, History, and Democratic Dispositions in Austria, Poland, Hungary and the Czech Republic*. Innsbruck: Studien Verlag.

Olsen, J. (1999): *Nature and Nationalism: Right-Wing Ecology and the Politics of Identity in Contemporary Germany*. New York: St Martin's Press.

Olsen, J. (2000): The perils of rootedness: On bioregionalism and right wing ecology in Germany, *Landscape Journal*, 19(1/2): 73–83. http://dx.doi.org/10.3368/lj.19.1–2.73

O'Neill, S. J. (2013): Image matters: Climate change imagery in US, UK and Australian newspapers, *Geoforum*, 49: 10–19. https://doi.org/10.1016/j.geoforum.2013.04.030

O'Neill, S. J. and Smith, N. (2014): Climate change and visual imagery, *WIREs Climate Change*, 5: 73–87. https://doi.org/10.1002/wcc.249

Polyakova, A. and Shekhovtsov, A. (2016): On the rise: Europe's fringe right, *World Affairs*, 179(1): 70–80. https://doi.org/10.1177%2F0043820016662746

Rose, G. (2016): *Visual Methodologies: An Introduction to Researching with Visual Materials*. London: Sage.

Saraceni, M. (2003): *The Language of Comics*. London: Routledge.

Scheiring, G. (2020): *The Retreat of Liberal Democracy: Authoritarian Capitalism and the Accumulative State in Hungary*. London: Palgrave.

Singer, P. (2002): *Animal Liberation*. New York: Ecco Press.

Sontag, S. (2004): *Regarding the Pain of Others*. London: Penguin.

van Leeuwen, T. (2008): New forms of writing, new visual competencies, *Visual Studies*, 23(2): 130–135. https://doi.org/10.1080/14725860802276263

Warlaumont, H. (1995): Advertising images: From persuasion to polysemy, *Journal of Current Issues & Research in Advertising*, 17(1): 19–31. https://doi.org/10.108 0/10641734.1995.10505023

Wilkin, P. (2018): The rise of 'illiberal' democracy: The Orbánization of Hungarian political culture, *Journal of World-Systems Research*, 24(1): 5–42. https:// doi.org/10.5195/jwsr.2018.716

Wodak, R. (1999): *The Discursive Construction of National Identity*. Edinburgh: Edinburgh University Press.

Wodak, R. (2009): The semiotics of racism: A critical discourse-historical analysis. In: J. Renkema (ed.), *Discourse, of Course: An Overview of Research in Discourse Studies*. Amsterdam: John Benjamins, 311–326.

10

Homeland, cows and climate change: the visualisation of environmental issues by the far right in India

Mukul Sharma

Geographical entity, bounded by the mighty Himalayas in the North and the Mahasagar in the South is known as Bharat, Hindustan or India. The inhabitants of this land are designated as Bharti (or Bhartiya), Hindus or Indians. [...] The contribution of the Hindus in various fields of knowledge and thought has been admirable. Their views on the importance of a sustainable environment and the existence of bio-diversity may provide solace to the strife-torn world which is facing worst climate crisis today. (Shukla, 2018: 59)

Introduction

Thus explains an article in the *Organiser*, a widely circulated weekly English-language magazine published in Delhi since 1947 and affiliated with the Hindu nationalist organisation *Rashtriya Swayamsevak Sangh* (National Volunteer Organisation, RSS). The article recalls Hindu epics and religious texts that, according to the writer, contain deep environmental consciousness and remind Indians of their glorious tradition of protecting mother earth and the fatherland. Included in this article are two visuals, one showing a woman wearing traditional ornaments and praying to the sacred Peepal tree (*Ficus religiosa*) and the other showing a group of devotees, mostly women, dipping in the river and offering prayers to the Sun God – both giving force to the claim that this is a people rooted in nature/culture. Several such texts and visuals in the *Organiser* show how RSS – the progenitor and controller of many organisations (together called the RSS 'family' of organisations), including the ruling, far-right nativist and authoritarian Bharatiya Janata Party (BJP, see Mudde, 2019) which has governed India, including many of its states, since 2014 (Rehman, 2019) – has been active on environmental issues in multiple ways.

These organisations represent a Hindutva politics that projects India as fundamentally a Hindu society, defines Muslims and minorities as aggressors and outsiders, and works towards recreating a golden past based on caste, hierarchy and a majoritarian nation. They espouse a Hindu system of thought, knowledge and communication, which, allegedly, constructs our experiences of the environment. They carry out regular activities and campaigns on specific environmental issues, and selectively target practices, people, places and politics, either to condemn and attack them for various ecological reasons or to glorify a leader, such as Prime Minister Narendra Modi, for his holiness, guidance and action to save the earth. Indeed, the regular flow of environmental texts and visuals in the *Organiser*, which openly states the 'positive impact of RSS on NDA Government' (Singh, 2015), epitomises a range of representational modes: ancient, Vedic, cosmic, mystic and mythical; sacred gods, goddesses, animals, rivers and places; networks of energy, power, electricity, production and transmission; mighty missiles, rockets, machines, technology, successes of science and scientists; and an entourage of visuals of the Supreme Leader, spread across its issues.

Against this background, this chapter scrutinises the environmental politics of Hindutva by asking the following question: What characterises the visual environmental communication of the *Organiser*, representing Hindutva, and how does it construct ideal Indian subjects, in relation to 'others', mother earth and the fatherland? How do Hindu nationalists visualise the role of science, technology, climate change and renewable energy in representing a great awakening of the motherland? And what are the specific characteristics of the far-right environmental politics in India, which are different from the West?

In responding to these questions, this chapter offers an analysis of 250 issues (roughly fifty each year) of the *Organiser* published during the first five-year term of BJP rule in India (2014–2019), to understand the visual culture of the far right's politics of the environment. In these issues, I have located eighty articles and news reports related directly (climate change and renewable energy) or indirectly (agriculture and science) to the environment. Most articles and news reports feature images (photographs, maps, sketches or cartoons): seventy-two in total. In my analysis, I have investigated all these articles, news reports and images, taking an inductive approach to identify definite trends that emerge from the data.

While extensive academic writings on Hindu nationalism and the far right in contemporary India have also provided important intellectual resources, my analysis of environmental material in the *Organiser* brings out some new trends and developments in the politics of the far right in India. Amid a diversity of environmental texts and visuals in the *Organiser*, this contribution focuses on four prominent themes which have been identified on the basis of their frequency in the analysed material: first, the envisioning of a great natural Hindu 'motherland' and it's past, present and future;

second, icons of the mother, embodied in river and animal, and her enemies; third, climate change and renewable energy; and fourth, the eulogising of Modi as an environmental saviour. Several other themes, such as agriculture, organic farming, food, sanitation, cleanliness, pollution, cities, urban development and natural disasters, also appear in the magazine and are tangentially referred to.

As such, this chapter is situated at the intersection of the emerging field of studies on the far right and the natural environment (Olsen, 1999; Forchtner, 2019a; Malm and The Zetkin Collective, 2021) and the burgeoning field of visual studies in South Asia (Pinney, 2004; Davis, 2007; Ramaswamy, 2014), and a noticeable 'visual turn' in the region, involving new producers and viewers, environments and places, where visuals acquire a materiality of their own and open multiple ways of meaning-making (Freitag, 2014). The widespread use of images and media by Hindu religious politics has drawn the attention of South Asian scholars (Kapur, 1993; Rajagopal, 2001). However, the entanglements between visuality, the Hindu Right and the 'natural' environment, including visuals around history, culture, religion, myths, memory and modernity, have escaped their attention. Indeed, environmental narratives can often buttress a regressive politics, which has been referred to as 'right-wing ecology' (Olsen, 1999), and feed into the spread of far-right politics, ideology and practice. This relationship has drawn considerable academic attention in Europe. In a key contribution to this field, Olsen (1999) identifies its ideological content in terms of pollution of an environmental order that harps on natural human belonging to a particular place, culture and ethnicity. More recent studies notice a growing link between a range of far-right actors, environmental themes and communication in Europe and beyond. Far-right discourses on the 'natural' environment provide a solid base for their wider identity politics (Forchtner, 2019b). In India, the convergence between Hindu nationalism and environmental politics has been identified around ultranationalism; the yearning for a Brahminical Hindu religion, tradition and culture; emphasis on authority, social order, unity and discipline; and an implicit hostility towards Muslims, Dalits and Christians (Sharma, 2012). However, there has been no significant study to understand the links between Hindutva politics and environment following the ascendancy of BJP and Modi to power in the country.

It is the visual component of such politics which takes centre stage in this chapter. Applying 'Heidegger's idea of modernity as an age in which the world is primarily experienced as a picture' (Sinha, 2007: 188), the centrality of image practices in India also enables an exploration of historical links between the visual images and the experience of modernity. This chapter positions the visuality of far-right environmental politics at a critical time, when for the first time in independent India, the far right is at the helm of governmental power and is actively propagating policies and actions in the sectors of energy, climate change, science, technology, land and water, to make India a modern, powerful and developed country.

With this brief introduction, the chapter moves to the four main themes present in the magazine: first, visualising the naturescape (geographically, historically and scientifically) as a great Hindu motherland for which people are ready to kill and willing to die; second, religious iconography of mother, embodying river and animal; third, championing concerns of climate change and renewable energy; and fourth, the portrayal of Modi as a great environmental leader. The chapter closes with a summary of the main arguments.

The great Hindu motherland/homeland: natural and scientific

According to Kaur (2007), Indian nationalist visual representation is premised on several interrelated themes. These include: figurative ideals, individuated as heroes/heroines or collectivised as an ideal group of people; iconic events; representations of gender; constructions of 'others'; presentations of space, nature and territory; indices of national progress and modernisation; and aniconic emblems that evoke the national ideal. Thus, visuals of nature and natural contours, land and landscapes, rivers, mountains, forests, people and animals help to construct a homeland. Notions of belonging and identity within a unique homeland are always defined in terms of what is supposedly internal, exclusive, religious and cultural. Thus, a nation comes to be embodied in nature and its representations, and such embodiment can allegedly not be shared with non-national others. Environmental protection coalesces with the nationalist imperative of preventing the nation from being polluted. A Hindu culture comes to be valorised and equated with the national culture, and a process that might be called political synonymising – the creation of a singular identity via eliding or collapsing separate concepts into each other – is brought out (Sharma, 2012).

The *Organiser* sees Bharat as the motherland: 'this Bharat is so carved out by Mother Nature that our sub-continent is a world of its own with an inalienable soul of the highest Everest-high esoteric wisdom, enshrined in our Vedic culture' (Rangarajan, 2016: 23). This text visualises the motherland – her body, arms, feet, head and hair – with land, river and mountain. A map of the 'motherland' is placed prominently in the middle of the page, where the figure of a mother is seen holding the saffron flag on top of the geographic entity of the country. Declaring that the time has come when everybody must hail the motherland, the article also warns of traitors and 'those who aggressed this holy land and subjugated the Rashtra'

(Rangarajan, 2016). Such maps, along with censuses and museums created by the colonial and post-colonial states, profoundly shape nationalist communities and ideologies (Anderson, 1991).

Motherland is sometimes used interchangeably with fatherland, man, *purusharthas* (manly power) and *dharma*. For example, one article states that: 'We believe in the oneness of Man and Nature. Right from the Vedic period till date the Indian life line has never deviated from this main line of thought' (Muralivallabhan, 2016: 56). Two visuals display a man holding the sampling of a plant, and five fingers of his rising palm, expressing five primordial, basic elements of the universe (fire, air, space, earth and water). A half-page coloured photograph (Figure 10.1) of RSS's chief and some of its top functionaries, who are on the stage of an exclusive training camp of their core volunteers, asks for vigilance and war against the invaders. The background of the stage is covered with a bright visual of the mighty Himalayas, with the following slogan prominently displayed in Hindi: '*Satya ka aadhaar lekar, hum Himalaya se khade hain*' ('We stand strong like the Himalayas with our basis in truth') (Pachpore, 2014: 44). The written texts and visuals together frame them in specific, political ways: Hindu's unity, purity, integration and balance, held safely in the mighty hands of Hindu men.

This illustrates the far right's 'matrix of integration', invoking the glorious tradition of a unified nature-nation-culture, while simultaneously subverting

Sarsanghachalak Shri Mohan Bhagwat speaking at the concluding ceremony of Sangh Shiksha Varg in Nagpur

10.1 RSS's chief with top functionaries

the 'disintegrative' identity politics of region, language, caste or gender that 'we get to see in the post-colonial polity' (Bharadwaj, 2018: 9). The nation is defined in geocultural units, where divinity and sacrality of landscapes, tradition and culture are the most prominent aspects of the Hindu *rajya* (nation). Indeed, and in contrast to post-colonial Indian states and institutions (recognised on the basic of democratic, federal and linguistic aspirations), the *Organiser* imagines society on the basis of divine geography, traditional Bharata (India), different collectivities such as *jati* or *sampardaya* (community), and civilisers/refiners. Visually, this is conveyed via, for example, photographs of Rameshwaram temple, with river water and a large number of devotees. Rameshwaram is associated with the Hindu myth of God Ram and his war against the demon-king Ravan. Since the 1980s, RSS, BJP and its associated bodies have polarised and mobilised the Hindu population in the name of Ram, promising the construction of his temple and the restoration of *ramrajya* (rule of Hindu God Ram), following the demolition of the Babri mosque by Hindutva forces in 1992. The mosque was built in the fifteenth century at Ayodhya in north India, which has been portrayed by Hindutva as the birthplace of the Hindu God Ram.

In this myth-making, Vedic and ancient Hindu India is projected as glorious and 'golden' in every sphere, place and space, including its village system, community, local knowledge, food, health, land, water and forest management. Industrialisation, Westernisation and colonisation have often been identified as enemies of a natural, harmonious and environmentally sound system, in this case a Hindu society. In the pages of the *Organiser*, there are repeated calls to return to the ancient natural Hindu system, which involves various dimensions. Take, for example, the following articulation of traditional villages and the village ecosystem:

> Guruji believed that our villages had all the required trades and solutions for all. He was of the view that our villages had about 360 '*Jatis*' and each *Jati* was a profession, an expertise in an art. *Jati* was not merely a caste but a skill in a particular trade. [...] Further, each profession had sub-classifications within them which in modern terms can be seen as super specialisations. [...] This entire ecosystem made our villages self-sufficient. (Vaidyaraj, 2018: 73)

In a picture, Guruji Ravinder Sharma, the promoter of traditional arts, science, technology and social organisation, and founder of *Kala Ashram* (House of Arts), is seen amid a background of a vast spread of land, sitting and making small idols of Hindu gods. Accompanying it are other visuals that display rural artefacts and villagers, working collectively on a fire/dust bowl with their hands and equipment. The visuals, as prominently displayed as the text, not only strengthen the author's basic argument of the Indian village being a great ecosystem, but expand it further by single-handedly focusing on caste-based rural knowledge and the artisan system. Caste-divisions, hierarchies and subjugation of Dalits and low-caste people do not find any mention in this constructed 'ideal' village ecosystem.

In its environmental language and imagery, post-2014, the far right has also been trying to blur the binaries between the West and India, tradition and modernity, rural and urban. The major markers of such divisions – science, technology, industry, city, development and globalisation – have been at times embraced in this projection. Indeed, BJP rule has also seen the RSS go through a series of modulations: Modernity, development, science and technology have resurfaced; they are now embraced, not any longer outright rejected, but nevertheless repackaged through nativism. The simultaneous presence of natural and scientific, past and future, described through myth and (as we will see soon) missile, creates a new hybrid Hindu world. The writers in the *Organiser* explain how such a world of sophisticated science and technology (including knowledge of astronomy and nuclear physics, engineering and climate change) existed in the great Hindu motherland, which was culturally sound and environmentally sustainable. These developments, they argue, were suppressed under Muslim and colonial rule; however, they have been revived under the BJP government and must be taken further. In this changed rhetoric, motherland and modernity strengthen each other and provide a new rationale to Hindu readers to comprehend the changing stances of RSS and BJP.

Relevant articles in the *Organiser*, such as 'A Return to India's Glorious Scientific Past' (Kumar, 2015), 'Confluence in Science' (Manekar, 2017) and 'With Civilisation to Globalisation' (Diwan, 2018) are eye-catching in terms of their regularity and coverage. They highlight how ancient Indian science and technology, and its modern avatars, can bring glory, pride, confidence and power back to the motherland. Scientific visualisations hardly focus on its environmental aspects. The use of photographs as a visual medium of narrative is collaborated by the photographic-like pictures, such as spaces, waves, currents, stars, graphs and maps. Such imageries 'seem hyper-legible, but in fact they are far from transparent or direct' (Demos, 2017: 17), because they do not offer location data, ownership or legibility, and are carefully edited to show the positive examples of modern development.

Written texts and visuals in the *Organiser* focus on taking their ancient and contemporary understanding of science to the masses and highlight that Hindus are hailing new innovations and solutions for sustainable development. For example, 'Confluence in Science' (Manekar, 2017) is accompanied by four photographs (a minister, a child, a group of people and another mass of people) appreciating the 'true spirit of science by bringing traditional and modern stream together'. The caption of a three-column photograph of slogan-shouting people in front of many missiles reads: 'PROMISE OF

NATIONAL PRIDE: Visitors enjoying the grandeur and magnificence of BrahMos that adorn the Indian army' (Manekar, 2017: 35).

In sum, RSS's construction of motherland – its natural, social and economic contours – is based on a Hindu supremacist view where a majoritarian religious community presents a case for the return of a glorious, nostalgic past, and calls for aggression, masculinity and power in culture and religion, and unity and integration against enemies.

Icons of the mother: river and animal

RSS's devotion to motherland/homeland, and the provocative declarations of men's history and power to defend it, extend further to visualise rivers and places, animals and forests, as icons of mother. In metaphorical representations by Hindu nationalism in north India, the female body and the many faces of 'mother' – motherland, mother tongue, motherhood – have served as the most universal and potent symbols of imagining the nation (Gupta, 2001). Consequently, the icon of Mother India enables Hindu nationalist parties to make specific claims regarding ownership of land, exercise of sovereignty over it and legitimacy of rule (Ramaswamy, 2001).

It is thus not surprising that the *Organiser* too has regularly featured different images and figures of mother as representing environmental icons since 2014. On the one hand, the BJP in power has driven the RSS to reimagine the physical body of the nation as a river (Mother Ganga, Narmada or Saraswati) and, on the other hand, as mother cow. These environmental icons of mother are described as natural, ideal, pure and generous, living amid danger, destruction and pollution. The mothers that emerge from the river and the animal are Hindu culture and religion specific, and are emblematic of passive female figures. In nationalistic politics, the nation-space has been frequently conceived as a passive, vulnerable woman, who enables the establishment of heroism of the active, masculine man (Grewal and Kaplan, 1994). In a new Hindu world, where many things are destabilised, the mother provides a stable, personal, emotional and traditional setting. The mother touches heart and soul, as well as boils one's blood. What is powerful is the continued production of an active, strong, passionate and heroic male body of environmental politics, which must deal decisively with the enemies of the mother.

First, and concerning 'Mother Ganga', Modi (2014) himself spoke of 'feeling like a child when he returns to his mother's lap'. Two articles published in the *Organiser*, 'Namami Gange' (*Organiser*, 2015b) and 'Hey Gange' (Sirohi, 2017), display similar aspects of cultural and ecological politics of the RSS around rivers. 'Namami Gange' spreads a photograph of the river on top of the article, displaying its everyday cultural and religious forms, such as water, temples, buildings, people and boats. The author describes the Ganga River vividly as 'Mother Ganga', as 'the heart of the world's one of the richest civilisations' and stresses the extent to which Indians are 'emotionally attached to the river' (Das, 2015). 'Hey Gange' also has a four-column top spread of two photographs of the river, along with water, mountain, construction and erosion, where the written text focuses on 'pollution', 'vigorous action against those who cause pollution' and 'most strict action [...] against those who pollute the Ganga' (Sirohi, 2017: 43). Several researches have shown that in its campaigns, the RSS constantly refers to purity and pollution, particularly cultural pollution. The image of a pure, scared Mother Ganga (Figure 10.2), descending from the heavens, has been created for its 'unique power of salvation', 'purification' and killing of 'evil spirits' (Misra, 2019: 43).

The concept of pollution has been central in the right-wing ecology of the Western world where foreign, alien and 'other' human or non-human species are seen as the central cause of the defilement of natural and social worlds (Olsen, 1999). In the environmental imaginary of Germany's extreme right, an ideal citizen and state is characterised by purity, order and stability (Forchtner, 2019). The RSS takes this concept to another, aggressive level. Slogans like '*Pukarti hai Maa, Pukarti hai Bharti, Khoon se Tilak Karo aur Goliyon se Aarti!*' ('Calls Mother, calls Bharat, Mark your forehead with blood and worship with bullets') and '*Jis Desh mein Shastr aur Shaastr ki Puja Hoti Hai, Who Kabhi Parajit Nahi Hota!*' ('A country where arms and religious scriptures are worshipped, can never be defeated') help in crystallising feelings for a pure and sacred river flowing amid an ethnically and culturally homogenous, naturally existing nation. Hindu national identity becomes the pre-eminent sense of identity and belonging, and environmental politics is made synonymous with the protection of various elements of that identity (Sharma, 2001).

A campaign around 'servicing Mother/Goddess Narmada' river in the Madhya Pradesh state, launched by the BJP government, not only focuses on pollution but builds a visual of a 'cradle with natural Shivalinga (representation of the Hindu God Shiva) from where the Narmada originates' (Kumar, 2017: 24). Portraits and group photographs of the state chief minister, Modi, RSS functionaries and *sadhus* (renunciant, holy man) are prominently displayed, where they are shown performing religious rituals to purify the river. The texts are visualised in a continuum of Hindu imageries and imaginations, conveying an aggressive, nationalist meaning. The importance of mother rivers in the environmental politics of the Hindu right leads the *Organiser* to run a four-page photo essay on the 'resurgence of Sarasvati

An artistic impression of Gangavataran

10.2 Mother Ganga descending from the heavens

Ethos': An endeavour 'to resurrect the spiritual and cultural legacy attached to the Vedic heritage river and to restore its glory enshrined in scriptures' (Bharadwaj, 2017: 30) in the BJP-ruled Haryana state. After BJP's acquisition of power, the RSS has tried to revive the river Sarasvati, to bolster their idea of a golden age of Hindu India before the invasions of Muslims and Christians (Nair and Daniel, 2015).

Second, and along with the mother river, the RSS constructs the mother cow as a living, motherly figure that is imperative for the economic, environmental, political and emotional rejuvenation of the community and the country. The cow has a complex historical trajectory in India and, symbolising a sacred entity, has religious and cultural rooting in Hindu society. In ecological and economic terms, there is an 'entire cattle complex' where the agro-economic system, ecology and people are closely interrelated (Harris, 1966). At the same time, the sacred cow as mother becomes a significant trope for the reassertion of religious and national identities (Sharma, 2018). Peter van der Veer (1994) links the Hindu love for mother cow and the protection of her body to Brahmanical rituals, devotional religion, the metaphor of a nurturing mother goddess and the usefulness of her products. This sacred symbol has also become a way to establish sacred spaces, in a process of sanctification and group solidarity (Yang, 1980). Pinney (1997) points to the vital significance of visuals of cows in the organisation and ideology of cow protection movements during the colonial period and demonstrates how images of the cow were invested with the divine. In numerous lithographs, the cow becomes a proto-nation, a space that embodies the Hindu cosmology. Post-2014, BJP and RSS have renewed these planks and markers of the cow protection movements through new and strict legislation, accompanied with aggressive campaigns.

The spread of the cultural artefact of the cow is multifaceted. There are a large number of written texts and images devoted to her, which are saturated with Hindu idioms. For example, 'Cow Protection: Cow is a Cultural Symbol' (Kashyap, 2017) refurbishes an earlier, ubiquitous image of the cow, in whose body several Hindu gods are residing. A calf is at her udder and a woman sits before the calf holding a bowl, waiting for her turn. This woman is labelled: 'The Hindu'. Behind the cow, above her tail, is a representation of Krishna labelled 'Dharmraj', and in front of the cow, above her head, is a man with a drawn sword labelled 'Kaliyug'. The upper-caste Hindus expiated on the meaning of the image, by identifying the sword-man as the immediate threat to the cow. The overtly Hindu symbolism of the cow is usually accompanied with images and written texts of the killing, slaughtering and smuggling of cows, often targeting Muslims as the chief culprits, even to the extent of defending their lynching by Hindutva groups. Indeed, Muslims have become the key targets of the cow protection movement in contemporary times. An article titled 'Bring an End to Cow Slaughter' has an image of a sadhu holding a banner with the slogan 'Don't Slaughter Your Mother Cow' and begins with Muslim-bashing:

> Asaduddin Owaisi and so many other Muslims as well as secularists tell us that they have so-called freedom to eat whatsoever they want to eat. Yes, you have the freedom to do whatsoever you want to. But you also have the freedom to urinate. But do you pass water openly in the public? No [...] you should be aware of the environmental hazards of cow slaughter as well. (Das, 2015: 25)

To sum up this section, it appears that Mother Ganga and mother cow are cursed by pollution and Muslims, and urgently need protection through action by militant Hindu conservationists. The ecological use of the idiom of mother combines emotion with impulse, glorification of Hindu culture and religion with solemnity of everyday worship, and nature with nationalism.

Climate change and renewable energy

The links between conservatism, right-wing nationalism, xenophobia and climate change have been researched widely in the context of the USA and Europe. There is a significant level of climate change denial among conservative white males in the United States (McCright and Dunlop, 2011) and studies have shown how the growth of right-wing nationalism in Europe has contributed to an increase in climate change denial (Ernstrom, 2021), which is also linked with such right-wing parties' exclusionary sociocultural issues and institutional distrust (Jylha et al., 2020). However, researchers have also pointed out that some far-right populist parties, for instance France's *Rassemblement National* (National Rally), are adopting climate protection policy positions, showing much more flexibility and adaptability than previously anticipated, and using these issues strategically for the benefit of their organisation (Oswald et al., 2021). Indeed, some have acknowledged climate change, incorporating such a stance to blame immigrants and to advocate stronger borders, which has been referred to as 'ecobordering' (Turner and Bailey, 2021).

In India, climate change has been a significant political and economic project of the Hindu nationalists to propagate their vision of a 'New India'. From the RSS to the BJP, Hindu far-right groups have emphasised the glory of ancient and 'natural' Hindu India, condemned the West and promoted the renewable energy sector to mitigate climate change. Such patterns of assent and action create positive channels between three core constituencies: Hindutva organisations, BJP-run states and big industry, as they work closely in championing certain kinds of climate solutions. In line with this, visuals that are abstract and scientific, photographs of natural disasters and peoples' misery, and images of dedicated organisational efforts and political leadership at local and national levels, bring to the fore Hindu nationalist politics and mega-modern industrial projects.

The BJP Election Manifesto for 2014 highlighted 'climate change mitigation activities' at its 'centre of thoughts and actions', and promised to take initiatives like 'cleaner production', 'cleaner fuels', 'carbon credit', 'ecological audit', 'pollution control', 'green building' and 'environment technology'. It also promised to accord renewable energy the 'highest priority' (Bharatiya Janata Party, 2014). In December 2015, the cover of the *Organiser* displayed a full-size image of the Eiffel Tower, with a cover story titled 'Paris Climate 2015: Towering Task'. The latter explained in stark terms that the issue of climate change is related to national security, terrorism and the stability of the country, calling for Paris to be turned into 'a unifying ground for the world' to tackle climate change and terrorism, something the magazine viewed as 'a towering task and the role of Bharat will be critical in this process' (*Organiser*, 6 December 2015, cover page).

Another article on the Paris Climate Summit called it 'an attempt to save the world' from instability, insecurity and disasters (Dubey, 2015c: 13). Several such articles on climate change and its impact are image-driven, exposing readers to a deluge of photos of destruction and disasters. The images are placed within an overarching story of climate disorders and threats to the country. Reproduced in high numbers, such images create various degrees of fear, anxiety and concern. Human misery, loss of lives and displacement loom large in these times of climate change. Fear communication arouses emotional responses and mediates belief and behaviour change. In Hindutva politics, fear is enmeshed within the broader contours of contested political, social and cultural issues, with a series of disturbing and frightening communications about Muslims, Pakistan, China, terrorists, the killing of cows and conversions (Omar, 2021). Amid this, calls are made to awaken the great Hindu nation to be a strong superpower.

In contrast, popular print articles and images on the RSS's conceptualisation and visualisation of climate change never deal with issues like social and economic justice, climate equity, caste, gender, industry, fossil fuel, mining, large dams, nuclear projects, natural resources, displacement, development and capitalism (Bidwai, 2012).

Interestingly, and against the backdrop of climate change, the Indian far right extensively focuses on renewable energy and new sources of power. Alongside an immense faith in the past and future of Indian science and technology, the RSS rides on the shoulders of the Modi-led government to seize the opportunity of 'Powering Bharat' (2015), and 'Energise India' (Dubey, 2015a, 2015c), through a vast expansion of industry-energy endeavours led by state and private-public enterprises. The RSS mentions little about local, micro, decentralised and people/community-initiated renewable energy pedagogy. The need to transform energy production, distribution, storage and consumption, in the context of renewables, is never discussed. Instead, the renewable energy sector, especially solar and wind, becomes an extension of the big corporate and capital-driven power sector, forming a particular nexus of political, economic, technological and global coalescences.

The *Organiser*'s articles on renewable energy display pictures and pathways of big growth, targets and a capacity-driven 'sunrise' sector in India, and take pride in claiming the following:

> In the face of rising pollution, depleting natural resources and the looming threat of climate change, Renewable Energy is fast becoming a mantra across the world. Indian tradition has long recognised the energy emanating from the Surya (Sun), Varuna (Water), Vayu (Wind), and Gau (biofuel). It is therefore, befitting that India should aim to be the Clean Energy Capital of the World. And India has started working towards it, and it was clearly reflected when the Prime Minister, Narendra Modi said that 'India is now thinking in Gigawatts rather than Megawatts when it comes to renewable'. (Singh, 2016: 24)

The high capacity and overall renewal target of 175 GW by 2022 also claimed to 'set a direction and commitment to travel creating an attractive market for global investors' (*Organiser*, 2017b: 29). Indeed, public-private power/coal/renewal energy companies have regularly advertised in the *Organiser*, displaying their commitment for a clean and green India. Researchers have shown the convergence of neoliberalism and Hindutva, resulting in the creation of a hindutvatised neoliberal subjectivity (Chhachhi, 2020). It has also been pointed out how neoliberalism and Hindutva share common, deeper class interests and political goals by 'articulating shared notions of a bounded, unitary and individual-based conceptions of society' (Gopalakrishnan, 2006: 2803).

The *Organiser* grants substantial space to the subject of climate change and renewable energy, and for multiple industrial and developmental protagonists who claim to follow the path of green and sustainable development. Sectors such as urban development ('Smart Cities: Reshaping Urban Life', Organiser Bureau, 2016), nuclear energy ('Nuclear Security Summit: One Hurdle Down, a Few to Go', Nayan, 2016), natural gas ('Energising Pipeline Diplomacy', 2016), big dam ('Sardar Sarovar Project: An Engineering Miracle', Pandya, 2017), mining ('Upscale Mining', Sehgal, 2015), natural resources like land ('Land Acquisition Bill Is Farmer Friendly', Singhal, 2015) and water ('Mainstreaming the Water Transport', Dubey, 2015b), material infrastructure ('Mining New Gains in Infrastructure', *Organiser*, 2017a), and its cultural forms ('Six Steps to the Renaissance', Kak, 2018), together build a ground for green growth. These articles make a strong case of how Indian scientific and technological progress can better harness the potential of gas and mining, big dams and infrastructure for the grandeur of Bharat and its modern developments.

The visuality of renewable energy and its associated industries, in contrast to climate change imageries, presents bright photos, diagrams and pictures of solar panels, grid infrastructure and wind turbines, thus providing an aesthetic composition to various economic and industrial activities. Images of renewable energy are merged with engineering, science and technology. They are carefully choreographed to support the tone of the text. In addition, images are also used to demonstrate the success of such measures in transforming people and community lives. These images make big industry and capital right, justifiable, accessible and acceptable. Take the *Organiser*'s focus issue on renewable energy, with the cover story on 'Energise India: To Energise India Promoting Clean and Green Energy with Cost Effective Innovations Is Inevitable to Realise Future Development Potential' (Dubey, 2015b). The story has fifteen photos depicting people, villages, darkness and light, agriculture, solar panel, a wind turbine, a city, a political leader and expert; four diagrams and sketches showing waves, water, currents and statics; and four advertisements from power companies, claiming to green the world. They are organised in such a way that renewable energy, people, the corporate sector, growth and development merge into a single natural-industrial frame.

Coming to an end of this section, climate change and renewable energy have clearly emerged as new sites of environmental politics of the Hindu nationalists, where both appear to be inextricably intertwined. The focus on climate change does deal with its impact on the human population, floods, droughts and disasters, and the individual-organisational roles of the 'nationalists' and the 'Hindus' (*Organiser*, 2015a, 2019) in supporting a community in crisis. However, the RSS gives industries, scientists and technocrats a leading role in addressing climate change, and then in the same breath positions the mega renewable energy sector to address the problem. Climate change and corporate activities go together in its vision, something that is also visible in the choice and circulation of images.

Modi: evolution of environmental legitimacy

Explaining the political authority of governments in South East Asia, Alagappa (1995) underscores how rationales such as normative goals, performance, personal authority and international support have been critical for their legitimation. However, according to him (Alagappa, 1995), since legitimation on the basis of these rationales is highly contingent and subject to periodic erosion and crisis, there is always a search for a new and more durable basis of authority. In this respect, the natural environment becomes a new constituent element in the politics of far-right leaders.

Modi as the prime minister, and a RSS propagandist in the past, personifies the governmentality and politicality of the far right in relation to the environment. Indeed, in his persona as the environmental saviour of the nation, the dominant environmental themes discussed previously in this chapter are merged. The written texts and visuals on and of Modi are not only about a strong and decisive personality but also underline his vision for a new Bharat based on RSS ideology. Salient features of Modi's personality and his personal authority are continuously expanded to solidify the image of a supreme leader. This has been characterised as 'populist-authoritarianism in India' under the 'strongman' Modi, who claims a legacy of the poor and the marginalised based on his past, and the power of the rich and the corporate based on his current stature (Gudavarthy, 2019). In European countries, 'the politics of fear' brought populist right-wing politics to the centre stage, which further entrenches social divides of nation, gender and body (Wodak, 2015). In India today, goals of environment and development are increasingly deployed to legitimise Modi and his government and to promote a far-right agenda. Indeed, the persona of Modi appears prominently in projections of government and BJP/RSS-led environmental activities. Modi himself uses his image on multiple media platforms to create a positive and edifying impression about his personality, leadership and power. Diverse images and visuals of Modi – strong, active, cheerful, communicative, energetic and agile, both indoors and outdoors – have been crafted and displayed by his official and organisational networks to make him ever visible in the Indian political landscape.

In 2014, Modi's visit to Banaras and the naming of himself as the 'Ganga-son' provided an interesting starting point to Modi and the RSS for unfolding their environmental politics. The primary metaphors in this event were Hindu religiosity, sacrality, purity of mother and Modi, which were magnified with large visuals of him (*Organiser*, 2014a, 2014b). Since then, Modi has repeatedly visited the river, and the Hindu right refurbished its old ideas of a pure and pollution-free Ganga into a political project. Uma Bharti, a hardcore Hindu nationalist leader, was made minister of the newly created Ministry of Ganga Rejuvenation in 2014.

Since 2014, Modi's environmental image has moved forward, expanded and come to encompass many themes in the pages of the *Organiser*. For example, 'It's Time to Deliver: Modern Industry and Environment Friendly' (Organiser Bureau, 2014), 'Beautifying Banaras' (Pandey, 2015) and 'Clean India Campaign' (Clean India Campaign, 2016).

Energy, climate change, smart-green cities and urban development have been recurrent themes for Modi since 2016. The *Organiser* has continuously published on these issues since 2014, and has particularly focused on Modi in print and visual mediums. Extensive design and layout, including coloured pictures, quotes, sketches, boxes and top–bottom spreads of visuals, have been employed to prominently, prolifically and intimately place Modi in the public domain as an environmental saviour. Here are a few examples: 'Narendra Modi-led Government has given a new edge to the gas pipeline diplomacy as one of the cornerstones of meeting Bharat's growing energy needs' (Rao, 2016), 'International Solar Alliance: Let Us Turn to Sun' (Bureau, 2016), 'PM Narendra Modi Dedicates the Sardar Sarovar Dam to the Nation' (Pandya, 2017: 38), 'Indian Prime Minister Narendra Modi and President of France Emmanuel Macron Inaugurated a 75 MW Solar Power Plant in Mirzapur' (Organiser Bureau, 2018: 20). In 2019, cyclone Fani struck the Indian states of Odisha and West Bengal, causing severe human and environmental damage. The *Organiser*'s cover story, 'Cyclone Fani' (Organiser Bureau, 2019), represented the disaster, climate change and people affected, along with the work done by the RSS, through a multitude of texts and visuals. The captions of the photos read: 'Odisha's spiritual city, Puri, ravaged in an unseasonal cyclone', 'RSS Sahsarkaryavahk distributing relief to the cyclone affected people', 'RSS workers distributing relief to Fani cyclone affected people' and 'RSS swayamsevaks restoring road connectivity'. Along with this, the magazine placed a long article titled 'Not "Fani" but "Modi Wave" Rattles Didi', which also carried a photograph of Modi – victorious and aggressive, with both his hands raised in the air – to showcase that Modi had triumphed over damaged caused by Fani in the West Bengal state. The BJP has particularly concentrated on West Bengal in the past few years for spreading its Hindutva politics, as it is a state in which power has remained elusive for them. The article utilises written text and visual imagery of the cyclone to articulate a political point, anchored in Modi and his vision of India.

In sum, Prime Minister Modi has extensively used environmental issues, especially of Ganga, cow, climate change and renewable energy, in strengthening his political image. His environmental texts and visuals have a variety of modes, which are often knitted together through narratives of the great motherland and the power of a strong nation and leader. His images of 'taking holy dips' (Figure 10.3) or focusing on climate change are meant for 'the elections for future Bharat' where 'the identity of India or Bharat itself is part of this bitter electoral battle' (Frawley, 2019: 21). As such, Modi's environmental leadership and its visual portrayal is intertwined with Hindu nationalist politics in intimate ways.

Conclusion

Themes of a glorious Hindu Bharat and community, the great past and present of Bharatiya science and technology, the need for a strong nation and leader, and defence of motherland, river and animal, form an integral part of contemporary discourse of the far right in India, which are also rooted in narratives of modernity and development. In the context of my research questions – How does Hindutva visual environmental communication

PM Modi taking holy
dip in Prayagraj during
Kumbh 2019

April 7, 2019 | Organiser.org

10.3 'PM Modi taking holy dip'

constructs ideal Indian subjects? How does climate change and renewable energy gets prominence in national awakening? And what are the specific environmental characteristics of Hindu nationalist forces? – at least four significant political themes are visible: first, a return to the ancient, traditional and indigenous caste-based village system; second, the launch of a mega 'green' industrial development, based on the application of Indian science and technology; third, the overarching role of a central authority; and fourth, ideological and physical attacks on Muslims. Simultaneously, they invoke polarised notions of community and environment, which emphasise, and find justification in, exclusive, violent, weaponised and centralised resource management. Relations between environment, people and culture have often been explained in a linear narrative by the Hindu right: Bharat versus West, indigenous versus foreign, mother versus others, Hindu versus Muslim and purity versus pollution. Yet the far right also shows flexibility towards adopting new strategies for articulating the challenge of climate change, which feed into their standard environmental narratives. Some distinctive trends have emerged post-2014 regarding far-right and environmental communication in India: embracing a narrative of climate change and renewable energy; targeting Muslims for natural and social pollution; promoting a caste-based, aggressive Hindutva; and state-initiated, mass-based environmental campaigns.

The RSS and the BJP have skilfully combined governmentality with politics, Hindu nationalism with environmental ideology and green practice with corporate interests to undertake massive organisational and political outreach activities on environmental issues. In *Environmentality: Technologies of Government and the Making of Subjects*, Agrawal (2005) describes how various strategies of power, knowledge and statistics create particular environments as domains fit for government, and how different sets of new relations – governmentalised communities, regulatory communities and the constitution of environmental subjects – change the politics of the environment. Through its written texts and images, *Organiser* helps in carving out a distinct environmental public sphere where individuals and collectives are actively mobilised around a sectarian ecological ideology that can even justify the killing of the perceived 'other' in the name of animals, food and pollution.

The triangle of RSS, BJP and Modi – principal faces of the contemporary far right in India – are resourceful and conscious about the use of media and communication for their political and governmental agenda. At a time when the media transform religion and religious consciousness in South Asia (Babb and Wadley, 1997), the RSS has designed a regular flow and, at times, flooding of images for their environmental communication. The streams of visuals discussed in this chapter expand the Indian far right's ideological outreach and magnify its political appeal, aiding the rise of a new, aggressive and hyper-Hindu environmental subject which stands up for far-right agendas and activities.

References

Agrawal, A. (2005): *Environmentality: Technologies of Government and the Making of Subjects*. Durham, NC: Duke University Press.

Alagappa, M. (ed.) (1995): *Political Legitimacy in South East Asia: The Quest for Moral Authority*. Stanford: Stanford University Press.

Anderson, B. (1991): *Imagined Communities: Reflections on the Origin and Spread of Nationalism*. London: Verso.

Babb, L. A. and Wadley, S. S. (eds) (1997): *Media and the Transformation of Religion in South Asia*. Delhi: Motilal Banarsidas.

Bharadwaj, A. (2017): Resurgence of Sarasvati ethos, *Organiser*, 12 March 2017: 31–33.

Bharadwaj, S. (2018): Matrix of integration, *Organiser*, 13 May 2018: 9–11.

Bharatiya Janata Party (2014). BJP Manifesto 2014. www.bjp.org/bjp-manifesto-2014 (accessed 1 March 2023).

Bidwai, P. (2012): *The Politics of Climate Change and the Global Crisis: Mortgaging our Future*. Hyderabad: Orient Blackswan.

Bureau (2016): International Solar Alliance: 'Let us turn to sun,' *Organiser*, 31 July 2016: 45.

Chhachhi, A. (2020): Neoliberalism, Hindutva and gender: Convergence and contradictions in the provision of welfare, *Feminist Dissent*, 5: 50–93.

Clean India Campaign (2016): *Organiser*, 2 October 2016: 44–45. https://doi.org/10.31273/fd.n5.2020.759

Das, N. (2015): Bringing an end to cow slaughter, *Organiser*, 21 September 2015: 25.

Davis, R. H. (ed.) (2007): *Picturing the Nation: Iconographies of Modern India*. Hyderabad: Orient Longman.

Demos, T. J. (2017): *Against the Anthropocene: Visual Culture and Environment Today*. Berlin: Sternberg Press.

Diwan, M. (2018): With civilisation to globalisation, *Organiser*, 7 October 2018: 28–29.

Dubey, J. P. (2015a): Energise India, *Organiser*, 19 July 2015, 8–10.

Dubey, J. P. (2015b): Mainstreaming the water transport, *Organiser*, 4 October 2015: 38–39.

Dubey, J. P. (2015c): Powering BHARAT, *Organiser*, 27 December 2015, 13–15.

Ernstrom, U. (2021): Climate change denial strongly linked to right-wing nationalism, *Chalmers*. www.chalmers.se/en/departments/tme/news/pages/climate-change-denial-strongly-linked-to-right-wing-nationalism.aspx (accessed 14 February 2022).

Forchtner, B. (ed.) (2019a): *The Far Right and the Environment*. London: Routledge.

Forchtner, B. (2019b): Nation, nature, purity: extreme-right biodiversity in Germany, *Patterns of Prejudice*, 53(9): 285–301.

Frawley, D. (2019): Future Bharat, *Organiser*, 24 February 2019: 21–22.

Freitag, S. B. (2014): The visual turn: Approaching South Asia across the disciplines, *South Asia: Journal of South Asian Studies*, 37(3): 398–409.

Gopalakrishnan, S. (2006): Defining, constructing and policing a 'New India': Relationship between neoliberalism and Hindutva, *Economic and Political Weekly*, 41(26): 2810–2813.

Grewal, I. and Kaplan, C. (eds) (1994): *Scattered Hegemonies: Postmodernity and Transnational Feminist Practices*. Minneapolis: University of Minnesota Press.

Gudavarthy, A. (2019): *India after Modi: Populism and the Right*. Delhi: Bloomsbury.

Gupta, C. (2001): The icon of mother in late colonial North India: 'Bharat Mata', 'Matri Bhasha' and 'Gau Mata', *Economic and Political Weekly*, 36(45): 4291–4299.

Harris, M (1966): The cultural ecology of India's sacred cattle, *Current Anthropology*, 7(1): 51–66.

Jylha, K. M. Strimling, P. and Rydgren, J. (2020): Climate change denial among radical right-wing supporters, *Sustainability* 12: 1–15. https://doi.org/10.3390/su122310226

Kak, S. (2018): Six steps to the renaissance, *Organiser*, 18 March 2018: 29–33.

Kapur, A. (1993): Deity to crusader. In: G. Pandey (ed.), *Hindus and Others: The Question of Identity in India Today*. New Delhi: Viking. 74–109.

Kashyap, S. (2017): Cow is a cultural symbol, *Organiser*, 13 August 2017: 42.

Kaur, R. (2007): Spectacles of nationalism in the Ganapati *Utsav* of Maharashtra. In: R. Davis (ed.), *Picturing the Nation: Iconographies of Modern India*. Hyderabad: Orient Longman, 206–241.

Kumar, P. (2015): A return to India's glorious scientific past, *Organiser*, 8 March 2015: 22–23.

Kumar, P. (2017): Turning the tide, *Organiser*, 26 February 2017: 24–27.

Malm, A. and The Zetkin Collective (2021): *White Skin, Black Fuel: On the Danger of Fossil Fascism*. London: Verso.

Manekar, S. (2017): Confluence in science, *Organiser*, 23 May 2017: 34–35.

McCright, A. M. and Dunlop, R. E. (2011): The denial of climate change among conservative white males in the United States, *Global Environmental Change*, 21(4): 1163–1172. https://doi.org/10.1016/j.gloenvcha.2011.06.003

Misra, N. (2019): The mother of all rivers, *Organiser*, 24 February 2019: 43–45.

Modi (2014): *Organiser*, 18 May 2014: 8.

Mudde, C. (2019): *The Far Right Today*. Cambridge: Polity Press.

Muralivallabhan, TV. (2016): Sustainable development *mantra*, *Organiser*, 10 April 2016: 56–57.

Nair, R. J. and Daniel, F. J. (2015): Battling for India's soul, state by state, *Reuters*. www.reuters.com/article/us-india-rss-specialreport/special-report-battling-for-indias-soul-state-by-state-idUSKCN0S700A20151013 (accessed 14 February 2022).

Nayan, D. R. (2016): Nuclear security summit: One hurdle down, a few to go, *Organiser*, 10 July 2016: 30–31.

Olsen, J. (1999): *Nature and Nationalism: Right-Wing Ecology and the Politics of Identity in Contemporary India*. New York: St. Martin's Press.

Omar, M. (2021): The Muslim 'threat' in right wing narratives: A critical discourse analysis, *SSAI Working Paper Series*. www.soas.ac.uk/south-asia-institute/publications/working-papers/file152729.pdf (accessed 14 February 2022).

Organiser (2014a): 11 May 2014: 8.

Organiser (2014b): 18 May 2014: 8.

Organiser (2015a): Namami Gange, *Organiser*, 31 May 2015: 34–35.

Organiser (2015b): Relief operation by Swayamsevaks, *Organiser*, 10 May 2015: 11.

Organiser (2017a): Making new gains in infrastructure, *Organiser*, 1 October 2017: 23.

Organiser (2017b): Time for Bharat to take the lead, *Organiser*, 2 July 2017: 28–29.

Organiser (2019): RSS stands with cyclone-hit Odisha, *Organiser*, 26 May 2019: 46–47.

Organiser Bureau (2014): It's time to deliver, *Organiser*, 1 June 2014: 6–21.

Organiser Bureau (2016): Smart cities: Reshaping urban life, *Organiser*, 14 February 2016: 16–18.

Organiser Bureau (2018): Uttar Pradesh: Changing the socio-economic landscape in the state, *Organiser*, 2 September 2018: 19–20.

Organiser Bureau (2019): Cyclone Fani, *Organiser*, 19 May 2019: 6–9.

Oswald, M. T., Fromm, M. and Broda, E. (2021): Strategic clustering in right-wing-populism? 'Green policies' in Germany and France, *Zeitschrift für Vergleichende Politikwissenschaft*, 15: 185–205. https://doi.org/10.1007/s12286-021-00485-6

Pachpore, V. (2014): Govt should emulate Shivaji's governance, *Organiser*, 22 June 2014: 44.

Pandey, D. S. K. (2015): Beautifying Banaras, *Organiser*, 1 March 2015: 34–35.

Pandya, A. B. (2017): Sardar Sarovar project: An engineering miracle, *Organiser*, 1 October 2017: 38-40.

Pinney, C. (1997): The nation (un)pictured? Chromolithography and 'popular' politics in India, 1878–1995, *Critical Inquiry*, 23(4): 834–867. https://doi.org/10.1086/448856

Pinney, C. (2004): *'Photos of the Gods': The Printed Image and Political Struggle in India*. London: Reaktion Books.

Rajagopal, A. (2001): *Politics after Television: Hindu Nationalism and the Reshaping of the Indian Public*. Cambridge: Cambridge University Press.

Ramaswamy, S. (2001): Maps and mother Goddesses in modern India, *Imago Mundi*, 53: 97–114. https://doi.org/10.1080/03085690108592940

Ramaswamy, S. (2014): *Goddess and the Nation: Mapping Mother India*. Delhi: Zubaan.

Rangarajan, S. P. V. (2016): Bharat Mata Ki Jai: Bharat as the 'Motherland', *Organiser*, 1 May 2016: 22–23.

Rao, R. (2016). Energising pipeline diplomacy, *Organiser*, 10 January 2016: 20–21.

Rehman, M. (ed.) (2019): *Rise of Saffron Power: Reflections on Indian Politics*. Abingdon: Routledge.

Sehgal, A. (2015): Upscale mining, *Organiser*, 8 March 2015: 10.

Sharma, I. (2018): Cow as a sacred national symbol: (Un)making of the idea of India. Unpublished manuscript.

Sharma, M. (2001): Nature and nationalism, *Frontline*, 3 February 2001: 94–96. https://frontline.thehindu.com/other/article30249823.ece (accessed 14 February 2022).

Sharma, M. (2012): *Green and Saffron: Hindu Nationalism and Indian Environmental Politics*. Ranikhet: Permanent Black.

Shukla, D. S. P. (2018): Being Hindu: Bonded naturally, *Organiser*, 18 March 2018: 59–61.

Singh, S. (2015): Positive impact of RSS on NDA government, *Organiser*, 31 May 2015: 19.

Singh, S. (2016): The electrifying effect, *Organiser*, 31 July 2016: 24–26.

Singhal, S. (2015): Land Acquisition Bill is farmer friendly, *Organiser*, 29 March 29 2015: 32.

Sinha, A. J. (2007): Visual culture and the politics of locality in modern India: A review essay, *Modern Asian Studies*, 41(1): 187–220. http://doi.org/10.1017/S0026749X06002356

Sirohi, S. (2017): Hey Gange, *Organiser*, 30 April 2017: 42–43.

Turner, J. and Bailey, D. (2021): 'Ecobordering': casting immigration control as environmental protection, *Environmental Politics*, https://doi.org/10.1080/09644016.2021.1916197

Vaidyaraj, P. (2018): Decolonising the village ecosystem, *Organiser*, 19 April 2018: 72–73.

Veer, P. v. d. (1994): *Religious Nationalism: Hindus and Muslims in India*. Berkeley: University of California Press.

Wodak, R. (2015): *The Politics of Fear: What Right-Wing Populist Discourses Mean*. London: Sage.

Yang, A. A. (1980): Sacred symbol and sacred space in rural India: Community mobilization in the 'anti-cow killing' riot of 1893, *Comparative Studies in Society and History*, 22(4): 576–596.

11

Double vision: local environment and global climate change through the German far-right lens

Bernhard Forchtner and Jonathan Olsen

The concept of ecology contains the word οἶκος, house. This means that we are dealing with limiting parameters in both sustainability and ecology. The desire for a *global* ecology faces the same dilemma as someone struggling to extend a love for one's neighbour [*Nächstenliebe*] to a far-away stranger [*Fernsten*], to offer family-like solidarity to all of humanity: It works for poetry. However, in reality it rarely occurs.

That is why environmental protection and climate protection are not just two pairs of shoes, but as different as real shoes and fairytale seven-mile boots. Environmental protection is concrete, climate protection is abstract. Environmental protection is achievable, while when it comes to climate protection, it is simply not possible to know anything for certain. Environmental protection is regional while climate protection should be global. It really is not possible to make political or ideological capital out of environmental protection; meanwhile climate protection is already the most powerful substitute religion in the Western world. (Honorary chairman of the German far-right party Alternative for Germany Alexander Gauland, 2019: 52f)

Introduction

October 2021, two men and their magazine. As with previous issues of the German far-right eco-quarterly *Die Kehre* (The Turning), Jonas Schick, editor in chief, and Jörg Dittus, contributor, introduce issue seven of the 'Magazine for Nature Protection' on its YouTube channel (DK, 2021a). In contrast to previous issues, however, Schick starts by reflecting on the difficulty of visually capturing the complexities of the issue's topic, post-growth, on the cover page. The latter shows a massive harvester in the background, one rusted and falling apart, with the rest of the image displaying a farmer on an old tractor who ploughs a healthy-looking field. Not only does Schick's reflection on putting post-growth into a picture illuminate the contours of how the far right imagines the natural environment, it also makes explicit the significance of images in communicating such ideas.

While not every far-right actor engages intensely (and visually) with environmental questions, something this chapter and various contributions to this volume vividly illustrate, visual representations often play a critical role in positioning subjects (see the Introduction to this volume). They are regularly the first thing we look at, they aim to situate us before we engage with the written word, and they do so through a mode which seemingly does not argue but 'simply depicts'. Indeed, images convey emotions and knowledge, and attempt to interpellate readers in a mode more 'innocent' than the written word. They thus warrant particular attention.

Importantly, they also do so with regard to the contrast outlined by Gauland above, that is, between an ideological affinity towards environmental protection (though this is not realised uniformly) and various types of climate obstruction (though, again, not uniformly so, and certainly not reducible to outright climate change denial). In fact, *Die Kehre*'s very first editorial criticised 'the current narrowing of ecology to "climate protection"' (Schick, 2020: 1) next to an image of wind turbines. This contrast has long been indicated, for example by Forchtner and Kølvraa (2015; see also Chapter 8 in this volume), who argue that the natural environment and climate change mobilise nationalism's nature differently. Indeed, a considerable number of far-right actors show an affinity towards 'their' natural environment, that is, a beautiful and bounded territory which has evolved together with the nation. This 'national ecosystem' shall remain pure, a bedrock of the national community which connects past, present and future. While such ideas have not been limited to Germany, it has probably been nowhere more extensively analysed than with regard to the case of Germany. Here, the imaginary of an essentialised and exclusionary 'eco-communion' between 'nation' and 'homeland' (see the Introduction in this volume) has existed since the nineteenth century (Geden, 1996; Olsen, 1999; Staudenmaier 2011 [1995]; for an overview, see Forchtner and Özvatan, 2019). In turn, climate change has been primarily characterised by types of obstruction, from outright denial of the evidence for anthropogenic climate change to criticism of ways in which knowledge is (allegedly) created and publicly debated, as well as policy responses (see van Rensburg, 2015 for a general model; see Lockwood, 2018; Forchtner, 2019a; Malm and The Zetkin Collective, 2021 on the far right and climate change). Where this contrast exists, it might be explained via reference to the ethno-communal core of far-right thought, that is, one which celebrates the particularity of this or that ethnic community and its 'right' to strive within a bounded territory. The nation, in this reading, manifests itself as *ipso facto* worthy of existence and protection – as does its natural environment. While there can be a Herderian respect and acknowledgement of another nation and its natural space, oftentimes within a broader ethnic 'civilisation', affective energies are focused on 'our' territory. Conversely, the global is viewed with suspicion if not rejected outright for its supposedly abstract, general and levelling tendencies. This is precisely what 'the climate' has been associated with. Climate action is rejected not simply because responses might involve international cooperation and loss of sovereignty, threaten fossil fuel(led) masculinities and foreground the workings of a 'cosmopolitan', global elite. Moreover, and beyond such specific points, discussions about how climate change is addressed have fed into an imaginary of an Orwellian 'one world', one which challenges the very primacy of the concrete and particular, the local/regional/national, and, thus, the distinctiveness of nationalists' nature and identity.[1]

Against this background, this chapter asks: What similarities/differences exist in how local/regional/national environment and global climate change are visually articulated? Utilising quantitative and qualitative means, we analyse 346 images across 127 contributions published in four key German far-right publications between January 2020 and July 2021. We thus contribute knowledge of the role(s) images play in far-right environmental communication and suggest an analytical procedure to do so comprehensively. More specifically, this exploration of the visual articulation of local environment and climate change within one investigation enables us to illuminate the tension between these two domains of far-right environmental thinking, that is, their different roles (though a few, basic similarities exist too) which, we argue, are fundamentally motivated by binaries of local/regional/national–global, concrete–abstract and particular–general. This tension should not be rationalised away as cynical opportunism or ignored as 'not really environmentalist' (see Staudenmaier, 2021: 165; see also Voss, 2014; Lubarda, 2023), but should be seriously considered so as to better understand both the far right's relation to the natural environment and the possible appeal of some far-right conceptions of environmental protection/climate change beyond far-right milieus.

Following this introduction, we first offer a historical overview of how the German far right has made sense of the natural environment across the two domains of local environment and climate change. Subsequently, we discuss our methods of data collection and analysis. Third, we present our findings – illustrating that the aforementioned tension is real and, in some cases, takes particularly complex forms – and, finally, provide a conclusion.

A brief overview of the German far right's approach to the natural environment and climate change

At the outset, we note that it is well past time that scholarship covering the far right's engagement with environmental questions should dispense with the statement that such a discussion will 'surprise' the reader who expects concern for the environment to come only from the political left. As has been well chronicled, far-right concerns for the natural environment can be found in the early nineteenth century in Germany. Here, Romantic, anti-French and anti-Enlightenment elements were present, leading, for example, Ernst Moritz Arndt and Wilhelm Heinrich Riehl to imagine *völkisch* connections between 'land and people', something which led the twenty-first century ecofascist group Greenline Front to proclaim that Arndt and Riehl are the 'fathers of the *völkish* environmentalism' (GF, n.d.). At the turn of the twentieth century, environmental ideas were articulated largely by the *Heimatschutz* or 'protection of the homeland' movement, itself often infused with nationalist, *völkisch* and Social Darwinist streams of thought (Geden, 1996; Olsen, 1999; Biehl and Staudenmeier, 2011 [1995]). This wider 'nature and nationalism' tradition (Olsen, 1999) culminated most infamously in the ecofascist, National Socialist marriage of *Blut und Boden* (Blood and Soil). To be sure, scholars have pointed to the ambivalent nature of 'how green were the Nazis' (for example, Brüggemeier et al., 2005; Biehl and Staudenmeier, 2011 [1995]; see Forchtner and Özvatan, 2019 for a review; Malm and The Zetkin Collective, 2021: 470 see only 'nature-related *rhetoric*'). As such, while infrastructure modernisation and war were hardly 'green', aspects of the earlier *völkisch* environmental tradition were carried over into the National Socialist regime.

During the second half of the twentieth century, a nationalistic and exclusionary politics of nature increasingly retreated into the background, giving way to a more universalistic environmental politics, epitomised by the rise of the (ultimately left-wing) Green party. Nevertheless, aspects of the earlier nature and nationalism tradition survived. Remaining engaged throughout the 1950s and 1960s, the far right vigorously attempted to hold (and gain) ground in the 1970s and 1980s, especially as a new generation of New Right activists emerged and fashioned new theories (for example, 'ethnopluralism') to make their ideology relevant to modern politics and society (Jahn and Wehling, 1991; Geden, 1996; Olsen, 1999; Biehl and Staudenmeier, 2011 [1995]). In the last thirty years, relevant studies have focused on both far-right political parties, such as *Die Republikaner* (The Republicans) and the *Nationaldemokratische Partei Deutschlands* (National Democratic Party of Germany, NPD), and publications, such as the now defunct eco-quarterly *Umwelt & Aktiv* (*Environment & Active*, see Hurd and Werther, 2016; Forchtner and Özvatan, 2019). Notably, however, the main themes in such communication have been quite consistent over the last decades.

First and foremost, 'nature's laws' are seen as encompassing the human as well as non-human world: A particular reading of nature is thus made into a model for the social and political order. In the domain of the natural environment, such concerns for natural laws which one ignores at great peril are visible in, for example, opposition to genetically modified organisms; indeed, the NPD (2007) has long and loudly proclaimed 'GMO-slop – No Thanks!' Second, nations/cultures are seen as shaped by the distinctive ecosystem in which they develop, as expressions of a particular environment or landscape (Olsen, 2000) – but also as shaping this land and, thus, as evolving within '"ethno-scape[s]" in which a people and its homeland become increasingly symbiotic' (Smith, 2009: 50). A now classic effect of such a belief is opposition to wind turbines based on concern over the nation's cultural landscape, as when the youth wing of the far-right party *Alternative für Deutschland* (Alternative for Germany, AfD) demands 'stop the defacement of cultural landscapes' written in front of wind turbines and a darkened sky (Young Alternative, 2019). Third, environmental protection is equated with the defence of the pure national community. Thus, far-right actors offer themselves up as the 'true environmentalists' by defending the homeland, its imagined pure community and its natural spaces. To quote Björn Höcke (DK, 2021b: 32), the unofficial leader of the AfD's *völkisch* wing and co-leader of the party in the federal state of Thuringia, 'those who love their homeland also want to protect the natural spaces that preserve its natural conditions of life'. Because of this eliding from nature-to-nation protection, it is easy to link an anti-immigrant politics with an environmental politics. Just as foreign species threaten the biological balance of a unique ecosystem, so too are foreigners seen as threats to the native population. Finally, environmental problems are largely seen as resulting from liberalism and (global) economic practices, an alienation from the rooted national community. As Götz Kubitschek (DK, 2020d: 33), one of the most important New Right thinkers in Germany today, argues in an interview with *Die Kehre*, contemporary environmental problems stem from a 'false feeling of a global community, a one-world-family. Mass society and uprootedness [from one's homeland] are per se destructive, levelling, inorganic, and unecological.'

To be sure, far-right actors in Germany have only inconsistently tilled the field of environmental protection, regularly ignoring the issue or even engaging in knee-jerk, anti-environmental opposition to what is viewed as a 'left-wing' topic. For example, while notable projects, such as *Umwelt & Aktiv* (2007–2019) and *Die Kehre* (2020–), have attempted to put forward far-right views on environmental issues, the AfD has not, even in the view of Schick (DK, 2020b; 2020e), engaged seriously. While the AfD's absence from comprehensive environmental policy-making is especially visible in its climate obstruction (on the multidimensional notion of climate obstruction in general – encompassing denial, delay and inaction – see Ekberg et al., 2022; on the AfD in particular, see for example Boecher et al., 2022; Forchtner and Özvatan, 2022; Küppers, 2022; see Quent et al., 2022; Sommer et al., 2022 for relevant, book-length analyses with a focus on Germany), much of the literature on the far right and the environment has demonstrated that even those who show a specifically far-right concern for how to respond to environmental despoliation – irrespective of whether 'their' solutions would solve these crises – often oppose climate-related measures (Forchtner, 2019b). Indeed, while outright denial does not dominate, opposition to meaningful mitigation is common, for example via reference to 'economic decline'. Overall, the analysis thus needs to account for nuances, including explicit acceptance of human-made climate change. But why, how and to what effect is such complexity present?

Analysing images in (written) context: data and method

We analyse visualisations of the German far right's relationship with its natural environment by considering four key print publications between the beginning of January 2020 and the end of July 2021. These publications cover a wide spectrum of the German far right, thus providing access to pictures with considerable circulation and impact within the far right. They thus allow for a comprehensive analysis of ideology conveyed through imagery. Our sources include the weekly *Junge Freiheit* (Young Freedom), which was once under observation by North Rhine-Westphalia's Office for the Protection of the Constitution but is currently backing the (purported) 'moderate' faction within the AfD. The monthly *Compact* also backs the AfD, though in a less intellectual, more strident way (and is now officially considered as 'proven extreme right' by the German Federal Office for the Protection of the Constitution), while the monthly *Deutsche Stimme* (German Voice) is the party newspaper of the extreme-right NPD. These three are well established within the German far-right media ecosystem. In contrast, *Die Kehre* is a newcomer, one which, at the beginning of 2020, took the place of *Umwelt & Aktiv*. The latter had close links to the NPD and thus differs from *Die Kehre*, which is firmly situated within the New Right. *Die Kehre* takes its name from the German philosopher Martin Heidegger's work on technology – work which has long inspired the New Right, including his fear of a future 'bloodless universalism' and a 'debased technocratic globalism' (quoted in Göpffarth, 2020: 256) – and, in contrast to *Junge Freiheit*, *Compact* and *Deutsche Stimme*, focuses exclusively on environmental issues.

Concerning *Compact* and *Deutsche Stimme*, we collected all contributions which included a keyword (established deductively, before being complemented inductively) in the title/lead paragraph.[2] In the case of *Junge Freiheit* and *Die Kehre*, due to the amount of data, we limited ourselves to the cover page and sections 'Page 2', 'Topic', 'Forum' and 'Nature & Technology' (though excluding very short reprints which are never accompanied by images in the latter section) in the case of the former, and excluded very short contributions on the first pages of *Die Kehre*. Across all publications, we excluded the table of contents, editorials, book/film reviews and letters to the editors. In total, this sampling procedure resulted in a corpus comprising 346 images across 127 contributions; depending on whether these belong to the domain of global climate change or local environment, articles were assigned to one of two subcorpora. This left us with the following sample: fifty-nine images across forty-three contributions derive from *Junge Freiheit* (thirty-seven/twenty-five and twenty-two/eighteen images/contributions concern local environment and global climate change respectively); forty-nine images across fifteen contributions are from *Compact* (thirty/nine and nineteen/six images/contributions concern global climate change and local environment respectively); sixty-seven images across thirty contributions were culled from *Deutsche Stimme* (forty-four/sixteen and twenty-three/fourteen images/contributions concern local environment and global climate change respectively); and 171 images across thirty-nine contributions came from *Die Kehre* (131/thirty and forty/nine images/contributions concern local environment and global climate change respectively). As *Die Kehre* is thus responsible for about half of all images, at times we pay special attention to its communication.

Having established a corpus, we adopted a four-step analytical procedure to understand the environmental communication of these actors. This procedure largely follows the example of an analysis of German climate change communication by far-right actors between July 2018 and December 2019 (Forchtner, in press; see also the wider literature on visual environmental communication reviewed in the Introduction to this volume). First, we coded the valorisation of each image (that is, is the thing depicted presented as positive–negative–unclear within the entire contribution, thus taking into account the multimodal nature of meaning). Next we conducted a descriptive content analysis of the dominant topic in each image. Third, we carried out an interpretative analysis of the dominant frame conveyed through each image (taking also into account written captions/superimposed text), drawing on Entman's (1993: 52) definition of framing. Our quantitative analysis prepared the ground for a final, qualitative analysis of two paradigmatic images which we use to reflect on and explore the wider implications of visual communication in detail. This multilevel procedure aims to offer a comprehensive account of the far right's visual environmental communication in Germany to which we now turn.

Two pairs of shoes? Analysing the articulation of global climate change and local environment

In the following, we introduce the role played by images in the two domains of, first, global climate change and, second, local environment – moving from analyses of quantified valorisation, topics and frames to qualitative analyses of images.

Global climate change

A total of 115 images across 50 contributions deal with climate change. Of those 115, 78 are valorised negatively (thirty-three are valorised positively and four are unclear). While this tells us that images too serve an antagonising function in the climate change communication of the far right, this distribution becomes even more meaningful in comparison to images on local environment where, as we point out below, the distribution of negative and positive valorisation is almost upside-down, indicating the very different roles of these two domains.

However, before we address valorisation in the local environment corpus, we turn to dominant topics in the far right's climate change communication (Table 11.1).[3,4] The antagonising nature of these images is already visible in the main category coded: 'Actors/people'. The biggest group, 'Environmentalists', is almost exclusively valorised negatively (nine out of ten), though, interestingly, only one of these images shows the climate activist Greta Thunberg. This contrasts sharply with the misogynist representation of Thunberg in a similar corpus covering July 2018 to December 2019 (Forchtner, in press), indicating that after an initial period in which Thunberg and her activism had to be signified (the period covering the rise of Fridays for Future protests and the European Parliament Elections in 2019 in which climate change featured prominently), this signification is now completed (arguably, a similar process has been visible in the past with regard to Al Gore). In contrast, the second-largest subcategory, 'Ordinary people/workers', exclusively features 'victims' and positively valorised opponents of climate action and policy. This is the 'silent majority', the 'pure people' constructed by the far right.

Turning to 'Policies and technologies/architecture', the subcategory of 'Green policy and technology' features wind turbines (nine times, valorised exclusively negatively – it is notable that new technologies are valorised overwhelmingly negatively) and their harmful effects on birds (twice). This hostility is no surprise and in line with existing research; indeed, Otteni and Weisskircher (2021) demonstrated that the construction of wind turbines has a positive impact on the electoral success of the AfD. However, while

Table 11.1 Topics present in the visual climate change communication of the German far right

Topics			Number of images (total/files)
Actors	People	Environmentalists	10/8
		Ordinary people/workers	8/7
		Politicians	6/6
		Miscellaneous	12/11
		Total	36/25
	Non-people	Media	5/4
		Miscellaneous	3/3
		Total	8/6
	Total		44/27
Policies and technologies/ architecture	Green policy and technology		26/16
	Fossil fuel-related policy and technology		7/4
	Miscellaneous		8/6
	Total		41/22
Natural environment and lands			13/8
Graphs and figures			9/7
Miscellaneous			8/8
Total			115/50

(visual) arguments against wind turbines as damaging wildlife and increasing land consumption are sometimes used polemically to articulate a particularistic environmentalism, *Die Kehre* combines the latter with attacks against high levels of energy consumption as the underlying problem.

Finally, 'Graphs and figures', although the smallest category (for more on this type of images, see Chapter 12 in this volume), is noteworthy as it contains only one outright denialist figure, which draws on the climate-sceptic German think tank the European Institute for Climate & Energy, which has close links with the AfD (Moreno et al., 2022).

Turning to the framing of climate change (Table 11.2), we start by pointing to the significance of classic framings, such as 'Climate policies cause economic harm' (individual and national economic pain is a problem caused by the politics of, for example, a detached, globalist elite which can only be halted through supporting the right) and 'Climate change irrationalism' (alarmism, hysteria and quasi-religious delusion as problems caused by, for example, the political elite and is separated from the far right's own standards of

Table 11.2 Frames conveyed via the visual climate change communication of the German far right

Frames	Number of images (total/files)
Climate policies cause economic harm	23/15
Climate change irrationalism	20/11
Climate policies harm the environment	16/9
Special interests drive the climate debate	9/8
Old ways are good ways	9/6
Greens and their policies are a threat	8/5
Miscellaneous	14/10
Unclear	16/12
Total	115/50

rationality and sanity). This, once again, plays with the slogan that environmental concern is neither left nor right (Olsen, 1999), with the far right offering allegedly non-ideological insight, for example when Walter Rauch from the *Freiheitliche Partei Österreichs* (Freedom Party of Austria; DK, 2020a: 35) claims to give voice to 'common sense'. Of a different kind is the frame 'Climate policies harm the environment' (environmental problems are highlighted as being caused by ignorant and harmful climate policies which need to be overcome) which is, for example, connected to the aforementioned critique of wind turbines.

Unsurprisingly, the images which convey frames discussed so far are predominantly valorised negatively, though this changes in the case of 'Old ways are good ways' (the contemporary age is viewed as largely decadent and destructive, caused by liberalism/modernity, while old, traditional ways offer, at least philosophically, a way forward).

We close this section with a qualitative discussion through which we aim to capture more richly the meanings that are circulating. No doubt, large segments of the German far right remain tied to well-known tropes which they also enforce through visuals. For example, *Deutsche Stimme* (DS, 2020) thematises wind turbines as a threat to birds under the title 'The killer with sharp edges', accompanied with a collage of a bird flying into wind turbines. The close-up image of the individual bird presumably attempts to create horror in the face of what is going to happen and disgust vis-à-vis those who claim to stand up for the environment but allow this to happen, such as the Greens.

Another image, this time in *Compact*, illustrates the economic harm climate policies allegedly cause through the depiction of an 'everyday memorial'. Here, two posters on the wall at the centre of the onlookers' gaze proclaim 'No coal. No work. No future. Lusatia' and 'Our work. Our homeland. Our future. Lusatia' while the floor in front features numerous candles. The site thus acts as a shrine, evoking religious meaning, with a sign ('Societal compromise 2038') naming the culprit: climate policies. It mourns the loss of coal and, thus, a particular *Heimat* (homeland; here: Lusatia, a region in the east of Germany), conveying a deep sense of despair. More specifically, it conveys fear of the loss of masculinity embodied by coal mining, similar to what is communicated in, for example, an image depicting a man standing in front of wind turbines and showing his empty pockets (Compact, 2020; for an analysis of a variant of this image, see Forchtner, in press). In that image, a binary of threatened male labour (similarly evoked by this image of a shrine) and allegedly female renewables (or climate policies more generally) is evoked; as such, all these images reproduce 'breadwinner masculinities' (Hultman et al., 2019). As Daggett (2018) reminds us, modern industrial society was built on the burning of fossil fuels that secured (male) working-class jobs as well as white patriarchal rule. Thus, 'extracting and burning fuel was a practice of white masculinity' that 'could be crudely equated with virility' (Daggett, 2018: 32). At the same time, the image reproduces the identity-forming aspect of coal in certain regions, a phenomenon brilliantly discussed by Allen (2022) in her study of Polish miners. Similarly relevant in this context is a study on mining in the United States which stresses 'class, race, and gender dynamics of place-based identities and moral economies tied to mining' as being 'a key part of the micropolitics of right-wing populism' (Kojola, 2019: 377).

However, the image we want to consider in detail (Figure 11.1, Beleites, 2020: 11) moves beyond such widely circulating tropes. Indeed, together with Figure 11.2 it captures the aforementioned complexities in *Die Kehre*'s discussions of climate change and enables us to discuss the nuance characterising the visual communication of what is the main medium in our corpus.[5]

This image is taken from the very first, full article in *Die Kehre*, entitled 'Human-Made Overheating: On the Entropy of Industrial Society' (superimposed over two smokestacks). This title seems to suggest a serious concern for human-made climate change, different from what is often associated with the far right. However, while accepting a 'civilisation-depending' rise in CO_2 (Beleites, 2020: 7), the author goes on to claim that 'human-made CO_2-emissions are probably not the cause, but a necessary *concomitant* of' overheating, a development which can only be stopped via 'a general renunciation of [the] competition-driven growth dynamic' (Beleites, 2020: 11). As such, man is both responsible and not: not responsible, because human-made CO_2 is not driving the malaise; responsible because of humanity's lack of self-control. In this way, the causes of climate change are framed as very much a matter of culture and ideas: Although global capitalism is, to

11.1 Hell on Earth

be sure, a culprit, it is morality itself which needs to change, a position which obfuscates clear policy choices. The harmful metabolism, that is, the relationship between man and nature, has already been thematised by Karl Marx – with capitalism being the way in which this metabolic process is currently organised. Building on Marx, O'Connor (1988) argues that capitalism is now experiencing its 'second contradiction', this time between (1) capitalist production relations and productive forces and (2) the environment, and Foster (1999) discusses the 'metabolic rift' between humanity and nature. However, while the far right does point to this rift, the causes often become 'idealised', that is, less a matter of how our metabolism with nature is societally organised than a protest against liberalism and modernity. In other words, capitalism is indeed made responsible; as de Benoist, in an interview with *Die Kehre* (DK, 2020c), proclaims: 'Anyone who speaks of ecology without questioning capitalism should better remain silent.' Yet what often is visible to the reader is more the concern over a productivist culture than capitalism per se. Beleites (2020: 9) thus calls for a 'growth-critical perspective' which 'recognize[s] the conditions of humanity and the restoration of environmental relationships appropriate for humans, those which are mirrored in the inner world of humans'. This sentiment is also illustrated by Kubitschek, who argues in favour of a kind of eco-asceticism, or as he expresses it: '"ecological inertia" [...] it is best when there is little going on' (DK, 2020d: 32).

Accordingly, Figure 11.1 evokes the Romantic criticism of Blake and the Satanic mills uttered in the former's early nineteenth-century poem 'And did those feet in ancient time', of 'dark Satanic Mills' of the Industrial Revolution. Indeed, this is a pit in which humans have lost themselves, or, as the caption states: 'Symbol of an overheated society – steaming chimneys and high-voltage lines as far as the eye can see.' This is realised through a number of visual semiotic choices (see Machin and Mayr, 2012: 49–56), such as, first (and arguably most powerfully): colour. That is, the image is soaked in orange light, with the sun only breaking through in the upper-right corner. The dominant colour, while potentially signifying awe and beauty – think of romantic sceneries which see the sun rising – conveys a heated, truly hellish world. There is no green space, no nature in this image. Yes, there is ground, presumably green, but not only is this ground too cast in orange light, it also serves only to carry symbols of our failing culture: power lines and steaming chimneys. Second, these symbols make the image distinctively uniform, as modernity allegedly is too, that is, the same features repeat themselves. Third, the long-distance shot strengthens the impressions described so far as viewers are not given any promising particularity, for example a flower breaking through the ground. Instead, there seems to be no 'outside' of this world, only the threat of an all-consuming modern culture.

There is thus a certain terrorising dullness to the image, one which in the eyes of *Die Kehre* signifies modernity as such. It is this perception of modernity as horrifying monotony which helps to explain why even the recognition of rising CO_2 emissions as a problem involving humans does not necessarily result in the acceptance of scientifically grounded policies to mitigate climate change. After all, such support would, ultimately, align this position with what the far right views as abstract and general. This stands in stark contrast to the affective investment visible in images of natural distinctiveness, of particularity and the concrete representing the local/regional/national. Thus, and unsurprisingly, Beleites (2020: 13) calls for 'regionalisation instead of globalisation', something which brings us to the visualisation of locality.

Nature and the local environment

As mentioned above, the analysis of basic valorisation of local nature illustrates a sharp difference between this domain and climate change. In contrast to climate change, the 231 images across 77 contributions falling into this category show that the far right predominantly valorises nature and the local environment positively (132 are valorised positively, 72 negatively and 27 unclear).

With regard to topics present in the investigated images (Table 11.3), the category of actors yields results that are similar and different to the domain of climate change. For example, 'Environmentalists' (and 'Environmental organisations') are often present, but are, this time, predominantly positively valorisation: These include images of Pentti Linkola, often admired by the far right, who is portrayed in *Die Kehre* in 2021. 'Politicians' stand out too, though these resemble images in the domain of climate change as they both include 'others', such as politicians associated with the Green party, and positively valorised ones, such as Gauland. 'Media' too is largely valorised

Table 11.3 Topics present in the visual communication of nature of the German far right

Topics			Number of images (total/files)
Actors	People	Environmentalists	14/6
		Politicians	10/6
		Miscellaneous	34/19
		Total	58/25
	Non-people	Media	13/10
		Environmental organisations	8/5
		Tractors	6/5
		Miscellaneous	3/3
		Total	30/18
	Total		88/35
Nature	Heritage and land(scape)		28/13
	Agriculture, plants and fruit		20/10
	Animals		17/11
	Forest		12/6
	Miscellaneous		1/1
	Total		78/41
Policies and technologies/ architecture	Houses		26/10
	Pollution		4/4
	Miscellaneous		15/7
	Total		45/16
Graphs and figures			9/8
Miscellaneous			11/11
Total			231/77

positively, with, for example, no images of mainstream magazines allegedly reproducing 'climate hysteria'.

'Nature' is dominated by pictures of 'Heritage and land(scape)': They feature almost exclusively in *Die Kehre* and *Deutsche Stimme*, are valorised positively and parade nature monuments and the homeland. To some extent, this category is the paradigmatic site of far-right engagement with the natural environment, depicting that which is particular and deeply engrained in 'who we are', and which must therefore be preserved as pure. Concern for the natural environment is also visible with regard to the subcategory 'Animals', which are commonly valorised negatively – not because they are viewed as standing in the way of economic progress, but because they illustrate the negative consequences of others' actions, as in the depiction of death (birds) and threats to biodiversity (including 'invasive' species). A similar, 'environmentalist' logic underlies the depiction of 'Agriculture, plants and fruit' and 'Forest', as well as most uses of 'Graphs and figures'.

Under 'Policies and technologies/architecture', 'Pollution' concerns waste (unsurprisingly rejected) while 'Houses' covers both traditional and modern houses (largely the former, valorised positively), playing a function similar to that of 'Heritage and land(scape)' in that the local, the rooted, is stressed as desirable. In turn, 'the other' takes the form of modern housing which is connected to a levelling global modernity.

Turning to the frames conveyed (Table 11.4), the first six frames can all be subsumed under far-right, pro-environment stances: 'Protect the

Table 11.4 Frames conveyed in the visual communication of nature of the German far right

Frames	Number of images (total/files)
Protect the environment/sustainability is needed	35/15
Placing/rootedness is important	33/11
Far-right thinking is worth listening to	20/6
Listen to nature	18/6
Biodiversity must be protected	13/8
Globalism is destroying the environment	13/7
Greens are bad	13/7
Old ways are good ways	12/5
Protect our farmers	9/4
People as an environmental issue	4/4
Miscellaneous	26/12
Unclear	35/19
Total	231/77

environment/sustainability is needed' (environmental destruction is identified as a problem caused by liberalism/materialism/modernity/global capitalism and, thus, the environment needs to be protected); 'Placing/rootedness is important' (individuals/collectives are increasingly not bounded which is a problem caused by liberalism/materialism/modernity/globalism – placing/rootedness are the solution); 'Far-right thinking is worth listening to' (given the contemporary malaise caused by liberalism/materialism/modernity/global capitalism, listening to far-right thinkers and their sometimes 200-year-old wisdom offers a way forward); 'Listen to nature' (environmental issues, and beyond, are caused by ignorance towards the eternal laws offered by nature – we need to listen again), reminiscent of Olsen's (1999) conceptualisation of 'eco-naturalism' as one of three defining elements of right-wing ecology; and 'Globalism is destroying the environment' (environmental issues are caused by globalism, for example the shipping of products from China to Europe just so that we can consume cheaply, but this has to change). The latter has been highlighted in the case of the French Front National/National Rally in the European Parliament (Forchtner and Lubarda, 2023) and is arguably a frame easily adopted by opponents of the far right (as is 'Biodiversity must be protected' which concerns the threat to 'native species', see Olsen, 1999). Hence, opponents need to be particularly careful as such framing can go hand in hand with a call for borders (and essentialised identities).

These 'environmentalist' frames are followed by one demonising Greens (mirroring climate change communication). Finally, 'Old ways are good ways' (already present in climate change communication) is conveyed via, for example, the topic of 'Heritage and land(scape)' introduced earlier. Once again, it is not the global and abstract, modern ways of accelerated movement and displacement which are celebrated, but the local and particular, offering a path forward in the face of destructive global modernity.

What is surprising is that 'People as an environmental issue', covering also 'overpopulation', is hardly present. This is notable considering that the 1970s in particular saw 'overpopulation' and neo-Malthusian thinking being endemic and that it is often claimed to be of central importance in the far right today (for example, Malm and The Zetkin Collective, 2021). However, our study illustrates that it is not overly prevalent in far-right visual environmental communication (see also Forchtner and Özvatan, 2019; Forchtner and Lubarda, 2023). This is not to say that 'overpopulation' is not mentioned, that 'othered' populations are welcomed or that, for example, interviews with far-right activists would not illustrate its significance. For now, however, it suggests that such a frame either does not play a major role in published far-right communication (in Germany) or is segmented to such a degree that it is not mobilised (even though it can connect far-right and 'mainstream' or even left-wing actors, as can other frames mentioned above).

Following this overview of images circulated by the German far right when discussing the local/regional/national, we now turn, again, to a broader discussion of this stance articulated via an image.

Figure 11.2 (Eichberger, 2020: 14) is taken from an article in *Die Kehre* and, due to the multimodal arrangement, offers a straightforward pictorialisation of place-rootedness, of (stereo)typical Alpine scenery. As such, this is also a particular homeland, which is different from (for example) north Germany and therefore conveying the bioregional dimension of this contribution. This is a romanticised rural homeland of fields, forests and mountains – in contrast to depictions of alienated, modern urban spaces. Place is concrete and particular, it offers identity and, indeed, the cottage gives off the appearance of growing almost organically from the ground. In other words, the cottage (and the community it symbolises) is rooted, not implanted; authentic, not artificial. Considering the symbol of the cottage further, it is noticeably situated off-centre and in the background, as if it were just another natural feature within the depiction of the landscape. The human and socially constructed thus becomes naturalised as well as 'put into its place' as the most obvious sign of human penetration of the land does not take centre stage.

This naturalisation is intentional, as the article addresses bioregionalism, a theory that suggests that human communities, if they are to be truly ecologically harmonious, should reflect natural/bioregional boundaries. Most bioregionalist theories convey a certain anti-modernism: Environmental problems are conceptualised as 'coterminous with modernity's homogenizing impulses' (Olsen, 2000: 73). Thus, the task is to reintegrate human communities back into their own unique natural spaces. The appeal of such theories to the far right rests not only in the overlap between a naturalisation of the social, with 'nature's laws' as a purported guide, but also because human communities are seen as bounded, closed and organically growing out of a set of natural spaces. Protection of the environment, thus, becomes synonymous with the protection of the homeland. As such, the sympathetic viewer is called to protect this place, something also conveyed through positioning viewers as gazing down over 'our' space. Such a guardian-like stance is also articulated by Gauland (DK, 2020b: 36), who describes environmental protection as the 'attempt to preserve the old environment as far as possible as a homeland and as a way to enable identity'.

Further notable symbols include the aforementioned forest and depictions of the field: The latter almost dominates the image, especially as the overcast sky does not attract the viewer's attention. A bright, blue sky would have done so and given the image a less sombre tone (it would have also backgrounded the relatively light and fresh colours in the front of the image); as it stands, Figure 11.2 is dominated by rather dark colours, possibly evoking 'earthish', 'rootish' associations. The field is furthermore highlighted

11.2 '»Against the selling out of the homeland« – bioregional identity contra the disappearance of place'

through focus, a semiotic resource to give salience to a detail (Machin and Mayr, 2012: 55); here, it enables the display of individuality, the concrete and particular, and beauty via leaves and flowers in the front (before they bend into the wider scenery, the homeland).

Taking a step back, and recalling the gendered character of images discussed in the previous section, we note that Figure 11.2 too conveys a particular masculinity representative of the wider masculinity conveyed by communicating environmental protection. Here neither 'industrial/breadwinner masculinities'

(Hultman et al., 2019) nor 'petro-masculinity' (Daggett, 2018) but what we call a far-right, 'masculine/muscular environmentalism' is foregrounded (see also Chapter 5 in this volume), one which purports to protect and defend 'our' bounded places (in contrast to climate protection which is associated with the moving, the abstract and the feminine).[6]

Considering this image illustrates the type of sensitivity the far right shows when addressing concrete and local/regional/national natural environments: one reproducing ethno-communal identity, one protecting that which is close so as to avoid losing ourselves. It is thus no surprise, pointing once more to Kubitschek (DK, 2020d: 31), that the far right views ecology as 'concentric', 'from the close to the distant'. What can be closer than homeland, what can be more distant than climate?

Conclusion

This chapter's point of departure came from two observations. First, that some on the far right do voice concern for the natural environment, and that it is important to consider the visual component of such a voice which gives further impetus and emotional force to far-right visualisations, from affection for the homeland to disgust towards those (actions) which allegedly harm it. Second, we emphasised the contrast between such environmental protection sentiment and stances vis-à-vis climate change. Investigating similarities/differences in the multimodal articulation of local/regional/national environment and global climate change, we found that any similarities are largely limited to the 'othering' of Greens and the likes of liberalism/materialism/modernity/global capitalism (and appropriate 'old ways'), while a virtuous, 'rooted' *Umwelt-* or *Naturschutz* (environmental and nature protection respectively) mobilises an aesthetic and symbolic repertoire which is juxtaposed with the universal and abstract problem of climate change and policy for its mitigation. Through comparing valorisations, topics, frames and semiotic choices in a corpus of 346 images in German far-right media, we have illustrated that this difference is significant, at least in Germany.

Research has long indicated that the far right's hostility to the issue of climate change is not universal (for example, Lubarda, 2023), and an escalating climate crisis might well lead more of these actors to channel their ethnonationalism and authoritarianism into climate-friendly paths, though with no less exclusionary effects. How this is going to develop remains an empirical question, but while the ideological affinity towards environmental protection might well facilitate such changes, there are 'good' ideological reasons for why modes of obstruction, instead of climate championship, might remain. Indeed, there is a tension at the heart of nationalist ideology due to the global character of climate change, one even visible in cases where global cooperation is accepted, but not without affirming the primacy of the nation and its sovereignty. The path ahead is thus not determined but will depend on the performance of ideology in particular contexts and the interaction of a variety of mechanisms.

As we have stressed throughout, the association of climate with the abstract, general and global is a key mechanism behind this unease, which all too often leads to various forms of climate obstruction.[7] Here, several layers are at work. At its widest, philosophical level, the global is contrasted with the bounded and local, and as such it is also connected to a critique of the modern, the uniform and the fluid. At a more concrete level, rejection of (unbound) capitalism and marketisation might go hand in hand with favouring a bounded, national market. This unease is furthermore based in a masculine/muscular environmentalism which, while ready to defend the space 'we' are rooted in, is far less invested in the protection of the abstract and global climate. This is certainly not restricted to Germany, as even the 'master theorist' of the contemporary New Right, de Benoist (DK, 2020c: 35f), criticises 'overemphasing climate change' (which he accepts as being human-made) at the expense of attention given to, for example, the destruction of the soil and poisoning of the oceans. This 'overemphasing', he (DK 2020c) argues, is driven by a 'globalist' rhetoric (which is moralistic, apocalyptic and hysterical) while what is needed instead is multilayered action at the 'local level'. As we have noticed, such longing for the local can easily serve as a 'site' through which the far right connects to the centre and even left.

Against this background, and in a world ravaged by economic and environmental crises, could it be that an urgently felt need for community will manifest itself in an increased desire for 'our' rootedness in a landscape/soil, one which reflects the solidity of 'our' being? If so, then anything having to do with 'the climate' and related transnational issue or policies will continue to face suspicion – this, although the Earth might be on fire or under water.

Notes

1 The local, regional and national are, of course, not identical. Nevertheless, the real distinction for the far right is between global and non-global (local/regional/national), since the latter is understood as that in which a particular community can be *rooted* (unlike in the case of the global). We mostly speak of local for pragmatic reasons.

2 Keywords were: *agriculture*, biodiversity, *bioregional*, carbon dioxide, *climate*, CO_2, *eco*, *energy*, *environment*, *farmer* (*Bauer*), *forest*

(*Wald/Forst*), genetically modified, greenhouse effect, invasive species, *nature*, *overfish*, overpopulation, species protection, *sustainable*, waste (*Müll*). The asterisks are used in database searches to include variations. For example, overfish* would also show overfishing, etc.

3 'Total' stands for how often the topic (or frame, see below) was counted; 'files' stands for the number of different articles in which the topic (or frame) was present.

4 Tables show topics (or frame, see below) which were coded at least four times across four texts; otherwise they were subsumed under 'Miscellaneous'.

5 We note that Figures 11.1 and 11.2 are generic images, but that their circulation in far-right contexts allows for a reading of the far right's interpretative frameworks.

6 Veit (2022) too has addressed the far-right relationship between nature protection and climate denial, pointing to anti-feminism playing a 'linking function'.

7 On the issue of global climate change and place – a global sense of place – see Praskievicz (2022).

References

Allen, I. (2022): Heated attachments to coal: Everyday industrial breadwinning petro-masculinity and domestic heating in the Silesian home. In: K. Iwińska and X. Bukowska (eds), *Gender and Energy Transition*. Cham: Springer, 189–222.

Beleites, M. (2020): Die menschengemachte Überhitzung: Zur Entropie der Industriegesellschaft, *Die Kehre*, 1: 6–13.

Biehl, J. and Staudenmaier, P. (2011 [1995]): *Ecofascism Revisited: Lessons from the German Experience*. Porsgrunn: New Compass Press.

Boecher, M., Zeigermann, U., Berker, L. and Jabra, D. (2022): Climate policy expertise in times of populism: Knowledge strategies of the AfD regarding Germany's climate package, *Environmental Politics*, 31(5): 820–840.

Brüggemeier, F. J., Cioc, M. and Zeller, T. (eds) (2005): *How Green Were the Nazis? Nature, Environment, and Nation in the Third Reich*. Athens, OH: Ohio University Press.

Compact (2020): Dossier, *Compact*, April 2020: 43.

Daggett, C. (2018): Petro-masculinity: Fossil fuels and authoritarian desire, *Millennium*, 47(1): 25–44. https://doi.org/10.1177%2F0305829818775817

DK (2020a): 'Umwelt- und Naturschutz sind eine Frage des Hausverstands': Gespräch mit Walter Rauch (FPÖ), *Die Kehre*, 1: 34–36.

DK (2020b): Nachhaltigkeit als konservatives Prinzip: Interview mit dem AfD-Fraktionsvorsitzenden im Deutschen Bundestag Dr. Alexander Gauland, *Die Kehre*, 2: 34–40.

DK (2020c): 'Wer von Ökologie spricht, ohne den Kapitalismus in Frage zustellen, sollte besser schweigen': Interview mit dem französischen Philosophen Alain de Benoist, *Die Kehre*, 3: 32–38.

DK (2020d): 'Entortung und Masse sind per se destruktiv, nivellierend, unorganisch, unökologisch': Interview mit Götz Kubitschek, *Die Kehre*, 4: 30–34.

DK (2020e): 'Die Kehre #2': Was ist Nachhaltigkeit? www.youtube.com/watch?v=KcRn8rhwNbc (accessed 22 December 2021).

DK (2021a): 'Die Kehre #7': Postwachstum. www.youtube.com/watch?v=KcRn8rhwNbc (accessed 22 December 2021).

DK (2021b): 'Wer sein Land liebt, will auch dessen natürliche Lebensgrundlagen erhalten': Interview mit dem AfD-Landesvorsitzenden in Thüringen Björn Höcke, *Die Kehre*, 5: 30–35.

DS (2020): Gefahr für die Tiere: Die Killer mit den scharfen Krallen, *Deutsche Stimme*, 1: 20.

Eichberger, H. (2020): 'Gegen den Ausverkauf der Heimat': Bioregionale Identität wider das Verschwinden des Ortes, *Die Kehre*, 4: 14–21.

Ekberg, K., Forchtner, B., Hultman, M. and Jylhä, K. M. (2022): *Climate Obstruction: How Denial, Delay and Inaction are Heating the Planet.* London: Routledge.

Entman, R. (1993): Framing: Toward clarification of a fractured paradigm, *Journal of Communication*, 43(4): 51–58.

Forchtner, B. (2019a): Climate change and the far right, *WIREs Climate Change*, 10(5). https://doi.org/10.1002/wcc.604

Forchtner, B. (ed.) (2019b): *The Far Right and the Environment: Politics, Discourse and Communication.* London: Routledge.

Forchtner, B. (in press): Thunberg, not iceberg: Visual melodrama in far-right climate-change communication in Germany. In: I. Allen, K. Ekberg, S. Holgersen and A. Malm (eds), *Political Ecologies of the Far Right.* Manchester: Manchester University Press.

Forchtner, B. and Kølvraa, C. (2015): The nature of nationalism: Populist radical right parties on countryside and climate, *Nature & Culture*, 10(2): 199–224. https://doi.org/10.3167/nc.2015.100204

Forchtner, B. and Lubarda, B. (2023): Towards a physiognomy of climate change communication by the far right: Scepticisms and beyond in the European Parliament, *Environmental Politics*, 32(1): 43–68.

Forchtner, B. and Özvatan, Ö. (2019): Beyond the 'German forest': Environmental communication by the far right in Germany. In: B. Forchtner (ed.), *The Far Right and the Environment: Politics, Discourse and Communication.* London: Routledge. 216–236.

Forchtner, B. and Özvatan, Ö. (2022): De/legitimising Europe through the performance of crises: The far-right Alternative for Germany on 'climate hysteria' and 'corona hysteria', *Journal of Language and Politics*, 21(2): 208–232.

Foster, J. (1999): Marx's theory of metabolic rift: Classical foundations for environmental sociology, *American Journal of Sociology*, 105(2): 366–405. https://doi.org/10.1086/210315

Gauland, A. (2019): Nachhaltigkeit als konservatives Prinzip. In: A. Gauland (ed.), *Nation, Populismus, Nachhaltigkeit: Drei Vorträge.* Schnellroda: Antaios, 51–82.

Geden, O. (1996): *Rechte Ökologie: Umweltschutz zwischen Emanzipation und Faschismus.* Berlin: Elefanten Press.

GF (n.d.): Arndt and Riehl: Fathers of the völkish-environmentalism. https://greenlinefront.blogspot.com/2016/09/arndt-and-riehl-fathers-of-volkish.html (accessed 22 December 2021).

Göpffarth, J. (2020): Rethinking the German nation as German *Dasein*: Intellectuals and Heidegger's philosophy in contemporary German New Right nationalism, *Journal of Political Ideologies*, 25(3): 248–273.

Hultman, M., Björk, A. and Viinikka, T. (2019): Far-right and climate change denial: Denouncing environmental challenges via anti-establishment rhetoric, marketing of doubts, industrial/breadwinner masculinities enactments and ethno-nationalism. In: B. Forchtner (ed.), *The Far Right and the Environment: Politics, Discourse and Communication*. London: Routledge, 121–135.

Hurd, M. and Werther, S. (2016): The militant media of neo-Nazi environmentalism. In: H. Graf (ed.), *The Environment in the Age of the Internet*. Cambridge: Open Book Publishers, 139–170.

Jahn, T. and Wehling, P. (1991): *Ökologie von rechts: Nationalismus und Umweltschutz bei der Neuen Rechten und den 'Republikanern'*. Frankfurt am Main: Campus.

Kojola, E. (2019): Bringing back the mines and a way of life: Populism and the politics of extraction, *Annals of the American Association of Geographers*, 109: 371–381.

Küppers, A. (2022): 'Climate-soviets', 'alarmism', and 'eco-dictatorship': The framing of climate change scepticism by the populist radical right Alternative for Germany, *German Politics*. https://doi.org/10.1080/09644008.2022.2056596

Lockwood, M. (2018): Right-wing populism and the climate change agenda, *Environmental Politics*, 27(4): 712–732. https://doi.org/10.1080/09644016.2018.1458411

Lubarda, B. (2023): *Far-Right Ecologism: Environmental Politics and the Far Right in Hungary and Poland*. London: Routledge.

Machin, D. and Mayr, A. (2012): *How to Do Critical Discourse Analysis: A Multimodal Introduction*. London: Sage.

Malm, A. and The Zetkin Collective (2021): *White Skin, Black Fuel: On the Danger of Fossil Fascism*. London: Verso.

Moreno, J. A., Kinn, M. and Narberhaus, M. (2022): A stronghold of climate change denialism in Germany: Case study of the output and press representation of the think tank EIKE, *International Journal of Communication*, 16: 267–288.

NPD (2007): Genfrass – Nein Danke! *Der Ordnungsruf*, 1: 1.

O'Connor, J. (1988): Capitalism, nature, socialism: A theoretical introduction, *Capitalism, Nature, Socialism*, 1(1): 11–38. https://doi.org/10.1080/10455758809358356

Olsen, J. (1999): *Nature and Nationalism. Right-Wing Ecology and the Politics of Identity in Contemporary Germany*. New York: St. Martin's Press.

Olsen, J. (2000): The perils of rootedness: On bioregionalism and right wing ecology in Germany, *Landscape Journal*, 19(1–2): 73–83. http://dx.doi.org/10.3368/lj.19.1-2.73

Otteni, C. and Weisskircher, M. (2021): Global warming and polarization: Wind turbines and the electoral success of the greens and the populist radical right, *European Journal of Political Research*. https://doi.org/10.1111/1475-6765.12487.

Praskievicz, S. (2022): Ground truth: Finding a 'place' for climate change, *Progress in Environmental Geography*, https://doi.org/10.1177/27539687221127035.

Quent, M., Richter, C. and Salheiser, A. (2022): *Klimarassismus: Der Kampf der Rechten gegen die ökologische Wende. Wie Rechtsaußenparteien den Klimawandel für sich nutzen*. Munich: Piper.

Schick, J. (2020): Editorial, *Die Kehre*, 1: 1.

Smith, A. (2009): *Ethno-Symbolism and Nationalism*. London: Routledge.

Sommer, B., Schad, M., Kadelke, P., Humpert, F. and Möstl, C. (2022): *Rechtspopulismus vs. Klimaschutz? Positionen, Einstellungen, Erklärungsansätze*. Munich: oekom.

Staudenmaier, P. (2021): *Ecology Contested: Environmental Politics between Left and Right*. Porsgrunn: New Compass Press.

van Rensburg, W. (2015): Climate change skepticism: A conceptual re-evaluation, *SAGE Open*, 5(2): 1–13. https://doi.org/10.1177/2158244015579723

Veit, K. (2022): 'Gender-Ideologie' und 'Klimahysterie': Der Natur-Geschlechter-Nexus im rechten und extrem rechten Denken, *ZRex – Zeitschrift für Rechtsextremismusforschung*, 2(1): 141–158. https://doi.org/10.3224/zrex.v2i1.09

Voss, K. (2014): *Nation and Nature in Harmony: The Ecological Component of Far Right Ideology*. Unpublished PhD thesis. Florence: Italy.

Young Alternative (2019): Windkraft-Ausbau: Stoppt die Verschandelung unserer Landschaften! Press release, 16 December 2019. https://jungealternative-nrw.de/aktuelles/pressemeldungen/ (accessed 22 December 2021).

12

Talking heads and contrarian graphs: televising the Swedish far right's climate denialism

Kjell Vowles

Introduction

In early September 2018, leading up to the Swedish parliamentary elections when Greta Thunberg had started her school strike, the far-right online video channel SwebbTV published an interview with Lars Bern. Bern, a doctor of technology and former industrial leader who has long spread doubt about climate change science (Ekberg and Pressfeldt, 2021), was invited to speak about 'the environmental movements' scare-mongering' (SwebbTV, 2018a). To dismiss the threat of rising temperatures, he used several graphs. One was a distorted figure showing temperature reconstructions taken from the first Intergovernmental Panel on Climate Change (IPCC) report in 1990 while another was published in a Swedish popular science magazine in 1997. These cherry-picked graphs aimed to discredit not only the environmental movement but also institutions such as the IPCC. During the year and a half that followed, denial of climate science became widespread among far-right media in Sweden, and SwebbTV played an important role (Vowles and Hultman, 2021). Through engagement with the climate change countermovement, SwebbTV helped facilitate a far-right discourse in which climate change is a hoax.

Images, in general, are powerful in both increasing the emotional impact of a message and simplifying complex arguments (see the Introduction to this volume). Climate change graphs, in particular, specialise in the latter as they communicate science. They also speak to the former in making a political statement on how to act. They come with a claim of objectivity, of representing the material world, and thus can add weight to any argument. This also makes them useful for spreading disinformation. This study analyses all graphs used by SwebbTV in its climate programmes during the years 2018–2019, a period when legacy media reported extensively on climate change following Greta Thunberg's Fridays for Future movement and several extreme weather events (Nacu-Schmidt, et al., 2019). By analysing the graphs used by SwebbTV, this study both adds understanding to how the far right engages with climate science and contributes to the scarce scholarly literature on contrarian climate graphs. Specifically, it asks: First, what type of graphs are used by SwebbTV to visualise climate science; and second, where have the graphs been taken from?

SwebbTV, short for Swedish web-tv, is a nationalist video channel displaying all elements of far-right ideology pointed out by Wodak (2019: 27): *fearmongering* in arguing that the nation is under attack; *scapegoating* in blaming immigrants, feminists, legacy media and international institutions, pointing to a supposed *saviour* in far-right media finally telling the truth; and that this will *change* Sweden and return it to the glorious patriarchal, homogenic and industrially prosperous community of the past. One important strategy of SwebbTV's self-proclaimed truth-telling is the use of graphs. By, figuratively speaking, redrawing the graphs to argue that there is no climate change to worry about, SwebbTV, represented mainly by men who are exclusively white, is also drawing the boundaries of the community. The boundaries are protecting it against activists such as Greta Thunberg, by signalling that the case for climate change mitigation is baseless.

In the subsequent parts of this chapter, I start by introducing the Swedish climate change countermovement and the Swedish far-right media ecosystem. Subsequently, I review the literature on graphs and how they have been used to spread doubt about climate science, before offering a detailed analysis of the graphs used by SwebbTV. I conclude with a discussion around how the climate change denial of SwebbTV can be understood.

The climate change countermovement and the far-right media ecosystem

Fossil fuel companies knew about the dangers of climate change as long ago as in the 1960s and 1970s (Aronowsky, 2021). But when climate change rose up the international political agenda in the late 1980s, the fossil fuel industry in the Unites States teamed up with conservative foundations to create a countermovement casting doubt about the science (for example, McKie, 2017; Brulle, 2019). These efforts were replicated elsewhere. In Sweden the Climate Realists (formerly the Stockholm Initiative) was formed in the late 2000s, consisting mainly of older men who, like Lars Bern, had held prominent positions within academia, industry or media and who contested anthropogenic climate change (Anshelm and Hultman, 2014). As in the case of Bern on SwebbTV, it has been a deliberate tactic by the countermovement to make contrarian scientists visible in the media to give the impression that there is no scientific consensus (Boykoff, 2011). Also, once again, just like Bern, they have often used graphs to back up their argumentation (Schneider et al., 2014), as such visualisations are claimed to depict the world as it is, removed from all interpretation by corrupt institutions such as the IPCC.

The Swedish far right is, of course, not alone in spreading climate change denialism. Several parties of the European far-right have expressed such arguments during the 2010s (Forchtner, 2019; Malm and The Zetkin Collective, 2021). Indeed, several studies have shown how nationalistic and conservative values are correlated to opposition to climate change science (for example, McCright and Dunlap, 2011; Jylhä et al., 2020). Among this electorate, mistrust of legacy media and public institutions is also more widespread (Andersson and Oscarsson, 2020), making it more susceptible to climate disinformation. Previous research on online countercultures has shown how contrarian arguments have become part of an 'alliance of antagonisms' where opposition to climate change politics becomes entangled with anti-feminism and anti-immigration (Kaiser and Puschmann, 2017). In the case of SwebbTV, this alliance is manifest.

Several far-right alternative media outlets have appeared in Sweden during the last decade, ranging from anti-democratic extreme right to anti-liberal radical right (Rydgren, 2018). What ties them together is that they position themselves as corrective of legacy media, which is by default a corrupt mouthpiece of an equally besmirched elite (Holt, 2019). The way information is spread between the different media is characterised by the propaganda feedback loop. While legacy media outlets will call out anyone who publishes untrue stories, media in the propaganda loop will target those straying from the ideological line (Benkler et al., 2018). SwebbTV has played a central role in doing precisely that. It allows other far-right alternative media to dismiss anyone wanting action on climate change simply by referencing interviews on SwebbTV, whose guests from the countermovement are portrayed as scientific authorities. This made SwebbTV the most referenced source for climate change information within the Swedish far-right media ecosystem, which reached about 10 per cent of the Swedish population, in the years 2018–2019 (Vowles and Hultman, 2021).

SwebbTV started in 2015. The main programme host and legally responsible publisher is Mikael Wilgert, who was previously active within the main Swedish radical-right party the Sweden Democrats (Freje Simonsson, 2020). Another host is an active politician in the extreme-right party Alternative for Sweden. Initially, SwebbTV mainly focused on what it calls mass migration. Climate change became prominent after the summer of 2018, though the first programmes concerning the issue were broadcast as far back as 2017. SwebbTV started on YouTube but was expelled in December

2020 for breaking the rules regarding hate speech and disinformation about COVID-19. While based on YouTube, 'climate alarm' was one of four themed playlists. Now the playlists have been removed, but in a programme discussing the future of the channel, Mikael Wilgert states that SwebbTV will continue to work against the 'dark agenda' of the globalists, focusing on climate, immigration, gender and, most recently, health (SwebbTV, 2019a).

Visualising science through climate change contrarian graphs

To understand the use of graphs by the climate change contrarian movement, we need to look at the role that figures play in communicating science. In the late nineteenth century, mechanical objectivity became the scientific norm. Technological innovations in photography and measuring instruments promised to remove subjectivity from science. No personal judgement or interpretation should affect results; to that end it would be best to replace human language with photos and instrumentally generated graphs that supposedly show the world in its truest form (Daston and Galison, 1992). While feminist scholarship and science and technology studies have shown that all science is entangled in layers of human and structural interpretation (Merchant, 1989), the scientific image has kept an aura of authority. During the twentieth century, continued trust in numbers made formulas and graphs a communicative tool which seemingly minimised the need for intimate knowledge. As such, it was part of a democratic turn whereby institutional governance should be based on objective data rather than the personal, and perhaps partisan, judgement of public officials. However, as Porter (2020: xv) argued, this trust in numbers 'is trust in a very specific sense, implying often a radical distrust of people and institutions'. This (dis)trust has made numbers key elements of deception and propaganda. Huff (1954: 8) observed how the 'secret language of statistics, so appealing in a fact-minded culture, is employed to sensationalize, inflate, confuse, and oversimplify'. This becomes even more so as the scientific graph asks a lot of the viewer; if important information is left out, if data is cherry-picked, if axes are outdrawn or shrunk, a trained and critical eye is needed.

Graphs and charts are influential visual tools. They have been used extensively in climate communication by the IPCC and, to some extent, also by news media (Schneider, 2012; Rebich-Hespanha et al., 2015). Although there has been an increasing interest in news media's use of climate change visuals, its usage of graphs has received little scholarly attention. In recent reviews of the literature from a media and communications perspective, graphs are not discussed in depth (Hansen, 2017; Culloty et al., 2019). This is in line with, for example, O'Neill's (2020) longitudinal study of climate images in the press (2001–2009) which only finds them in one publication: the *Wall Street Journal*. Looking at a longer time period (1969–2009), Rebich-Hespanha et al. (2015) find the use of scientific graphs in the United States' print media to be noteworthy as the skills needed to understand them might distance some readers. Moreover, others might be drawn to the idea of understanding something complicated and, when it comes to arguing against the scientific consensus such as in the case of SwebbTV, to be able to expose something others cannot see. Thus, the understanding of graphs is not solely about scientific literacy but about pre-existing beliefs and ideology (Schneider et al., 2014: 34). The visual graphs on SwebbTV not only simplify a complex message but also create a strong emotional response of being in opposition to the political elite. Indeed, images can tie together a network of associations and affects (Carah, 2014); the contrarian graphs presented by mainly older, white men on a nationalistic video channel help to tie together an alliance of anti-immigration, -feminism and -climate change policies.

Scientific climate change graphs have a political dimension as they implicitly include a recommendation on how to act (Schneider, 2012). This has led to climate graphs, and none more so than Michael Mann's so-called hockey stick-graph, becoming contested images. Mann's graph, first published in 1998, used proxy data to reconstruct past temperatures and showed how present warming is unprecedented during at least the last 700 years. Initially, there was a legitimate scientific discussion about the proxy data, which led to methodological improvements and subsequent publications that confirmed the original findings. Nevertheless, the figure has remained one of the most popular targets of the climate change countermovement (for an in-depth analysis, see Ryghaug and Skjølsvold, 2010; Mann, 2014). The latest turn was in 2019 when a court dismissed a libel lawsuit that Mann had brought against the contrarian scientist Tim Ball. The court dismissed the case because Mann and his counsel had let it linger too long, but the climate change countermovement saw it as definitive proof that the hockey stick was broken, an argument that soon appeared on SwebbTV (for example, 2019b: 33:35).

Given their presence in contrarian climate communication, blogs specialising in debunking climate change denial myths, such as skepticalscience.com in English and mathsnilsson.se in Swedish, have long been meticulously picking apart erroneous and misleading graphs. However, there is little analysis of the use of contrarian graphs in the peer-reviewed literature, with Mellor (2009) and Schneider et al. (2014) being notable exceptions. Schneider et al. (2014) offer a classification scheme that is applied to examples taken from climate change contrarian blogs, books and reports, while Mellor (2009) analyses the contrarian documentary *The Great Global Warming Swindle*, originally broadcast in the United Kingdom. Similar to SwebbTV programmes, the visual setting of *The Great Global Warming Swindle* is mainly talking heads, interspersed with graphs and clips from other news media. Graphs and talking heads are standard documentary techniques that promise an indexical link between the film and the world it claims to represent. Mellor (2009: 144) notes that graphs 'are perhaps the most highly indexical of the representational techniques of science, tracing as they do data gathered from the material world'. *The Great Global Warming Swindle*, however, invokes this technique to mislead the audience as the indexical link is broken. The following analysis adds to these investigations by offering the, to my knowledge, first analysis of graphs based on systematic data collection within any part of the climate change countermovement.

Methods and empirical material

This study is based on all the programmes posted on SwebbTV's YouTube channel under the themed playlist 'climate alarm' between the beginning of January 2018 and end of December 2019, a period when Greta Thunberg and Fridays for Future rose in popularity. In total the dataset consists of fifty-four programmes or thirty-two hours and twenty-four minutes of video. The parts related to climate were coded, resulting in twenty-two hours of coded material. The majority of the programmes (thirty-eight) are studio programmes, where the most common format shows the channel host Mikael Wilgert interviewing a guest, usually Lars Bern, who is presented as the channel's political and scientific commentator. The non-studio programmes are either external lectures or shorter interviews with activists or political party volunteers, as well as one news bulletin.

Every new visual setting was coded according to its main feature (for example, 'studio', 'graphs', 'street shot', 'boats'). When a clip was shown from another TV-media, this was coded only as 'clip from TV-media', even though there might have been several different visual settings within the clip. All images were coded to just one code, unless for example a graph was cut inside the frame of the studio view, then this was coded both as 'studio' and 'graph'. The most common visual setting depicts people sitting in a studio or being on stage in case of an external event. This takes up 98 per cent (twenty-one hours and thirty-one minutes) of the coded playback time. In this setting, eighteen hours and fifty-three minutes show males only, two hours and one minute show both males and a female, and thirty-seven minutes show only a female. Apart from the studio setting, the only other reoccurring visual settings are clips from other news media, which is shown for 3 per cent of the coded time (thirty-nine minutes), and scientific graphs which is shown 3.5 per cent of the coded time (forty-six minutes). The former is mainly used to show how legacy media, and especially public service media, is 'fake news' according to SwebbTV. The latter engages in climate science, and in total fifty-five graphs were used eighty-six different times (counting each time a graph appeared in a different programme).

Schneider et al. (2014) have distinguished the following five classes for graphs used by the climate change countermovement. The conceptualisation helps describe how the graphs are deceptive. The classifications are not mutually exclusive, and many graphs contain elements from more than one.

1. Correct reproduction of up-to-date scientific graphs: To highlight ongoing discussions and uncertainties in climate change, as well as to show how the world is still fossil fuel dependent.
2. Misinterpretation of correct graphs: To make a faithful reproduction of a graph such as a temperature series, but to claim the findings are something other than they are.
3. Cherry-picking of obsolete results: To deliberately use old data or graphs that have become obsolete due to later findings within climate science.
4. Classic cherry-picking: To carefully select data that supports your case and claiming it to be representative, for example to take temperature at one location to represent the global mean. Cherry-picking can be used when visualising the data in charts, by hiding parts of a graph or by extending or suppressing an axis.
5. Data or image manipulation: To manipulate data points or to mislabel an axis.

To answer the two research questions posed in the introduction – first, on the type of graphs used by SwebbTV to visualise climate science, and second, on where these graphs have been taken from – I classify the graphs according to the above and trace their origins. Beyond the research questions, I explore the arguments being made through the graphs.

Analysing men who cherry-pick data

The main visual setting on SwebbTV is two men talking to each other, occasionally showing a graph of temperatures, sea-level rise or oil consumption. This is a rather dry setting. It is far removed from, for example, the black-sheep cartoon used by the Swiss People's Party or the ironic memes used by extreme-right groups in the Nordic countries (Doerr, 2017; Hakoköngäs et al., 2020; Askanius, 2021). Instead of appealing to emotion, the graphs appeal to the objectivity of science and the trust in numbers. Of all the graphs used on SwebbTV, only two are from actual peer-reviewed articles. One is Mann's hockey stick, which is presented as fake, and one is an image taken from a 1997 paper showing a model of the world's energy budget (SwebbTV, 2019c: 33:50). A further four are updated graphs where the originals appeared in peer-reviewed literature and twenty are taken from official sources such as the Permanent Service of Mean Sea Level (PSMSL). Of these, most are either cherry-picked data, not representative of global or future climate change trends, or graphs that portray the continued, expansive use of fossil fuel. Of the remaining graphs, sixteen are taken from blogs, seven are created by prominent members of the international climate change countermovement and not published in peer-reviewed literature, and six are taken from sources such as self-published books, popular science magazines and newspapers. These figures show, once again, how the debate over anthropogenic climate change is not a scholarly discussion taking place in peer-reviewed literature (as previously found by, for example, Cook et al., 2016). Rather, these contrarian claims continuously circulate via propaganda feedback loops.

Of the graphs used on SwebbTV, most are true to the data but remain misleading. By using examples from the different classifications, the next section illustrates how this happens.

Correct reproduction of up-to-date scientific graphs

Graphs of this type serve several purposes on SwebbTV. One is to show correct graphs just to claim they are false, for example a graph from the Swedish Meteorological and Hydrological Institute (SwebbTV, 2019d: 23:11). Another is to use graphs explaining basic physics (for example, SwebbTV, 2019e: 4:51) to argue that while there is a naturally occurring greenhouse effect, we cannot know how temperatures are affected by increased CO_2 emissions. A graph produced by a researcher at the conservative Cato institute, which has long spread doubt about climate science (Oreskes and Conway, 2011: 190), is used in four programmes (for example, SwebbTV, 2019f: 1:20:29). This graph, which has been updated continuously since it first was published in a peer-reviewed paper, shows little change in global tropical cyclone activity. While it is produced according to scientific procedures, SwebbTV does not mention that cyclones are predicted to become more intense, a trend that has been observable since the 1970s (Seneviratne et al., 2021: 90).

Eight of the correctly reproduced graphs show carbon emissions, energy use or the amount of carbon dioxide in the atmosphere. They are used fifteen times to make three arguments. The first argument is that rising emissions do not correspond to rising temperatures (for example, SwebbTV, 2018b: 8:32). The second is that Sweden's emissions do not matter on a global level and that global decarbonisation, where more than 80 per cent of energy use is fossil fuel based, is unrealistic (for example, SwebbTV,

2019g: 34:07). This argument overlooks both Sweden's high per capita emissions and high historical emissions, and makes action on climate change impossible, as any region can be said to be too small to make a global difference. Indeed, such an argument has been commonly used in nationalistic opposition to climate change mitigation, pointing to other countries, most often China, instead of considering 'our' role (Lamb et al., 2020). The third argument is that rising emissions prove that politicians are not really concerned about climate change, but rather want to raise taxes and create supranational governance (for example, SwebbTV, 2018c: 11:33). This argument does acknowledge the world's failure to curb emissions yet flips it on its head. Rising emissions are here not a failure related to political and societal inertia but a sinister conspiracy, in which the global elite has created the climate hoax as a means to other political ends. It ties into the anti-establishment rhetoric of the far right. It also connects to an anti-Semitic discourse, as when Greta Thunberg's sailing voyage to the USA is claimed to have been masterminded by George Soros and the Rothschilds (SwebbTV, 2019b: 43:13).

Misinterpretation of correct graphs

The most frequently used graph in this category is the satellite temperature measurements produced by scientists at University of Alabama, Huntsville (UAH). The satellite measurements have been widely used by the climate change countermovement as they, especially when first published, showed less warming than measurements at surface level. They have later been adjusted to correct technical issues and biases in the data, which has led to smaller discrepancies compared to other temperature records. The graphs from UAH are used in six different programmes: they indicate considerable warming, though SwebbTV claim it is nothing to worry about. It is worth noting how updated baseline periods hide warming. Temperature anomalies are measured against a thirty-year baseline period, and in the UAH set this is moved at the end of each decade. In the graphs on SwebbTV, the baseline years are 1980–2010, a period that had already experienced a significant amount of warming. When the graph states that the anomaly is +0.32°C (SwebbTV, 2019d: 28:03), temperatures are approximately one degree above preindustrial levels.

Shifting baselines also point to the idea of new normalities, as well as how we learn to adopt to gradual change, both culturally and environmentally. Moving away from the far right, Norgaard (2002) has argued how the normalisation of climate change helps the citizens of a Norwegian town to reproduce global environmental privilege, where the rich, mainly white and male, high emitters of the Global North can adapt but the where the Global

South suffers the worst consequences. Norgaard notices that different cultural tools are used in the everyday to construct senses of order and innocence, which allows the people of the town to normalise climate change even though they are seeing the effects through snowless ski slopes. What is described by Norgaard as a somewhat subconscious phenomenon of cultural inertia can, however, also be used more deliberately. When SwebbTV uses graphs that subtly normalise past warming, they are purposely normalising Swedish environmental privileges.

Cherry-picking of obsolete results

With regard to the third type of graphs, the most frequently used comes from the contrarian book *Falskt Alarm* (*False Alarm*, the latest version of the book is Pettersson, 2020: 35) by a professor emeritus in biochemistry at Lund University (Figure 12.1, top pane). This graph is used in four different programmes on SwebbTV (for example, 2018d: 12:21), and is a reconstruction of a schematic graph used in the first IPCC assessment report in 1990 (Figure 12.1, middle pane, IPCC, 1990: 202), which shows temperatures during the last 1,000 years. The data can be traced to climatologist Hubert Lamb, who plotted the temperature of central England using measurements and proxy data in 1965 (Jones et al., 2009). The graph shows unusual warmth during the thirteenth and fourteenth centuries, but the first data point in the central England temperature series is from 1659, so the medieval warm period is reconstructed by Lamb using proxy data available to him at the time. The temperature record is just for central England, meaning that there is no way of knowing from Lamb's reconstruction if the warm medieval period was global in scope. Later scientific findings have shown that while parts of the globe warmed, others cooled, and that the period is not comparable to the heating happening today. Although the figure has, thus, not been presented in later IPCC reports, it has frequently been used to claim that the IPCC supresses results not supporting the theory of anthropogenic global warming. In *Falskt Alarm*, the x-axis has been compressed, which makes the medieval warm period look even warmer (as previously noted by Nilsson, 2019). Similar to this figure, a counter-graph to the hockey stick created by Ball (for example, SwebbTV, 2019b: 34:08) appears to be based on the 1990 IPCC graph. Using both figures, SwebbTV turns to obsolete reconstructions that are nearly seventy years old, instead of using the state-of-the-art science as presented in later assessment reports by the IPCC (Figure 12.1, bottom pane, Masson-Delmotte et al., 2013). Comparing the graphs in Figure 12.1 shows how cherry-picking can be visualised. In the SwebbTV graph (top pane), all uncertainty is removed by including only one temperature record, whereas the IPCC graph (bottom pane) plots all relevant reconstructions (in different colours in the original graph).

Bild 9. *Jordens temperatur-utveckling sedan år 900* (Källa: IPCC, 1990)

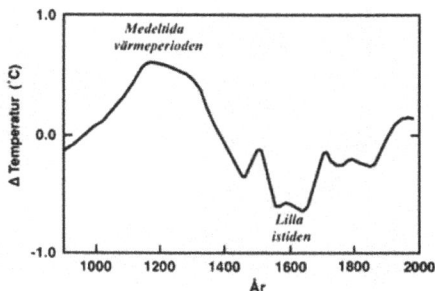

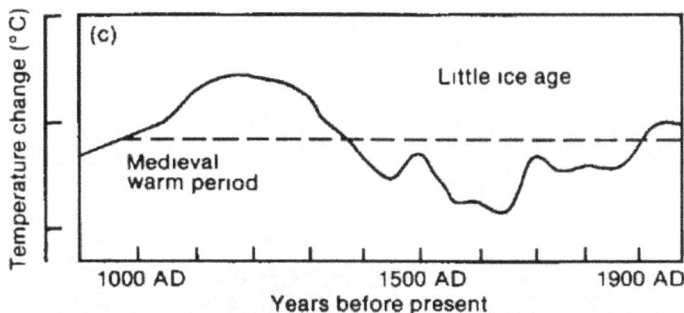

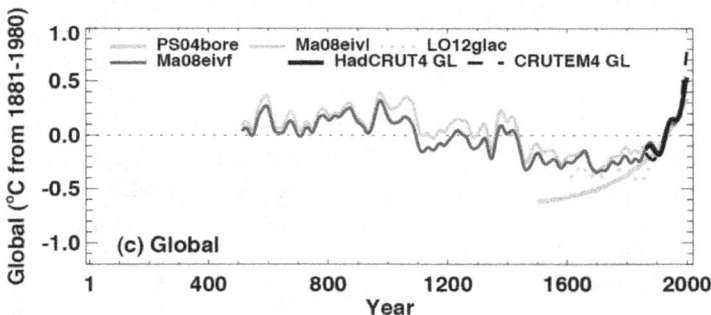

12.1 The top pane shows the graph used in SwebbTV taken from the book *Falskt alarm*; the graph is based on a figure in the first IPCC report 1990 (middle pane) which is a reconstruction of Central England temperatures; in the SwebbTV-version, the x-axis has been compressed, making the medieval warm period look warmer; this is a case of cherry-picking an obsolete graph, showing temperature at one specific location, rather than using global temperature reconstructions available in later IPCC reports (bottom pane)

Classic cherry-picking

Nearly half of the graphs used on SwebbTV can be classified as classic cherry-picking. Six are taken from PSMSL (psmsl.org) and show sea-level changes at one single tide gauge. One example, Figure 12.2, shows linear

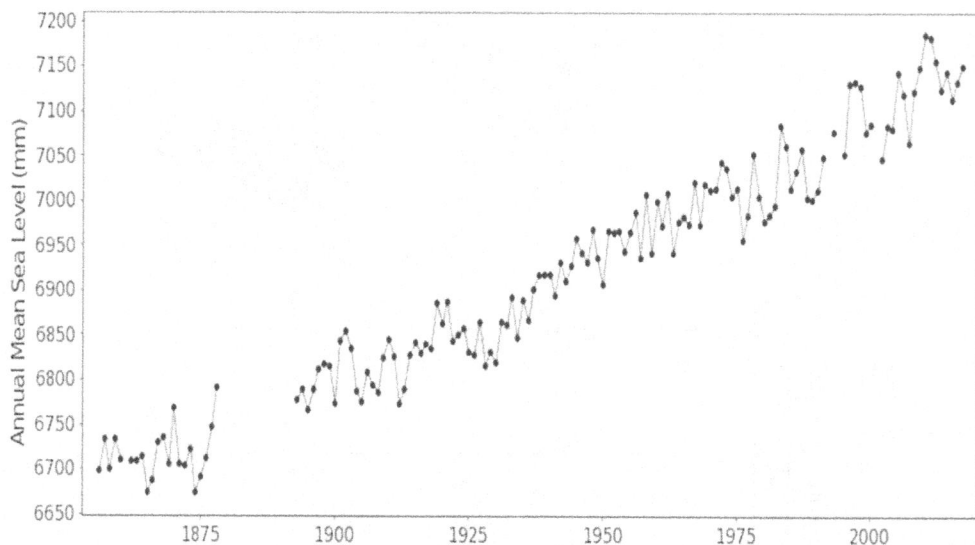

12.2 Annual mean sea level as measured by tide gauge at the Battery, New York

sea-level rise in New York during the twentieth century which is used in six different programmes (for example, SwebbTV, 2019h: 21:49). SwebbTV argues that the linear rise in New York disproves the notion of accelerating global sea-level rise, yet there is no argument for why New York would be representative of the global mean. Tide gauge data need careful handling to reproduce global trends, and contrary to what SwebbTV claims, peer-reviewed reproductions do show accelerating sea-level rise, just as satellite measurements do (IPCC, 2021)

SwebbTV graphs that use cherry-picked data include three slightly different graphs, each showing temperatures in Greenland over the past 10,000 years reconstructed with data from an ice core drilled by the second Greenland Ice Sheet Project (GISP2) in 1993 (for example, SwebbTV, 2019e: 16:21; worth noting in this particular version of the graph is the compressed second y-axis that understates the increase in atmospheric CO_2). The original version of this graph has been traced by Skeptical Science (2011) to a 2010 post at the United States denialist blog wattsupwiththat.com. While the GISP2 data follows the paleoclimate standard of setting 1950 as year 0, the blog version puts 2000 as year 0, therefore misleading the viewer that the temperature record stretches to the present day. While this has been corrected in the small print on two of the graphs shown on SwebbTV, this is never explained to the viewer (for example, SwebbTV, 2019i: 23:32). The last measurement in the GISP2 ice core is from 1855, so the graphs do not include any temperature rise during the last 150 years. Despite this, SwebbTV use them to claim that the climate crisis is nothing to worry about.

Of the cherry-picked graphs, three are created by Nils-Axel Mörner, an invited guest to one of the programmes (SwebbTV, 2019h). Mörner was a professor emeritus of paleogeophysics at Stockholm University and conducted research funded by denialist think tanks (Readfearn, 2018). One of Mörner's (2018: 53) graphs is from a paper published by Scientific Research Publishing, a predatory publisher not implementing proper peer-review (Beall, 2017). The paper claims to compare 'Anthropogenic Global Warming' with 'Natural Global Warming'. Cherry-picking a thirty-year temperature cycle, Mörner concludes that the latter is real while the former lacks empirical evidence. According to the dates specified on the paper, it took three weeks from submission to publication: a quick peer-review for any paper, not to mention one aiming to prove the entire scientific community wrong.

The fact that most of their graphs are classic cherry-picking suggests that SwebbTV are seeking to appear trustworthy. Extensive use of manipulated graphs would be easier to contest and would undermine SwebbTV's claim of looking at the data. Indeed, Forchtner et al. (2018) notice how far-right media in Germany is not anti-science as such, but they are against what is seen as the corrupt mainstream science of political institutions. The same can be said with regard to the graphs and alleged expertise used at SwebbTV. Bern is an engineer with a doctoral degree, and when he shows graphs correctly portraying the data, even if they are cherry-picked, it lends authority to the arguments.

Data and image manipulation

The only graph on SwebbTV (2019c: 36:25) where plotted data simply do not correspond to axis labels is credited to a meteorologist and a climatologist running a private weather forecasting service (Figure 12.3). The graph claims to chart global temperatures between 2500 BC and 2040 AD, with widely fluctuating warm and cold periods. The y-axis lacks a scale; instead, the parts of the graph above the x-axis are coloured orange and labelled as 'very warm' or 'warm' and the parts below are coloured blue and marked as 'cold' or 'very cold', with no further definition of those terms. A textbox accompanying the graph states that 'Whenever SOLAR RADIATION has DECREASED and VOLCANIC ACTIVITY has INCREASED, global temperatures SUDDENLY PLUMMET, often within weeks or months' (capitalisation in original). However, the x-axis is supposed to cover more than 4,500 years and cannot show such detail. Neither do the dates of events marked on the graph add up to the years proposed on the x-axis.

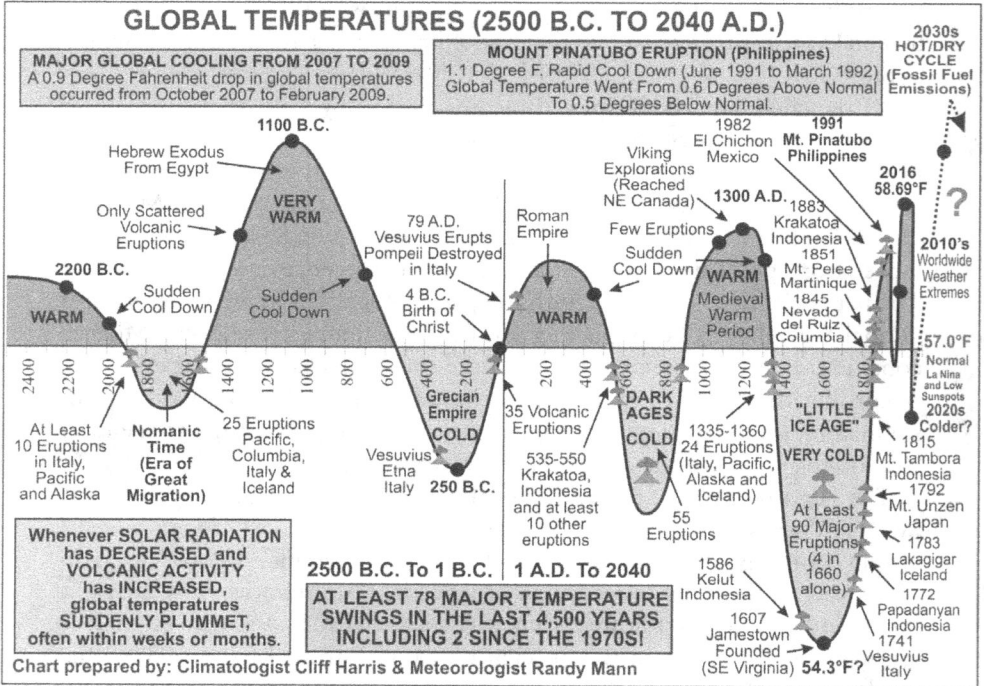

GLOBAL TEMPERATURES (2500 B.C. TO 2040 A.D.)

MAJOR GLOBAL COOLING FROM 2007 TO 2009
A 0.9 Degree Fahrenheit drop in global temperatures occurred from October 2007 to February 2009.

MOUNT PINATUBO ERUPTION (Philippines)
1.1 Degree F. Rapid Cool Down (June 1991 to March 1992)
Global Temperature Went From 0.6 Degrees Above Normal To 0.5 Degrees Below Normal.

2030s
HOT/DRY CYCLE
(Fossil Fuel Emissions)

1100 B.C.
Hebrew Exodus From Egypt
Only Scattered Volcanic Eruptions
2200 B.C.
Sudden Cool Down
WARM
VERY WARM
Sudden Cool Down
79 A.D. Vesuvius Erupts Pompeii Destroyed in Italy
4 B.C. Birth of Christ
Roman Empire
WARM

1982 El Chichon Mexico
1991 Mt. Pinatubo Philippines
Viking Explorations (Reached NE Canada)
1300 A.D.
Few Eruptions
Sudden Cool Down
WARM
Medieval Warm Period
1883 Krakatoa Indonesia
1851 Mt. Pelee Martinique
1845 Nevado del Ruiz Columbia

2016 58.69°F
?
2010's Worldwide Weather Extremes

57.0°F
Normal La Nina and Low Sunspots
2020s Colder?
1815 Mt. Tambora Indonesia
1792 Mt. Unzen Japan
1783 Lakagigar Iceland
1772 Papadanyan Indonesia
1741 Vesuvius Italy

2400 2200 2000 1800 1600 1400 1200 1000 800 600 400 200 | 200 400 600 800 1000 1200 1400 1600 1800

At Least 10 Eruptions in Italy, Pacific and Alaska
Nomanic Time (Era of Great Migration)
25 Eruptions Pacific, Columbia, Italy & Iceland
Vesuvius Etna Italy
Grecian Empire
COLD
250 B.C.
35 Volcanic Eruptions
535-550 Krakatoa, Indonesia and at least 10 other eruptions
DARK AGES
COLD
55 Eruptions
1335-1360 24 Eruptions (Italy, Pacific, Alaska and Iceland)
"LITTLE ICE AGE"
VERY COLD
At Least 90 Major Eruptions (4 in 1660 alone)

Whenever SOLAR RADIATION has DECREASED and VOLCANIC ACTIVITY has INCREASED, global temperatures SUDDENLY PLUMMET, often within weeks or months.

2500 B.C. To 1 B.C. | 1 A.D. To 2040
AT LEAST 78 MAJOR TEMPERATURE SWINGS IN THE LAST 4,500 YEARS INCLUDING 2 SINCE THE 1970S!

1586 Kelut Indonesia
1607 Jamestown Founded (SE Virginia)
54.3°F?

Chart prepared by: Climatologist Cliff Harris & Meteorologist Randy Mann

12.3 Graph claiming to show temperature changes over millennia

Despite this, the graph is used by SwebbTV to claim that the current warming is natural and not anthropogenic.

Conclusion

Understanding the spread of climate denial on the far right is central to understanding some of the obstacles towards a transition to a low-carbon society. As Wanvik and Haarstad (2021) have recently argued, the rupture caused by populist parties opposing transitional policies is inherent to the transition itself. The shift to a low-carbon society is not just a matter of diffusing and upscaling low-carbon technology, as it unseats deeply held power structures. This unseating can both create a democratic opportunity to listen to marginalised voices and provoke an antagonistic reaction from those being unseated. The climate change denialism of SwebbTV should therefore not be seen as a twig getting stuck in the spokes of the bike wheel but as a hammer designed to break it. Any forceful mitigating policies will receive pushbacks from those that stand to lose the most. For the far right, this is the imagined homogenic, patriarchal and industrial-prosperous community (Vowles and Hultman, 2022). To defend it, several far-right actors in Sweden have turned to denialism, spreading it through their own media ecosystem, which stands in firm opposition to legacy media. This, again, points to one of the problems with the information deficit model: the idea that the lack of action on climate change is due to a lack of knowledge. The case of SwebbTV shows how the spread of scientific knowledge within legacy media is once again met with the increased circulation of disinformation, in this case visualised via deceptive graphs. Fischer (2019: 141) has argued that the validity of different types of knowledge for social actors is dependent on ideology, and 'knowledge that does not contribute to a move in a particular ideological direction, while possibly true, is seen to be either of no interest, irrelevant or problematic'. When the scientific knowledge of climate change becomes a threat to economic or ideological interests, whether they be concerned with fossil fuel capitalism or far-right nationalism, this has often been fought through the circulation of dissenting views. By inviting their own supposed scientific experts and spreading contrarian graphs, SwebbTV feeds an ideologically appealing counter-knowledge to the Swedish far-right.

In response to the research questions concerning types of graphs and their origin, I notice two things. First, the most common graphs on SwebbTV concern classic cherry-picking (twenty-six), followed by the correct reproduction of up-to-date scientific graphs (sixteen), misinterpretation of correct graphs (eight), cherry-picking of obsolete results (four) and image manipulation (one). This suggests that even though SwebbTV oppose institutions such as the IPCC, they are trying to stay true to the data. Second, only six of the graphs on SwebbTV originate in peer-reviewed literature. The rest are either from official sources from which the data are cherry-picked, or from other sources such as blogs, self-published books or created by contrarian scientists but not published in academic journals. This shows how the debate about anthropogenic global warming is not a debate taking place in academia.

The graphs on SwebbTV are mainly presented by white men sitting in the studio. Here the graphs tie into far-right discourses of Sweden being perceived to be threatened by mass migration and feminism. Over the two years covered by this study, climate change increased in prominence on SwebbTV – just as it did in legacy media – when Thunberg and the Fridays for Future movement pushed climate change towards the top of the political agenda. In his history of climate politics and the Keeling curve, Howe (2014:

208) writes that the 'models and curves of climate science have ... tended to mask the moral, social, and political questions that global interdependence raises about a comfortable and wealthy fossil fuel-driven lifestyle that ultimately carries social and environmental costs for the rest of the globe'. Through the school strikes in 2019, the Thunberg-led movement managed to step away from the curve and make those questions visible. In response, SwebbTV claimed to go back to the data and to trust the numbers instead of the IPCC. By visualising contrarian science through graphs, the channel sought to paint climate change mitigation as another threat to a nation in decay, while presenting SwebbTV as the righteous proponents of the truth.

References

Andersson, U. and Oscarsson, H. (2020): (Parti-)politiserat institutionsförtroende. In: U. Andersson, A. Carlander and P. Öhberg (eds), *Regntunga skyar SOM-rapport 76*. Gothenburg: University of Gothenburg, 41–56.

Anshelm, J. and Hultman, M. (2014): A Green Fatwā? Climate change as a threat to the masculinity of industrial modernity, *NORMA*, 9(2): 84–96. https://doi.org/10.108 0/18902138.2014.908627

Aronowsky, L. (2021): Gas guzzling Gaia, or: A prehistory of climate change denialism, *Critical Inquiry*, 47(2): 306–327. https://doi.org/10.1086/712129

Askanius, T. (2021): On frogs, monkeys, and execution memes: Exploring the humor–hate nexus at the intersection of neo-Nazi and alt-Right movements in Sweden, *Television & New Media*, 22(2): 147–165. https://doi.org/10.1177/1527476420982234

Beall, J. (2017): List of publishers, 12 January 2017. https://web.archive.org/web/20170112125427/https://scholarlyoa.com/publishers/ (accessed 15 September 2021).

Benkler, Y., Faris, R. and Roberts, H. (2018): *The Propaganda Feedback Loop*. Oxford: Oxford University Press.

Boykoff, M. T. (2011): *Who Speaks for the Climate? Making Sense of Media Reporting on Climate Change*. Cambridge: Cambridge University Press.

Brulle, R. J. (2019): Networks of opposition: A structural analysis of U.S. climate change countermovement coalitions 1989–2015, *Sociological Inquiry*, 91, 603–624. https://doi.org/10.1111/soin.12333

Carah, N. (2014): Curators of databases: Circulating images, managing attention and making value on social media, *Media International Australia*, 150(1): 137–142. https://doi.org/10.1177/1329878X1415000125

Cook, J., Oreskes, N., Doran, P., Anderegg, W., Verheggen, B., Maibach, E., Carlton, S., Lewandowsky, S., Skuce, A., Green, S., Nuccitelli, D., Jacobs, P., Richardson, M., Winkler, B., Painting, R. and Rice, K. (2016): Consensus on consensus: A synthesis of consensus estimates on human-caused global warming, *Environmental Research Letters*, 11(4). https://doi.org/10.1088/1748-9326/11/4/048002

Culloty, E., Murphy, P., Brereton, P., Suiter, J., Smeaton, A. and Zhang, D. (2019): Researching visual representations of climate change, *Environmental Communication*, 13(2): 179–191. https://doi.org/10.1080/17524032.2018.1533877

Daston, L. and Galison, P. (1992): The image of objectivity, *Representations*, 40: 81–128.

Doerr, N. (2017): Bridging language barriers, bonding against immigrants: A visual case study of transnational network publics created by far-right activists in Europe, *Discourse & Society*, 28(1): 3–23. https://doi.org/10.1177/0957926516676689

Ekberg, K. and Pressfeldt, V. (2021): Market governance, obstruction, and denial: Neoliberal environmental thought and policy in Sweden, 1988–2015. Online workshop organised by Harvard University and Uppsala University.

Fischer, F. (2019): Knowledge politics and post-truth in climate denial: On the social construction of alternative facts, *Critical Policy Studies*, 13(2): 133–152. https://doi.org/10.1080/19460171.2019.1602067

Forchtner, B. (2019): Climate change and the far right, *WIREs Climate Change*, 10(5). https://doi.org/10.1002/wcc.604.

Forchtner, B., Kroneder, A. and Wetzel, D. (2018): Being skeptical? Exploring far-right climate-change communication in Germany, *Environmental Communication*, 12(5): 589–604. https://doi.org/10.1080/17524032.2018.1470546

Freje Simonsson, J. (2020): SwebbTV:s grundare om egna kanalen: 'Liknar en Ding Ding Värld', *Medierna*, 17 April 2020. https://sverigesradio.se/artikel/7469499 (accessed 14 February 2022).

Hakoköngäs, E., Halmesvaara, O. and Sakki, I. (2020): Persuasion through bitter humor: Multimodal discourse analysis of rhetoric in Internet memes of two far-right groups in Finland, *Social Media + Society*, 6(2): 1–11. https://doi.org/10.1177/2056305120921575

Hansen, A. (2017): Using visual images to show environmental problems. In: A. F. Fill and H. Penz (eds), *The Routledge Handbook of Ecolinguistics*. New York: Routledge, 179–195.

Holt, K. (2019): *Right-Wing Alternative Media*. London: Routledge.

Howe, J. P. (2014): *Behind the Curve: Science and the Politics of Global Warming*, Seattle: University of Washington Press.

Huff, D. (1954): *How to Lie with Statistics*. New York: Norton.

IPCC (1990): *Climate Change: The IPCC Scientific Assessment*. Cambridge: Cambridge University Press.

IPCC (2021): *Climate Change 2021: The Physical Science Basis. Contribution of Working Group I to the Sixth Assessment Report of the Intergovernmental Panel on Climate Change*. Cambridge: Cambridge University Press. www.ipcc.ch/report/ar6/wg1/#FullReport (accessed 14 February 2022).

Jones, P., Briffa, K., Osborn, T., Lough, J., van Ommen, T., Vinther, B., Luterbacher, J., Wahl, E., Zwiers, F., Mann, M., Schmidt, G., Ammann, C., Buckley, B., Cobb, K., Esper, J., Goosse, H., Graham, N., Jansen, E., Kiefer, T., Kull, C., Küttel, M., Mosley-Thompson, E., Overpeck, J., Riedwyl, N., Schulz, M., Tudhope, A., Villalba, R., Wanner, H., Wolff, E. and Xoplaki, E. (2009): High-resolution palaeoclimatology of the last millennium: A review of current status and future prospects, *The Holocene*, 19(1): 3–49. https://doi.org/10.1177/ 0959683608098952

Jylhä, K. M., Strimling, P. and Rydgren, J. (2020): Climate change denial among radical right-wing supporters, *Sustainability*, 12(23): 10226. https://doi.org/10.3390/ su122310226

Kaiser, J. and Puschmann, C. (2017): Alliance of antagonism: Counterpublics and polarization in online climate change communication, *Communication and the Public*, 2(4): 371–387. https://doi.org/10.1177/2057047317732350

Lamb, W. F., Mattioli, G., Levi, S., Roberts, T. J., Capstick, S., Creutzig, F., Minx, J. C., Müller-Hansen, F., Culhane, T. and Steinberger, J. K. (2020): Discourses of climate delay, *Global Sustainability*, 3. https://doi.org/10.1017/sus. 2020.13

Malm, A. and The Zetkin Collective (2021): *White Skin, Black Fuel: On the Danger of Fossil Fascism*. London: Verso.

Mann, M. E. (2014): *The Hockey Stick and the Climate Wars: Dispatches from the Front Lines*. New York: Columbia University Press.

Masson-Delmotte, V., Schulz, M., Abe-Ouchi, A., Beer, J., Ganopolski, J., González Rouco, J. F., Jansen, E., Lambeck, K., Luterbacher, J., Naish, T., Osborn, T., Otto-Bliesner, B., Quinn, T., Ramesh, R., Rojas, M., Shao, X. and Timmermann, A. (2013): Information from paleoclimate archives. In: T. F. Stocker, D. Qin, G.-K. Plattner, M. Tignor, S. K. Allen, J. Doschung, A. Nauels, Y. Xia, V. Bex and P. M. Midgley (eds), *Climate Change 2013: The Physical Science Basis. Contribution of Working Group I to the Fifth Assessment Report of the Intergovernmental Panel on Climate Change*. Cambridge: Cambridge University Press, 383–464.

McCright, A. M. and Dunlap, R. E. (2011): Cool dudes: The denial of climate change among conservative white males in the United States, *Global Environmental Change*, 21(4): 1163–1172. https://doi.org/10.1016/j.gloenvcha.2011. 06.003

McKie, R. E. (2017): *Rebranding the Climate Change Counter Movement: A Critical Examination of Counter Movement Messaging through a Criminological and Political Economic Lens*. Doctoral thesis, Newcastle: University of Northumbria.

Mellor, F. (2009): The politics of accuracy in judging global warming films, *Environmental Communication*, 3(2): 134–150. https://doi.org/10.1080/17524030902916574

Merchant, C. (1989): *The Death of Nature: Women, Ecology, and the Scientific Revolution*. New York: Harper & Row.

Mörner, N.-A. (2018): Anthropogenic global warming (AGW) or natural global warming (NGM), *Voice of the Publisher*, 4: 51–59. https://doi.org/10.4236/ vp.2018.44005

Nacu-Schmidt, A., Boykoff, M. and Katzung, J. (2019): *Media and Climate Change Observatory Special Issue 2019: A Review of Media Coverage of Climate Change and Global Warming in 2019*. Boulder: University of Colorado, Boulder.

Nilsson, M. (2019): Falskt Alarm om falskt alarm om klimatet, *Maths Nilsson, författare*, 22 April 2019. https://mathsnilsson.se/2019/04/22/falskt-alarm-om-falskt-alarm-om-klimatet/ (accessed 14 September 2021).

Norgaard, K. M. (2002): Climate denial and the construction of innocence: Reproducing transnational environmental privilege in the face of climate change, *Race, Gender & Class*, 19(1–2): 80–103.

O'Neill, S. (2020): More than meets the eye: A longitudinal analysis of climate change imagery in the print media, *Climatic Change*, 163(1): 9–26. https://doi.org/10.1007/s10584-019-02504-8

Oreskes, N. and Conway, E. (2011): *Merchants of Doubt: How a Handful of Scientists Obscured the Truth on Issues from Tobacco Smoke to Global Warming.* New York: Bloomsbury Press.

Pettersson, G. (2020): *Falskt Alarm: Klimatfrågan ur vetenskaplig aspekt.* Stockholm: Elsa Widding AB.

Porter, T. M. (2020): *Trust in Numbers: The Pursuit of Objectivity in Science and Public Life.* Princeton, NJ: Princeton University Press.

Readfearn, G. (2018): Climate denial group with Trump admin ties is funding sea level research in questionable journals, *DeSmog*, 18 January 2018. www.desmogblog.com/2018/01/18/climate-denial-co2-coalition-trump-morner-funding-sea-level-research-dodgy-journals (accessed 18 December 2018).

Rebich-Hespanha, S., Rice, R. E., Montello, D. R., Retzloff, S., Tien, S. and Hespanha, J. P. (2015): Image themes and frames in US print news stories about climate change, *Environmental Communication*, 9(4): 491–519. https://doi.org/10.1080/17524032.2014.983534

Rydgren, J. (2018): The radical right: An introduction. In: J. Rydgren (ed.), *The Oxford Handbook of the Radical Right.* Oxford: Oxford University Press, 1–13.

Ryghaug, M. and Skjølsvold, T. M. (2010): The global warming of climate science: Climategate and the construction of scientific facts, *International Studies in the Philosophy of Science*, 24(3): 287–307. https://doi.org/10.1080/02698595.2010.522411

Schneider, B. (2012): Climate model simulation visualization from a visual studies perspective: Climate model simulation visualization, *WIREs Climate Change*, 3(2): 185–193. https://doi.org/10.1002/wcc.162

Schneider, B., Nocke, T. and Feulner, G. (2014): Twist and shout: Images and graphs in skeptical climate media. In: B. Schneider and T. Nocke (eds), *Image Politics of Climate Change: Visualizations, Imaginations, Documentations.* Bielefeld: transcript, 153–186.

Seneviratne, S., Zhang, X., Adnan, M., Badi, W., Dereczynski, C., Di Luca, A., Ghosh, S., Iskandar, I., Kossin, J., Lewis, S., Otto, F., Pinto, I., Satoh, M., Vicente-Serrano, S., Wehner, M. and Zhou, B. (2021): Weather and climate extreme events in a changing climate. In: V. Masson-Delmotte, P. Zhai, A. Pirani, S. Connors, C. Péan, S. Berger, N. Caud, Y. Chen, L. Goldfarb, M. Gomis, M. Huang, K. Leitzell, E. Lonnoy, J. Matthews, T. Maycock, T. Waterfield, O. Yelekçi, R. Yu and B. Zhou (eds), *Climate Change 2021: The Physical Science Basis. Contribution of Working Group I to the Sixth Assessment Report of the Intergovernmental Panel on Climate Change.* Cambridge: Cambridge University Press. www.ipcc.ch/report/ar6/wg1/downloads/report/IPCC_AR6_WGI_Chapter_11.pdf (accessed 14 February 2022).

Skeptical Science (2011): Confusing Greenland warming vs global warming, *Skeptical Science*, 31 January 2011. https://skepticalscience.com/archive.php?r=1140 (accessed 14 September 2021).

SwebbTV (2018a): Lars Bern 6 September del 1: om miljörörelsens skrämselpropaganda, *SwebbTV*, 6 September 2018. https://swebbtv.se/w/p5vZhq5x9qLPxkFNCwWUS5 (accessed 14 February 2022).

SwebbTV (2018b): Lars Bern om SVT fake news nr 4 inför FNs klimatkonferens i Polen, *SwebbTV*, 13 December 2018. https://swebbtv.se/w/1fL61GpQMswVKqyfBhntdu (accessed 14 February 2022).

SwebbTV (2018c): Tekn: Dr Lars Bern kommenterar SVT fake news nr 2 i 'Dokument Utifrån', *SwebbTV*, 17 November 2018. https://swebbtv.se/w/1tdeNUAiF4 FDYRqH3cR6YQ (accessed 14 February 2022).

SwebbTV (2018d): Lördagsintervju 31 med Peter Stilbs: kan vi lita på vetenskapsprogrammen, *SwebbTV*, 27 October 2018. https://swebbtv.se/w/msvfj3F8 HBeiJy7GdQJwQW (accessed 14 February 2022).

SwebbTV (2019a): Nyårshälsning från Swebbtv och ett stort tack till alla er som bidrar till att Swebbtv växer, *SwebbTV*, 31 December 2019. https://swebbtv.se/w/5ZaQSmVbe7uHqbbNw33hYN (accessed 14 February 2022).

SwebbTV (2019b): Fjärde statsmakten nr 16 med Lars Bern om en stat i förfall, *SwebbTV*, 4 September 2019. https://swebbtv.se/w/i8QaTVR49WgfZrN3oH3Xh7 (accessed 14 February 2022).

SwebbTV (2019c): Lördagsintervju nr 65 med f.d. VD för Sandvik P-O Eriksson om koldioxiden – livets gas, *SwebbTV*, 10 November 2019. https://swebbtv.se/w/ mvWYjgF16e8mLpByb5QZCp (accessed 14 February 2022).

SwebbTV (2019d): Fjärde statsmakten nr 18 med Lars Bern om SVT Agenda fake news, *SwebbTV*, 19 November 2019. https://swebbtv.se/w/bqZ3ae95DXTJ2L6bmVjwZw (accessed 14 February 2022).

SwebbTV (2019e) Del 6 höstkonferens 2019 Elsa Widding: barnen och vetenskapen – Om klimatet, *SwebbTV* (16 October 2019). https://swebbtv.se/w/ kRjKD4FT5A3Un2SwNNgs8d (accessed 14 February 2022).

SwebbTV (2019f): Fjärde statsmakten nr 3 med Lars Bern om SVTs klimatbedrägeri i Ekdal och Ekdal, *SwebbTV*, 28 February 2019. https://swebbtv.se/w/ 1jZDuD9XwV7KvK1s66fd9P (accessed 14 February 2022).

SwebbTV (2019g): Fjärde statsmakten nr 23 med Lars Bern om feministisk snöröjning, CO2 skatt, Agenda 2030 mm, *SwebbTV*, 29 October 2019. https://swebbtv.se/w/ mLyUDeC7XGJtMgUKjB5hLu (accessed 14 February 2022).

SwebbTV (2019h): Lördagsintervju 40 – havsforskare Nils-Axel Mörner om klimatet: Hur är det egentligen, *SwebbTV*, 25 January 2019. https://swebbtv.se/w/ scS8afYvJYK5tb9p2go3fr (accessed 14 February 2022).

SwebbTV (2019i): Lördagsintervjun nr 54 med energiexpert Elsa Widding om klimat- och energipolitiken, *SwebbTV*, 29 June 2019. https://swebbtv.se/w/ dQqBhq1AgSVvBTfgqznsm4 (accessed 14 February 2022).

Vowles, K. and Hultman, M. (2021): Scare-quoting climate: The rapid rise of climate denial in the Swedish far-right media ecosystem, *Nordic Journal of Media Studies*, 3(1): 79–95.

Vowles, K. and Hultman, M. (2022): Dead white men vs. Greta Thunberg: Nationalism, misogyny, and climate change denial in Swedish far-right digital media, *Australian Feminist Studies*, 36(110): 414–431. https://doi.org/10.2478/njms-2021-0005

Wanvik, T. I. and Haarstad, H. (2021): Populism, instability, and rupture in sustainability transformations, *Annals of the American Association of Geographers*, 111(7): 1–16. https://doi.org/10.1080/24694452.2020.1866486

Wodak, R. (2019): The trajectory of far-right populism: A discourse-analytical perspective. In: B. Forchtner (ed.), *The Far Right and the Environment: Politics, Discourse and Communication*. London: Routledge, 21–37.

13

The (paranoid) style of American climate politics: a comparative visual rhetoric analysis of web design by far-right and left conspiracists in the United States

Lauren Cagle

Introduction

In late 2018, my colleague Jim Ridolfo posted on Facebook about a flyer he had found in his home mailbox in Lexington, Kentucky, where we both work at the University of Kentucky. The flyer was six 8.5 × 11 inch pages, front and back, in bold colours, with a mix of text and images (Figure 13.1). The text appears to be mostly in Times New Roman font, occasionally bolded, with a few sans serif sections of text apparently copied and pasted from other sources. Throughout, the type is small and densely packed, except for pockets of white space produced by lists of unshortened URLs. While some of the text is formatted in a standard black-on-white colour scheme, much of it pops off the page in primary shades of red, blue and green.

The flyer opens with what might seem at first glance to be an innocuous question: 'Did You Know [*sic*] that Lexington, Kentucky City Council [*sic*] has signed us up as Members of ICLEI [International Council for Local Environmental Initiatives], Agenda 21, Agenda 2030, and the United Nations?' The following question (all in red, partially underlined), however, quickly dispels any sense of innocuousness:

> Did you know that our Planning Commission, Utility Companies, University of Kentucky, and many others have taken money to install LED Lights (with Cameras and Recorders inside), Wireless Utility Meters, and other smart technology to use as <u>Mass Surveillance Devices in order to have complete control over all of us?</u> (Underlining in original)

The phrase 'complete control over all of us' is a flag as red as the type it is written in; such sweeping claims, particularly about top-down control of society, are immediately suggestive of conspiracising. Over its remaining pages, the flyer goes on to explicate these initial claims, laying out the broad

13.1 Page one of the six-page ICLEI conspiracy theory flyer found in
Lexington, KY

strokes of a well-established conspiracy theory: what I refer to here as the
'United Nations Agenda 21 conspiracy theory' or 'UNA21 conspiracy theory'
for short.

The UNA21 conspiracy theory centres on the United Nations' adoption
of Agenda 21 at the United Nations Conference on Environment and
Development, held in June 1992 in Rio de Janeiro, Brazil. Agenda 21, also
known as the Rio Declaration on Environment and Development, and the
Statement of Principles for the Sustainable Management of Forests, is described

by the UN as 'a comprehensive plan of action to be taken globally, nationally and locally by organisations of the United Nations System, Governments, and Major Groups in every area in which human impacts [*sic*] on the environment' (United Nations, n.d.). The UNA21 conspiracy theory posits that this plan is not actually about environmental protection but rather is a conspiracy to eliminate national sovereignty and impose global governance (Southern Poverty Law Center, 2014; Trapenberg Frick, 2014; Mahl et al., 2021). While some versions of this conspiracy theory focus exclusively on the plan, some go so far as to claim that anthropogenic climate change (ACC) itself is a hoax spread by the United Nations in service of its conspiratorial world governance goals.

Seemingly every aspect of our modern lives is the subject of one conspiracy theory or another, so it is not surprising that the environment is no exception. In this chapter, I rely on Douglas et al.'s (2019: 4) definition of conspiracy theories as 'attempts to explain the ultimate causes of significant social and political events and circumstances with claims of secret plots by two or more powerful actors'. Climate change in particular is ripe for conspiracising; as Uscinski et al. (2017) note in their review of climate change conspiracy theory research, 'individuals with elevated levels of conspiratorial thinking are more likely to deny the existence and severity of anthropogenic climate change', leading such individuals to make a host of claims about different kinds of secret plots involving climate change. It is worth noting that climate conspiracy theories represent a somewhat amorphous subset of the broader phenomenon of climate change denial and scepticism, often spread through deliberate misinformation campaigns (Dunlap and McCright, 2011).

In the USA in particular, climate change conspiracising presents a particular draw for the far right, given that political party affiliation is one of the key factors determining belief in the scientific consensus on ACC, and that conspiracy thinking can in fact further partisan rejection of scientific evidence, particularly on the right (Uscinski and Olivella, 2017). The USA is a two-party system, with the Democratic Party representing left or progressive views and the Republican Party representing right or conservative views. As of 2018, while more than 50 per cent of registered Democratic voters nationwide believed in the scientific consensus on ACC, not a single congressional district had greater than 50 per cent of registered Republicans who held this belief (Mildenberger et al., 2020). Within that context, the UNA21 conspiracy theory is of particular interest to studies of environmental rhetoric because it has been taken up by actors on both the left and right of the political spectrum. Studying this conspiracy theory thus provides us with an opportunity to compare the far right's rhetorical strategies with the left's framing and presentation of the same general content.

Against this background, this chapter presents a comparative rhetorical analysis of the visual strategies used by US conspiracy theorists on the left *and* on the far right in their promulgation of the UNA21 conspiracy theory and concomitant framing of climate change, sustainability and the UN as existential threats to democracy and freedom. The visual texts used for analysis are drawn from the homepages of two websites used to spread this conspiracy. For the left version of the conspiracy theory, I analyse the website 'Democrats Against UN Agenda 21' (democratsagainstunagenda21.com, DAUNA21) and for the far right, I analyse the site 'Freedom Advocates[SM]' (freedomadvocates.org, FA). Both sites contain claims that climate change is a 'hoax' or 'fraud' or otherwise non-scientific ploy being exploited to justify government and foreign actor overreach. Climate change conspiracising is a necessary component of the broader conspiracy about UNA21 serving anti-democratic goals. In comparing these two texts, I focus not on the linguistic content but rather on layout, type, colour schema and other elements of document design. While such design features can, and often are, used to create what I term below the 'paranoid visual style', my comparison of these texts demonstrates that such a style is not as consistent a feature of far-right conspiracist websites as we might expect. This comparison thus yields the primary takeaway from this study: that simply identifying, let alone combatting, conspiracist disinformation by far-right actors requires readers to resist normative assumptions about what conspiracist, mainstream or well-reasoned texts *look* like.

I begin by reviewing the literature on the far right and the environment in the USA, highlighting the relative dearth of scholarship in this area compared to work on the European context. While much work has been done in the US context on the intersections of politics and the environment, far-right environmental communication specifically has received less direct attention, with most work focusing on the European context (for example, Forchtner et al., 2018; Forchtner, 2019c; Malm and the Zetkin Collective, 2021). Subsequently, I introduce the two source sites, one left and one far right, I use to develop a visual comparison with a focus on document design. Having introduced these two UNA21 conspiracy theory websites, I briefly describe my analytic methods, then present findings from my comparative analysis of two key and interrelated visual elements of these sites' homepages: First, the template underlying each website's homepage, and second, the typeface formatting on those pages. I conclude with a discussion of the findings, which suggest that conspiracist document design is extremely inconsistent across texts, making it difficult to pinpoint visual 'fingerprints' of this type of communication. Moreover, the relative appearance of professionalism and centrism in some UNA21 conspiracist texts can obscure or even confuse the underlying left or far-right politics animating them.

Focusing on document design as a form of visual rhetoric

The vast majority of scholarship on the rhetoric of the far right, whether environmental or otherwise, focuses on their language-based symbolic action, such as speeches, website text and manuals – though work on these groups' visual rhetoric, such as the German far right's visual memes (Bogerts and Fielitz, 2019) and their broader multimodal aesthetics (Forchtner and Kølvraa, 2017), has been increasingly emerging. However, little has been published on perhaps the most mundane aspect of textual visual rhetoric: document design, including colour schemes, layout and text formatting. In the general context of far-right communication, certainly, memes and visual symbols are more immediately arresting and arguably more important, given their role in recruitment and in-group identification. For conspiracy theories in particular, though, I would argue that the mundane elements of visual rhetoric necessitate study as well, specifically because of how they impact audience reception of conspiracist rhetoric.

To make this point: Compare the professionally formatted text on the page you are reading right now with the design of the flyer in Figure 13.1. Most likely, you have an intuitive sense of the relative credibility of each of these texts, even if you had not read a single word of either of them. On the flyer, the overwhelming nature of the dense text, the screaming of the primary colours, the distortion of the images, the crowding of it all to the very edges of the page combine to create a visual analogue to what Hofstadter (1964) famously called 'the paranoid style in American politics': a 'sense of heated exaggeration, suspiciousness, and conspiratorial fantasy'. In short, the paranoid-appearing document design of the flyer alone would lead you to read it differently from how you read this chapter, even had you no idea of either texts' provenance. The paranoid style, as Hofstadter describes it, is precisely that: a style. Characterising a text or speaker as engaging in the paranoid style is not to cast aspersions on its content but merely to say something descriptive about the presentation of that content, marked by paranoic features such as 'personal invective', 'vivid' villains and an appeal to incessantly 'apocalyptic' stakes (Hofstadter, 1964). These features may be apparent in fine-grained stylistic elements such as word choice or much higher-level elements such as organisational patterns. But, importantly, Hofstadter notes that this style is not unique to the contemporary far right of his time, although they do seem to monopolise it more than other political groups.

In the same vein, I do not argue that we can tell conspiratorial communication on sight, based purely on the visual style of document design; rather, I argue that it is risky to *assume* that we can do so based on the kind of comparison I just made. Conspiracy theorists may have as much access to and proficiency with desktop publishing tools as any other author. In fact, as we will see later in this chapter, online publishing makes it even easier for conspiracy theory discourse to obscure itself via a veneer of visual professionalism, as so much online and digital publishing now relies on either social media platforms that flatten all texts into the same look and feel or website-hosting platforms that advertise their vast library of professional-looking templates to attract non-technical users to their service. These forms of self-publishing invite authors to default to the platforms' visual design; authors must make more conscious efforts to deviate from certain of those defaults, such as line spacing, element margins and padding, and – for social media posts – text formatting (Gallagher, 2015). Given this homogenisation of web publishing due to templates, we can hardly rely on the paranoid visual style as a foolproof standard with which to identify conspiracy theory communication.

Defining the ideological political spectrum in the United States

The study of the far right, while long present in the European context, is much less well developed in US-centric scholarship. As Mudde (2018: xi) put it, the far right, as recently as 2008, was 'dominating academic and political debates on European politics in the twenty-first century. In the U.S., in sharp contrast, terms like "radical right" and "far right" featured sparsely in the political debate and generated little interest from scholars or students.' But, as Mudde goes on to note, the 2016 US presidential election shoved far-right ideologies into the political limelight, thanks to then candidate Donald Trump espousing far-right views, such as the notions that ethnonationalism should drive immigration policy or that the country should be led by a strongman authoritarian, who just happened to be himself.

The relative recency of this increased attention to the far right in the USA perhaps explains the challenge of developing a general definition of the American far right. That said, our lack of a general or shared definition is not indicative of how well established the far right's political influence actually is. In the US two-party political system, one party – the contemporary Republican Party – increasingly qualifies as far right, certainly in comparison to conservative parties in other nation-states. Moreover, the Republican Party's embrace of Trumpism evidences its commitment to ethnonationalism and authoritarianism, two broad criteria offered by Forchtner (2019a) to characterise the far-right end of the ideological spectrum. A full discussion of the Republican Party's historical and contemporary status as a far-right party is beyond the scope of this chapter, in part because this study follows recent work on far-right environmental and climate communication in focusing on non-party actors to examine far-right visual communication online outside the bounds of institutionally sanctioned communication (for example, Forchtner, 2019b; Forchtner, 2019c). It is worth noting, however, that in their 2012 platform, the Republican National Convention avowed: 'We *strongly* reject the U.N. Agenda 21 as *erosive* of American sovereignty, and we oppose any form of U.N. Global Tax' (2012 Republic Platform, 2012: 45, emphasis added). Additionally, UNA21 conspiracy theorists have moved their organising offline in some striking ways, successfully stymieing sustainable urban planning efforts across the country, from California to Alabama (Hurley and Walker, 2004; Trapenberg Frick, 2014; Southern Poverty Law Center, 2014; Trapenberg Frick et al., 2015). The UNA21 conspiracy theory is thus clearly not limited to the fringes in the USA, raising the stakes for scholars interested in cataloguing and combatting it.

In the USA, ethnonationalism and authoritarianism take shape somewhat differently from their European parallels, making it all the more important to add to the existing US-centric scholarship on the far right. The American far right in particular differs in terms of its attitude towards the state. The deep libertarian strain running through much of the US far right creates a strong undercurrent of what appears to be *anti*-authoritarianism, insofar as individual rights and freedoms are seen as inviolable and encroached upon by an overreaching federal government led by progressive crusaders for the 'nanny state'. Of course, authoritarianism can be a matter of social-psychological attitudes, rather than or in addition to pro-statism (Adorno et al., 2019), leading anti-government sentiments in the USA to often co-exist in unselfconscious tension with calls for or belief in the authoritarian regulation of others, such as ethnonationalist border controls or the rejection of pregnant persons' bodily autonomy and right to abortion. Mudde (2018: 1–2) further distinguishes between the radical right and the extreme right: the former accepts democracy while the latter opposes it outright on the grounds of belief in a natural hierarchy among men, which makes some superior to others. The key feature uniting these two, though, is opposition to liberalism and multiculturalism. What the US and European far right *do* share in terms of authoritarianism is a strong rejection of what they perceive as authoritarian overreach by groups or institutions at the wrong scale. For example, a global intergovernmental organisation is suspect, whereas for the US far right a local militia group might not be (Crothers, 2019), particularly among the anti-government set of right-wing extremists (Jackson, 2019).

The left–right distinction between the two sites under analysis here is apparent not only in their self-declared identification (for example, the 'Democrats' of democratsagainstunagenda21.com), but also in the disparate values they appeal to in their explanations of the supposed conspiracy to use UN Agenda 21 to advance a communitarian world government. Both sites offer a downloadable or purchasable text explaining the UNA21 conspiracy theory. The left-wing site links out to a self-published 119-page Amazon ebook titled *Behind the Green Mask: U. N. Agenda 21*, with authorship attributed to Rosa Koire, the most visible individual behind the site. The right-wing site offers a download of a sixteen-page 'white paper', whose authorship is attributed to 'Freedom Advocates'. The latter text deploys precisely those appeals one might expect of a US organisation with a self-declared focus on freedom: personal property and negative rights. There is no acknowledgement in this white paper that environmental protection is a worthwhile value, let alone something that is worth imposing on the individualistic values of personal property protection and freedom from the imposition of others' values.

In contrast, Koire's ebook imagines a reader who does value environmental protection. Within the first several pages, she uses the second person to speak directly to this imagined audience (see Goffman, 1956): 'Will you be accused of not caring about the planet if you question Sustainable Development?' (Koire, 2011: 3). On the following page, Koire makes this stereotypically US left commitment to environmental values even more explicit: 'So I'm not against making certain issues a priority, such as mindful energy use, alternative energy sponsorship, recycling/reuse, and sensitivity to all living creatures' (Koire, 2011: 4). To be clear, Koire's argument is also driven by a presumed zero-sum conflict between individualistic and communitarian regimes, with a focus on property rights; Koire herself was a real estate professional, so is particularly concerned with land use issues raised by various property rights frameworks. The veneer of left values might obscure this, and in fact seems to be an attempt to attract support for this conspiracy theory from the left in part by framing traditionally conservative viewpoints (in the contemporary USA) about the primacy of negative rights as a non-partisan matter that is relevant to anyone concerned about government overreach.

Neither the far right nor the left holds a monopoly on conspiracising; both are susceptible to conspiracies that appeal to their various ideological commitments and values. What is interesting about the UNA21 conspiracy theory is, in part, that it is so appealing to both sides, despite the gulf between their ideological commitments.

Sites for comparison: left versus far-right websites focused on the UN Agenda 21 conspiracy theory

To illustrate how visual document design cannot be relied upon to metonymically represent the presence or absence of far-right environmental rhetoric and conspiracies, I turn to two US websites dedicated to the UNA21 conspiracy theory. For the left version of the conspiracy theory, I analyse the website DAUNA21, and for the far right, I analyse the site FA. Comparing these two sites in particular allows us to see how the 'paranoid visual style' may in fact demarcate a conspiracy theory website but *not* a far right one; as the below analysis demonstrates, the far-right conspiracy site's design makes it appear reasonable and professional, especially in comparison to the leftist site conveying an identical conspiracy theory.

The former site was created in 2010 (democratsagainstunagenda21.com, n.d.) by Rosa Koire, the founder of three additional anti-Agenda 21 groups and associated websites: the Post Sustainability Institute, the Santa Rosa Neighborhood Coalition and the now defunct Stop Plan Bay Area. Koire, a self-professed feminist lesbian Democrat, calls Agenda 21 a worldwide effort to 'inventory and control all land, all water, all minerals, all plants, all animals, all construction, all means of production, all energy, all education, all information, and all human beings in the world' (Koire, n.d.). The full conspiracy theory encompasses a number of topics, including climate change, which is cast as a false flag operation intended to justify global domination. For example, in one blog post, Koire writes that '[t]he Climate Change threat is a stage, a phase designed to prepare us for more restrictions and limitations'; there and elsewhere on her sites, climate change is cited as the hoax or fraud used by the UN and related stakeholders to push Agenda 21 and sustainable development goals.

From her four sites, Koire links out to dozens of other fringe sites, contributing to an expansively networked corner of the web where conspiracy theories about climate change, gun rights, pharmaceuticals, COVID-19 and so on butt up against and bleed into each other. Her content is concentrated on two sites: DAUNA21 and 'Santa Rosa Neighborhood Coalition'.

On both of these content-dense sites, a blog feature accounts for the vast majority of that content. Publication dates show that the DAUNA21 website is more central to Koire's public communication than any of the other sites; its most recent post was published on 25 January 2021, while the 'Neighborhood Coalition' site blog has not been updated since May 2017.

While Koire's self-identification clearly aims to locate her outside the far right, her conspiracist take on Agenda 21 and her connections to the far right make her a prime example of the kinds of unlikely coalitions that fringe beliefs can sometimes build (on such overlaps, see also Chapter 9 in this volume). These connections are apparent in her appearances in far-right media (such as her guest spots on infamous conspiracist Alex Jones's show) and hyperlinks from her sites out to indisputably far-right sites, including freedomadvocates.org, the second site under examination here. Understanding these connections as coalition-building makes sense of what would otherwise be an ideologically incoherent set of texts; Koire can claim to be left and appeal to left values, and yet also promote far-right content that aligns with her views on sustainability and climate change.

The second website, FA, claims the tautological 'Freedom Advocates' as its copyright holder. While the website claims to 'represent a cross-section of people from all political parties and backgrounds who are united in the principles of individual liberty, equal justice and the constitutional administration of government', only one individual 'research fellow' is listed: Patrick Wood, 'an economist by education, a financial analyst and writer by profession and an American Constitutionalist by choice'.[1] While no birthdate or age is listed, Wood is described as having 'studied elite globalization policies since the late 1970's', making him likely well into his sixties or seventies. In addition to FA, Wood publishes the more topically eclectic 'Technocracy News and Trends' (technocracy.news). FA clearly appeals to traditional US conservative values, which is apparent in the following list of 'areas' the website intends to promote discussion on: constitutional government, private property, individual and family autonomy and sustainable development/ Agenda 21. Although the final item is the central subject of the website, the first three further underscore that Wood's concern is not overreach in response to valid environmental concerns but overreach using the environment as an excuse to undermine conservative and libertarian principles of government. The climate conspiracising is also buried more deeply on this site than on Koire's: the top-level pages rarely mention climate or climate change. However, a number of linked PDFs and slide decks contain standard climate conspiracy talking points: A document titled *The Ultimate War: Globalism vs. America* contains the claim that '[s]o much of the Agenda 21 invasion at the local level relies on the man-made global warming fraud. But national and international "consensus" on man-caused climate change has dissipated', while a slide deck purporting to be an overview of ICLEI includes a slide on 'Climategate' that includes non-sequitur mentions of Marx, Engels and Lenin as well as a slide titled 'Carbon Dioxide (CO2): Fiction'.

Wood's websites are also shot through with hallmarks of far-right discourse and its promotion of ethnonationalism and authoritarianism. FA uses a number of xenophobic and white supremacist dog whistles, including referring to sustainable development's proponents as 'socialists' and 'cultural marxists'. Anti-Muslim sentiment also crops up throughout the site: for example, a 2012 PowerPoint slide hosted on FA names the Organization of Islamic Capitals and Cities and the Islamic Development Bank as adherents of sustainable development, and we are meant to enthymematically understand that it is support by Muslim organisations that should further our suspicions about UNA21. The distinctly American far-right tension between anti-government authoritarianism and promotion of authoritarian attitudes is also apparent, as when Wood endorses private ownership of federal lands and the abolishment of fiat monetary systems as ways to protect local sovereignty against national and international overreach.

While these two conspiracists and their multiple websites present a large corpus of textual and visual material, I rely in this analysis on comparing the homepages of their two primary websites: DAUNA21 and FA. These two websites contain the bulk of each of these writers' conspiracising about UN Agenda 21 and climate change, and their homepages present a kind of 'cover' for each site. Although a reader could arrive at a website via a search engine link to a different subpage, the homepage remains the welcoming or landing page presenting the most public face of a website. As such, the homepages enable the comparison of likely the most intentionally designed pages on these sites, as well as the pages most likely to be seen by the largest share of visitors to the sites.

Comparing left and far-right conspiracies

To make direct comparisons between the left and far-right UNA21 conspiracy theory websites, I examine document design on the sites through two inter-related frames, each of which focuses on different portions of an overlapping set of individual design elements. That is, I analyse both the site templates, including layout and colour schemas, and the sites' typeface formatting, including size, font, colour and formatting elements. This comparison aims to answer two interrelated research questions:

1. What similar or different visual document design elements characterise these conspiracist texts on the left and the far right?
2. How can this rhetorical analysis of document design inform efforts to identify and intervene in the circulation of misinformation and disinformation?

Comparison 1: site templates

Over the past three decades, scholars of visual rhetoric and technical communication have conclusively demonstrated the rhetorical importance of document design and the concomitant need to take it seriously as an object of visual analysis. As Kinross (1989) argued, even simple choices such as portrait versus landscape orientation, or the design of a table's borders, can affect the rhetorical functions of a text and how a reader makes meaning from it. Given that, as Arola (2009: 12) puts it, 'the template encourages particular understandings of the self and of others', any analysis of a website's visual design and its rhetorical impacts must acknowledge how the site uses templates (or does not, keeping in mind that many contemporary websites are based on pre-existing templates, which have often been composed by expert designers and not the particular website creator). Many of the companies employing these expert designers who produce such templates, moreover, offer a (limited/limiting set of) graphical user design interfaces, which allow creators with no coding knowledge or experience to customise their websites. For example, Weebly, the company which hosts Koire's DAUNA21, advertises its 'beautiful themes created by top designers [that] make your website look polished and professional on any device' (weebly.com/websites). Wordpress, the platform on which FA is built, makes similar claims; creators can use it to '[s]tand out with professionally-designed themes' (wordpress.com). Any direct comparison of DAUNA21 and FA, then, must account for the fact that both have been created using website builders and content management systems that offer predesigned templates.

Comparing the DAUNA21 and FA website templates, FA is the most professional-appearing one: its layout, colour scheme and text formatting all bespeak constraint and awareness of norms around professional communication. It uses a WordPress template called 'MH Corporate'; as of this writing, the theme costs \$49, so is an investment, particularly given that literally thousands of free WordPress themes are available to any website creator. Figure 13.2 provides a side-by-side comparison of the base MH

13.2 Side-by-side comparison of MH Corporate WordPress template (left) and freedomadvocates.org (right), which is based on that template

Corporate default page template and the FA homepage, which is clearly designed from that template.

This side-by-side comparison allows us to determine which design choices are specific to FA itself; the most prominent are, first, the addition of a callout box at the top of the main content column with a three-column set of action items just beneath it, and, second, the change in colour scheme, incorporating the navy and yellow of the FA header along with a complementary muted blue as the background to either side of the website's content.

In contrast, DAUNA21 appears to veer sharply away from its underlying Weebly theme (called 'Light'). Unlike the side-by-side comparison of FA and its base theme in Figure 13.2, in which the similarities are immediately visible, Figure 13.3 shows that DAUNA21's base theme is not visually apparent in the final form of the edited website.

Whereas the base template reads as clean and professional, with significant white space between elements, a simple top-level menu and a 2:1 column layout with a narrow sidebar to the right of the main content colum, DAUNA21 revises that template to be crammed and busy. The top-level menu becomes a left sidebar with far more menu links than in the template, the centre content column fills the screen with a barely interrupted flow of text, and the right sidebar is now equally full of text rather than short links

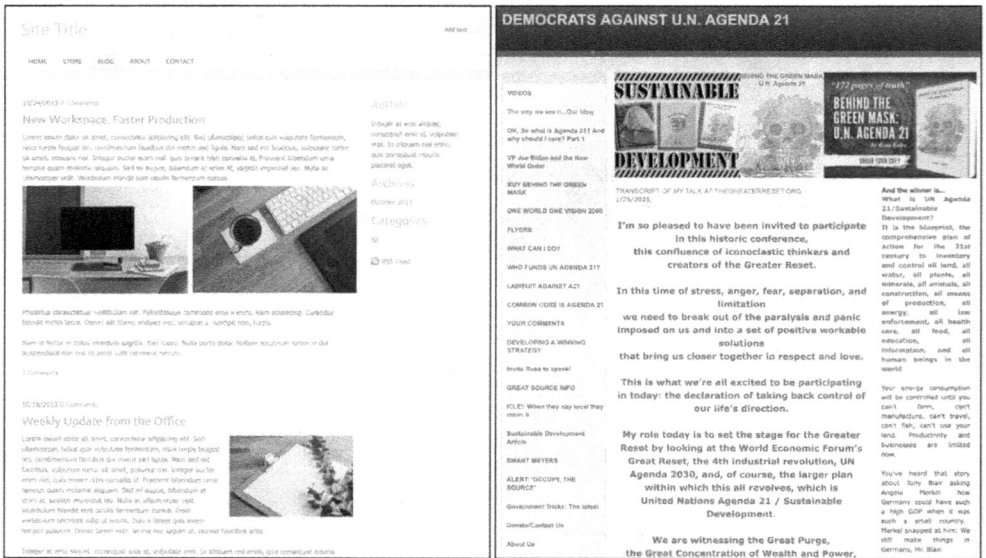

13.3 Side-by-side comparison of Weebly Light theme (left) and democratsagainstunagenda21.com (right), which is based on that template

surrounded by whitespace. The text in the centre column and right sidebar is fully justified rather than left-justified, as in the template. In place of images breaking up the content in the main column, DAUNA21 only has one image on this landing page: a dark, multicoloured collage of images functioning as a header across the centre column and right sidebar. The darkness of that collage echoes the heaviness of the black and red full-page header above, against which the small, light-grey text with the site title strains to stand out. The overall impression of this site, despite it having been built on the foundation of a professional-appearing minimalist Weebly theme, is closer to the paranoid visual style of the flyer I opened this chapter with. That said, elements from the original theme do pop out on occasion, as with regard to the webpage's contact form.

The similarities between the contact forms confirms that Weebly Light is in fact the base theme for DAUNA21; the website creator, Rosa Koire, has clearly chosen to individualise her site far more than is the case for FA.

Setting the FA and DAUNA21 homepages side by side further underscores the relative professionalism of the former and the paranoid styling of the latter (Figures 13.2 and 13.3). Among other elements, the relative readability and impression of neutrality conveyed by FA compared to DAUNA21 results from, first, the use of left-justification rather than full justification, which is harder to read (Hooper and Hannafin, 1986; Trollip and Sales, 1986). Second, this impression is arguably due to the sparing use of emphasis via placement and text styling, as making everything a focal point, which DAUNA21 arguably does, means nothing stands out as a focal point (Tufte, 1990). Third, a coherent muted blue and yellow colour palette is used rather than an array of colours, some muted and some bold primaries such as red and yellow, which conveys for Western readers alarm and high emotion and can affect perception of website trustworthiness (Alberts and van der Geest, 2011). Notably, these differences and the overall effects they add up to are not attributable to different theme choices; they are necessarily a result of design choices imposed by the site creators *after* base themes have been selected. The fact that both are based on templates thus makes it all the more interesting that the far-right website does in fact appear professional, while the other hews closer to the paranoid visual style of the flyer this chapter opened with.

Comparison 2: text formatting

Text formatting can be one of the most impactful elements of document design (Brumberger, 2003): text can be styled in perhaps literally infinite configurations, each configuration contributing differently to the visual rhetoric of an overall design. Some, though not all, of the textual formatting features designers have control over in digital designs such as websites are: typeface, font, size, colour, text decorations such as underline and strike-through, letter case schemas (for example, all caps, small caps, title case, mixed case, etc.) and, finally, line design, especially in relation to justification, leading and kerning. Of course, these features may overlap with the design elements already discussed in relation to site templates: Line design is as much a matter of layout as of text formatting, and the colour of the text is a piece of the overall colour palette of a design. It is worth attending to text formatting as a specific design feature, however, because of how central it is to the paranoid visual style gestured at in the introduction.

The paranoid visual style of text design is marked, most dramatically, by excess. There is an excess of typefaces, fonts, sizes, colours, text decora-tions, capitalisation schemas and line designs. This excess could also be understood as a lack of consistency: no one set of text formatting choices is allowed to dominate the design, so the design becomes cluttered with inconsistent formatting lacking any visual logic justifying the many, often sudden, changes.

Referring back to Figures 13.1 and 13.3 (in comparison to Figure 13.2), this contrast between constrained and excessive text formatting becomes visible. FA appears to use only two typefaces on its homepage, one serif and one sans serif. The fonts within those typefaces vary, but in ways that mirror the structural logic of the page: Serif fonts are used only for major elements, such as the site title and the above-the-fold callout box; the serif site title is several orders of magnitude larger than any other text on the page; and sans serif headings are larger than sans serif body text. The vast majority of the text on the page is in the same neutral black; hyperlinks are in blue, consistent with web design norms; a few phrases are emphasised by a shift to green (an interesting choice, given the fact that green is associated with environmentalism in the USA, a value which this far-right climate conspiracy site notably elides); and all other non-black text is in a colour that contrasts well with a non-white background (as with the yellow site title layered over a muted blue-grey background).

The excess of DAUNA21's text formatting stands in stark contrast. The homepage alone uses at least four typefaces and at least eight fonts, including serif and sans serif fonts in varying sizes, bolded and italicised. Type occurs in three shades each of grey and blue, as well as black, red, yellow and green. Occasionally, text is fully capitalised in captions underneath videos linked at the bottom of the main content column. The left sidebar menu links have four capitalisation schemas: all caps (for example, 'ONE WORLD ONE VISION 2050'), title case (for example, 'Sustainable Development Article'), sentence case (for example, 'Invite Rosa to speak!') and mixed case inconsistent with Standard American English orthographic rules (for example, 'Government Tricks: The latest').

On each website, any one text formatting design choice may communicate with readers in a particular way. For example, typefaces communicate different types of credibility (Brumberger, 2003; Shaikh, 2007; Smits and van der Sar, 2015), and since the advent of digital writing, all caps is often read as shouting (Goetz, 2016). As such, FA might already be read as more approachable or credible, simply because of the reliance on the theme's typefaces and lack of all caps. But the contrast between these sites' use of text formatting is not a matter of one-to-one comparison of particular choices, but rather the total number of choices each site's designer imposes on the reader.

In rhetorical terms – FA's restrained use of textual formatting and DAUNA21's excessiveness – each function as visual analogues to the rhetorical figures of *aschematiston* and *periergia*, respectively. FA's visual *aschematiston*, or 'the absence of ornamental or figured language' (Zimmerman, 1997: 740), is reminiscent of contemporary exhortations to plain language to make information accessible and thereby enhance its credibility, in part by disappearing any sense of that information having been designed at all. DAUNA21's excessive stylisation, in contrast, draws attention to itself as a designed object; it is unsurprising, perhaps, that the relevant rhetorical figure of *periergia*, or 'excessive elaboration of a point' (Quintillian, cited by Arner, 1972: 80), has most frequently been cited in literary scholarship investigating poesis. Of course, though, the question of credibility is part of a larger question of reader response; in other words, credibility is not to be found in the essence of a text but rather in the interpretive space between text and reader. We cannot, therefore, make universal claims as to whether *aschematism* or *periergia* is more or less credible. Rather, we can observe that the textual formatting of a website contributes to its overall visual rhetoric in a way that might, but does not necessarily, demarcate it as conspiracist in a way non-conspiracist scholars of rhetoric or other readers outside the conspiracist discourse community would expect.

Conclusion

In this chapter, I have attempted to respond to Forchtner's (2019a) call in his interdisciplinary review of scholarship on climate change and the far right for more comparative studies and studies on visual rhetoric. This study provides a comparison of specific instances of left and right versions of climate change conspiracising by analysing the latter in the US far right and left. Much of the analysis is not necessarily specific to environmental communication, save that the sites of comparison focus on climate change conspiracy theories. Yet I would argue that such distinctions are already blurry, as conspiracy theories rarely sort themselves easily into distinct categories, and those engaged in conspiracy thinking may not constrain themselves to engagement with a single conspiracy theory. Thus, this chapter contributes to both environmental communication scholarship and to conspiracy scholarship more generally.

In addition, this comparative study demonstrates that our visual analysis must account not just for imagery but also the contributions of document design to a text's visual rhetoric. In fact, in the case of climate change conspiracising, document design may provide a way into understanding visual rhetoric that is otherwise stymied, given how climate change does not lend itself to the aesthetically driven communications the far right typically uses in relation to the environment (Forchtner and Kølvraa, 2017). Indeed, on these two websites I have compared, there are not that many images, but there are many opportunities nonetheless to make visual comparisons. And yet we must be careful to distinguish between our expectation of conspiracising being marked by design excess, which constitutes an easy analogue to the paranoid style, and the reality that conspiracist content online is equally likely to be presented within a constrained design aesthetic.

The paranoid visual style is a real marker of certain kinds of discourse, but it cannot be taken as a definite marker, nor can its absence be used to judge a text reasonable. Indeed, even though the far-right FA website's self-presentation looks reasonable by many standards, a quick perusal of its content quickly reveals its true character. Engagement with the content of the written rhetoric itself remains vital for identifying and categorising conspiracist texts. While this conclusion may seem trivial, it remains true that readers use at-a-glance clues, such as the relative professionalism of document design, to judge a text's credibility. Given the cases examined here, it is crucial that analysts (and readers more generally) resist that urge and rely on consistent ways to identify, and ultimately combat, the environmental disinformation and conspiracist rhetoric promulgated by the far right and others.

Notes

1 See www.freedomadvocates.org/wp-content/uploads/2014/06/Patrick-Wood-bio-2012.pdf (accessed 14 February 2022).

References

2012 Republic Platform (2012): Republican National Party.

Adorno, T., Frenkel-Brenswik, E., Levinson, D. J. and Sanford, R. N. (2019): *The Authoritarian Personality*. New York: Verso.

Alberts, W. A. and van der Geest, T. M. (2011): Color matters: Color as trustworthiness cue in web sites, *Technical Communication*, 58(2): 149–160.

Arner, R. D. (1972): The smooth and emblematic song: Joel Barlow's 'The Hasty Pudding', *Early American Literature*, 7(1): 76–91.

Arola, K. L. (2010): The design of web 2.0: The rise of the template, the fall of design, *Computers and Composition*, 27(1): 4–14. https://doi.org/10.1016/j.compcom.2009.11.004

Bogerts, L. and Fielitz, M. (2019): 'Do you want meme war?': Understanding the visual memes of the German far right. In M. Fielitz and N. Thurston (eds), *Post-Digital Cultures of the Far Right: Online Actions and Offline Consequences in Europe and the US*. Bielefeld: transcript, 137–153.

Brumberger, E. R. (2003): The rhetoric of typography: The awareness and impact of typeface appropriateness, *Technical Communication*, 50(2): 224–231.

Crothers, L. (2019): *Rage on the Right: The American Militia Movement from Ruby Ridge to the Trump Presidency*. Washington, DC: Rowman & Littlefield.

democratsagainstunagenda21.com   (n.d.).   https://www.whois.com/whois/democratsagainstunagenda21.com (accessed 7 November 2021).

Douglas, K. M., Uscinski, J. E., Sutton, R. M., Cichocka, A., Nefes, T., Ang, C. S. and Deravi, F. (2019): Understanding conspiracy theories, *Political Psychology*, 40(S1): 3–35. https://doi.org/10.1111/pops.12568

Dunlap, R. E. and McCright, A. M. (2011): Organized climate change denial. In: J. S. Dryzek, R. B. Norgaard and D. Schlosberg (eds), *The Oxford Handbook of Climate Change and Society*. Oxford: Oxford University Press, 144–160.

Forchtner, B. (2019a): Climate change and the far right, *WIREs Climate Change*, 10(5). https://doi.org/10.1002/wcc.604.

Forchtner, B. (2019b): Nation, nature, purity: Extreme-right biodiversity in Germany, *Patterns of Prejudice*, 53(3): 285–301. https://doi.org/10.1080/0031322X.2019.1592303.

Forchtner, B. (ed.) (2019c): *The Far Right and the Environment: Politics, Discourse and Communication*. London: Routledge.

Forchtner, B. and Kølvraa, C. (2017): Extreme right images of radical authenticity: Multimodal aesthetics of history, nature, and gender roles in social media, *European Journal of Cultural and Political Sociology*, 4(3): 252–281. https://doi.org/10.1080/23254823.2017.1322910

Forchtner, B., Kroneder, A. and Wetzel, D. (2018): Being skeptical? Exploring far-right climate-change communication in Germany, *Environmental Communication*, 12(5): 589–604. https://doi.org/10.1080/17524032.2018.1470546

Gallagher, J. R. (2015): The rhetorical template, *Computers and Composition*, 35: 1–11.

Goetz, M. K. (2016): Switching to lowercase messaging: A capital idea, *Journal – American Water Works Association*, 108(2): 48–51. https://doi.org/10.5942/jawwa.2016.108.0033

Goffman, E. (1956): *The Presentation of Self in Everyday Life*. New York: Anchor Books/Doubleday.

Hofstadter, R. (1964): The paranoid style in American politics, *Harper's Magazine*, November 1964. https://harpers.org/archive/1964/11/the-paranoid-style-in-american-politics/ (accessed 14 February 2022).

Hooper, S. and Hannafin, M. J. (1986): Variables affecting the legibility of computer generated text, *Journal of Instructional Development*, 9(4): 22–28. https://doi.org/10.1007/BF02908315

Hurley, P. T. and Walker, P. A. (2004): Whose vision? Conspiracy theory and land-use planning in Nevada County, California, *Environment and Planning A: Economy and Space*, 36(9): 1529–1547. https://doi.org/10.1068/a36186

Jackson, S. (2019): *A Schema of Right-Wing Extremism in the United States*, policy brief, The Hague: International Centre for Counter-Terrorism.

Kinross, R. (1989): The rhetoric of neutrality. In V. Margolin (ed.), *Design Discourse: History, Theory, Criticism*. Chicago: University of Chicago Press, 131–143.

Koire, R. (2011). *Behind the Green Mask: UN Agenda 21*. Post Sustainability Institute Press.

Koire, R. (n.d.): *OK, So What Is Agenda 21? And Why Should I Care? Part 1*. DEMOCRATS AGAINST U.N. AGENDA 21. www.DEMOCRATSAGAINSTUNAGENDA21.com/ok-so-what-is-agenda-21-and-why-should-i-care-part-1.html (accessed 7 November 2021).

Mahl, D., Zheng, J. and Schäfer, M. S. (2021): From 'NASA lies' to 'reptilian eyes': Mapping communication about 10 conspiracy theories, their communities, and main propagators on Twitter, *Social Media + Society*, 7(2): 1–12. http://dx.doi.org/10.1177/20563051211017482

Malm, A. and The Zetkin Collective. (2021): *White Skin, Black Fuel: On the Danger of Fossil Fascism*. New York: Verso.

Mildenberger, M., Marlon, J., Howe, P. and Leiserowitz, A. (2020): Democratic and republican views of climate change (2018), *Yale Program on Climate Change Communication*. http://climatecommunication.yale.edu/visualizations-data/partisan-maps-2018/ (accessed 14 February 2022).

Mudde, C. (2018): *The Far Right in America*. Abingdon: Routledge.

Shaikh, D. (2007): *Psychology of On-Screen Type: Investigations Regarding Typeface Personality, Appropriateness, and Impact on Document Perception*. PhD thesis. Wichita, KA: Wichita State University.

Smits, T. and van der Sar, R. (2015): *The Right Font for the Job: The Effect of Typeface-Product Congruency on Attitude towards the Ad*. Presented at the Etmaal van de Communicatiewetenschap, 2–3. February 2015, Antwerp, Belgium. https://lirias.kuleuven.be/1860028 (accessed 14 February 2022).

Southern Poverty Law Center (2014): *Agenda 21: The UN, Sustainability and Right-Wing Conspiracy Theory*. Southern Poverty Law Center. www.splcenter.org/20140331/agenda-21-un-sustainability-and-right-wing-conspiracy-theory (accessed 14 February 2022).

Trapenberg Frick, K. (2014): The actions of discontent: Tea Party and property rights activists pushing back against regional planning, *Journal of the American Planning Association*, 79(3): 190–200. https://doi.org/10.1080/01944363.2013.885312

Trapenberg Frick, K., Weinzimmer, D. and Waddell, P. (2015): The politics of sustainable development opposition: State legislative efforts to stop the United Nation's Agenda 21 in the United States, *Urban Studies*, 52(2): 209–232. https://doi.org/10.1177/0042098014528397

Trollip, S. R. and Sales, G. (1986): Readability of computer-generated fill-justified text, *Human Factors*, 28(2): 159–163. https://doi.org/10.1177/001872088602800204

Tufte, E. (1990): *Envisioning Information*. Cheshire, CT: Graphics Press.

United Nations (n.d.): *Agenda 21*. UN Sustainable Development Goals Knowledge Platform. https://sustainabledevelopment.un.org/outcomedocuments/agenda21 (accessed 6 November 2021).

Uscinski, J., Douglas, K. and Lewandowsky, S. (2017): Climate change conspiracy theories. In: M. Nisbet, S. Ho, E. Markowitz, S. O'Neill, M. Schäfer and J. Thaker (eds), *The Oxford Encyclopedia of Climate Change Communication*. Oxford: Oxford University Press.

Uscinski, J. E., and Olivella, S. (2017): The conditional effect of conspiracy thinking on attitudes toward climate change, *Research & Politics*, 4(4). https://doi.org/10.1177/2053168017743105.

Zimmerman, B. (1997): A catalogue of rhetorical and other literary terms from American literature and oratory, *Style*, 31(4): 730–759.

Looking back, looking forward: some preliminary conclusions on the far right's visualisation of its natural environments

Bernhard Forchtner

Looking back

In these concluding remarks to the edited volume *Visualising Far-Right Environments: Communication and the Politics of Nature*, I bring together findings from the preceding thirteen chapters. The volume was compiled with the aim of making an essential contribution to our knowledge about the intersection of the natural environment and the far right. As such, it departed from the recognition of the particular significance of the role of images and the visual mode more generally in drawing boundaries between *us* and *them*, in creating (emotional) bonds. Furthermore, the contributions to this volume showcase a wide range of approaches to how to analyse such communication. Finally, and at least as important, the volume does so with regard to cases within Europe and beyond, as the far right today is undoubtedly a global phenomenon. Thus, the contributions analyse the visualisation of different themes; the presence (or absence) of historically and culturally resonant ideas of nature, for example Romantic, *völkisch* or overtly fascist ones; the relation between depictions of local/regional/national sites vis-à-vis global ones, from landscape to climate change; and the emotions at play. At times, the contributions comment on overlaps between far-right and centrist/left-wing visual communication, as in Chapter 9 on aesthetic practices in Hungary. Against this background, the aim of what follows is not to offer a synthesis – for that, the landscape appears much too diverse. However, based on the comprehensive and systematic analyses of images and multimodal environmental communication offered in previous chapters, a handful of preliminary observations can be made.

At the outset, contributors were not asked to focus on specific thematic areas, but rather to decide themselves whether their chapters would investigate a particular environmental issue or offer an overview of respective visual communication. One outcome has been the finding that the nation's physical territory – the affirmation of landscape and 'homeland' – often takes centre stage. Of course, those studies which deliberately focus on other issues, such as graphs in climate obstruction in Sweden (Chapter 12) and the 'paranoid visual style' of climate-related conspiracy theory websites (Chapter 13), cannot be expected to address this aspect. However, many of those chapters which provide more general introductions to visual environmental communication by party and non-party far-right actors noted the significance of 'the land'. This includes, for example, extreme-right actors in Australia and New Zealand (Chapter 2), as well as the National Socialist Movement in the United States (Chapter 3). It also includes the cases of France (Chapter 8), Germany (Chapter 11), India (Chapter 10), Spain (Chapter 4) and South Africa (Chapter 1) – all indicating the centrality of the aesthetic and symbolic dimension of 'the land'. Indeed, rural idylls and 'ethnoscapes' (Smith, 2009: 50) more generally are omnipresent and, as Aguilera-Carnerero exemplarily puts it in Chapter 4, the 'countryside [is imagined] as the backbone of the nation'. However, the affirmation of 'the land' in this volume is arguably not just a result of the far right's focus on territory but also due to this volume's focus on visuality. After all, images are particularly capable of depicting 'beauty', stirring emotions and conveying 'eco-communion' (see the Introduction to this volume).

The visual mode is furthermore adept at establishing intertextual links to earlier, historical ideas of nature. As I have just mentioned, traditional representations of the rural are regularly evoked. However, going beyond a visualisation of the pastoral, the rural is also approached as a site of 'modernisation', with Burnett (Chapter 1) explicitly noting that wider changes in style in the South African far right unfold in tandem with the performance of 'our' belonging to 'an Afrikaner ethnoscape'. Similarly, Jones (Chapter 3) points to the translation of Blood and Soil ideas for a modern audience, while Carle (Chapter 8) notes that parts of the French far right are 'subtly quoting an ideological and iconographic background that owes much to the *völkisch* movements'.

The ways in which these actors assure themselves of their deep connection with the homeland, of course, differ. For example, in settler-colonial cases, such as Australia and New Zealand (Chapter 2), South Africa (Chapter 1) and the United States (Chapter 3), visually asserting ownership and performing rootedness (or 'implantment') unfolds within a different context than is the case in, for example, France. Across these cases, however, these homelands play affective roles; see, especially, Burnett (Chapter 1), though also Vicenová et al. (Chapter 7). What makes the latter's chapter on the Slovakian far right particularly interesting is the emotive economy indicated, one in which 'positive' emotions, such as pride, are related to the natural environment, while negative emotions (anger and hate) are mobilised concerning non-green issues. In contrast, Pietiläinen (Chapter 6) speaks of positive emotions too (hope and joy), but does so in relation to depictions of Arctic exploitation. Indeed, these (and other) chapters illustrate the importance of 'the feeling of place': the emotional economy of territory.

To be clear, the centrality of the rural in general and of the emotions attached to it is not surprising, but its prevalence is notable when compared with climate change. While the ideological disconnect between nationalism and climate change (Conversi, 2020), populism and climate change (Huber et al., 2021) and the far right and climate change (Lockwood, 2018; Forchtner, 2019; Malm and The Zetkin Collective, 2021) has been noted, debates and visualisations of climate change remain central among the wider public. While some chapters point to an acceptance of anthropogenic climate change (for example, Chapters 9 and 10), with others noting such acceptance though they do not find much discussion in the analysed material (for example, Chapters 3 and 7), there are also those cases in which various forms of climate obstruction play a role (Chapters 4, 11, 12 and 13). There thus remains a diverse range of stances when it comes to anthropogenic climate change.

And yet, what Moore and Roberts (2022: 46) aptly describe as the 'fractured and fractious landscape' of the far right is also true when it comes to stances towards environmental issues more broadly, with far-right actors not only divided on climate change but also at times regarding territory. As such, the particular (read: exclusionary and particularistic) concern for the natural environment some of them display is mirrored by other actors' ignorance. In *Visualising Far-Right Environments*, this is probably most clearly illustrated by the cases of the Spanish Vox (Chapter 4) and the Izborskii Club in Russia (Chapter 6). The latter, in particular, does not relate to nature Romantically but in terms reminiscent of Merchant's (1983 [1976]) classic study of the scientific revolution sanctioning the exploitation and domination of nature and women. Here there are images introducing us to the Russian Arctic as a site to be dominated and penetrated, an empty land in which white masculinity can assert itself through the archetypes of soldier, worker and scientist/explorer.

Furthermore, Pietiläinen's (Chapter 6) and even more so Christou's (Chapter 5) chapters employ gender as a core analytical category in their analyses. Other chapters too point to the far right's gendered understanding of the natural environment, as in Sharma's discussion of the 'great Hindu motherland' (Chapter 10) and Carle's argument that the think tank *Institut Iliade* depicts women in harmony with nature while men are depicted antagonistically (Chapter 8). While the issue of ecological masculinities has attracted wider attention (for example, Pulé and Hultman, 2021), most of the research investigating gender in the context of the far right and the environment has concerned climate change (but see, for example, Darwish, 2021). In this volume, Forchtner and Olsen (Chapter 11) juxtapose the presence of a visualised 'masculine/muscular environmentalism' manifest in concerns for the natural environment with the widely received notions of 'industrial/ breadwinner masculinities' (Hultman et al., 2019; see also Chapter 12 in this volume) and 'petro-masculinity' (Daggett, 2018) emerging in work related to climate change, while Burnett (Chapter 1) points to the significance of traditional white masculinity in the figure of the farmer.

Considering the physical territory and its appreciation, both Jones (Chapter 3) and Campion and Phillips (Chapter 2) point to outdoorsmanship and health as sites through which the natural environment becomes (visually) meaningful to the far right. This mirrors Westberg and Årman's (2019) study and points to the recreational, experiential dimension of engaging with nature. While far-right environments have commonly been approached through the analysis of written text, the 'banal', bodily dimension of such immersion in the 'national ecosystem' warrants further ethnographic investigation. Such practices furthermore point to 'eco-action' (Tarant, 2019), for example: a beach clean-up. This takes centre stage in Chapter 3, though it is also mentioned in Chapter 5, Chapter 2 and Chapter 7. In fact, given the focus on visuals in this volume, the widespread analysis of online platforms via which such activism could easily be shared and the potential strategic value of such actions, one could have imagined more of such visualisation.

Looking forward

Besides calling for more studies so as to provide both empirical insights and the testing of ideas and concepts in contexts around the world, I, finally, point to four specific aspects which came to mind while reading the thirteen chapters. These points – certainly not an exhaustive list – aim to push the visual analysis of far-right environments further to provide a more comprehensive understanding of such communication and their (potential) consequences. However, before I turn to these points, I note that it has become clear over the course of this volume that analysing images systematically must become the default in studies of far-right environments. Due to being in the relatively early stages of investigating visual environmental communication by the far right, most chapters draw on qualitative multimodal discourse analysis/semiotic analysis to illustrate patterns emerging from their respective cases (though regularly supported by quantitative content analysis). However, in light of the visual nature of our everyday culture, a multimodal focus should indeed not stand out any longer, even though this will admittedly not always be possible due to lack of access to material because of deplat-forming (see Chapters 5 and 7) and copyright concerns/issues around consent to reproduce images might prevent their inclusion.

Works able to incorporate visuals should, first, address reception: While audience research is not limited to visual aspects and adds another set of practical difficulties, the polysemic nature of images calls for such enquiry (see O'Neill and Nicholson-Cole, 2009 for a classic study on climate change visuals and reception). Besides interviews and focus groups, surveys and eye-tracking (for the latter, see, for example, Lindholm et al., 2021) would be ways to understand what environmental images mean and how they are processed. This would also be useful in research into the overlap between right and centre/left (Chapter 9) or when comparing them (Chapter 13).

Second, the analysis of visuals also lends itself to a longitude focus to understand the changing nature of visual environmental communication, particularly in light of cultural and technological changes in recent decades. In this volume, most chapters cover a period of a few years, with studies on Russia and Slovakia covering the longest time periods, both from 2013 to 2021. Here again, practical issues often stand in the way of doing longitudinal research as far-right groups are often short-lived, while even those with a long history might not have produced relevant material. Ideally, however, we should learn more about the content and form of such communication over the long term to grasp far-right environmental/ecological imaginaries in changing historical contexts.

Third, what are the affordances of different platforms and genres, from newspapers to Instagram? Are there differences, for example, due to the easy way of circulating imagery via social media? How does this affect which themes circulate and are foregrounded? Furthermore, and considering social media in particular: What changes with the inclusion of the sonic mode and the movement of images, be it in short videos on, for example, Twitter or longer ones shared via YouTube? Arguably, the focus on visuals that this volume has championed should be extended to also capturing these developments as videos are created and shared with increasing ease. Examples of analysing such crucial multimodal texts in this volume are provided by Burnett (Chapter 1) and, though less central, Aguilera-Carnerero (Chapter 4).

Finally, the persuasiveness of the visual mode should not be separated from, but has to be viewed as interwoven with, the narratives the far right tells. Given the foundational status of narrative as being constitutive of social identities (Somers, 1994) and the seduction of the narrative mode (Bruner, 1991), visual environmental communication by the far right is also worth focusing on through the analytical lens of narrative. Indeed, even still images can either support the written narrative or evoke narratives themselves, be it because of a panel structure, such as in comics, or because individual images represent actions (Bateman, 2014: 55–71). Such a focus on narrative could follow various avenues – including, for example, a structuralist consideration of actants (*subject* and *object*, *helper* and *opponent*, *sender* and *receiver*; Greimas, 1983) and a formalist one of plots (Frye, 1957). With regard to the former, Chapter 10 illustrates that the purity desired by the far right in India currently draws on the strength of a particular subject – Prime Minister Narendra Modi – who is visually/multimodally narrated as an environmental saviour (see also Chapter 5 in this volume), while opponents are, for example, Muslims. More broadly, reconstructing Greimas' actantial model can facilitate comparison between (environmental and beyond) narratives by 'carving out' their constitutive parts. Concerning plot, melodrama has been discussed in environmental communication research more generally (Schwarze, 2006; Kinsella et al., 2008), and with regard to the far right in particular (Daggett, 2020; Forchtner, in press). Beyond the melodramatic genre, with its polarising and oversimplifying characteristics, but also engaging, unifying aspects, narrative genres offer further ways to understand how meaning is visually/multimodally constructed – and how counter-communication could react. For example, alternatives to melodrama could be employed in some situations to potentially facilitate reflexivity, as in the case of irony or tragic elements via which the attraction of consumerism could be compromised (Niemelä-Nyrhinen and Uusitalo, 2021; see the example of the far-right Hungarian Our Homeland in Chapter 9).

No doubt, there are further paths which this edited volume has left unexplored. And as the natural environment is likely to remain, among other things, a grand setting for the political theatre of the far right and a site of 'ethno-communal beauty and existence in need of protecting', as well as a site to be dominated and exploited, and one via which its political opponents are attacked, further investigations are certainly needed while environmental crises will keep unfolding. In offering insights into the visual environmental communication of the far right around the world, *Visualising Far-Right Environments: Communication and the Politics of Nature* hopefully offers resources for and inspires such critical enquiry.

References

Bateman, J. A. (2014): *Text and Image: A Critical Introduction to the Visual/Verbal Divide*. London: Routledge.

Bruner, J. (1991): The narrative construction of reality, *Critical Inquiry*, 18(1): 1–21.

Conversi, D. (2020): The ultimate challenge: Nationalism and climate change, *Nationalities Papers*, 48(4): 625–636.

Daggett, C. (2018): Petro-masculinity: Fossil fuels and authoritarian desire, *Millennium*, 47(1): 25–44.

Daggett, C. (2020): The melodrama of climate change denial, *Green European Journal*. www.greeneuropeanjournal.eu/the-melodrama-of-climate-change-denial/ (accessed 11 June 2021).

Darwish, M. (2021): Nature, masculinities, care and the far-right. In: M. Hultman and P. Pulé (eds), *Men, Masculinities, and Earth Contending with the (m)Anthropocene*. Cham: Palgrave Macmillan, 183–206.

Forchtner, B. (2019): Climate change and the far right, *WIREs Climate Change*, 10(5): 1–11.

Forchtner, B. (in press): Thunberg, not iceberg: Visual melodrama in far-right climate change communication in Germany. In: I. Allen, K. Ekberg, S. Holgersen and A. Malm (eds), *Political Ecologies of the Far Right*. Manchester: Manchester University Press.

Frye, N. (1957): *Anatomy of Criticism: Four Essays*. Princeton, NJ: Princeton University Press.

Greimas, A. J. (1983): *Structural Semantics: An Attempt at a Method*. Lincoln: University of Nebraska Press.

Huber, R., Greussing, E. and Eberl, J.-M. (2021): From populism to climate scepticism: The role of institutional trust and attitudes towards science, *Environmental Politics*. https://doi.org/10.1080/09644016.2021.1978200.

Hultman, M., Björk, A. and Viinikka, T. (2019): The far right and climate change denial: Denouncing environmental challenges via anti-establishment rhetoric, marketing of doubts, industrial/breadwinner masculinities enactments and ethno-nationalism. In: B. Forchtner (ed.), *The Far Right and the Environment*. London: Routledge, 121–135.

Kinsella, W., Bsumek, P., Walker, G., Check, T., Rai Peterson, T. and Schwarze, S. (2008): Narratives, rhetorical genres, and environmental conflict: Responses to Schwarze's 'Environmental Melodrama', *Environmental Communication*, 2(1): 78–109.

Lindholm, J., Carlson, T. and Högväg, J. (2021): See me, like me! Exploring viewers' visual attention to and trait perceptions of party leaders on Instagram, *The International Journal of Press/Politics*, 26(1): 167–187.

Lockwood, M. (2018): Right-wing populism and the climate change agenda, *Environmental Politics*, 27(4): 712–732.

Malm, A. and The Zetkin Collective (2021): *White Skin, Black Fuel: On the Danger of Fossil Fascism*. London: Verso.

Merchant, C. (1983 [1976]): *The Death of Nature: Women, Ecology, and the Scientific Revolution*. New York: HarperOne.

Moore, S. and Roberts, A. (2022): *The Rise of Ecofascism, Climate Change and the Far Right*. Cambridge: Polity Press.

Niemelä-Nyrhinen, J. and Uusitalo, N. (2021): Aesthetic practices in the climate crisis: Intervening in consensual frameworks of the sensible through images, *Nordic Journal of Media Studies*, 3(1): 164–183.

O'Neill, S. and Nicholson-Cole, S. (2009): 'Fear won't do it': Promoting positive engagement with climate change through visual and iconic representations, *Science Communication*, 30(3): 355–379.

Pulé, P. and Hultman, M. (eds) (2021): *Men, Masculinities, and Earth: Contending with the (m)Anthropocene*. Cham: Palgrave Macmillan.

Schwarze, S. (2006): Environmental melodrama, *Quarterly Journal of Speech*, 92(3): 239–261.

Smith, A. D. (2009): *Ethno-Symbolism and Nationalism*. Abingdon: Routledge.

Somers, M. (1994): The narrative constitution of identity, *Theory and Society*, 23(5): 605–649.

Tarant, Z. (2019): Is brown the new green? The environmental discourse of the Czech far right. In: B. Forchtner (ed.), *The Far Right and the Environment*. London: Routledge, 201–215.

Westberg, G. and Årman, H. (2019): Common sense as extremism: The multi-semiotics of contemporary national socialism, *Critical Discourse Studies*, 16(5): 549–568.

Index

14 words 37

Abascal, Santiago 1, 83–86, 92, 94–97, 99
aboriginal 44, 59
abortion 85, 154, 280
Academia Christiana (France) 166–167, 169–170, 174–177, 182
Action Group Resistance Kysuce (Slovakia) 146
Action Zealandia (AZ) 14, 44, 46, 48, 50, 53–59
activism 46
    ecological/environmental 64, 66, 110, 192–193, 197, 236, 297
    see also collecting garbage; beach clean ups; eco-action(s); litter; outdoor(s); picking up trash; rubbish
Adopt-a-Highway 64–65, 67–69
    see also National Socialist Movement
aesthetic(s) 3–4, 6, 8, 11, 44, 50, 67–68, 105, 114, 167–168, 172–173, 175, 179–181, 220, 247, 278, 290, 294–295
'aestheticisation of politics' 8
AfD *see* Alternative for Germany
affect 6, 9, 14, 30–31, 36–37, 231, 241, 257, 295
    affective economy/economies 13, 30
    affective public(s) 24, 26, 31
    see also emotion(s)/emotional/emotive

AfriForum 26–28, 30
Afrikaans
    popular culture 26, 28, 38
    press 29
Afrikaner Resistance Movement (South Africa) 24, 26–27
Afrikaner Weerstandsbeweging see Afrikaner Resistance Movement
Afrikaners
    identity 28–29, 31, 37–38
    nationalism 27
    population 26
Agenda 21 274–275, 280–284
agrarianism 96
agriculture/agricultural 11, 25, 29–30, 32, 37, 73, 160, 170–171, 181, 190, 207–208, 220, 242–243, 248
Akčná Skupina Vzdor Kysuce see Action Group Resistance Kysuce
alarmism 237
Almodóvar, Pedro 92
Alps/Alpine 7, 172, 245
alt right 5
Alternative for Germany (AfD) 13, 160, 229, 233–234, 236–237
Alternative for Sweden 255
ambelopoulia 110
American Nazi Party 66
Americanisation 177
angle (camera) 10, 34, 68, 88, 133, 136, 138, 191, 193–194, 200
anthropocentric 53, 56, 92, 196

anticolonialism 182
Anti-Defamation League 56
anti-elitist 111
anti-Enlightenment 232
anti-establishment 150, 261
anti-fascist 65–66, 70, 76
anti-feminism 249, 255, 257
anti-globalist 155, 160
anti-intellectualism 87
anti-Muslim
   Othering in India 206–208, 212,
     215–218, 223–224
   rhetoric 87
   sentiment 283
anti-nuclear 197
Antipodean Resistance (Australia) 48,
   52
anti-Roma 63, 146, 149, 156,
   193–194
anti-Semitic/Semitism 4, 24, 49, 57,
   149, 261
   see also Jewish, Judaism
anti-speciesism/speciesist 96, 99
anti-urbanism 66
Aoraki 56
Aotearoa 53, 55
apartheid 24, 26–30, 32, 38
Arndt, Ernst Moritz 232
Aryan 54, 67, 130
aschematism/aschematiston 289
autarky 91, 112, 153
authoritarian(ism) 4–5, 83, 85–86,
   125, 127–128, 130, 140, 182,
   188, 200–201, 206, 221, 247,
   279–280, 283
authority 4, 11, 47, 73, 91, 112, 138,
   140, 182, 187, 193, 208,
   220–221, 223, 256, 265
   anti-authority 111

'banal globalism' 7
Bardem, Javier 92
Barrès, Maurice 173
beach clean–ups 53, 56, 58, 297
   see also collecting garbage; eco-
     action(s); litter, picking up trash,
     rubbish
bees 192–193, 197, 199
Bern, Lars 253–255, 258, 265
Betyársereg (Hungary) 189

Bharti, Uma 221
Bharatiya Janata Party (BJP) (India)
   206–208, 211–218, 221–222,
   224
biodiversity 166, 179, 190, 192–193,
   197, 243–244, 248
bioregional/bioregionalism 198,
   245–246, 248
birds 6, 110, 132, 179, 236, 238,
   243
birth rates 49
BJP *see* Bharatiya Janata Party
Black South Africans (representation)
   as labour 34, 37
   as vengeful 29
   as violent 30
blog(s) 104, 257, 260, 264, 267, 282
Blood and Soil 5, 63, 78, 232, 295
Blut und Boden see Blood and Soil
Boer
   commando 35–37
   nationalism 26
   rebels 35
Bousquet, François 171
Brannen, Robert 66
bucolic 44, 173
bullfighting 84, 90, 96, 99
Burton, Virginia Lee 66
bushland 50–52
bushwalk(s) 52, 54, 58

camping 44, 73
capital/capitalist/capitalism 2, 166,
   182, 218, 220, 239–240, 244,
   247–248
   fossil (fuel) capitalism 126, 129,
     267
   fossil fuel capital 141
Carlson, Tucker 28
Carpathian Basin 197, 202
Casanova, Eduardo 92
Casapound Italia 50
caste 207, 211–212, 216, 218,
   223–224
Catholic(s) 84, 94–95, 166–167, 169,
   174–175
Cato institute 260
Chapman, Kyle 53
Charlottesville 64, 66–67
Christchurch 5, 45–46, 48, 54, 57

Christian
  Amazon 177
  and ESNS 158–159
  and Othering in India 208, 215
  and Reconquista 95
  and The People's Youth 149
  and Vox 94
  ecologism 201
  god-fearing family 37
  heritage 27
  praise 36
  prayer 35
  Southlanders 24
Christianity 176
Christou, Christos 108
cityscapes 50
civilisation(s) 17, 49, 56, 139, 168,
  177, 212, 214, 231, 239
  Arctic 130, 133, 135, 139–140
  European 172, 182
  Russian 125, 135, 139
  Soviet 135
climate change 3, 7, 10–12, 14–16, 76,
  107–108, 110–112, 118, 120,
  129, 153, 160, 188, 190, 192,
  196–197, 199, 206–209, 212,
  217–224, 229–232, 235–239,
  241–242, 244, 247–249,
  253–255, 259–261, 267–268,
  296–298
  acceptance 7, 75–76, 193, 217, 234,
    296
  as a hoax 253, 261, 276–277, 282
  countermovement 7, 253–261
  conspiracising 276–290
  denial 111, 150, 217, 230, 254–
    255, 257, 266, 276
  obstruction 7, 112, 230, 233,
    247–248, 295–296
  scepticism 6, 12, 16, 111, 151, 160,
    237, 276
'Climategate' 283
clouds 35–36, 136
Cold War 27, 71
collecting garbage 159, 161
  see also eco-action(s); beach clean
    ups; litter; picking up trash;
    rubbish
colonialism 52, 55, 132, 139, 177, 182
Colucci, Burt 76

comic(s) 13, 191, 194, 299
Compact 234–235, 238–239
connotation 98, 105, 113–115,
  117–118
conservatism/conservative 28, 38, 43,
  72, 83–85, 107, 109–110, 168,
  171, 186, 190, 217, 254–255,
  260, 276, 279, 281, 283
Conservative Revolution 166, 173
conspiracist(s) 16, 274, 277, 282, 284,
  289
  content online 290
  disinformation 277
  document design 277
  information 16
  rhetoric 278, 290
  take on Agenda 21
  texts 277, 284, 290
  websites 277
conspiracy 54, 261, 276–277, 280
  scholarship 290
  site's design 282
  talking point 283
  thinking 276, 290
conspiracy theory/theories/theorists 24,
  43, 96, 275–282, 290
  websites 277, 284, 295
conspiratorial 276, 278
  ideologies 72
  narratives 73
consumerism 54, 166, 171, 299
Cortés, Hernán 94
cosmopolitan
  elites 7, 92, 151, 179–180, 231
  hysterics 1, 9
counter-terrorism 48
cow(s) 15, 206, 213, 215–218, 222
criticism of economic growth 54,
  239–240
  see also degrowth; post-growth
crypto-fascist discourse 78
Csereklye, Krisztina 191, 193
cultic milieu 14, 72, 78
'cultural marxists' 283
custodians 59, 67–68, 96, 99
custodianship 14, 64, 69
cyclone(s) 222, 260

Dalits 208, 212
Danube 188, 199

DAUNA21 *see* Democrats Against UN Agenda 21
de Benoist, Alain 166–167, 171, 174, 182, 240, 248
de la Rey, Koos 28
decadent/decadence 49, 66, 189, 238
decay/decaying 5, 49, 66, 70–71, 197, 268
deforestation 67, 172, 192–193, 197
degeneration 65
degrowth 166–167, 170
    see also criticism of economic growth; post-growth
Democrats Against UN Agenda 21 (DAUNA21) (United States) 277, 280, 282, 284–289
denotation 105, 113–118
Deutsche Stimme see German Voice
Dialogue for Hungary 189
Die Kehre see The Turning
Die Land (South Africa) 26, 31–32, 34–36
Die Republikaner see The Republicans
disinformation 253, 255–256, 267, 284, 290
Dittus, Jörg 229
Dominion Movement (New Zealand) 46, 53, 56
drought(s) 25, 35–36, 38, 220
du Plessis, Jay 33
du Toit, Ruhan 33
Dugin, Alexandr 130
Duke, David 28
Dúró, Dóra 189

eco-action(s) 7, 14, 54, 56, 58, 64, 297
    see also collecting garbage; beach clean ups, litter; picking up trash; rubbish
eco-asceticism 240
ecobordering 11, 58, 91, 111, 217
ecocentric/ecocentrism 53, 56
eco-communion 4, 6–7, 10, 230, 295
ecofascism 14, 17, 43–44, 49–50, 52–53, 56, 65, 92, 111–112
ecofascist 5, 11, 45, 47, 49–50, 52–54, 59, 65, 73, 76–78, 96, 111, 232
ecofeminism 107

ecologism 17, 110, 112, 189, 195, 199
    Christian 201
    syncretic 166
    see also far-right ecologism
ecology 16, 45, 84–86, 91, 166–168, 170–172, 176, 179, 216, 229–230, 240, 247
    civilisational 168–169, 177
    Identitarian 173
    integral 167
    patriotic 168, 170
    right-wing 174, 208, 214, 244
    rooted 166
    völkisch 166
eco-modernisation discourse 188
eco-nationalism 112, 188
eco-naturalism 5, 244
    see also naturalism
eco-organicism 5
    see also organicism
eco-socialism 187
ELAM *see* National Popular Front
Eléments (France) 171
emotion(s)/emotional/emotive 1, 3, 6, 9, 12, 15–16, 30–31, 37, 94, 99, 106, 126, 135, 139–140, 147–148, 150–153, 155–156, 158, 160–161, 181, 187, 213–215, 217–218, 230, 247, 253, 257, 259, 287, 294–296
    see also affect
enclave nationalism 26–27
entitativity 53, 58–59
Environment & Active (Germany) 59, 232–234
environmentalism 5, 17, 43, 63–64, 71, 74, 77–78, 92, 105, 110, 120, 167, 179, 187, 189, 288
    anti-immigration 5
    far-right 5, 109
    German neo-Nazi 11
    masculine/muscular 247–248, 297
    particularistic 237
    völkish 232
Erdoğan, Recep Tayyip 116
Espinosa de Los Monteros, Iván 85
ethno-communal 5, 7, 230, 247, 299
ethnocracy 194

ethnonationalism/ethnonationalist 4–5, 17, 130, 188, 247, 279–280, 283
  Afrikaner 24, 26, 29, 37–38
ethnopluralism/ethnopluralist 4, 17, 167–168, 173, 177, 232
ethnoscape(s)/ethno-scape 5, 29, 37, 45, 52, 168, 172, 176, 233, 295
European Institute for Climate & Energy (Germany) 237
Evola, Julius 53

FA *see* Freedom Advocates
Facebook 13, 15, 112, 147, 162, 170, 187, 190–192, 195–196, 198, 274
family farm 29, 31
farm murders 24, 28–30, 37
farmer(s) 26, 28, 30, 34–37, 86, 91–94, 96–97, 99, 172, 179–180, 219, 229, 243, 248, 297
farming and Afrikaner identity 28, 30
far-right ecologism 91, 105, 112, 120, 141, 187, 191–193, 195, 201
  see also ecologism
fascism(s) 8, 29, 56, 64–66, 72, 111
  European 5
  see also ecofascism
fascist 3, 5, 8, 16, 24, 38, 49–50, 53, 56, 63–66, 69, 72–74, 77, 84, 294
  clerical 146, 149
  international networks 27
  neo-fascist 125, 127–128, 130
  see also ecofascist
fatherland 206–207, 210
  see also motherland
fauna and flora 172
feminine 13, 176, 247
feminism/feminist 87, 107–108, 254, 256, 267, 282
Fidesz (Hungary) 188, 196, 200
field(s) (environment) 32, 35–36, 110, 172, 177, 229, 245
First World War 197
forest(s) 1, 6–7, 57, 154–155, 158–159, 161, 172–173, 209, 211, 213, 242–243, 245, 248, 275, 297
fossil fuel(s) 111, 125–127, 129–130, 133, 135, 139–141, 218, 231, 237, 239, 259–260, 267–268
  industry 7, 129, 132–133, 254

Fox News 28
Franco, Francisco 84, 93
Freedom Advocates (FA) (United States) 277, 281–290
Freedom Party of Austria 10, 13, 99, 238
Fridays for Future 188, 236, 253, 258, 267
Front National (France) 6, 182, 244
  see also National Rally
Fülöp, Erik 191–192
Fuerza Nueva (Spain) 84
Futurists 8

Ganga 15, 213–215, 217, 221–222
Gauchon, Pascal 171
Gauland, Alexander 229–230, 242, 245
genetically modified organisms 233
German Voice (Germany) 234–235, 238, 243
  see also NPD
GISP2 *see* Greenland Ice Sheet Project
Global North 261
Global South 14, 107, 194
globalisation 58, 87, 177, 182, 212, 241, 283
globalism/globalist 7, 234, 237, 243–244, 248, 256, 283
God Ram 211
Golden Dawn (Greece) 83, 108–110, 112
Grant, Madison 4
'green patriotism' 111
great replacement theory 43, 167, 171, 176
green economy 197
green growth 219
Green Homeland (Hungary) 189–194, 196, 201
green parties 111, 189, 197, 201
Green party (Germany) 232, 242
Greenland Ice Sheet Project (GISP2) 264
Greenline Front 86, 232
greens 186, 238, 243–244, 247
greenwashing 126, 195

Haeckel, Ernst 4
harmony with nature 43, 65, 151, 296
Hatvannégy Vármegye Ifjúsági Mozgalom (Hungary) 189
'heartland' 29

Heidegger, Martin 208, 234
Heimatschutz movement *see* homeland
    protection movement
Herrington, Cliff 66
hiking 44, 159
Himmler, Heinrich 111
Hindu gods 211, 216
Hlinka's Slovak People's Party 149
Hlinkova slovenská ľudová strana see
    Hlinka's Slovak People's Party
Höcke, Björn 233
hockey stick 257, 259, 262
Hofmeyr, Steve 26, 28, 30, 33, 37
Holocaust denialism 149
homeland protection movement
    (Germany) 4, 7, 232
humoristic 89
hunting 84, 96, 99, 106, 108, 111,
    192
Hyperborea 130
hysteria/hysterical/hysterics 1, 9, 237,
    243, 248

ICLEI *see* International Council for
    Local Environmental Initiatives
identitarian/Identitarian 48, 54, 56, 86,
    166–167, 171, 175
Identitarian Block 167, 171
Identitarianism 172
idyllic 94, 187, 194
illiberal democracy 188
imaginary 9, 29, 45, 47, 52, 58, 119,
    135, 177, 181, 230
    environmental/ecological 6, 214
    Green Homeland's 192
    'one world' 231
    Russia 140
    South Africa 32, 34
imperialist 125, 128, 130, 134
indigenous 54–55, 129, 139–140, 182,
    223–224
industrialisation 44, 110, 181–182,
    211
Instagram 13–14, 90, 162, 169–171,
    175, 182, 298
Institut Iliade (France) 166, 169–174,
    296
Intergovernmental Panel on Climate
    Change (IPCC) 253, 255–256,
    262–264, 267–268

International Council for Local
    Environmental Initiatives (ICLEI)
    274–275, 283
International Solar Alliance 222
intersectional 107, 187, 194
'invasive species' 1, 6, 44, 106, 243,
    249
IPCC *see* Intergovernmental Panel on
    Climate Change
irony 10, 299
Islam 56
Islamic 283
    extremism 45
    State 47, 85
Islamophobia 4
Izborskii Club (Russia) 15, 125,
    127–128, 130–141

Jewish 48, 63
Jobbik (Hungary) 77, 189–191
Johnson, Greg 5
Jones, Alex 282
Juan Carlos I 85
Judaism 49
Junge Freiheit see Young Freedom
Jünger, Ernst 173
Juvin, Hervé 166, 168–171, 177–180,
    182

Kawarau 54, 56
Koire, Rosa 281–283, 285, 287
Kotarac, Andrea 168
Kotleba, Marian 148, 152, 155
Kotlebovci – People's Party Our
    Slovakia (ĽSNS) 15, 146–162
Ku Klux Klan 51–52, 73
Kubitschek, Götz 233, 240, 247

Lads Society (Australia) 48
landscape(s) 1, 3, 10, 14, 17, 29,
    32–33, 36–38, 44–45, 49–50,
    52–53, 55–59, 63–64, 66, 69–72,
    77–78, 84, 94, 128, 151,
    158–159, 161, 168, 170,
    172–173, 176–177, 179–182,
    187, 209, 211, 221, 233, 245,
    248, 294–296
Le Gallou, Jean-Yves 167, 172, 182
League (Italy) 86, 96
    see also Northern League

Lega Nord see Northern League,
    League
*Lehet Más a Politika – Magyarország
    Zöld Pártjasee see* LMP –
    Hungarian Green Party
Lennon, John 194
Le Pen, Marine 6, 83, 97, 182
Les Antigones (France) 171
Les Localistes see The Localists
Leza, Blas de 94
LGBT(+) 13, 68, 76
liberalism 182, 186, 233, 238, 240,
    244, 247, 280
    market 26
    see also neoliberal/neoliberalism
libertarian 280, 283
Linkola, Pentti 242
litter 67–70, 77
    see also collecting garbage; beach
        clean-ups; eco-action(s); picking
        up trash; rubbish
Little House on the Prairie 66, 74
LMP – Hungarian Green Party (LMP)
    187–190, 196–201
localism 15, 166–167, 169–172, 174,
    180
locus amoenus 194
locus terribilis 194
Los Indignados (Spain) 85
L'SNS *see* Kotlebovci – People's Party
    Our Slovakia
Ľudová mládež see The People's Youth
Lukie (character in *Treurgrond*) 30–31

machismo 111
Manichean 112, 193–194, 196, 200
Manichaeism 91, 187, 193, 200
Mann, Michael 257, 259
Māori 44, 54–56, 59
Marx, Karl 240, 283
masculine/masculinities/masculinity 7,
    14–15, 33–34, 87, 104–105,
    107–108, 110, 112–113, 116,
    118–119, 125, 127, 135,
    137–141, 213, 231, 239,
    246–248, 296–297
    industrial/breadwinner 7, 119, 239,
        246, 297
    see also muscular ELAMites
materialism 54, 244, 247

Mátra Power Plant 196, 199
Maukatere 57
mechanical objectivity 256
melodrama 299
meme(s) 10, 13, 64, 76, 89–90, 259,
    278
metabolic rift 240
metapolitical/metapolitics 14–15,
    166–167, 169, 180–181
Michaloliakos, Nikos 108
militia 24, 280
Mineworkers Union (South Africa) 27
misinformation 276, 284
misogynist 10, 236
Mi Hazánk see Our Homeland
Modi, Narendra 15, 96, 207–209,
    213–214, 218–224, 299
Mörner, Nils-Axel 265
motherland 15, 104–105, 113–114,
    207, 209–210, 212–213, 222,
    296
    see also fatherland
Mourning Ground (South Africa)
    30–31, 37
MultiChoice (South Africa) 26
multimodal/multimodally/
    multimodality 2–3, 11–15, 26,
    31–32, 37, 64, 77, 88–89, 92,
    98–99, 119, 169, 176, 235, 245,
    247, 278, 294, 297–299
muscular ELAMites 117
    see also National Popular Front
music 28, 32–37, 63, 172
    video 14, 26, 32
mysticism 91, 112, 150
mythology 95, 105, 113–115, 117–119

National Democratic Party of
    Germany (NPD) 232–234
National Front (New Zealand) 53
National Party (South Africa) 27
National Popular Front (ELAM)
    (Cypris) 15, 104–106, 108–120
National Rally (France) 6, 83, 97,
    166–168, 171, 177, 179–181,
    217, 244
    see also Front National
National Socialism 4, 49, 66, 78
National Socialist Movement (NSM)
    (United States) 14, 63–78, 295

National Socialist Network (NSN) (Australia) 14, 45–46, 48–54, 56, 59

National Volunteer Organisation (RSS) (India) 15, 206–207, 210–218, 220–222, 224

Nationaldemokratische Partei Deutschlands see National Democratic Party of Germany

native species 193

nativism/nativist/nativity 4, 44, 58–59, 76, 83, 86–87, 96, 99, 105, 109, 150, 201, 206, 212

natural order 17, 43–45, 50, 52, 58

naturalism 91, 112, 187, 193
  see aslo eco-naturalism

Nazi(s) 24, 27, 50, 52, 63, 66, 73, 111, 128, 232
  Germany 4, 27, 63

Nazism 65–66, 73

neoliberal/neoliberalism 31, 58, 85, 119, 188, 219
  see also liberalism

neo-Malthusian 5, 178, 244

neo-Nazi(s) 1–2, 11, 24, 27, 63–64, 66, 68, 75, 109, 146, 148–149

neo-Nazism 11, 65–66

neo-pagan(s) 166–167, 171–173, 177

New Force see *Fuerza Nueva*

New Right 5, 166–167, 171–173, 182, 232–234, 248

Nietzsche, Friedrich 173

Niezgoda, Fabien 171

nomadic/nomadism 92, 168, 174

Northern League (Italy) 13
  see also League

northern sea route 129, 140

nostalgia 28, 30, 32, 38, 74, 91, 99, 110, 112, 135, 151, 180–181, 187

Nouvelle Droite see New Right

NPD see National Democratic Party of Germany

NSM see National Socialist Movement

NSM Magazine 64, 69–72, 76

NSN see National Socialist Network

nuclear
  icebreaker 136–137
  energy 155, 196, 219

Odinist(s) 45, 49

Orbán, Viktor 188, 196

organicism 91, 112, 187
  see also eco-organicism

Ortega Smith, Javier 97

Ossewa Brandwag see Oxwagon Sentinel

Our Homeland Movement (Hungary) 187, 189–192

outdoor(s)
  activities and pursuits 14, 44, 51, 56, 63–65, 73, 77, 221
  life 38, 151

overconsumption 107, 192

overpopulation 5, 43, 70, 167, 244, 249

Oxwagon Sentinel (South Africa) 27

palingenetic 77, 111, 119

Papayiannis, Linos 110, 115

paramilitary 24, 146

Párbeszéd Magyarországért see Dialogue for Hungary

pastoral 86, 96, 295

Partido Popular see People's Party

patriarchal/patriarchy 37, 106, 107, 128, 239, 254, 267

People's Party (PP) (Spain) 84–86

periergia 289

Permanent Service of Mean Sea Level (PSMSL) 260, 263

Peterman, Alexandr 137–138

Philip VI 85

photograph(s)/photography 2, 29, 70, 78, 113, 117, 170, 176, 207, 210–212, 214, 217, 222, 256

picking up trash 114, 117
  see also collecting garbage; beach clean ups; eco-action(s), litter; rubbish

Pioneer group (Australia) 53

pirate parties 187

Podemos see We Can (Spain)

pollution
  air 190, 192, 196–197, 199
  land 190, 197, 243
  plastic 192–193, 197, 199
  water 190, 192–193, 197, 199, 214, 221

polysemic/polysemy 3, 9, 24, 44, 174, 187, 298
populism 83–84, 86–87, 89–90, 94, 96, 98, 188, 200, 239, 296
post-growth 229
  see also criticism of economic growth; degrowth
PP *see* People's Party
prepper commando 35
productivist 4, 167, 240
Prokhanov, Alexandr 128, 133–136
PSMSL *see* Permanent Service of Mean Sea Level
puppy 196
purity 5–6, 11, 63, 66, 76–77, 87, 104–106, 111, 115, 118, 210, 214, 221, 224, 299
Putin, Vladimir 128, 135

racial/racially 4, 34, 37, 43–45, 49, 54, 58, 63, 65, 76, 127, 139, 175, 194
racialised/racialisation 25, 127–128, 131, 133
Rajoy, Mariano 84–85
Rauch, Walter 238
Reclaim Australia 45
Reconquista 95–96
Rassemblement National see National Rally
renewable energy 15, 154–155, 160, 196–197, 207–209, 217–220, 222–224, 239
  see also wind turbines
Republican(s) (United States) 96, 276, 279–280
Riehl, Wilhelm Heinrich 232
Roche, Simon 28, 38
Rockwell, George Lincoln 66
Rodríguez Zapatero, José Luis 85
Roets, Ernst 28, 30
Roma *see* anti-Roma
Romantic 3, 4, 7, 11, 16, 74, 149–150, 161, 173, 232, 241, 294
Romanticism 111
Roodt, Darrel 30
rootedness 5, 15, 168–169, 172, 174, 176, 243–245, 295
RSS *see* National Volunteer Organisation

rubbish 59, 70, 172, 194
  see also collecting garbage; beach clean ups; eco-action(s); litter; picking up trash
rural 14, 29, 31, 33, 36, 38, 50, 63, 66, 73–74, 77, 84, 86, 91, 94, 96–97, 99, 146, 168, 172, 175–176, 179, 181, 211–212, 245, 295–296
Russian strategy 130
Russkie strategii see Russian strategy

sacred
  flame 64, 66
  truth(s) 72–73
Salvini, Matteo 96
Sánchez, Pedro 86
Saraswati 213
Schick, Jonas 229–230, 233
Schmuck, Erzsébet 197
Schoep, Jeff 66–67, 70, 76
sea-level 259, 263–264
Second World War 27, 65, 146, 148, 158
semiological/semiology 113, 190–191
semiotic(s) 10, 15, 26, 31, 83, 88–89, 94, 113, 186–188, 190–191, 195, 241, 246–247, 297
sensational signs 30–31, 37
settler(s) 14, 29–30, 33, 44, 52, 72, 295
  autochthony 29
  colonialist attitude 64
Shilingarov, Artur 135
Sierra Club 70–71
Slovak Conscripts 146
Slovak Revival Movement 146
Slovak Togetherness – National Party 146, 148–149
Slovenská pospolitosť – Národná strana see Slovak Togetherness – National Party
Slovenské hnutie obrody see Slovak Revival Movement
Slovenskí Branci see Slovak Conscripts
Social Darwinist 4, 232
social democrats 187
Socialist Party (Spain) 86
Sokszínű vidék (Hungary) 192
South African War (Second Anglo-Boer War) 28

South Africa
  Constitution 27
  democratic transition 27
Southern Cross 56
Southlanders (South Africa) 24–26, 28, 35, 38
sovereignty 7, 94, 105, 111, 159, 167, 171, 177–178, 200, 213, 231, 248, 276, 280, 284
Soviet Union 128–129
Spencer, Richard 5, 28
spirituality 91, 112, 133, 150, 187
Sports Fans for Animals (Hungary) 192
stewardship 77, 189
Stormtrooper (United States) 64, 67–70, 72
Štúr, Ľudovít 150
Suidlanders see Southlanders
sustainability/sustainable 54, 58, 111, 153–154, 206, 212, 219, 229, 243–244, 249, 275, 277, 280–283, 288
swastika(s) 24, 26, 38, 73–74
SwebbTV 16, 253–268
Sweden Democrats 255
Swedish Meteorological and Hydrological Institute 260
Swiss People's Party 259
Szent Korona Rádió (Hungary) 192
Szurkolók az Állatokért
  see Sports Fans for Animals

Tarrant, Brenton 43
Tasman Forth 53
Telegram 11, 48, 50–51, 53, 56–57
terra nullius 64
Terre'Blanche, Eugene 24, 26
terrorism 5, 76, 218
text formatting 2, 278–279, 285, 287–289
The Great Global Warming Swindle 257–258
The Localists (France) 168
The Movement for a Better Hungary
  see Jobbik
The People's Youth (Slovakia) 149
  see also ĽSNS
The Republicans (Germany) 232
The Turning (Germany) 229–230, 233–235, 237, 239–243, 245

think tank(s) 166–167, 169–171, 237, 265, 296
Third Reich 4, 65
Thunberg, Greta 236, 253–254, 258, 261, 267–268
Tiso, Jozef 150
Tisza 193, 199
Toroczkai, László 189
tragic 299
trans-Tasman 46
Treurgrond see Mourning Ground
Trianon 196–199, 201
Trump, Donald 28, 69, 95–96, 279
trust in numbers 256, 259
Turistamagazin (Hungary) 192
Turner, Frederic Jackson 139
Twitter 11–12, 14, 24–26, 35, 90, 112, 162, 171, 180, 298
typeface(s) 277, 284, 288–289

Uhrík, Milan 148
Unite the Right rally 28, 64
United Patriots Front (Australia) 45, 48
University of Alabama, Huntsvill (UAH) 261
uprooting 176
urban 66, 76, 84, 208, 212, 219, 221, 245, 280
urbanisation 44

van Blerk, Bok 28, 33
van Jaarsveld, Bobby 33
Vedic 207, 209–211, 215
vegan/veganism 86, 96, 99
velocity 31, 33, 35, 88
Venner, Dominique 167, 171, 173, 182
Vidal-Quadras, Aleix 85
violence 13, 30, 36–37, 66, 109
völkisch 3–4, 16, 111, 166, 173, 174, 181, 232–233, 294–295
volunteer/volunteering 67, 104, 109–110, 117–119, 210, 258
Vox (Spain) 1–2, 14, 83–86, 88–99, 296

water 24–25, 37–38, 70, 74–75, 77, 109, 117, 132, 155–156, 158, 174, 190, 192–193, 196–197, 199, 209–211, 214, 216, 219–220, 248, 282

wattsupwiththat.com 264
We Can (Spain) 85, 90
web template(s) 277, 279, 284–288
White Aryan Resistance (United States)
    67
white futurity 37–38
'white genocide' *see* farm murders
white supremacy/supremacist 25–27,
    37, 49, 56, 283
wilderness 29, 52, 71, 173
wildlife 96, 132, 189, 237
Wilgert, Mikael 255–256, 258

wind turbines 1, 12, 170, 178–181,
    219–220, 230, 233, 236–239
Wood, Patrick 283

Yeltsin, Boris 128
Young Freedom (Germany) 234–235
YouTube 13, 16, 24–26, 38, 64, 90,
    182, 229, 255–256, 258, 298

Zengő 188
Zöld Ellenállás 192
Zöld Hazánk see Green Homeland

EU authorised representative for GPSR:
Easy Access System Europe, Mustamäe tee 50,
10621 Tallinn, Estonia
gpsr.requests@easproject.com